Lecture Notes in Computer Science

Edited by G. Goos, J. Hartmanis and J. van Leeuwen

Springer
*Berlin
Heidelberg
New York
Barcelona
Hong Kong
London
Milan
Paris
Singapore
Tokyo*

Dennis Dams   Rob Gerth
Stefan Leue   Mieke Massink (Eds.)

Theoretical and Practical Aspects of SPIN Model Checking

5th and 6th International SPIN Workshops
Trento, Italy, July 5, 1999
Toulouse, France, September 21 and 24, 1999
Proceedings

 Springer

Volume Editors

Dennis Dams
Eindhoven University of Technology, Department of Electrical Engineering
and Department of Mathematics and Computer Science
5600 MB Eindhoven, The Netherlands
E-mail: d.r.dams@ele.tue.nl

Rob Gerth
Intel Microprocessor Products Group, Strategic CAD Laboratories
5200 NE Elam Young Parkway, JFT-104 Hillsboro, OR 97124-6497, USA
E-mail: robgerth@ichips.intel.com

Stefan Leue
University of Waterloo, Department of Electrical and Computer Engineering
Waterloo, Ontario N2L 3G1, Canada
E-mail: sleue@uwaterloo.ca

Mieke Massink
C.N.R.-Ist. CNUCE
via Santa Maria 36, 56126 Pisa, Italy
E-mail: mieke@gongolo.cnuce.cnr.it

Cataloging-in-Publication data applied for

Die Deutsche Bibliothek - CIP-Einheitsaufnahme

Theoretical and practical aspects of SPIN model checking : 5th and 6th
international SPIN workshops, Trento, Italy, July 5, 1999, Toulouse, France,
September 21 and 24, 1999 ; proceedings / Dennis Dams ... (ed.). - Berlin ;
Heidelberg ; New York ; Barcelona ; Hong Kong ; London ; Milan ; Paris ;
Singapore ; Tokyo : Springer, 1999
 (Lecture notes in computer science ; Vol. 1680)
 ISBN 3-540-66499-8

CR Subject Classification (1998): F.3, D.2.4, D.3.1

ISSN 0302-9743
ISBN 3-540-66499-8 Springer-Verlag Berlin Heidelberg New York

© Springer-Verlag Berlin Heidelberg 1999
Printed in Germany

Typesetting: Camera-ready by author
SPIN: 10704313   06/3142 – 5 4 3 2 1 0   Printed on acid-free paper

Organization

Organization of 5thSPIN99

Program Committee

Dennis Dams (Eindhoven University, The Netherlands)
Mieke Massink (CNR-Ist. CNUCE, Italy)
Gerard Holzmann (Bell Laboratories, USA)
Ed Brinksma (Univ. of Twente, The Netherlands)
Marco Daniele (ITC-IRST, Italy)
Bengt Jonsson (Uppsala University, Sweden)

Local Organization

Adolfo Villafiorita

Referees

R. Alur	L. Holenderski	M. Nilsson
D. Bošnački	B. Jonsson	A. Nymeyer
D. Dams	R. Kaivola	J. Nyström
M. Daniele	J.-P. Katoen	T. Ruys
G. Faconti	D. Latella	N. Sidorova
M. Geilen	G. Lenzini	R. de Vries
S. Gnesi	M. Massink	

Organization of 6thSPIN99

Organizers

Rob Gerth (Intel Corp., USA)
Gerard Holzmann (Bell Laboratories, USA)
Stefan Leue (University of Waterloo, Canada)

Referees

K. Etessami	M. Kamel	P. Tysowski
R. Gerth	G. Karjoth	M. Zulkernine
J.-C. Grégoire	S. Leue	
G. Holzmann	W. Liu	

Preface

Increasing the designer's confidence that a piece of software or hardware is compliant with its specification has become a key objective in the design process for software and hardware systems. Many approaches to reaching this goal have been developed, including rigorous specification, formal verification, automated validation, and testing. Finite-state model checking, as it is supported by the explicit-state model checker SPIN, is enjoying a constantly increasing popularity in automated property validation of concurrent, message based systems. SPIN has been in large parts implemented and is being maintained by Gerard Holzmann, and is freely available via ftp from `netlib.bell-labs.com` or from URL `http://cm.bell-labs.com/cm/cs/what/spin/Man/README.html`.

The beauty of finite-state model checking lies in the possibility of building "push-button" validation tools. When the state space is finite, the state-space traversal will eventually terminate with a definite verdict on the property that is being validated. Equally helpful is the fact that in case the property is invalidated the model checker will return a counterexample, a feature that greatly facilitates fault identification. On the downside, the time it takes to obtain a verdict may be very long if the state space is large and the type of properties that can be validated is restricted to a logic of rather limited expressiveness. However, looking at the number and type of practical applications it seems that finite-state model checking technology is moving towards becoming engineering practice. This development can largely be attributed to the relative ease of handling and the potential for automation of the validation process which makes this technology accessible to the software designer and even the domain expert.

The SPIN workshop series was initiated by Jean-Charles Grégoire who hosted the first SPIN workshop in October 1995 at INRS Télécommunications in Montréal. Its success led to subsequent SPIN workshops held in New Brunswick (August 1996), Enschede (April 1997) and Paris (November 1998). At a time when the number of formal methods events is increasing, two conferences expressed interest in hosting SPIN workshops in 1999: the Federated Logic Conference (FLoC'99) held in Trento in June/July, and the World Congress on Formal Methods in the Development of Computing Systems (FM'99) held in Toulouse in September. In order to give SPIN-related research an exposure at both events it was decided to organize two SPIN workshops in 1999. However, both events were to focus on different aspects. The *5th International SPIN Workshop on Theoretical Aspects of Model Checking (5thSPIN99)* was held on July 5, 1999 as a satellite workshop of FLoC'99, while the *6th International SPIN Workshop on Practical Aspects of Model Checking (6thSPIN99)* was held as a user group meeting within FM'99 on September 21 and 24, 1999.

5thSPIN99 featured an invited talk by John Rushby, 6 research paper presentations that were selected out of 12 submitted papers, an overview of SPIN release 3.3.0 by Gerard Holzmann, an invited tutorial by Kousha Etessami, and a panel discussion. 6thSPIN99 offered a keynote address by Dan Craigen, an invited tutorial by Rob Gerth, 12 research paper presentations that were selected out of 25 submitted papers, and two tool demonstrations. Papers presented at both workshops are included in this volume.

Acknowledgements. The editors of this volume wish to thank all referees for their tremendous help in putting together a strong program for both workshops. Stefan Leue thanks Piotr Tysowski and Mohammad Zulkernine for their support in organizing the paper review process for 6thSPIN99 and for their aid in putting this volume together. Dennis Dams and Mieke Massink are grateful to the FLoC'99 organization, and in particular to Adolfo Villafiorita, for their support. They also wish to thank Bell-Labs and C.N.R.-Ist. CNUCE for their support of the initiative. Rob Gerth and Stefan Leue wish to express their gratitude to Dines Bjørner for initiating the idea of a SPIN workshop during FM'99, and to the FM'99 organizers for hosting the event.

September 1999

Dennis Dams
Rob Gerth
Stefan Leue
Mieke Massink

Table of Contents

Integrated Formal Verification: Using Model Checking with Automated Abstraction, Invariant Generation, and Theorem Proving*

John Rushby

Computer Science Laboratory
SRI International
333 Ravenswood Avenue
Menlo Park, CA 94025, USA
rushby@csl.sri.com

Abstract. Mechanized formal methods that use both model checking and theorem proving seem to hold most promise for the future. Effective use of both technologies requires they be recast as methods for calculating properties of specifications, rather than merely verifying them. The most valuable properties are those that contribute to the development of invariants and property-preserving abstractions. We outline an architecture for verification tools based on iterated use of such capabilities.

1 Introduction

The advent of model checking not only introduced useful tools, such a SPIN, it also brought a different focus to the field of formal methods. This new focus stressed tools and automated analyses over mathematical derivations performed by hand, and was targeted towards refutation (i.e., finding bugs) more than verification. Many of those who worked on traditional formal verification tools (those based on theorem proving) welcomed the new interest in pragmatics and the sanction that it provided for use of more effective methods of deduction, such as decision procedures. (Formerly, decision procedures had been spurned in some quarters because mechanized verification had—mistakenly, in my view—been identified with the activity of proof in mathematics, rather than with calculation in engineering.)

Some verification tools were extended to incorporate model checking by making a model checker available as a back-end proof procedure—in PVS, for example, a model checker (due to Geert Janssen) is used as a decision procedure for Park's μ-calculus restricted to finite types, and CTL model checking is implemented as a derived proof procedure on top of that [14]. Conversely, some

---

* This research was supported by DARPA through USAF Rome Laboratory Contract F30602-96-C-0204, and by the National Science Foundation contract CCR-9509931.

developers of model checkers provided lightweight theorem proving as a front end to overcome limitations in plain model checking [13].

Most users and developers of theorem proving and model checking tools now accept that both technologies are needed, but each tends to see the "other" technology as a supporting player, relegated to the role of a front- or back-end adjunct to their primary tool. In contrast, I believe that significant further advances will be made only by "symmetrically" integrated verification environments in which theorem proving and model checking are seen as equal partners and are used in an iterative, interleaved fashion to provide capabilities such as abstraction and invariant generation, as much as to perform direct verification.

A couple of projects have started to explore the development and use of these symmetric approaches; they include SAL (Symbolic Analysis Laboratory) at SRI and Stanford (with substantial input from Berkeley), and VeriTech at The Technion. In the remainder of this short paper, I will sketch the architectures employed in these systems and some of the techniques used. The systems themselves are still inchoate, and their utility has not yet been demonstrated, so the approach they embody should be regarded as somewhat speculative at present.

2 Common Intermediate Languages

Mechanized formal analysis starts from a description of the problem of interest expressed in the notation of the tool to be employed. Construction of this description often entails considerable work: first to recast the system specification from its native expression in C, Esterel, Java, SCR, UML, Verilog, or whatever, into the notation of the tool concerned, then to extract the part that is relevant to the analysis at hand (the order of these two steps can be reversed), and finally to reduce it to a form that the tool can handle (e.g., finite state). If a second tool is to be employed for a different analysis, then a second description of the problem must be prepared, with considerable duplication of effort. Notice that only the final analysis is automated: the translation, extraction, and reduction steps are all performed by hand (an exception is the *Java PathFinder* [9] which provides model checking for Java via an automated translation into Promela, the language of SPIN). The reasons for this lack of automation seem economic rather than technical: with m source languages and n tools, we would need $m \times n$ translators, either m or n "extractors," and n "reducers." This situation naturally suggests use of a common intermediate language, where the numbers of tools required could be reduced to $m + n$ translators and perhaps as few as one extractor and one reducer.

Successful use of an intermediate language seems more promising in this domain than in programming (where the failure of the UNCOL project in the 1960s is still remembered) because we are interested primarily in concurrency issues, where transition relations already provide a widely-accepted semantic foundation.

A useful intermediate language cannot provide just bare transition relations, however, for we will want to support various transformations and analyses on the intermediate representation and these will be inefficient or ineffective if too much of the structure and "intent" of the original specification is lost by flattening it out into a plain transition relation. For these reasons, the SAL intermediate language provides both synchronous and asynchronous forms of composition; distinguishes input, local, and output variables; provides state update via both single-variable assignments (a style often used for hardware specification) and guarded commands (where several state variables may be updated simultaneously—a style often used in protocol specification), and a module structure. Because SAL is an environment where theorem proving as well as model checking is available, absence of causal loops in synchronous systems is ensured by generating proof obligations, rather than by more restrictive syntactic methods. For example, the following pair of assignments is acceptable in SAL because we can prove that X is causally dependent on Y only when A is *true*, and vice-versa only when it is *false*—hence there is no causal loop.

```
X = IF A THEN NOT Y ELSE C ENDIF
Y = IF A THEN B ELSE X ENDIF
```

While there are as yet no automated translators into the SAL language (we hope others will write those if the rest of the system proves effective), we do have translators from SAL to SMV (for model checking), to PVS (for theorem proving), and to Java (for animation).

3 Syntactic Transformations

A number of generally-useful transformations can be defined on systems specified in an intermediate representation. A canonical "extractor" could perform backward slicing on variables to yield just that part of a large system specification that is relevant to a given property [7]. We suspect that many of the complexities of program slicing (e.g., interprocedural data flow and global variables) are much reduced when this technology is applied to specifications rather than imperative programs. (Conversely, we believe that effective automated theorem proving could improve the precision of classical program slicing.)

Other transformations could perform syntactic "reductions" on the state space of a specification. These may, but do not always need to be, property-preserving. For example, a reduction commonly employed in model checking arbitrarily reduces the size of large or infinite data types to small concrete values: the maximum number of messages in a queue may be reduced from n to 3, for instance. Such *downscaling* may preserve neither soundness (model checking the downscaled instance may fail to reveal bugs in the original) nor completeness (bugs may be found in the downscaled instance that are not present in the original), but can nonetheless be effective in exposing real bugs quite cheaply.

Yet other reductions may be property-preserving: examples may include some defined by abstract interpretation and those associated with partial order reductions. One of the attractions of an intermediate representation is that it may make techniques such as partial order reduction, presently provided only by SPIN, more widely available.

4 Semantic Transformations

The real power of integrated verification environments only becomes apparent when we consider transformations whose own construction or justification exploits the model checking or deductive capabilities available in the environment. Property-preserving abstractions are the main transformations of this kind. The utility of such abstractions in model checking is well known [5, 12], and the topic of interest is how to develop useful abstractions by largely automatic means. To illustrate some of the issues, I use the following trivial transition system.

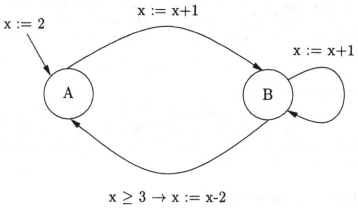

This system is truly trivial, in that it does not involve concurrency; it features two control locations, A and B, and a single integer-valued state variable x, which can be incremented by one when control is at either location, and decremented by two when control is at B and x is at least three. Initially, control is at A and x has the value two; the goal is to show that x is at least two whenever control is at B.

This system cannot be model checked directly because it is not finite-state (its state variable x can grow arbitrarily large). We could downscale the system by restricting x to some arbitrary minimum and maximum values—say zero and five, respectively—but then we will have to modify the description to do something other than increment when x is at its maximum value, and to do something other than decrement if this would take it below its minimum value, and then we may wonder about the relationship between the original and the downscaled system descriptions, and the interpretation of any results obtained by model checking.

If we wish to draw conclusions about the original system on the basis of model checking a reduced system, then we must ensure that the reduced system is a property-preserving abstraction of the original. Before doing this, however, I wish to set the stage for combined approaches by illustrating how properties of infinite-state systems can be established by theorem proving.

Theorem proving can be used to establish an invariant property (implicitly, those are the only kind of properties considered here) by showing that the property is true in the initial system state and that it is preserved by all transitions of the system. If we feed our example into PVS [15], it quickly discharges three of the four proof obligations and terminates with the following unproven subgoal.

```
[-1]      pc(pre!1) = A
[-2]      pc(post!1) = B
[-3]      x(pre!1) = 0
  |-------
[1]       x(pre!1) + 1 ≥ 2
```

PVS displays proof goals in this "sequent" form; the interpretation is that the conjunction of the formulas above the line should imply the disjunction of formulas (here there is only one) below the line. An expression such as `pc(pre!1)` = A is interpreted as asserting that the control location (or "program counter," hence the abreviation `pc`) in state `pre!1` is A (the !1 suffix is added to ensure that Skolem constants have unique names). This particular sequent is inviting us to consider the case of a transition from A to B, where the value of x is initially zero. Plainly, the invariant is not satisfied in this case (hence the unprovable formula below the line, which reduces to $1 \geq 2$). From our understanding of the system, however, we can see that this case cannot arise, because x must be at least one when control is at A. In order to convince the prover of this, however, we must add it to the invariant as an additional fact to be proven: the invariant is said to be *strengthened* by adding the extra conjunct. In general, the process of establishing an invariant by theorem proving involves inspecting failed subgoals to deduce plausible additional conjuncts, strengthening the invariant by adding these conjuncts, and repeating the process until the proof succeeds. In one example of this kind, 57 such strengthenings were required to verify a bounded retransmission communications protocol [10]; each conjunct was discovered by inspecting a failed proof, and the process consumed several weeks.

A more integrated approach to this problem is one that uses theorem proving to justify a property-preserving finite state abstraction of the system, and then model checks the abstraction. Given a concrete state space with transition relation tr_c and initial states and desired invariant characterized by predicates $init_c$ and p_c, respectively, we need to find a (finite) abstract state space with an abstraction function abs from concrete states to abstract ones, together with an abstract transition relation tr_a and predicates $init_a$ and p_a on the abstract states, such that the following verification conditions hold.

1. $init_c(cs) \supset init_a(abs(cs))$,
2. $tr_c(pre_c, post_c) \supset tr_a(abs(pre_c), abs(post_c))$, and
3. $p_a(abs(cs)) \supset p_c(cs)$

where cs, pre_c, and $post_c$ are concrete states, formulas are implicitly universally quantified over their free variables, and $\supset$ indicates logical (material) implication. Then we will have

$$invariant(p_a)(init_a, tr_a) \supset invariant(p_c)(init_c, tr_c),$$

and the antecedent can be established by model checking.

A particularly useful form of abstraction uses a collection of boolean variables to define the abstract state space, where each variable abstracts some predicate over the concrete state space [17]. This is called *predicate abstraction* (or sometimes *Boolean abstraction*) and we can apply it to our example by using just a single abstract variable that abstracts the predicate $x \geq 2$. Using insight, we can postulate the following as a suitable transition relation under this abstraction.

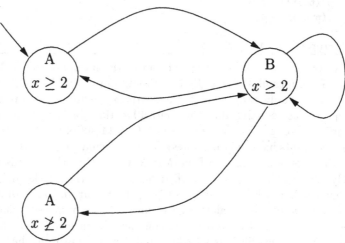

We can see by inspection that the desired invariant is satisfied in this system, so it remains to show that the postulated transition relation is a true abstraction of the original. The first and third of the verification conditions listed previously are discharged trivially by PVS, but the second yields the following sequent.

```
[-1]      pc(postc!1) = B
[-2]      x(prec!1) = 0
  |-------
[1]       x(prec!1) + 1 ≥ 2
```

Similar to the subgoal that arose in the invariance proof, this is inviting us to consider the case of a concrete transition into B from a state in which x is zero. Also similar to the original invariance proof, we see that this troublesome case can be eliminated by using the fact that $x \geq 1$ is a global invariant of the concrete system—but then we will again need to establish that this is indeed an invariant. As this example illustrates, justification of abstractions generally requires invariants. For the bounded retransmission protocol mentioned earlier, 45 invariants were needed to justify a proposed finite-state abstraction.

Now static analysis can easily establish that $x \geq 1$ is an invariant of our example system, so one way to enrich an integrated verification environment is by adding a static analysis component (e.g., [4]) that can deduce useful invariants. Justification of a given abstraction can then make use of such known invariants.

The alternative to justifying a given abstraction *a posteriori* is to construct one that is sound *a priori*: that is, the construction technique ensures that if the abstracted property is true of the abstraction so constructed, then the original property is true of the original system (the converse may not be so, however).

Several methods have been proposed for constructing abstracted transition relations for a given abstraction function. One way starts with the universal relation on the abstracted states; then, for each pair of abstract states, generates the verification condition that asserts that the arc between those two states can be removed (the condition is that there is no transition between any pair of original states that map to those abstract states). If the verification condition can be proved (using automatic proof procedures), then the transition can be omitted from the abstracted system description; if not, then it is conservative to include it. [2]. An alternative approach (specialized for predicate abstraction) develops the abstract transition relation by a forward reachability analysis; at each point it generates the verification conditions that lead to successor states with each given predicate true and with it false [18]. Both approaches can generate an abstracted specification for the bounded retransmission protocol in minutes; the first approach (which is implemented in an extension to PVS called InVeSt [3]) has the advantage that it preserves the structure of the original system description, the second (which is implemented in PVS itself) does not preserve structure but is generally faster and develops abstracted systems with fewer states.

Both these methods require the user to propose the abstraction function (and both work better when supplied with a collection of known invariants). For the case of predicate abstraction, it is natural to start by abstracting on subexpressions of the desired invariant that involve nonfinite variables. With our example system, abstracting on $x \geq 2$ yields the following abstracted system.

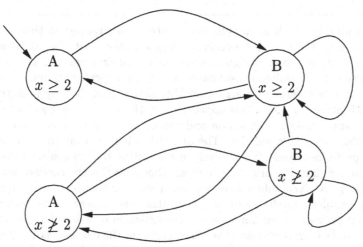

Unfortunately, we see that the abstracted invariant is not satisfied in this system (i.e., the state at the lower right is reachable). If, however, we take a counterexample trace generated by model checking the abstracted system—for example

$$\{A, \ x \geq 2\} \rightarrow \{B, \ x \geq 2\} \rightarrow \{A, \ x \not\geq 2\} \rightarrow \{B, \ x \not\geq 2\}$$

and then *concretize* it [1], we will obtain a trace such as

$$\{\text{A}, \ 2\} \ \rightarrow \ \{\text{B}, \ 3\} \ \rightarrow \ \{\text{A}, \ 1\} \ \rightarrow \ ?$$

in which it is impossible to find a final state that both concretizes the final abstract state and satisfies the concrete transition relation. This suggests that our initial abstraction is too coarse and that we should abstract on some additional predicates. Often, those appearing in guards are plausible candidates, but that is not the case here; however, inspection of the counterexample trace suggests $x \geq 1$ as a candidate. Abstracting on both $x \geq 2$ and $x \geq 1$ is a correct solution: it generates the same abstracted system that we previously generated by hand and sought to justify.

Using the abstractor built in to PVS version 2.3, this example is dispatched by a single proof strategy that combines abstraction and model checking when instructed to abstract on both $x \geq 2$ and $x \geq 1$.

```
|-------
{1}   FORALL (s: state): initial(s) IMPLIES AG(transition, prop)(s)

Rule? (ABSTRACT-AND-MC ("LAMBDA s: x(s)>=2" "LAMBDA s:   x(s)>=1"))

Starting computation of abstraction...abstraction computed in 4 seconds

calls to the decision procedure: possible: 38    performed: 34

MU simplification took 0.08 real, 0.05 cpu seconds
Q.E.D.
```

A difficulty in all these approaches involving abstraction is that the user must propose an abstraction function (or, equivalently, a set of predicates to be abstracted) that is strong enough to solve the entire problem: this is a substantial challenge that requires considerable insight or experimentation. A variant approach does not seek to construct an abstraction that directly preserves the property of interest: instead, this approach uses theorem proving as its top-level technique, and employs abstraction and model checking to help discharge the subgoals that are generated [16]. The attraction here is that theorem proving will have performed some case analysis in generating the subgoals, so that they will be simpler than the original problem. Therefore the abstraction needed to help discharge a given subgoal can be much simpler than one that discharges the whole problem; furthermore the predicates that appear in the formulas of the subgoal provide useful hints for the construction of a suitable abstraction. Another benefit from developing the abstractions in the context established by a theorem prover is that the prover keeps track of all outstanding proof obligations and subgoals, so that none can be forgotten or overlooked.

The techniques sketched in this section make fairly substantial use of both theorem proving and model checking, but they are still not truly integrated in

---

[1] "Concretization" is the inverse of abstraction; the inverse of the abstraction function is not a function, in general, so some approximation is required.

that model checking is used only to verify the final abstraction (though I did suggest how a counterexample trace could be used to aid diagnosis of an inadequate abstraction). The reason for this is that a traditional model checker returns very little information that can be used in subsequent analyses (basically, true/false plus possibly a counterexample in the latter case). However, it typically will have calculated a great deal of interesting information during its internal computation, and then thrown it away. For example, a symbolic model checker operating in the "forwards" mode calculates[2] the reachable states of its model. Now, the reachable states characterize the strongest invariant of a system, so a concretization of the reachable states of an abstracted system is certainly an invariant, and possibly a strong one, for the original system. This suggests a new way to calculate invariants that may help in the construction of abstracted system descriptions: construct some simpler abstraction (one for which already known invariants are adequate for its construction), and use a concretization of its reachable states as a new invariant that can help construct further abstractions. A practical difficulty in this approach is that the reachable state set calculated by a model checker is not usually made available externally and, in any case, it is usually represented by a data structure (a BDD) that is not directly suitable for input to a theorem prover. This difficulty has been overcome in the CMU version of the SMV model checker, where a `print` function, implemented by Sergey Berezin, provides external access to the reachable states.

An integrated combination of abstraction and reachability analysis similar to that sketched above is described in a recent paper by Abdulla et al [1]. Another related approach is described by Das, Dill, and Park [6].

5 Conclusion

A significant advance in the effectiveness and automation of verification for concurrent systems seems possible by combining techniques from model checking and theorem proving in a truly integrated environment. A key idea is to change the perception (and implementation) of model checkers and theorem provers from tools that perform verifications to ones that calculate *properties* (such as abstractions and invariants). By iterating through several such tools (together with tools for static analysis) operating on a common intermediate representation, it becomes possible to incrementally accumulate properties (e.g., invariants) that eventually enable computation of a substantial new property (e.g., an abstraction)—which in turn enables accumulation of further properties. By exploiting the combined power of several forms of mechanized formal analysis, proofs and refutations that currently require significant human effort (either in guiding a theorem prover or in constructing clever abstractions) will, I believe, soon become routine calculations.

---

[2] Or can calculate—it may terminate early if it discovers a reachable state that falsifies the desired property.

Acknowledgments

None of the work described here is mine; I have drawn freely on the research and insights of my colleagues Saddek Bensalem, David Dill, César Muñoz, Sam Owre, Vlad Rusu, Hassen Saïdi, N. Shankar, Eli Singerman, and Yassine Lakhnech. The SAL project is led at SRI by N. Shankar, and at Stanford by David Dill, and has benefitted from collaboration with Tom Henzinger at UC Berkeley.

I am grateful also to Dennis Dams and Mieke Massink for inviting me to the Fifth Spin Workshop, and for their careful reading of the first version of this paper.

References

1. Parosh Aziz Abdulla, Aurore Annichini, Saddek Bensalem, Ahmed Bouajjani, Peter Habermehl, and Yassine Lakhnech. Verification of infinite-state systems by combining abstraction and reachability analysis. In Halbwachs and Peled [8], pages 146–159.
2. Saddek Bensalem, Yassine Lakhnech, and Sam Owre. Computing abstractions of infinite state systems compositionally and automatically. In Hu and Vardi [11], pages 319–331.
3. Saddek Bensalem, Yassine Lakhnech, and Sam Owre. InVeSt: A tool for the verification of invariants. In Hu and Vardi [11], pages 505–510.
4. Saddek Bensalem, Yassine Lakhnech, and Hassen Saïdi. Powerful techniques for the automatic generation of invariants. In Rajeev Alur and Thomas A. Henzinger, editors, *Computer-Aided Verification, CAV '96*, volume 1102 of *Lecture Notes in Computer Science*, pages 323–335, New Brunswick, NJ, July/August 1996. Springer-Verlag.
5. Edmund M. Clarke, Orna Grumberg, and David E. Long. Model checking and abstraction. *ACM Transactions on Programming Languages and Systems*, 16(5):1512–1542, September 1994.
6. Satyaki Das, David L. Dill, and Seungjoon Park. Experience with predicate abstraction. In Halbwachs and Peled [8].
7. Matthew B. Dwyer and John Hatcliff. Slicing software for model construction. In *Proceedings of ACM SIGPLAN Workshop on Partial Evaluation and Semantics-Based Program Manipulation (PEPM'99)*, January 1999.
8. Nicolas Halbwachs and Doron Peled, editors. *Computer-Aided Verification, CAV '99*, number 1633 in Lecture Notes in Computer Science, Trento, Italy, July 1999. Springer-Verlag.
9. Klaus Havelund and Thomas Pressburger. Model checking Java programs using Java PathFinder. *Software Tools for Technology Transfer*, 1999. To appear.
10. Klaus Havelund and N. Shankar. Experiments in theorem proving and model checking for protocol verification. In *Formal Methods Europe FME '96*, volume 1051 of *Lecture Notes in Computer Science*, pages 662–681, Oxford, UK, March 1996. Springer-Verlag.
11. Alan J. Hu and Moshe Y. Vardi, editors. *Computer-Aided Verification, CAV '98*, volume 1427 of *Lecture Notes in Computer Science*, Vancouver, Canada, June 1998. Springer-Verlag.

12. C. Loiseaux, S. Graf, J. Sifakis, A. Bouajjani, and S. Bensalem. Property preserving abstractions for the verification of concurrent systems. *Formal Methods in System Design*, 6:11–44, 1995.

13. Ken McMillan. Minimalist proof assistants: Interactions of technology and methodology in formal system level verification. In Ganesh Gopalakrishnan and Phillip Windley, editors, *Formal Methods in Computer-Aided Design (FMCAD '98)*, volume 1522 of *Lecture Notes in Computer Science*, Palo Alto, CA, November 1998. Springer-Verlag. Invited presentation—no paper in proceedings, but slides available at http://www-cad.eecs.berkeley.edu/~kenmcmil/.

14. S. Rajan, N. Shankar, and M.K. Srivas. An integration of model-checking with automated proof checking. In Pierre Wolper, editor, *Computer-Aided Verification, CAV '95*, volume 939 of *Lecture Notes in Computer Science*, pages 84–97, Liege, Belgium, June 1995. Springer-Verlag.

15. John Rushby, Sam Owre, and N. Shankar. Subtypes for specifications: Predicate subtyping in PVS. *IEEE Transactions on Software Engineering*, 24(9):709–720, September 1998.

16. Vlad Rusu and Eli Singerman. On proving safety properties by integrating static analysis, theorem proving and abstraction. In W. Rance Cleaveland, editor, *Tools and Algorithms for the Construction and Analysis of Systems (TACAS '99)*, volume 1579 of *Lecture Notes in Computer Science*, pages 178–192, Amsterdam, The Netherlands, March 1999. Springer-Verlag.

17. Hassen Saïdi and Susanne Graf. Construction of abstract state graphs with PVS. In Orna Grumberg, editor, *Computer-Aided Verification, CAV '97*, volume 1254 of *Lecture Notes in Computer Science*, pages 72–83, Haifa, Israel, June 1997. Springer-Verlag.

18. Hassen Saïdi and N. Shankar. Abstract and model check while you prove. In Halbwachs and Peled [8], pages 443–454.

Runtime Efficient State Compaction in SPIN

J Geldenhuys and PJA de Villiers

Department of Computer Science, University of Stellenbosch,
7600 Stellenbosch, SOUTH AFRICA
{jaco,pja}@cs.sun.ac.za

Abstract. SPIN is a verification system that can detect errors automatically by exploring the reachable state space of a system. The efficiency of verifiers like SPIN depends crucially on the technique used for the representation of states. A number of recent proposals for more compact representations reduce the memory requirements, but cause a considerable increase in execution time. These methods could be used as alternatives when the standard state representation exhausts the memory, but this is exactly when the additional overhead is least affordable.

We describe a simple but effective state representation scheme that can be used in conjunction with SPIN's normal modes of operation. We compare the idea to SPIN's standard state representation and describe how SPIN was modified to support it. Experimental results show that the technique provides a valuable reduction in memory requirements and simultaneously *reduce* the execution time. For the cases considered an average reduction in memory requirements of 40% was measured and execution time was reduced on average by 19%. The proposed technique could therefore be considered to replace the default technique in SPIN.

1 Introduction

Model checking has been applied successfully to detect errors in systems of realistic size and complexity [1, 6]. SPIN is a well-known model checker that does on-the-fly state exploration to verify correctness claims stated as temporal logic formulae. With model checkers such as SPIN there are two main concerns: (1) the efficiency of state generation and (2) the amount of memory needed to store unique states. The state generation algorithm used in SPIN is highly efficient, but it seems possible to improve state storage.

Currently, SPIN must be used in *supertrace mode* to cope with large state spaces. This involves using a controlled partial search. The technique is based on hashing without collision detection and when collisions do occur, search paths are sometimes terminated prematurely. Unfortunately this means that errors could be missed.

A full state space exploration is always preferable, but this is only possible for much smaller models because all unique states must be stored in memory. One remedy is to reduce the state size by storing states in compacted form. Various state compaction techniques have been investigated, but all increase the execution time significantly [3, 5, 7]. In this paper we describe a state representation technique that is simple to implement. It does not only reduce the memory requirements, but often reduces the execution time as well. Section 2 describes the principles underlying our technique and Section 3 explains how the SPIN source code was modified to incorporate the proposed technique; results are presented in Section 4.

2 Proposed State Representation Technique

The global state of a PROMELA model consists of the values of the variables in all processes. Usually each state includes several data variables and a single location variable per process. These variables are aligned on byte boundaries because PROMELA supports various 8-bit, 16-bit and 32-bit types. Because one or more bytes are allocated to each variable, state sizes of more than a hundred bytes are not exceptional. Therefore, if all unique states are stored explicitly in uncompacted form, a model that generates a few million states quickly exhausts the memory available on typical workstations.

Most variables in validation models only assume a small subset of their potential values. An efficient technique to map these values onto consecutive integers would save a substantial amount of memory. One possible strategy is to enter unique states as they are encountered in lookup tables. This is the principle behind the approaches in [5, 7]. The position (index) in the table where a given state is entered then serves to identify the much larger state value. However, the overhead of manipulating these tables increases the execution time.

A significant reduction in state size is possible by simply placing tighter bounds on the ranges of variables and packing them into the minimum space required. This idea is the essence of the technique proposed here. Users can easily supply the information about the ranges of variables if the validation language supports user-definable types. For example, type definitions such as "ProcNumber = 0...4" are easy to use and provide enough information to store variables in compacted form.

A small example will illustrate the basic idea. Assume that a model contains three variables v_1, v_2, and v_3 which can respectively assume values from the ranges $0...4$, $0...2$, and $0...6$. Reflecting the number of different values each variable can assume, the compacted form V of each given state is computed as

$$V = v_3 + 7(v_2 + 3v_1)$$
$$= v_3 + 7v_2 + 7 \cdot 3v_1$$

Two constant factors are associated with each variable v_i. These factors, known as the lower and upper factors of each variable, are denoted by v_i^l and v_i^u respectively. In the example above, $v_3^l = 1$, $v_3^u = 7$, $v_2^l = 7$, $v_2^u = 7 \cdot 3 = 21$, $v_1^l = 21$, and $v_1^u = 7 \cdot 3 \cdot 5 = 105$. These factors are used as masks to extract and update the value of a specific variable in the compacted representation of a state.

Variables are manipulated by two basic operations which must be implemented as efficiently as possible. The operation *GetValue* used to extract the value of a given variable v_i from a compacted state V is simple: $v_i = (V \bmod v_i^u)$ $div\ v_i^l$. A simple adjustment is necessary to accommodate variables with non-zero offsets. The operation *SetValue*, which is used to change the value of a variable v_i to v_i', is a little more complex. The new compacted state V' is given by $V' = V + v_i^l \cdot (v_i' - v_i)$. The operations *GetValue* and *SetValue* represent the only overhead at execution time.

Assume that the number of values allowed for variable v_i is denoted by $|v_i|$ and that the lower and upper factors associated with v_i are denoted by v_i^l and v_i^u, respectively. The lower factor of variable v_1 is 1 and its upper factor is $|v_1|$. For $i > 1$ the lower and upper factors of variable v_i are given by

$$v_i^l = v_{i-1}^u$$
$$v_i^u = |v_i| \cdot v_i^l$$

These constants are computed only once for each variable and therefore contribute only a small constant overhead to the validation run. The number of bits required to store a compacted state with n variables is

$$\lceil \log_2 \prod_{i=1}^{n} |v_i| \rceil$$

For instance, the number of bits required to store v_1, v_2, and v_3 in the example above is $\lceil \log_2 5 \cdot 3 \cdot 7 \rceil = 7$.

3 Experimental Implementation Using SPIN

A detailed description of SPIN can be found in [4]. Most relevant here, is the format of the state vector as shown in Figure 1. The state vector stores the current state. It contains the number of processes (nr_pr), the number of queues (nr_qs), flags for cycle detection (a_t) and the contents of processes and queues. Each process (such as p_0) contains a unique identifier, its local state, the process type, and the values of its local variables. Each queue (such as q_1) contains the queue length, queue type, and the values of its elements. Unused elements are stored as zeros. The state vector is continually referenced as the values of variables are read and modified. It is kept in uncompacted form to speed up references to variables.

The SPIN verifier explores the state space in a depth-first manner, storing only the current execution path in a stack. The amount of memory required by the stack is not a serious concern; although the stack may sometimes contain several thousands of states, it is usually small relative to the size of the state space. A more serious problem is that in full search mode all unique states must be stored in a state table. In practice, the number of states that can be stored in the table determines the maximum size of models that can be handled. This is where compaction pays off: it makes it possible to store more states in the same amount of memory.

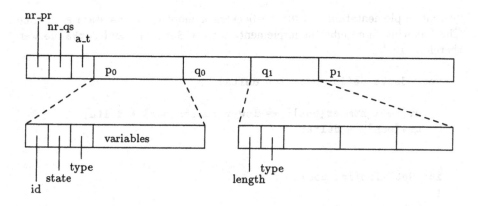

Fig. 1. Standard form of the state vector

It is not practical to store the entire compacted state as a single number and therefore variables are packed into subgroups called *cells*. Each cell is compacted separately and variables may not be split over more than one cell. This causes a small amount of space wastage, but speeds up the manipulation of variables. In the experimental implementation the state vector consists of an array of cells of type **unsigned long**. Each variable in the model is given a unique number, called its *position*. There are three tables: **cell_number** maps each position to the cell where it is stored, **lower_factor** maps each position to its lower factor, and **upper_factor** maps each position to its upper factor. The compacted state vector is stored in a global array variable called **sv**. The implementations of the SetValue and GetValue operations are simple:

```
void SetValue(int pos, int delta)
{
    sv[cell_number[pos]] += lower_factor[pos] * delta;
}

int GetValue(int pos)
{
    return sv[cell_number[pos]] %
        upper_factor[pos] / lower_factor[pos];
}
```

The **pos** parameter refers to the position of a variable, and the **delta** parameter of **SetValue** is the value $(v_i' - v_i)$, the difference between the old and new values of the variable.

However, this implementation of **GetValue** is too slow. A simple remedy is to keep an uncompacted copy of the current state in variable **usv**. For most models, the size of **usv** is less than 1 Kbyte. It is unnecessary to store **usv** in the state table, but, unfortunately, it must be stored on the stack to allow the current implementation of SPIN to backtrack more than one state at a time. The following more efficient implementations of SetValue and GetValue were therefore used:

```
void SetValue(int pos, int delta)
{
    sv[cell_number[pos]] += lower_factor[pos] * delta;
    usv[pos] += delta;
}

int GetValue(int pos)
{
    return usv[pos];
}
```

As new variables are created during the execution of a model, they are added to the state vector. This task is performed by the AddPosition routine. The parameter card indicates the cardinality ($|v_i|$) of the new variable.

```
void AddPosition(int card)
{
    if (MAXCELLVALUE / upper_factor[maxpos - 1] <= card)
    {
        /* use a new cell */
        lower_factor[maxpos] = 1;
        cell_number[maxpos] = cell_number[maxpos - 1] + 1;
    }
    else
    {
        lower_factor[maxpos] = upper_factor[maxpos - 1];
        cell_number[maxpos] = cell_number[maxpos - 1];
    }
    upper_factor[maxpos] = lower_factor[maxpos] * card;
    maxpos += 1;
}
```

The global variable maxpos stores the number of the highest position allocated so far. The test determines whether the new variable will fit into the current cell, or whether a new cell must be used. When a new cell is allocated, the last few bits of the previous cell are sometimes left unused. It is possible to minimize the number of bits wasted by reordering the variables, although this was not attempted in the current implementation.

Currently, a slightly restricted version of PROMELA is supported:

– Different orders of process activation along different execution paths are forbidden.

– No global channels are currently allowed. If necessary, models must be adapted so that the `init` process contains all channels, passing them to processes when they are created.
– The ranges of variables must start at 0.

It was necessary to make several modifications to the SPIN source code to implement the compaction technique: the PROMELA grammar was extended with a new data type, the translation of PROMELA statements was modified and a few other routines in the SPIN system were adapted to use the new state representation.

3.1 Modifications to the PROMELA Grammar

The range of each variable is needed and the simplest way to obtain this information is to ask the user to supply it. The PROMELA grammar was therefore extended to allow a new data type: **value** n. Instead of declaring a variable as

```
byte x;
```

we write

```
value 12 x;
```

which means that variable x can take on 12 different values ranging from 0 to 11. The declaration

```
mtype = { A, B, C, D };
```

is transformed into

```
#define A 4
#define B 3
#define C 2
#define D 1
#define mtype value 5
```

(The values for the messages were chosen to be internally consistent with the current SPIN implementation.) So, instead of

```
chan q = [4] of { mtype, int };
```

we could write

```
chan q = [4] of { mtype, value 6 };
```

In our opinion, it would be better to provide such user-definable types to replace the fixed types of PROMELA. This would allow users to place tighter bounds on the ranges of variables. The notation above was selected for its simplicity; it may be more convenient to also specify the lower bound, to allow types such as "$-2\ldots2$" and "$60\ldots70$". It may also be useful to allow user-defined subrange types instead of the scheme described above. As an example, a counter that can take on values 0 through 10 could then be declared as follows:

```
subrange Counter = 0...10;
Counter c;
```

3.2 Modification to the Manipulation of Variables

Normally SPIN translates PROMELA statements to code that performs operations
on the normal state vector shown in Figure 1. This system was modified so that
the generated code acts on the new compacted state vector. The most important
statements are accesses to local variables of processes.

A read access of variable x is translated as

```
GetValue(pos)
```

where pos is the position of x in the state vector. A write access, or assignment,
x = e, is translated as

```
SetValue(pos, e - GetValue(pos))
```

Turning to a more concrete example, consider the PROMELA statement

```
x = y + 2
```

where x and y are local variables of some process. This is normally translated as

```
case 6: /* STATE 5 - [x = (y+2)] */
   IfNotBlocked
   (trpt+1)->oval = ((int)((P2 *)this)->x);
   ((P2 *)this)->x = (((int)((P2 *)this)->y)+2);
   m = 3; goto P999;
```

In the modified version of SPIN the assignment is translated as

```
case 6: /* STATE 5 - [x = (y+2)] */
   IfNotBlocked
   pos = curproc+14;
   delta = (GetValue(curproc+15) + 2) - GetValue(pos);
   (trpt+1)->oval = delta;
   SetValue(pos, delta);
   m = 3; goto P999;
```

The main difference is that procedures GetValue and SetValue are used to
manipulate variables. The constants 14 and 15 in the example are the positions
of variables x and y relative to the start of the process to which they are local.
The starting position of the variables of a process is stored in curproc.

4 Results

A number of well-known PROMELA models were used to measure the effectiveness
of the compaction technique. Some of the models (leader, pftp, snoopy, and sort)
are part of the standard SPIN distribution, but were slightly modified to adhere

to the restrictions of our implementation. The other models (cambridge and slide) were collected from the Internet[1].

Table 1 shows the memory required (in Mbytes) followed by the time needed to complete each validation run (in seconds)[2]. The first column (marked SPIN) gives the results for the standard SPIN system. The next column (marked SPIN-C) is for the modified SPIN system with compact representation of states. The last column shows the ratio between the two systems for purposes of comparison.

Table 1. Comparison of standard SPIN against SPIN with the proposed compression technique (SPIN-C)

Model	SPIN		SPIN-C		Ratio	
	memory	time	memory	time	memory	time
cambridge	54.1	6.9	23.8	6.8	0.44	0.99
leader	91.7	12.6	33.2	7.7	0.36	0.61
pftp	66.6	8.9	26.5	7.3	0.40	0.83
snoopy	15.2	1.7	10.6	1.4	0.70	0.84
sort	3.7	0.3	4.4	0.2	1.19	0.77
sort(BIG)	130.7	22.6	70.4	14.7	0.54	0.65
slide	33.3	3.2	20.3	3.2	0.61	0.97
Average					0.60	0.81

Note that the technique works best for the larger models. A useful reduction in memory requirements was measured for most models, the average being 40%. More surprising, however, is that execution time was *decreased* on average by 19%.

As can be expected, the results differ from one model to the next. This is due to differences in the number of variables, the number of read and write accesses, and the structure of the state space. In fact, when models use large amounts of stack memory compared to the amount of state table memory, the technique does not seem to help at all.

For example, a model of six dining philosophers[3] yields a memory ratio of 1.89 and a time ratio of 1.11. This model is unusual because the stack reaches a depth of 152383 states, while the state table contains only 94376 states. For the majority of models, the situation is reversed. The execution time is longer in this case, since a substantial overhead is associated with pushing states onto the stack. This overhead comes from copying the uncompacted state vector to the stack. This overhead is avoided in SPIN's standard mode of operation because the uncompacted state vector is not stored in the stack. A substantial modification of the internal mechanisms of SPIN is required to address this problem, but

---

[1] http://cm.bell-labs.com/cm/cs/what/spin/Man/Exercises.html
[2] Tests were executed on a 400MHz Pentium II with 256 Mbytes of memory.
[3] http://www.ececs.uc.edu/~imutaban/miniproject/2Phase/2phase.html

this was not attempted since our goal was simply to test the feasibility of the technique in the context of SPIN.

More information about the models is given in Table 2. The first three columns give the size of the original SPIN state vector in bytes, the number of variables in each model, and the number of cells (of 4 bytes each) occupied by the compacted state vector. The last two columns contain the number of unique states and length of the longest path on the stack.

Table 2. More details about models

Model	SPIN	# variables	cells	states	depth
cambridge	64	52	5	728544	13004
leader	148	223	18	341290	148
pftp	140	109	11	439895	5780
snoopy	196	105	14	91920	12250
sort	140	92	16	15351	115
sort(BIG)	188	147	23	659683	202
slide	52	43	4	510111	51072

5   Discussion and Conclusions

Compact representation of states is crucial in verifiers like SPIN and various compaction techniques have been investigated by modifying the SPIN source code. In Table 3 a comparison is given for five such techniques. (Only the pftp and snoopy data are available for all techniques considered.) The measurements in the table were taken from the literature [3, 5, 7]. Although they were measured on different platforms and cannot be compared directly to each other, they provide a rough indication of the cost of each technique.

Because the platforms and validation models differ, it is difficult to draw general conclusions about the effectiveness of specific techniques. However, all compression techniques proposed thus far seem to increase execution times while the technique proposed in this article can *reduce* the runtime required. This is surprising. A possible explanation is that the reduction in state size—which speeds up state comparison and manipulation—must be more than enough to compensate for the compression overhead. On the negative side, only a fair amount of compression can be expected in general.

The impressive performance of some compression techniques rely on extra information that must be supplied by users. For example, it may be necessary to obtain information about the behaviour of variables from training runs [3, 5]. In addition, the most powerful technique considered ([3]) requires that users define an encoding for state information. To be fair, this extra time and effort cannot be ignored. The technique proposed here only needs information that can be derived automatically from the declaration of variables at compile time.

Table 3. Comparison of state compression techniques. The first four rows of measurements were taken directly from the literature, while the last two rows were measured on a 400MHz Pentium II.

Technique	pftp		snoopy	
	memory	time	memory	time
GETSs [3]	0.05	2.07	0.09	3.38
State compression [7]	0.25	1.24	0.17	0.29
Recursive indexing [5]	0.18	1.41	0.33	2.45
Two-phase compression [5]	0.15	2.42	0.22	3.23
Recursive indexing [5]	0.18	2.54	0.27	3.47
State compaction (proposed technique)	0.40	0.83	0.70	0.84

The technique relies on extra information regarding the minimum and maximum values assumed by variables. It is easy to obtain this information if user-definable types are used instead of the predefined fixed types of PROMELA. In fact, based on our experience with ESML [2]—a specification language similar to PROMELA—we know that it requires little extra effort of users to define the ranges of variables more precisely. When it comes to the implementation of such models, it is trivial to find the optimal representation for integer subranges.

We have demonstrated the feasibility of our idea in a well-known context by modifying the SPIN source code to test the technique. The results indicate that substantially larger models can be handled in full search mode, while reducing execution time as a bonus.

References

1. E. M. Clarke and J. M. Wing. Formal methods: state of the art and future directions. ACM Computing Surveys, 28(4):626–643, December 1996.
2. P. J. A. de Villiers and W. C. Visser. ESML—a validation language for concurrent systems. South African Computer Journal, 7:59–64, July 1992.
3. J.-Ch. Grégoire. State space compression in SPIN with GETSs. In Proceedings of the 2nd SPIN Workshop, 1996.
4. G. J. Holzmann. Design and Validation of Computer Protocols. Prentice Hall Software Series, 1991.
5. G. J. Holzmann. State compression in SPIN: recursive indexing and compression training runs. In Proceedings of the 3rd SPIN Workshop, 1997.
6. J. Rushby. Mechanized formal methods: progress and prospects. In Proceedings of the 16th Conference on the Foundations of Software Technology and Theoretical Computer Science, Lecture Notes in Computer Science #1180, pages 43–51. Springer-Verlag, December 1996.
7. W. C. Visser. Memory efficient state storage in SPIN. In Proceedings of the 2nd SPIN Workshop, 1996.

Distributed-Memory Model Checking with SPIN

Flavio Lerda and Riccardo Sisto

Dipartimento di Automatica e Informatica
Politecnico di Torino
Corso Duca degli Abruzzi, 24, I-10129 Torino (Italy)
e-mail: flerda@athena.polito.it, sisto@polito.it

Abstract. The main limiting factor of the model checker SPIN is currently the amount of available physical memory. This paper explores the possibility of exploiting a distributed-memory execution environment, such as a network of workstations interconnected by a standard LAN, to extend the size of the verification problems that can be successfully handled by SPIN. A distributed version of the algorithm used by SPIN to verify safety properties is presented, and its compatibility with the main memory and complexity reduction mechanisms of SPIN is discussed. Finally, some preliminary experimental results are presented.

1 Introduction

The model checker SPIN [4] is a tool widely used to verify concurrent system models. Its success depends on many factors, among which its amazing efficiency in performing model checking and its portability, i.e. the fact that, being written in ANSI C, it runs on most computer platforms.

The main limitation of SPIN, of course shared by all other verification tools based on reachability analysis, is that it can deal with models up to a given maximum size. As a model gets larger and larger, also the memory usage increases, and when the amount of memory used becomes greater than the available physical memory, the workstation is forced to use virtual memory. Since the memory is mainly allocated for a hash table, which is accessed randomly, the system will proceed slowly due to thrashing. In practice, it can be observed with SPIN that when the memory used is less than the physical available memory the performance of the model checker is excellent, and execution time is generally at most in the order of minutes, but as soon as the physical memory is exhausted the performance drops down dramatically. As a consequence, the maximum model size that SPIN can deal with depends essentially on the amount of physical memory that is available.

Various techniques are used by SPIN to reduce the amount of memory needed for verification, thus making the analysis of larger models possible. The main examples are state compression, partial order reductions and bit state hashing. A different technique that could be applied to further extend the size of the verification problems that can be successfully handled by SPIN is the use of a distributed-memory environment such as a network of workstations (NOW), which is ultimately a way to increase the amount of actually available physical memory, and to increase the speed of the verification process by exploiting parallel processing. In this paper we explore this possibility and present some preliminary results. Attention is focused here only on verification of safety properties such as deadlocks and assertions, and not on LTL model checking, which is left for further study.

As memory in SPIN is used mainly to store states, the distributed version of SPIN that we consider is based on a partition of the state space into as many state regions as the number of network nodes. Each node is assigned a different state region, and holds only the states belonging to that subset. In this way, the state table is distributed over a NOW. Each node computes the successors of the states that it holds and, if it finds any successors belonging to other state regions, it sends them to the nodes that are in charge of processing them. Of course, performance depends on how the state space is partitioned, the best results being obtained if the workload is well balanced and communication is minimized. In this paper we consider different possible approaches to the partitioning problem and compare them.

Another important issue that must be taken into consideration is that a distributed version of SPIN should not exclude the use of the other main memory and complexity reduction techniques available in the centralized version, such as state compression, partial order reduction, and bit state hashing. The approach that we consider in this paper is characterized by good compatibility with such mechanisms.

Since one of the strengths of SPIN stands in its portability and widespread use, we decided to develop an experimental distributed version of SPIN that can run on a very common platform: a NOW made up of heterogeneous workstations, interconnected with a standard 10Mbps Ethernet and using the TCP/IP protocol. Of course, more sophisticated communication infrastructures may yield better performance, but the basic environment that we considered is generally available to everyone, and its performance can be considered a reasonable lower bound.

A parallel/distributed version of a reachability analysis model checker, based on the Murφ Verifier [2], was proposed in [8]. The approach taken in [8] is similar to our one, but we use different ways to partition the state space. Moreover, in contrast with SPIN, the Murφ model checker uses a model where the computation of the next states may be quite complex, so with Murφ the most critical resource is not memory, but time. As documented in [8], there are cases where a verification run may take up to several days to complete. For this reason, the main purpose of the distributed version of Murφ is to speed up the verification process, exploiting parallel processing. With our distributed version of SPIN instead we mainly aim at making tractable models that otherwise would be intractable. Moreover, any speed up attained thanks to parallel processing tends to be obscured by communication overhead, which is generally predominant with respect to the short time taken by SPIN in computing the next states.

There has been also a previous proposal to develop a distributed model checker [1], in which the future state computation and the storage function are located at different nodes. This architecture is more complex than our one and the communication overhead is higher because each state is transferred at least two times over the network, since it has to go from the computation node that generated it to the storing node where it is kept for future reference and then back again from it to the computation node that must find its successors.

The rest of the paper is organized as follows. First, the distributed version of the SPIN verification algorithm is described, along with some implementation issues. Then the compatibility of this algorithm with the main memory and complexity reduction mechanisms of SPIN is discussed, and some preliminary experimental results are given. Finally, some conclusions are drawn and perspectives for further research are discussed.

2 The Distributed Verification Algorithm

2.1 The Centralized Algorithm

When SPIN must verify safety properties of a concurrent system, such as proper termination and state properties, it generates a verification program that makes a depth first visit of the system state space graph. The following pseudo code represents the centralized version of such a program:

```
procedure Start(start_state);
begin
  V := {}; { already visited states }
  DFS(start_state);
end;

procedure DFS(state);
begin
  if not state in V then
  begin
    V := V + state;
    for each sequential process P do
    begin
      nxt = all transitions of P enabled in state
      for each t in nxt do
      begin
        st = successor of state after t
        DFS(st);
      end;
    end;
  end;
end;
```

The procedure DFS makes a depth first visit of the graph, and is first called on the initial state (start_state). If the state to visit is not already present in the set of visited states V, it is added to V, and the DFS procedure is recursively called for each of its possible successors st. The computation of the successors consists of identifying the enabled transitions of the processes making up the model and determining the successor of the current state after each of such transitions. When an already visited state is found, the visit does not proceed any deeper.

For efficiency, the recursive DFS procedure is simulated by means of a user defined stack that contains the moves made from the initial state to the current state, along with all the information needed to restore the current state after a simulated recursive call of DFS(st). The set of visited states V is implemented by an hash table with collision lists, which is generally the most memory consuming data structure, its size being proportional to the number of states in the state graph. Also the stack data structure can consume a considerable amount of memory, because its size is proportional to the depth of the state graph, which, in some cases, can be comparable with the number of states.

2.2 The Distributed Algorithm

The idea at the basis of the distributed version of the verification algorithm is to partition the state space into as many subsets as the number of network nodes. Every node owns one of the state subsets, and is responsible for holding the states it owns and for computing their successors. When a node computes a new state, first it checks if the state belongs to its own state subset or to the subset of another node. If the state is local, the node goes ahead as usual, otherwise a message containing the state is sent to the owner of the state. Received messages are held in a queue and processed in sequence. When all queues are empty and all nodes are idle the verification ends.

The following pseudocode illustrates the algorithm used in the distributed version:

```
procedure Start(i, start_state);
begin
  V[i] := {}; { already visited states }
  U[i] := {}; { pending queue }
  j := Partition(start_state);
  if i = j then
  begin
    U[i] := U[i] + start_state;
  end;
  Visit(i);
end;

procedure Visit(i);
begin
```

```
      while true do
      begin
        while U[i] = {} do
        begin
        end;
        S := extract(U[i]);
        DFV(i,S);
      end;
    end;

  procedure DFV(i, state);
  begin
    if not state in V then
    begin
      V[i] := V[i] + state;
      for each sequential process P do
      begin
        nxt = all transitions of P enabled in state
        for each t in nxt do
        begin
          st = successor of state after t
          j := Partition(st);
          if j = i then
          begin
            DFV(i, st);
          end else begin
            U[j] := U[j] + st;
          end;
        end;
      end;
    end;
  end;
```

The nodes that participate in the algorithm execute all the same program, but each one of them calls the Start procedure with a different value of i, which is an integer index that identifies it. The set of visited states V is partitioned, V[i] being the subset assigned to node i, and Partition(s) being the function that takes a state s and returns the identifier of the node that owns s. Each node is coupled asynchronously with the other ones by means of an input pending requests queue. U[i] indicates the queue of node i. It is initially empty for every node but the one that owns the initial state.

Every node starts the visit (procedure Visit) waiting until a state is present in its input pending requests queue. At the beginning, only one node, the one that owns the initial state, has a non-empty queue and can proceed calling the DFV procedure. This procedure is almost the same as the previous procedure DFS. It performs a depth first visit of the state space graph, starting from the argument state, but the visit is restricted within the state space region owned by the node. The visit is not performed if the state has already been visited. If instead the state is new, it is added to the visited states set V[i]. Then each successor of the current state is computed in the usual way and checked with the Partition function. If the state st is local, i.e. it is owned by the same node, the procedure DFV is recursively called for that state, otherwise DFV is not called and the state is added to the pending requests queue of the corresponding node, which will continue the interrupted visit in its own state space region.

The main consequence of using this algorithm instead of the centralized one is that the visit does no longer follow the depth first order globally. From the correctness point of view, this is not a problem with the standard reachability analysis verification of safety properties that we consider in this paper, because it works with a non depth first visit as well. LTL verification instead needs a (nested) depth first visit to give the correct results so the algorithm presented here is not adequate for this kind of verification. Of course it would be possible to modify the algorithm to make the visit depth first, but this would cut off most of the parallel processing involved in the algorithm. From the memory usage point of view, a new data structure U[i] has been introduced, which increases the overall amount of memory needed. On the other hand, the non depth first order of the visit makes it possible to use a smaller stack structure, which can compensate for this memory increase. Moreover, the amount of memory needed for the pending requests queue can be bounded if some kind of flow control policy is applied.

2.3 The Partition Function

The Partition function that takes a state and returns the identifier of the region to which it belongs must depend exclusively on the state itself. Moreover, to balance the workload among the nodes, in terms of both memory and computation time, it should divide the state space evenly. Finally, to minimize communication overhead, it should minimize cross-transitions, i.e. transitions between states belonging to different regions.

A first simple possibility for partitioning is to use the same hash function that is applied to the state when it is stored in the hash table, as suggested in [8] for the parallelization of Murϕ. In the case of an homogeneous network of workstations, this solution can be implemented very easily in a distributed SPIN program working with the above algorithm, but in the case of an heterogeneous one it cannot be implemented unless the hash function used by SPIN is modified. In fact, state vectors, i.e. the binary representations that SPIN uses for states, are different on different computer architectures, and the hash function of SPIN depends on such representations. Another problem with the hash partition function is that, although as shown in [8] it statistically divides the state space evenly, it does not address the problem of minimizing the number of cross-transitions.

Here we propose also another way to solve the partitioning problem, that exploits the structure of the global system states in SPIN.

SPIN is used to verify models of systems made up of synchronously or asynchronously coupled concurrent processes, where each process is described by a state machine. In such models, a global state contains a state component for each concurrent process. Since a state transition generally involves only few processes, generally one process for local actions or asynchronous interactions and two processes for synchronous interactions, when the system evolves from one state to another state only few state components change, the majority of them remaining unaffected. Based on these considerations, a convenient yet simple partitioning rule consists of defining the partition subsets according to the values taken by just one of the state components. In practice, the state region to which a state belongs depends only on the state component of one of the concurrent processes making up the model, called the designated process. Such a process can be for instance the one in a particular position in the state vector or the first one of a particular type. A table gives the correspondence between the states of the designated process and the state space subsets. With this kind of partition function, cross-transitions are transitions that determine a state change in the designated process, and, because of the above considerations, they are a limited fraction of the total. Moreover, some preliminary experiments show that partitions generated in this way are sufficiently well balanced.

The intuitive results that have just been presented can be confirmed by a simple analysis of the average features of the two partition functions. Let P, S and T be respectively the number of processes, of states and of state transitions in the model to be analyzed. Also, let N be the number of nodes used for distributed-memory reachability analysis. In general, the partition function is a function $\pi : S \to \{1, ..., N\}$, mapping global states to integers in the range from 1 to N.

With hash partitioning, states are mapped randomly and uniformly over state space regions. Hence, the average fraction of states belonging to a given region is $1/N$. For what concerns cross transitions, let us consider a generic state $s \in S$, and let T_s be the set of transitions starting from s, and D_s be the set of destination states of transitions in T_s. If we assume that there are no self transitions (i.e. transitions that do not change the global model state), because of the uniform distribution of states over regions, we can say that the average fraction of elements of D_s belonging to the same state region of s is $1/N$. Hence, the average fraction of elements of D_s belonging to other regions is $1 - 1/N$, and this represents also the average fraction of cross-transitions. Although this result does not take into account self-transitions, it can be considered a good approximation, because generally the fraction of self transitions is negligible in that it is very uncommon that a transition does neither change the values of any of the variables nor the "program counter" of any of the processes in the model.

Let us now consider the case of a partition function that depends on one state component only. Each state s of the model to be analyzed is composed of several state components, $s_i \in S_i$, i.e. $s = (s_1, ..., s_m)$. Let s_d be the state component representing the state of the designated process, and $\pi_d : S_d \to \{1, ..., N\}$ be the local partition function defined on the designated process state space S_d. The partition function that we are considering is one such that $\pi(s_1, ..., s_m) = \pi_d(s_d)$. Let us assume that π_d is selected so as to divide S_d into N equally sized subsets. In this case, the average fraction of global states $s = (s_1, ..., s_m)$ such that $\pi_d(s_d)$ takes a given value is $1/N$, and this is also the average fraction of global states belonging to a given region. With a partition function depending on one state component only, a cross transition is a transition that implies a change in the designated process state component from s_d to s'_d, such that $\pi_d(s_d) \neq \pi_d(s'_d)$. Let k be the average number of processes involved in a transition, which is a value ranging between 1 and 2. Then, k/P represents the average fraction of processes involved in a transition. Assuming that each process has the same chance of being involved in a transition, k/P represents also the average fraction of transitions that a given process is involved into. So we can say that the designated process is involved on average in a fraction k/P of the transitions. If we call ϕ_d the fraction of cross transitions in the designated process state machine, i.e. the fraction of local transitions of the designated process such that the starting state and the ending state are mapped to different regions, then we can conclude that the average fraction of cross transitions in the global state machine is $\phi_d k/P$.

This simplified analysis shows that on average the two partition functions both divide evenly the state space. However, the average fraction of cross transitions is $(N-1)/N$ with hash partitioning whereas it is $\phi_d k/P$ with a partitioning function based on one state component only. It can be observed that the first ratio tends to approach 1 as N becomes large, whereas in the second one only the ϕ_d factor gets close to 1, the average fraction of cross transitions remaining always less than k/P.

2.4 Keeping Track of Error Traces

If an error is found during the visit of the state space graph, the verification program must produce the trace of the model actions that lead to the error. In the centralized version of the program, this is done simply traversing the stack structure. In the distributed version, a similar approach is possible, but each node must hold the whole stack, containing the moves from the initial state to the current state, and not only the part of it corresponding to the execution of the DFV procedure. To make this possible, the message used to send a state to another node contains not only the state representation, but also the path that leads to that state, represented as a sequence of moves. The receiver uses the state representation to decide if the state has already been visited and eventually discards the message. If instead the state is new, the path is added to a list of paths representing the U[i] queue. Later on, when a path is dequeued, it is used to recreate the corresponding state: the path is followed, and every move in it is executed. In this way, the stack is automatically initialized to contain the execution path that leads to the current state. When an error occurs, the node behaves as in the centralized program.

For efficiency, in our experimental implementation of the algorithm, paths sent together with state representations are not absolute, but relative to the previous path sent. Moreover, they are represented in a compact way, using a simple run-length compression. In this way, the average message sizes are kept within reasonable values.

2.5 Algorithm Termination

The distributed algorithm must terminate when the U[i] queues are all empty and all nodes are idle. The detection of this condition is a typical problem of a class of distributed algorithms, including parallel discrete event simulation, and can be solved in different ways [7]. Here we sketch a possible solution, which has been used in the experimental implementation of the algorithm.

We use a manager process that is in charge of starting the verification program in a predetermined set of network nodes, and of stopping it after having detected termination and collected the results. Each node sends to the manager a message when it becomes idle and a different one when it becomes busy, i.e. when its queue becomes non-empty. In this way, the manager has a local representation of the current status of all the nodes.

When the manager detects on its local copy that all nodes are idle, it asks for a confirmation, because the local copy of the manager could be non consistent with the actual status of the nodes. If in the meanwhile a node has received a new message containing a new state to be visited, and then has become busy, it sends back a negative acknowledgment. Positive acknowledgments also contain the total number of messages sent and received by the node. The manager commands the nodes to terminate if each of them sent a positive acknowledgment and the overall number of messages sent is equal to the overall number of messages received. If this is not the case, there are some messages still traveling in the network. In this case the manager does not know if such messages will cause a node to start a new visit, because they may contain already visited states, so the manager needs to reset the procedure and then ask for a new confirmation round from all the nodes again.

2.6 Other Implementation Issues

An experimental modified version of the model checker SPIN that generates a distributed version of the verification program according to the above algorithm has been implemented. The generated source files can be used to make both the centralized and the distributed versions of the program, depending on a macro definition.

One of the main objectives (and also a main problem to solve) was to get the verification work on a network of heterogeneous workstations. Our first try was to use the PVM library [3], which is a widely used package that provides a transparent message passing interface for networks of heterogeneous workstations. This possibility was later abandoned, because of the overhead introduced and because of the need to implement flow control over the PVM layer. In fact the PVM library buffers messages in the receiving machine memory without limitations, and this may cause memory overflow problems. We decided then to use the socket interface, that provides standard bidirectional connections where flow control is already implemented. On top of it we used an XDR (eXternal Data Representation) layer, to make the transfer of data between different architectures transparent. The program has been successfully tested on three different platforms: Intel - Linux, Alpha - Digital Unix, and Sparc - SunOS.

3 Compatibility with Memory and Complexity Reduction Mechanisms

Whenever a new technique to extend the capabilities of a tool like SPIN is introduced, it is important to verify that it is compatible with the memory and complexity reduction mechanisms available in the basic version of the tool, otherwise the implied risk is that the overall performance of the tool is not really extended by the introduction of the new technique, but possibly reduced.

In this section, the main reduction mechanisms of SPIN are considered and compatibility with each of them is discussed. Some of them have already been implemented in our experimental distributed version of SPIN, whereas others can be easily added.

3.1 State Compression

SPIN implements various schemes of compression, that are used for reducing the amount of memory needed for storing states, but whichever compression technique is used, the state is always computed in its uncompressed form, and then it is compressed before being stored. In the distributed version of the program, the hash table is divided into different sub-tables, and for each of them any compression mechanism can be applied for storing states, without limitations.

Although the use of any compression technique is always possible, there may be performance implications. In its simplest form, compression is a function f that transforms a state s into a compact representation $f(s)$. The original representation s can be retrieved applying the inverse of f. Other compression schemes are characterized by memory, i.e. the result of the compression function depends on the history of compression operations previously performed. In the distributed version of the program, two aspects play an important role: the kind of compression that is used (with or without memory) and the heterogeneity of the network nodes.

If the network nodes are homogeneous, the state representation is the same on any network node. If a memoryless compression scheme is used, states can be sent in their compressed form and the amount of memory needed to store states is the same as in the centralized version. Moreover, in this case compression contributes to reduce the communication overhead. If instead a compression scheme with memory is used, states must be sent in their uncompressed form, and compression must be performed at the receiver side, otherwise the receiver may not be able to reconstruct the uncompressed state from the compressed one. In addition, the behavior of the compression function may be different from the one in the centralized version.

In an heterogeneous environment, the representations of a given state differ from node to node. For this reason, the state must be transformed into a machine-independent representation such as XDR before being sent to another network node. Let us call g the function that transforms a state s into its machine-independent form $g(s)$. Since the compression mechanisms of SPIN work on the machine-dependent representation of s, in this case the sender must send $g(s)$, and the receiver will reconstruct s from $g(s)$ and then apply f before storing s.

In our experimental implementation we included the two main compression schemes of SPIN, i.e. standard compression and collapse compression.

3.2 Partial Order Reduction

SPIN uses a static partial order reduction technique [6], which is a means to avoid the exploration of some execution sequences that are not strictly required to prove the safety or liveness properties of the concurrent system being analyzed. When this reduction method is applied, the expansion step in which the successors of a state are computed is modified, with the aim of computing only a minimal subset of all the possible successors. The expansion step is performed expanding each concurrent process, i.e. computing the possible state transitions of each process, and, for each of such transitions, computing the global successor state. Before the actual expansion step is carried out, processes are examined sequentially, to identify the ones that can execute only so-called safe transitions [6]. In fact, it has been shown that it is enough to expand just one of such processes, provided that the successors fulfill a condition, known as the reduction proviso. The verification program computes the successors generated by the transitions of each of the above processes first, and as soon as it finds one of them that generates a set of successors satisfying the reduction proviso, it interrupts the expansion, thus ignoring the successors generated by the other processes. In the worst case, all the processes are expanded, and no reduction occurs. The reduction proviso can be different according to the kind of properties that reduction must preserve. If only safety properties must be preserved, as we assume in this paper, it is enough to require, as a reduction proviso, that there is at least one successor not contained in the stack [5].

In the distributed version of the verification program, the static information about which transitions are safe is known by all the nodes, so any node can make a preselection of the processes, and examine first those that can execute only such transitions. However a problem arises when one of the nodes must check if the reduction proviso is fulfilled. If some of the successors are stored outside the node that has computed them, such a node cannot know by itself if they are currently in the stack, because this information is hold by SPIN in the state table. Obliging any node to hold a copy of all the states currently in the stack is cumbersome and memory-consuming. This problem can be avoided taking a conservative (worst case) assumption: successors that are hold outside the node where they are computed are always assumed to be currently in the stack. In this way, safety properties are preserved, but it is possible that some of the reductions that are carried out in the centralized version of the program cannot be carried out also in the distributed version.

It is interesting to note that, if we consider specifically the case of a partition function that depends on one of the state components only, it is possible to increase the number of reductions that can be performed. The reason is that in this case any transition that does not involve the designated process is not a cross-transition, i.e. it leads to a successor state that is in the same region as the current state. Therefore, the reduction proviso can always be checked for all such transitions. Moreover, if the designated process is arranged so as to always be the last process that is examined in the preselection phase, it is expanded only when no other process can be expanded. In this way, the number of reductions performed is maximized, and, as an additional side-effect, the fraction of cross-transitions is further reduced. This happens because, whenever different alternative reductions can be applied, always a reduction without cross-transitions is selected.

3.3 Bit State Hashing

Bit state hashing is a complexity reduction mechanism that affects the way in which states are stored in the hash table. It can be considered as a compression mechanism with loss of information, because a state is stored in a single bit. Consequently, the considerations made for compression also apply for bit state hashing, i.e. the distributed version of the program is compatible with it.

4 Experimentation and Results

The experimental distributed version of SPIN has been tested on some test cases, to measure its performance. The testbed that has been used is a NOW composed of 300Mhz Pentium II Linux workstations with 64Mbytes of RAM each, interconnected with a standard 10Mbps Ethernet LAN. The selected test samples are all scalable using one or more parameters, and experiments have been carried out with values of the parameters that are critical for the workstations that have been used.

Table 1 contains the results obtained using three scalable samples named Bakery, Leader, and Philo. For each sample and each set of values of the parameters the number of states and transitions are reported. Of course, the number of states mainly influences memory usage while the number of transitions mainly influences computation time. The tests were executed on a single workstation with the original centralized program and on two and four workstations with the distributed one. For each test case the average memory usage per node in megabytes and the execution time in seconds are reported. All the results are referred to an exhaustive verification and have been obtained using the XDR layer and a partition function that depends on a single state component. Missing results mean that verification could not be completed because of memory allocation failure.

Bakery is a description of the Lamport's Bakery algorithm for mutual exclusion with N processes that make at most K attempts. The Bakery sample was tested using the standard compression and partial order reduction features of SPIN. Since partial order reduction can alter the number of states and transitions actually explored, the data in the second and third rows are those reported by the centralized version. The partial order reduction is slightly less effective on the distributed version, and its effectiveness decreases as the state subsets get smaller, so the numbers of states and transitions with the distributed version are greater than with the centralized version. While in the other samples the memory per node nearly halves when doubling the number of workstations, in this case the memory used decreases but not so rapidly. Nevertheless, it can be observed that, when the total memory usage is higher than the physical memory available on a single workstation (second and third columns), the distributed version performs better than the centralized one.

Leader is the leader election algorithm model that can be found in the SPIN distribution. It was compiled with collapse compression, but without partial order reductions. The Leader sample memory usage grows very fast. While with N=6 the distribution of the verification program is still not convenient because of the modest memory usage, with N=7 the load is too heavy for a single workstation, and gives the best results with 4 workstations. This is an example of a verification that cannot be completed on a single workstation, because of memory allocation failure, but can be completed on multiple workstations. The results of distributed verification with N=7 are not so good as they could be, because the partition function used in the experiment is not so fair. In fact, even if the average memory usage for each node is less than the physical memory, we found that at least one node was thrashing due to its higher number of states to visit.

Philo is a model describing the dining philosophers problem. It was compiled using collapse compression and no partial order reduction. Also with this sample the growth is very fast and we pass from N=12, where the most efficient technique is centralized verification, to N=14, where it is necessary to resort to distributed verification, and the best results are obtained with four workstations.

In the rest of this section, additional results are presented that are useful to analyze a few aspects of the experimental distributed version of SPIN.

Table 2 illustrates the differences in terms of number of messages exchanged, partition rates, and execution time when using different partition strategies. The partition rate is the ratio of the minimum to maximum values of the state space region sizes, which gives a measure of how the workload is balanced.

The first strategy, called ad hoc partitioning, is based on a user defined partition function that depends on a single state component, and is the same used in the previous tests. This function has been defined empirically, trying to obtain a well balanced partition. The second partitioning function, called hash partitioning, is the one based on the same hash function used by SPIN for the hash table. Finally, modified hash partitioning uses the same hash-based approach, while retaining the principle of having a partition function that depends on one

Table 1. Performances of centralized and distributed SPIN

Bakery				
Model Parameters		N=2 K=20	N=3 K=10	N=4 K=4
States		106063	1877341	2336892
Transitions		129768	2463669	3101854
1 workstation	Memory per node	4.68MB	76.45MB	103.06MB
	Execution time	1s	908s	6306s
2 workstation	Memory per node	3.01MB	39.7MB	53.57MB
	Execution time	2s	24s	481s
4 workstation	Memory per node	2.55MB	34.7MB	51.82MB
	Execution time	23s	235s	330s

Leader				
Model Parameters		N=5	N=6	N=7
States		41692	341316	2801653
Transitions		169690	1667887	15976645
1 workstation	Memory per node	3.78MB	24.57MB	-
	Execution time	2s	27s	-
2 workstation	Memory per node	2.52MB	12.92MB	109.5MB
	Execution time	3s	130s	6687s
4 workstation	Memory per node	1.89MB	7.1MB	55.40MB
	Execution time	23s	219s	4577s

Philo			
Model Parameters		N=12	N=14
States		94376	636810
Transitions		503702	3965261
1 workstation	Memory per node	18.1MB	-
	Execution time	11s	-
2 workstation	Memory per node	6.70MB	63.1MB
	Execution time	23s	248s
4 workstation	Memory per node	3.94MB	20.89MB
	Execution time	35s	196s

Table 2. A comparison of different partition functions

Test Sample	Partitioning	Messages	Partition rate	Execution time
Bakery (N=2,K=20)	Ad Hoc	38874	0.7749	10s
	Hash	883297	0.9870	113s
	Modified Hash	343340	0.7470	50s
Leader (N=6)	Ad Hoc	139293	0.7361	46s
	Hash	373023	0.9679	121s
	Modified Hash	113378	0.7161	45s
Philo (N=14)	Ad Hoc	242984	0.9155	155s
	Hash	1185761	0.9871	403s
	Modified Hash	234328	0.8961	155s

state component only. This is achieved computing the hash function on one state component only.

For the Bakery example, we decided to present the results obtained without partial order reduction, because when this mechanism is used the number of states varies with the partition function, and in this case we found that the variance was so high that verification could not be completed when using hash partitioning, so we were not able to give any data for this kind of partitioning. This result of course confirms the expected better performance of the partition functions based on one state component with respect to partial order reductions.

Another difference with respect to the experiments presented in Table 1 is that here the results are referred to experiments made without the XDR layer, because in our implementation hash partitioning works only with this configuration. The parameters for the samples are shown in the table. All the results are relative to a 2 workstations testbed.

The results show that hash partitioning gives the best results in terms of balancing, but the number of messages cannot be controlled. This causes an increment in network overhead due to an increased amount of data transferred, and, consequently, an increment in execution times. Partition functions depending on one state component only do not give perfectly balanced workloads, but they are the most effective ones in terms of completion time, because they give sufficiently well balanced partitions and, at the same time, a low number of cross-transitions.

Partition functions based on one state component only could be improved exploiting knowledge about the system behavior, and statistical data such as transition counts that SPIN can compute. For example, it is possible to let SPIN compute the transition counts for a smaller sized (scaled down) model and then using these data to drive the definition of the partitioning function for the bigger one. However, a manual definition of a good partition function is not always easy. A possible improvement may be to introduce a tool that, on a statistical base, automatically determinates the partition function.

Table 3. Evaluation of the overhead due to heterogeneity

Test Sample	Transfer	Memory per node	Execution time
Bakery (N=3,K=10)	Binary	9.36MB	21s
	XDR	13.3MB	24s
Leader (N=6)	Binary	50MB	46s
	XDR	149.9MB	130s
Philo (N=14)	Binary	142.3MB	155s
	XDR	195.0MB	248s

One of the main goals of the project was to develop a distributed version of SPIN that can run on a network of heterogeneous workstations. This requirement introduces an overhead, mainly due to internal representation conversions. Of course, when using an homogeneous network of workstations, conversions can be avoided, and the XDR layer can be eliminated. This can speed up the verification process, reducing message size, and hence network overhead, but also memory requirements and and computation time. Table 3 can be useful to evaluate the amount of overhead implied by the XDR layer. It reports the results obtained using unformatted binary transfer in an homogeneous architecture (Binary Transfer), and those obtained using platform independent transfers (XDR Transfer), in the same architecture. In this case partial order reduction does not affect the results, so it has been used in the Bakery sample.

5 Conclusions and Perspectives

We have described a distributed-memory algorithm for verification of safety properties and its experimental implementation within the SPIN model checker. It has been shown that the algorithm can extend the capabilities of a verification tool like SPIN, adding up the physical memory of several workstations interconnected via a standard LAN, so implementing a distributed virtual verifier. When this algorithm is applied, it becomes possible to deal with models larger than those that can be analyzed with a single workstation running the standard version of SPIN.

Since SPIN is very efficient in analyzing the models that fit in the physical memory of the machine where it runs, the distributed version of the verification program performs worse than the centralized version on such models. Therefore, the distributed version of SPIN may be useful as a complementary tool, to be used instead of the standard version when the model size exceeds the available physical memory.

The distributed algorithm that has been presented is compatible with the main techniques used by SPIN to improve performance. In particular, it is compatible with compression techniques, static partial order reduction techniques, and bit state hashing.

One of the most critical aspects of the distributed verification algorithm is the function that defines the partition of the state space graph. We have considered various possibilities and showed that a function that depends on a single state component is advantageous under several points of view, because it can yield not only sufficiently well balanced workloads, but also low communication overhead, and wide applicability of partial order reductions.

In this paper, the possibility of implementing a distributed LTL model checking based on a nested depth first visit of the state space was not considered. This is however an interesting area for future research. The main problem that remains to be solved is that the algorithm as it has been proposed here performs a non depth first visit of the state space. If we introduce some form of synchronization, the network nodes can be forced to perform a depth first visit. For example, each node would be obliged to wait for a reply from the destination node whenever it sends a message, and the destination node would communicate back when it has finished. This kind of algorithm would cut off most of the parallel processing, and its implications in terms of needed memory must be investigated.

Another important issue for further study on the distributed verification algorithm is the automatic generation of good partitioning functions. Of course, optimality cannot be achieved, because this is an np-hard problem, but good heuristics, such as the principle of having a partition function that depends on a single state component, can be found. This point has a relevant practical importance, because asking users to define partition functions by themselves may not be acceptable.

Finally, the experiments presented in this paper are only preliminary. We plan to perform more extensive tests to get additional experimental results and so be able to give a more comprehensive view of the performance of this technique and of its scalability.

References

[1] S. Aggarwal, R. Alonso, and C. Courcoubetis. Distributed reachability analysis for protocol verification environments. In P. Varaiya and H. Kurzhanski, editors, *Discrete Event Systems: Models and Application*, volume 103 of *LNCIS*, pages 40–56, Berlin, Germany, August 1987. Springer-Verlag.

[2] D. L. Dill. The murphi verification system. In Rajeev Alur and Thomas A. Henzinger, editors, *Proceedings of the Eighth International Conference on Computer Aided Verification CAV*, volume 1102 of *Lecture Notes in Computer Science*, pages 390–393, New Brunswick, NJ, USA, July/August 1996. Springer Verlag.

[3] J. Greenfield. An overview of the PVM software system. In *Ideas in Science and Electronics Exposition and Symposium. Proceedings: Albuquerque, NM, USA, May 1995*, volume 17 of *Annual Ideas in Science and Electronics Exposition and Symposium Conference*, pages 17–23. IEEE Computer Society Press, 1995.

[4] G. J. Holzmann. The model checker spin. *IEEE Trans. on Software Engineering*, 23(5):279–295, May 1997.

[5] G. J. Holzmann, P. Godefroid, and D. Pirottin. Coverage preserving reduction strategies for reachability analysis. In *Proc. 12th Int. Conf on Protocol Specification, Testing, and Verification, INWG/IFIP*, Orlando, Fl., June 1992.

[6] G. J. Holzmann and Doron Peled. An improvement in formal verification. In *Proc. Formal Description Techniques, FORTE94*, pages 197–211, Berne, Switzerland, October 1994. Chapman & Hall.

[7] D. M. Nicol. Noncommittal barrier synchronization. *Parallel Computing*, 21(4):529–549, April 1995.

[8] U. Stern and D. L. Dill. Parallelizing the murphi verifier. In *Proceedings of the Nineth International Conference on Computer Aided Verification CAV*, 1997.

Partial Order Reduction in Presence of Rendez-vous Communications with Unless Constructs and Weak Fairness

Dragan Bošnački

Dept. of Computing Science, Eindhoven University of Technology
PO Box 513, 5600 MB Eindhoven, The Netherlands
fax: +31 40 246 3992, e-mail: dragan@win.tue.nl

Abstract. If synchronizing (rendez-vous) communications are used in the Promela models, the `unless` construct and the weak fairness algorithm are not compatible with the partial order reduction algorithm used in Spin's verifier. After identifying the wrong partial order reduction pattern that causes the incompatibility, we give solutions for these two problems. To this end we propose corrections in the identification of the safe statements for partial order reduction and as an alternative, we discuss corrections of the partial order reduction algorithm.

1 Introduction

The issue of fairness is inherent and important one in the study of concurrency and nondeterminism, in particular in the area of the verification of concurrent systems. Since fairness is used as generic notion there is a broad taxonomy of fairness concepts. In this paper we confine our attention to the notion of weak fairness on the level of processes which is implemented in the Spin verifier. This means that we require that for every execution sequence of the concurrent program which is a composition of several processes, if some process becomes continuously enabled at some point of time (i.e. can always execute some of its statements), then at least one statement from that process will eventually be executed. This kind of fairness is most often associated with mutual exclusion algorithms, busy waiting, simple queue-implementations of scheduling, resource allocation. Weak fairness will guarantee the correctness of statements like eventually entering the critical region for every process which is continuously trying to do this (in the mutual exclusions) or eventually leaving the waiting queue for each process that has entered it (in the scheduling) [7].

Partial order reduction is one of the main techniques that are used to alleviate the problem of state space explosion in the verification of concurrent systems [16, 8, 11, 14] and it is indeed one of Spin's main strengths. The idea is, instead of exploring all the execution sequences of a given program, to group them in equivalence classes which are interleaving of independent program statements. Then only representatives for each equivalence class are considered. In practice this is realized such that from each state only a subset of the executable statements are taken.

Combining the algorithms for model-checking under weak fairness with partial order reduction is a prerequisite for the verification of many interesting properties to be feasible in practice. However, recently it was discovered that the two algorithms are not compatible when rendez-vous communications occur in the Promela models. As a result, in the present implementation of Spin the combination of weak fairness with partial order reduction when rendez-vous are used in the models is not allowed.

Another problem with Spin's partial order reduction in presence of rendez-vous occurs when the unless construct is used in the Promela models. The combination of this three Spin's features is also currently forbidden.

Interestingly, it turns out that both problems are caused exactly by the same pattern of wrong partial order reduction. After pointing out the incorrect reduction pattern we propose solutions for these problems. For each of the problems we discuss two kind of solutions, classified according to the two different phases of the verification in which they are implemented. The first kind of solutions corrects the identifications of so called safe statements for the partial order reduction algorithm. The marking of the statements as safe is done during the compilation of the Promela model, so we call this solutions static. The second kind are the dynamic solutions which are applied during the exploration of the state space and are in fact corrections of the partial order reduction algorithm.

In the next section we give the necessary preliminaries for the rest of the paper. Section 3 is devoted to partial order reduction and the concrete algorithm that is used in Spin. In Section 4 we discuss the problem with the unless construct and give two solutions (one dynamic and one static) to overcome it. Section 5 deals with the Spin's weak fairness algorithm. After location of the problem and the comparison with the unless case, we again propose both kind of solutions. The last section is a standard summary with some considerations about the future work.

2 Preliminaries

In this section following [11] and [5] we give semantics of the Promela programs (models) and their verification in terms of finite labeled transition systems.

We represent the programs as collections of processes. The semantics of the process P_i can be represented as a *labeled transition system* (LTS). An LTS is a quadruple $(S_i, s_{0i}, \tau_i, L_i)$, where S_i is a finite set of states, s_{0i} is a distinguished initial state, L_i is a set of program statements (labels), and $\tau_i : S_i \times L_i \to 2^{S_i}$ is a nondeterministic transition function. The transition function induces a set $T_i \subseteq S_i \times S_i$ of transitions. Every transition in T_i is the result of an execution of a statement from the process, i.e., $(s_i, s_i') \in T_i$ iff there exists a statement a such that $s_i' \in \tau_i(s_i, a)$. We introduce a function *Label* that maps each transition to the corresponding statement. For a statement a, with $Pid(a)$ we denote the process to which a belongs. (If two syntactically identical statements belong to different processes we consider them as different.) $En(a)$ denotes the set of states in which a is enabled. (The enabledness (executability) of a given statement is defined according to some additional rules that we do not consider here.) Given a state s and process p we say that p is enabled in s (or, more formally, write $s \in En(p)$) if there is a statement a such that $Pid(a) = p$ and $s \in En(a)$.

Now we can define the semantics of the program P that corresponds to the concurrent execution of the processes P_i as an LTS which is a product of the labeled transition systems corresponding to the component processes. The product LTS consists of: state space $S = \prod S_i$, i.e., the Cartesian product of the state spaces S_i from P_i's LTS; $s_0 = (s_{01}, \ldots, s_{0n})$; $L = \bigcup L_i$, the set of statements is union of the statements sets of the components; and the transition function is defined by: (i) if a is not a rendez-vous statement, then $(s_1, \ldots, s'_k, \ldots, s_n) \in \tau(s_1, \ldots, s_k, \ldots, s_n, a)$ iff $s'_k \in \tau_k(s_k, a)$; (ii)if a is a rendez-vous send, and there is a rendez-vous receive statement a', such that $Pid(a') \neq Pid(a)$, then $(s_1, \ldots, s'_k, \ldots, s'_l, \ldots, s_n) \in \tau(s_1, \ldots, s_k, \ldots, s_l, \ldots, s_n, a)$ iff $s'_k \in \tau_k(s_k, a)$ and $s'_l \in \tau_l(s_l, a')$. Note that in the case of rendez-vous communication the resulting transition is labeled with the rendez-vous send statement.

An execution sequence for the LTS is an infinite sequence $t_0, t_1, \ldots$ where $t_i \in T$, for all $i \geq 0$ and t_0 originates from the initial state, i.e. $t_0 = (s_0, s'_0)$ (for some s'_0) and for all adjacent transitions $t_{i+1} = (s_{i+1}, s'_{i+1}), t_i = (s_i, s'_i)(i \geq 0)$ it holds $s'_i = s_{i+1}$. The execution sequence can also be defined as a sequence of global system states. In order to relate the two options for a given transition $t_i = (s_i, s'_i)$ we define $State(t_i) = s_i$.

The most general way to represent the requirements on the program is by linear temporal logic (LTL) formula. In Spin the next-time-free LTL are used, which means that the formulae may contain only boolean propositions on system states, the boolean operators $\wedge$, $\vee$, ! (negation), and the temporal operators $\Box$ (always), $\Diamond$ (eventually) and U (until). For the verification purposes the LTL formulae are translated into Büchi automata.

A *Büchi automaton* is a tuple $A = (\Sigma, S, \rho, s_0, F)$, where Σ is an alphabet, S is a set of states, $\rho : S \times \Sigma \to 2^S$ is a nondeterministic transition function, $s_0 \in S$ is the initial state, and $F \subseteq S$ is a set of designated states. A *run* of A over an infinite word $w = a_1 a_2 \ldots$, is an infinite sequence $s_0 s_1 \ldots$ of states, where s_0 is the initial state and $s_i \in \rho(s_{i-1}, a_i)$, for all $i \geq 1$. A run $s_0 s_1 \ldots$ is *accepting* if there is some state from F that occurs infinitely often, i.e. for some $s \in F$ there are infinitely many i's such that $s_i = s$. The word w is *accepted* by A if there is an accepting run of A over w.

The transitions of the Büchi automaton that is obtained from the formula are labeled with boolean propositions over the global system states of the LTS corresponding to the program.

In order to prove the satisfaction of the LTL formula by the program, we further define the *synchronous* product of LTS (S_P, s_{0P}, τ, L) corresponding to the program P and the Büchi automaton $(\Sigma, S_A, \rho, s_{0A}, F)$ obtained from the negation of the LTL formula, to be an LTS extended with acceptance states, [1] with: state set $S_P \times S_A$, initial state (s_{0P}, s_{0A}), transition function $\tau : S_P \times$

---

[1] Although the proliferation of different formal models (LTS, Büchi automata, ex-

$S_A \times L$ defined as $(s_{2P}, s_{2A}) \in \tau(s_{1P}, s_{1A}, a)$ iff $s_{2P} \in \tau_P(s_{1P}, a)$ and there is a proposition $p \in \Sigma$ such that $s_{2A} \in \rho(s_{1A}, p)$ and p is true in s_{1A}, set of statements L, and set of designated acceptance states Acc defined such that $(s_P, s_A) \in Acc$ iff $s_A \in F$, i.e. we declare as acceptance states the states with second component belonging to the acceptance set of the Büchi automaton. Similarly as for Büchi automata we will say for an execution σ that it is acceptance execution if there is at least one state from Acc that occurs infinitely often in σ.

The satisfaction of the formula can now be proven by showing that there are no acceptance executions of the extended LTS. On the other hand, the existence of acceptance executions sequences means that the formula is not satisfied. From the definition of Büchi automata and extended LTS and following the reasoning from [5], for instance, it is straightforward to conclude that the extended LTS has an acceptance execution iff it has some state $f \in Acc$ that is reachable from the initial state and reachable from itself (in one or more steps) [5]. In the sequel we will call the underlying graph a *state space*. Thus, we have to look for *acceptance cycles* in the state space, i.e., for cycles that contain at least one acceptance state.

3 Partial Order Reduction

In this section we give a brief overview of the partial order reduction (POR) algorithm by Holzmann and Peled [11], that is considered throughout the paper. This algorithm is also implemented in Spin. We start with rephrasing some definitions from [11].

The basic idea of the reduction is to restrict the part of the state space that is explored by the DFS, in such a way that the properties of interest are preserved. To this purpose, the independence of the checked property from the possible interleaving of statements is exploited. More specifically, two statements a,b are allowed to be permuted precisely then, if for all sequences v,w of statements: if $vabw$ (where juxtaposition denotes concatenation) is an accepted behaviour, then $vbaw$ is an accepted behaviour as well. In practice, sufficient conditions for such permutability are used that can be checked locally, i.e., in a state. For this, a notion of "concurrency" of statements is used that captures the idea that transitions are contributed by different, concurrently executing processes of the system.

We first introduce some additional terminology. For $q \in En(a)$, $a(q)$ is state which is reached by executing a in state q. Concurrent statements (i.e. statements with different $Pids$) may still influence each other's enabledness, whence it may not be correct to only consider one particular order of execution from some state. The following notion of *independence* defines the absence of such mutual influence. Intuitively, two statements are independent if in every state where

---

tended LTS) that are used to represent the semantics and ultimately the state space might seem unnecessary, we use three different formal concepts in order to follow more closely [11] and [5], so that we will be able to reuse most of the results from these papers in a seamless way.

they are both enabled, they cannot disable each other, and are commutative, i.e., the order of their execution makes no difference to the resulting state.

Definition 1. The statements a and b are *independent* iff for all states q such that $q \in En(a)$ and $q \in En(b)$,

- $a(q) \in En(b)$ and $b(q) \in En(a)$, and
- $a(b(q)) = b(a(q))$.

Statements that are not independent are called dependent.

Note that a and b are trivially independent if $En(a) \cap En(b) = \emptyset$. An example of independent statements are assignments to or readings from local variables, executed by two distinct processes.

Also note that the statements a and b are considered to be independent even if a can enable b (and vice versa). The main requirement is that the statements do not disable each other. This is unusual in a sense, because in the literature a more strict definition prevails that does not allow that a statement can enable another statement (e.g. [16, 8]). The advantage of the subtlety in Definition 1 is that ensures a greater set of independent statements than the "classical" definition and consequently a better reduction of the state space. However, we must be careful with this, because as we will see later this feature is closely connected with the incompatibilities that we are discussing in this paper.

Another reason why it may not be correct to only consider only one particular order of execution from state s of two concurrent statements a and b is that the difference between the intermediate states $a(s)$ and $b(s)$ may be observable in the sense that it influences the property to be checked. For a given proposition p that occurs in the property (an LTL formula), and a state s, let $p(s)$ denote the boolean value of the proposition p in the state s. Then, a is *nonobservable* iff for all propositions p in the property and all states $s \in En(a)$, we have $p(s) = p(a(s))$. The statement a is said to be *safe* if it is nonobservable and independent from any other statement b for which $Pid(b) \neq Pid(a)$.

In the rest of the section we describe in a rather informal way the partial order algorithm from [11]. For the full details about the algorithm we recommend the original references [11, 14].

The reduction of the search space is effected during the DFS, by limiting the search from a state s to a subset of the statements that are enabled in s, the so-called *ample set*. Such an ample set is formed in the following way: If there is a process which has only safe statements enabled and all those transitions lead to a state which is not on the DFS stack, then the ample set consists of all the statements from this process only. Otherwise, the ample set consists of all enabled statements in s. It can be proven [11, 14] that the reduced graph obtained in this way preserves the properties of the original LTS, stated as an LTL formula. The condition that all transitions from the ample set must end out of the DFS stack, the so-called "cycle proviso", ensures that a statement that it is constantly enabled, cannot be "forgotten" by leaving it outside the ample set in a cycle of transitions.

While the cycle proviso is clearly locally checkable during a DFS, the condition that an enabled statement is safe is not, as the definition of safety requires independence from *any* concurrent statement. For instance, a sufficient condition for safety of a statement a that can be checked locally is that a does not touch any global variables or channels. Indeed, it is this condition that is implemented in Spin.

However, it will turn out that one solution for our incompatibility problems will be to correct (or better to say, refine) this safety criterion.

In [11, 14] it is shown that

Theorem 2. *If there exist reachable acceptance cycles in the state space the reduced search algorithm will report at least one of them.*

4   The unless construct

The unless construct is a mean for modeling exception handling routines and priority choices. Formally, it introduces partial ordering between the statements that belong to a same process. Its syntax is *stmnt* unless *stmnt*. The first (left-hand) statement is called *normal* or *main*, while the second (right-hand) is *escape* statement. [2] Semantically, the executability of the normal statement depends on the executability of the escape sequence. The escape sequence has higher priority than the normal statement, which means that the normal statement will be executed only if the escape statement is not executable. Otherwise the escape statement is executed and the normal statement is ignored (skipped). This dependence between the two statements of unless causes the problems when the partial order reduction is used and the escape statement is a rendez-vous communication.

Let us consider the motivating Promela example given in Figure 1. [3] (In the sequel we assume that the reader is familiar with Promela.) Suppose that both A and B are in their starting points, i.e. A is trying to execute its skip statement, while B is attempting to do its only statement. Obviously the higher priority rendez-vous send offer c!1 issued by B cannot find a matching receive, so the verifier should detect the assertion violation assert(false). [4] However, in the reduced search this is not detected, because of the incorrect partial order

---

[2] In general, both statements can be sequences of Promela statements. Also the unless construct can be nested. The results form this paper can be extended in a straightforward way for this general case.

[3] The example is distilled from a model made in the discrete time extension of Spin DTSpin [2]. The model was written by Victor Bos, who first draw our attention to the possible problems with the unless statement.

[4] Strictly speaking in this example we are considering a safety property that is not expressed as an LTL formula. The equivalent formulation of the property in LTL can be done in a straightforward way and the partial order reduction will fail because of the same reason as in the present case. We decided to use this version of the example for the sake of simplicity.

```
chan c = [0] of {bit}

active proctype A()
{
skip; c?1;
}


acive proctype B()
{
assert(false) unless c!1;
}
```

Fig. 1. Motivating example for unless statement.

reduction. The problem with the reduction occurs because the skip statement is not safe anymore. Namely, the criterion that a statement is safe if it does not affect any global objects is no longer true. Because of the specific property that the executability of the rendez-vous statement can be changed only because of the change of the location in the process (program counter), the statements like skip are not unconditionally globally independent according to the Definition 1.

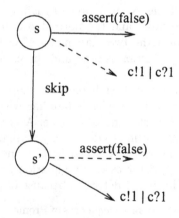

Fig. 2. Interdependence between the "safe" statements and the **unless** escape and normal statements.

The reason is depicted in Fig. 2. In the starting state described above the rendez-vous send c!1 is disabled, but with the execution of skip it becomes enabled. This means that skip has indirectly disabled assert(false) which was enabled in the starting state. In that way skip and assert(false) are not independent according to the Definition 1, because the net effect is that skip disables assert(false).

The problem can be solved both statically in compile time or dynamically during the exploration of the state space. The dynamic solution consists of checking whether in a given state there is a disabled rendez-vous statement (more precisely, rendez-vous send) which is a part of an escape statement and in that case the partial order reduction is not performed in the given state. The drawback of this solution is that it can be time consuming.

The static solution is to simply declare each statement which is followed by a rendez-vous communication (more precisely, by a rendez-vous receive) as unsafe. We use the term "followed" in a syntactical sense, taking into account all the cycles and jumps in the program. For example, the last statement of the body of an iteration is followed by the first statement of the body. Whether a given statement is followed by a rendez-vous can be checked by inspecting Spin's internal representation of the Promela program (abstract syntax tree). This can be done during the generation of the C source (pan.c) of the special purpose verifier for the program. Thus, the solution does not cause any time overhead during the verification. Its drawback with regard to the dynamic solution is that the reduction can be less effective because of an unnecessary strictness. It can happen that the reduction is unnecessarily prevented even when in the state that is considered by DFS there is no disabled rendez-vous send in unless construct or even there is no statement with an unless construct at all.

5 Fairness

A pattern very similar to the one from the previous section that causes the partial order reduction algorithm to fail in presence of rendez-vous communications, occurs when the weak fairness option is used in the verification. The weak fairness algorithm is also a very instructive example how the things can become complicated because of the feature interaction.

5.1 The Standard Nested Depth-First Search (NDFS) Algorithm

The weak fairness algorithm that we are going to present in the next subsection is an extension of the algorithm of Courcoubetis, Vardi, Wolper and Yannakakis [5] for memory efficient verification of LTL properties. The algorithm is a more efficient alternative to the usual computation of the strongly connected components of the underlying graph for the product LTS. It is also compatible with Spin's bit-state hashing, which is not the case with the strongly connected components algorithm. We start with the brief overview of this algorithm given in Figure 3.

The algorithm consists of two alternating depth first searches for exploration of the state space. When the first search retracts to an acceptance state the second search is started to check for a cycle through this acceptance state. If the second depth first search (DFS) closes a cycle, it is reported as an acceptance cycle. Otherwise, the first DFS resumes until the next acceptance state in postorder (if there is such a state). If no cycle is found than the property is successfully verified.

We need to work with two copies of the state space in order to ensure that the second DFS does not fail to detect a cycle by cutting the search because it has encountered a state visited already by the first DFS. To distinguish between states belonging to a different copy we extend the state with one bit denoting the DFS phase.

```
proc dfs(s)
    add {s,0} to Statespace
    for each successor s' of s  do
        if {s',0} not in Statespace then dfs(s') fi
    od
    if accepting(s) then seed:={s,1}; ndfs(s) fi
end

proc ndfs(s) /* the nested search */
    add {s,1} to Statespace
    for each successor s' of s do
        if {s',1} not in Statespace then ndfs(s') fi
        else if {s',1}==seed then report cycle fi
    od
end
```

Fig. 3. Nested depth first search algorithm.

The following theorem from [5] establishes the correctness of the algorithm

Theorem 3. *The algorithm in Fig. 3 reports a cycle iff there is an acceptance state reachable from the initial state that belongs to a nontrivial strongly connected component of the state space.*

Notice that the first DFS serves to order the acceptance states in postorder, such that the cycle checks can be done starting from the acceptance state which is removed first from the stack (i.e. first in postorder). It is important to emphasize that during the second DFS each state in the second copy of the state space is visited only once. This has (most of the time) an advantage over the straightforward solution to do the cycle check in preorder, i.e. starting a cycle check as soon as we visit an acceptance state. If we used preorder we would have to start the second DFS always from scratch. Although the memory requirements would be the same as for the postorder, the multiple visits to a same state can lead to a significant time overhead.

5.2   Description of the Weak Fairness Algorithm

We will consider weak fairness with regard to processes, i.e. we will say that a given execution sequence is fair if for each process that becomes continuously enabled starting at some point in the execution sequence, a transition belonging to this process is eventually executed. Formally

Definition 4. An execution sequence $\sigma = t_0 t_1 \ldots$ is fair iff for each process p the following holds: for all $i \geq 0$ such that $State(t_j) \in En(p)$ for all $j \geq i$, there is $k \geq i$ such that $Pid(Label(t_k)) = p$.

When model checking under fairness, we are interested only in fair acceptance runs (sequences). This means that we require the detected cycles to be fair, i.e. each continuously enabled process along the cycle contributes at least one transition to it.

The basic idea behind the weak fairness algorithm is to work in an extended state space instead of the original one. The extended state space consists of N copies of the original state space, where N is the number of processes. Whenever we are in the i-th copy and either we take a transition belonging to the process i or there is no executable transition that belongs to i, then we pass to the $((i + 1)modN) + 1$ copy. A cycle is then fair if and only if it passes through all the copies. This is because we are sure that all permanently enabled processes have contributed an action to the cycle.

The idea is quite straightforward and at first sight it seems that all we need is some counter which will indicate the copy of the state space we are passing through. However, the algorithm becomes more involved when we have to take care about the partial order reduction and try to improve it with some heuristics.

The weak fairness (WF) algorithm we are considering here is by Holzmann and it is a variant of the Choueka's flag algorithm [10]. This algorithm is also implemented in Spin as an extension of the nested depth first search algorithm.

For the WF algorithm we need a new extended state space. Its elements are quadruples of the form (s, A, C, b), obtained by extending each state s, apart from the bit b discriminating between the first and second DFS, with an additional bit A and an integer C. The variable C is the already mentioned counter that keeps track of the copy of the state space we are passing through. The role of A is to indicate that we have already passed through an acceptance state in the state space. We need this indicator because, as we will see in a moment, we will not always start the search from an acceptance state, but instead in a state when we are sure that all enabled processes have executed a statement, which often means that we have a better chance to close a fair cycle.

The standard NDFS model-checking algorithm is modified correspondingly for manipulation of the new variables and generation of the extended state space. The pseudo-code of the algorithm is given in Figure 4 and 5.

In the initial state A and C are zero. The values of A and C are changed according to the following three rules that apply both to the first and the second DFS.

- Rule 1: If A is zero in an acceptance state, then A is set to 1 and C is assigned the value $N + 1$, where N is the number of processes. (This rule is a kind of initialization that indicates that we have passed an acceptance state and a cycle check, i.e., a second DFS, is possibly needed.)
- Rule 2: If A is 1 and C equals the Pid number (increased by two) of the process which is being currently considered, then C is decreased by 1. (This rule is to keep track of the state space copy in which we are working. The technical difference is that the counter is increased instead of being decreased, as in the "naive" algorithm above.)
- Rule 3: If the condition of Rule 1 does not apply and if C is 1, then both C and A are reset to 0. (This rule is a preparation (initialization) for the second DFS.)

We have to use the counter not only in the second DFS, but also during the first DFS in order to keep the copies of the state space the same in both searches. This is important for the partial order reduction algorithm that we are going to use later. If those copies differ, the interaction between the nested DFS algorithm and the partial order reduction can produce incorrect results, as shown in [12].

Notice that if C is $i + 2$, then it is immediately decreased when we start exploring the statements (transitions) of a new process. This means that even if the process cannot perform any statement we will pass to a new state with a different counter number. This kind of transition in the state space we call a *default transition* and label it with a *default statement* meaning that the process is disabled and should not be taken into consideration for the cycle that is currently checked. We will see in the next subsection that these default transitions play a crucial role in the incompatibility with partial order reduction.

We mentioned above that unlike the standard NDFS in the WF algorithm the cycle check does not have to start in an acceptance state. Instead it starts in special states, which we simply call *starting states* in the sequel, and which have the property that $A = 1$, $C = 1$ and $b = 1$. Analogously to the standard NDFS, the cycle check starts after all the successors of the starting state are explored and the search returns back to the starting state. Also, let us emphasize that a starting state can "cover" several acceptance states in a sense that several acceptance states can be passed before the cycle check is started. The additional acceptance state that are passed after the first one do not "generate" new starting states because C stays unchanged. In this way we can often reduce the number of calls for the second DFS. Also by the lookahead for a possible fragment of a fair cycle, as we essentially do, we reduce the number of unsuccessful attepmpts to close a fair cycle.

5.3 Incompatibility with the Partial Order Reduction Algorithm

The incompatibility of the weak fairness algorithm with POR (and because of rendez-vous communications) was first discovered for the example given in Fig. 6 (by Dennis Dams):

```
proc dfs(s, A, C)
    add {s,A,C,0} to Statespace
    /* Rule 1 */
    if accepting(s) then
        if A == 0 then
            A = 1;
            C = N+1
        fi
    else
    /* Rule 3 */
        if C == 1 then
            A = 0;
            C = 0
        fi
    for each process i = N-1 downto 0 do
        /* Rule 2 */
        if A == 1 and C == i+2 then
            C = C - 1
        fi
        nxt = all transitions enabled in s with Pid(t)=i
        for all t in nxt do
            s' = successor of s via t
            if {s',A,C,0} not in Statespace then dfs(s',A,C) fi
        od
    od
    if A == 1 and C == 1 then
        seed:={s,A,C,1};
        ndfs(s,A,C)
    fi
end
```

Fig. 4. Weak fairness algorithm – first depth first search (continued in Figure 5).

In the model from Fig. 6 the LTL formula $\Diamond p$, where p is defined as $b ==$ *true*, is not valid even under fairness condition. This is because of the statement x = 0 in process C. Namely, because of this statement, the rendez-vous send c!1 from process B is no longer continuously enabled. Since, now there exists a fair cycle formed just by the statements from A and C, i. e. c!0; c?x; x = 0; c!0 ... along which the process B can be safely ingnored because it is not continuously enabled.

However, when partial order redcution was used the verifier uncorrectly showed that the forumula was valid. [5] So, the aforementioned fair cycle formed

---

[5] Note that if you try to run the example with the recent releases of Spin an error will be issued because of the incompatibility of fairness and partial order reduction in models with rendez-vous operations.

```
proc ndfs(s,A,C) /* the nested search */
   add {s,A,C,1} to Statespace
   /* Rule 1 */
   if accepting(s) then
      if A == 0 then
         A = 1;
         C = N+1
      fi
   else
   /* Rule 3 */
      if C == 1 then
         A = 0;
         C = 0;
      fi
   for each process i do
      /* Rule 2 */
      if A == 1 and C == i+2 then
         C = C - 1
      fi
      nxt = all transitions enabled in s with Pid(t)=i
      for all t in nxt do
         s' = successor of s via t
         if {s',A,C,1} not in Statespace then ndfs(s',A,C) fi
         else if {s',A,C,1}==seed then report cycle fi
      od
   od
end
```

Fig. 5. Weak Fairness Algorithm – second depth first search

by the processes A and C was not discovered. The reason for the failure is very similar to the one for the unless statements. Again the same pattern of a wrong partial order reduction because of the incorrect independence relation occurs. But this time the problem is with the difault meta transitions. Recall that those transitions only change the counter C in the fairness algorithm when all statements of the process which is currently considered are disabled. As ilustrated in Fig. 7 the problem is again caused by the rendez-vous statements.

With s is denoted the state in which process C is about to execute the statement x = 0, processes A and B are hanging on their rendez-vous sending statements, and the counter C from the WF algorithm equals the Pid of process B increased by 2. Then, the statement x = 0 is no longer safe, because it is dependent with the default transition (the decrement of C). Namely, because c!1 is disabled, according to the WF algorithm the default transition is enabled. After the execution of x = 0 the system passes in the state s' in which c!1 becomes enabled, and consequently the default transition is not possible. In the reduced search the statement c!1 is not considered at all. On the other

```
                    chan c =[0] of {bit};
                    bool b = false;

                    active proctype A()
                    {
                    starta:
                        c!0;
                        goto starta
                    }

                    active proctype B()
                    {
                    startb:
                        c!1; b = true;
                        goto startb
                    }

                    active proctype C()
                    { bit x;
                    startc:
                        c?x; x = 0;
                        goto startc
                    }
```

Fig. 6. Motivating example for the fairness algorithm.

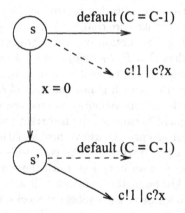

Fig. 7. Interdependence between the "safe" transitions and the default moves

hand in s', after $x = 0$, c!1 becomes enabled and must be included in the fair cycles. In this way during the reduced search the verifier never considers the fair cycle in which process B does not contribute a transition, which is, of course, wrong. There is an apparent analogy with the pattern from the unless case. By enabling a rendez-vous statement (transition) (c!1 in combination with c?x) we are preventing another transition (in this case the "meta" default transition) which is in discord with the independence definition.

As in the case of the unless construct two kind of solutions are possible.

The first solution is static and it is actually the same with the one for the problem with unless. [6] This is not surprising because we have the same problematic reduction pattern which we can avoid exactly in the same way by declaring as unsafe all statements that are safe according to the standard criteria in Spin, if they are followed by a rendez-vous receive statement.

We can also propose a dynamic solution which is analogous to the one for the unless case. In each state we need to check if there is a possibility of a default move caused by a rendez-vous communication. The partial order reduction is not performed if this is the case. Unlike in the unless case, this time the time overhead can be much smaller because we have to check the transitions from only one process - the one who's Pid satisfies $C = Pid + 2$.

However, we conjecture that there is a much more efficient dynamic solution that still allows reduction even in the state with a default move. In the new solution we use again the fact that we exactly know the possible problematic statements, or more precisely the Pid of the process which default move can cause the incorrect reduction.

In fact we correct the POR algorithm, while the same static criteria for safety of statements remain unchanged as in the standard POR. The change of the algorithm follows from the following reasoning. Because the problem is with the default move we should take care that we do not loose the counter decrement. To this end, before doing a reduction on a safe transition we first check if the process with Pid such that $C = Pid + 2$ can make a default move because no one of its transitions is enabled in the current state and in the same time contains a synchronous communication (which is not enabled, of course). If there is such a process we execute this default move before the reduction. In that way we do not loose the counter decrement because of the incorrect reduction. By decreasing C now another process can acquire the above problematic property to be blocked and to have a rendez-vous send while his Pid equals $C - 2$. We must obviously do the check described above in an iteration, until there are no processes with the problematic property. Although this solution will also exhibit a time overhead during the verification because of the necessary checks, it is reasonable to expect that this overhead will not be that significant. The new dynamic solution keeps of course the advantage over the static one that it can provide better reduction of the state space. Probably only the prospective practical implementations and tests on case examples can answer the question whether the possible timing overhead will be compensated by significantly less memory consumption. The

---

[6] The author owes this observation to Dennis Dams.

disadvantage for the practical implementation can be that the second dynamic solution (at least conceptually) seems more complicated than the static one.

As we stated above, our proposal is only a conjecture for the time being, because we are still checking the proofs. The idea is to show by an adaptation of the correctness proof from [11, 14] that with the small addendum described above the POR algorithm remains correct even when the reduction is done on in fact unsafe statements (with regard to the default move). This is because the LTL formulae do not refer to C which is a "meta" variable in the system and affects only the cycle fairness.

6 Conclusion

Promela's `unless` construct and the weak fairness algorithm are both incompatible with the partial order reduction algorithm when rendez-vous communications are present in the programs. We gave solutions to both problems by proposing a corrected identification of safe statements or changes in the partial order algorithm. It is hoped that the lessons learned from these problems will be helpful to avoid the interference of the partial order with the prospective new features of Spin.

A natural task for the future work would be the implementation of the solutions in Spin. In that regard the most promising looks the static solution with the correction of the criteria for safe statements. The only obstacle can be to find the successor of a given statement. The main problem in this context is the handling of the various Promela jump constructs (`break`, `goto`, etc.). Also the implementation of the first dynamic solution for the fairness should not be too involved. In the theoretical direction the correctness proof of the conjectured dynamic solution for fairness remains to be rechecked.

As a final remark, the compatibility with the weak fairness algorithm can be very important for the existing [2] and future extensions of Spin with real time, especially having in mind the work of [3] about zeno cycles in the real-time systems.

Acknowledgments The author is grateful to Dennis Dams, Gerard Holzmann, Victor Bos and Leszek Holenderski for their valuable information and comments.

References

1. Bengtsson, J., Jonsson, B, Lilius, J., Yi, W., *Partial Order Reductions for Timed Systems*, CONCUR'98, LNCS 1466, pp. 485-501, 1998.
2. Bošnački, D., Dams, D., *Integrating Real Time in Spin: a Prototype Implementation*, FORTE/PSTV'98, Kluwer, pp. 423-439, 1998
3. Bouajjani, A., Tripakis, S., Yovine, S., *On-the-Fly Symbolic Model-Checking for Real-Time Systems*, In Proc. of the 18th IEEE Real-Time Systems Symposium, pp. 232-243, IEEE, 1997

 4. Clarke, E., Emerson, E., Sistla, A., *Automatic Verification of Finite-state Concurrent Systems Using Temporal Logic Specifications*, ACM Transactions on Programming Languages and Systems, 8(2), pp. 244-263, 1986
 5. Courcoubetis, C., Vardi, M., Wolper, P., Yannakakis, M., *Memory Efficient Algorithms for the Verification of Temporal Properties*, Formal Methods in System Design I, pp. 275-288, 1992
 6. Dams, D., Gerth, R., Knaack, B., Kuiper, R., *Partial-order Reduction Techniques for Real-time Model Checking*, FMICS'98, CWI, pp.157-170, 1998
 7. Francez, N., *Fairness*, Springer, 1986
 8. Godefroid, P., *Partial Order Methods for the Verification of Concurrents Systems: An Approach to the State Space Explosion*, LNCS 1032, Springer, 1996
 9. Holzmann, G. J., *Design and Validation of Communication Protocols*, Prentice Hall, 1991. Also: `http://netlib.bell-labs.com/netlib/spin/whatispin.html`
10. Holzmann, G. J., Personal communication
11. Holzmann, G., Peled, D., *An Improvement in Formal Verification*, FORTE 1994, Bern, Switzerland, 1994.
12. Holzmann, G., Peled, D., Yannakakis *On Nested Depth First Search*, Proc. of the 2nd Spin Workshop, Rutgers University, New Jersay, USA, 1996.
13. Pagani, F., *Partial Orders and Verification of Real Time Systems*, Formal Techniques in Real Time and Fault Tolerant Systems FTRTFT 96, LNCS, 1996
14. Peled, D., *Combining Partial Order Reductions with On-the-Fly Model Checking*, Computer Aided Verification 1994, LCNS 818, pp. 377-390, 1994.
15. Vardi, M., Wolper, P., *Automata Theoretic Techniques for Modal Logics of Programs*, Journal of Computer and System Science, 32(2), pp. 182-221, 1986
16. Willems, B., Wolper, P., *Partial Order Models for Model Checking: From Linear to Branching Time*, Proc. of 11 Symposium of Logics in Computer Science, LICS 96, New Brunswick, pp. 294-303, 1996

Divide, Abstract, and Model-Check[*]

Karsten Stahl[**], Kai Baukus, Yassine Lakhnech, and Martin Steffen

Institut für Informatik und Praktische Mathematik
Christian-Albrechts-Universität zu Kiel
Preußerstr. 1–9, D-24105 Kiel, Germany
{kst,kba,yl,ms}@informatik.uni-kiel.de

Abstract. The applicability of model-checking is often restricted by the size of the considered system. To overcome this limitation, a number of techniques have been investigated. Prominent among these are data independence, abstraction, and compositionality. This paper presents a methodology based on deductive reasoning and model-checking which combines these techniques. As we show, the combination of abstraction and compositionality gives a significant added value to each of them in isolation. We substantiate the approach proving safety of a sliding window protocol of window size 16 using Spin and PVS.

1 Introduction

Model-checking [CE81,QS81] has proven a valuable approach for the formal, automatic verification of reactive systems. The size of the system to be verified limits, however, the applicability of this approach. First of all, many applications such as protocols use *infinite* data domains. This immediately renders the state space infinite, and hence, simple state exploration fails. Even when dealing with finite data, systems of parallel processes yield a state space exponential in the number of processes. This is known as the *state explosion* problem.

The obstacle of infinite data domains can be tackled by the *data independence* technique [Wol86]. Intuitively, a program is data independent if its behavior does not depend on the specific values of the data. In this case, many properties of the program stated over an infinite data domain can be equivalently expressed over finite domains that must contain enough elements. We call *safety* of data independence the requirement that the finite and infinite properties are equivalent.

Abstraction techniques are a prominent approach to address the state explosion problem (see e.g. [CGL94,BBLS92,Lon93,DGG94,Dam96]). Abstraction is a general approach [CC77] which allows to deduce properties of a concrete system by examining a more abstract —and in general smaller— one. Both systems are connected by an abstraction relation which is called *safe* with respect to a given property, if it preserves satisfaction of the property. This means, whenever the

---

[*] This work has been partially supported by the Esprit-LTR project Vires.
[**] Contact author.

property holds for the abstract system, it holds for the concrete one as well. In general, for a given concrete system, the abstract one depends on the property to be established. Therefore, in case the property to be verified is *global,* i.e., it depends on the exact behavior of all processes, it is hard to significantly abstract these components. It should be intuitively clear that the more local to a set of processes a property is, the more radically the remaining processes can be abstracted. Therefore, it is appealing to decompose a global property into a number of *local* ones which together imply the original one. Breaking a verification problem into more manageable subproblems is the essential idea of *compositional reasoning* (see e.g. [dRLP98] for a recent collection of relevant work in this field). To summarize, combining abstraction techniques and compositionality gives a significant added value to each of these techniques in isolation.

Verification of safety of data independence, of safety of abstraction, and of decomposition correctness is, in general, an undecidable problem that can be tackled using *deductive reasoning.* This is where theorem-proving comes in our approach.

The contribution of this paper is to explore the proposed methodology and to substantiate its applicability with a safety proof of a *sliding-window* protocol. The chosen variant of the protocol is inspired by the one implemented in *Mascara* [DPA+98], a medium-access layer for wireless ATM-networks, which uses a window size of 16. Judging from experience, model-checking directly the protocol with this window size is far beyond the reach of Spin or similar model-checkers. Using decomposition together with abstraction and data independence we were able to automatically verify the decomposed subproblems with the Spin model-checker [Hol91]. To verify the safety of the abstraction we used the theorem-prover PVS [ORSvH95].

The remainder of the paper is organized as follows: Section 2 explains the techniques used during verification. Section 3 contains the Promela model of the sliding window protocol. In Section 4 we present safety proof for the protocol. Finally, Section 5 contains concluding remarks and references to related work. The complete Promela code and the PVS derivation can be found at http://www.informatik.uni-kiel.de/~kst/sw/.

2   Verification Approach

The goal is to prove that a system $\mathcal{S}$, given as a parallel composition of a number of subsystems $\mathcal{S}_i$, satisfies a given property φ, that is

$$\mathcal{S}_1 \| \ldots \| \mathcal{S}_n \models \varphi \ .$$

In practice, when trying to apply model-checking in this setting, several problems occur. First, the data part is often infinite or at least very large. Second, the parallel composition of the $\mathcal{S}_i$'s leads to an exponential blowup of the state space of the overall system, which is known as the *state explosion problem.*

This paper presents a practical method to build abstract systems which can be handled by model-checkers. It is applied to a sliding window protocol taken from a wireless ATM protocol.

The methodology is based on three principles:

1. Decomposition of the property to prove,
2. data independence of the system, and
3. building abstractions.

2.1 Decomposition

We first *decompose* the property φ into a set of properties $\varphi_1, \ldots, \varphi_k$ which together imply φ, i.e., $\varphi_1 \wedge \ldots \wedge \varphi_k \implies \varphi$, such that each property φ_i is easier to establish than the original property φ. In order to derive φ_i, one can in turn use the principles of *data independence, abstraction,* and *decomposition*

As a guideline of a decomposition one should always try to introduce properties φ_i for which only a few processes are relevant, and which are therefore *local* to these processes. In such a case, this property can be shown with very abstract versions of the remaining processes.

2.2 Data Independence

For a property φ, we make use of the *data independence* [Wol86] of a system to change the input language, favorably reducing the alphabet of the input language to a finite set.

Data independence means that the system does not change the data received nor that it invents new data. For example, the system is allowed to compose the input to build new blocks in case it is later decomposed without change, or store some data and use it later unchanged. These assumptions can be checked syntactically and often hold for data-transmission protocols, and in particular, for the sliding window protocol of the following section.

When changing the input language, usually also the property φ has to be adapted yielding a property $\tilde{\varphi}$ over the new input language. The requirement $\tilde{\varphi}$ has to satisfy is that it holds for the program operating on the new input language if and only the original property holds for the program with the original input language.

For example, suppose we want to check that a process, given as input the increasing sequence of natural numbers starting from 0, first delivers a 0 as output. Since satisfaction of the property depends on whether 0 or *any other* value appears first, one can identify all values other than 0. In other words, under the assumption that the process is data independent, one can show the stated property with the restricted input language $0\,1^\infty$, using only a finite alphabet instead of the natural numbers.

2.3 Abstraction

Abstraction [CC77,CGL94,Lon93,DGG94,Kur94,LGS$^+$95,Dam96,Kel95] is the third technique we use. It is a general way of deriving properties for systems by investigating smaller, more abstract ones. In our specific setting, to establish a property φ local to component S_j, we create abstract versions $\widetilde{S}_l$ of the remaining processes S_l such that

$$\widetilde{S}_1\|\ldots\|\widetilde{S_{j-1}}\|S_j\|\widetilde{S_{j+1}}\|\widetilde{S}_n \models \varphi \quad \text{implies} \quad S_1\|\ldots\|S_n \models \varphi \ .$$

Of course, in general the part of interest might not consist of a single process S_j but of a set of processes. The connection between the concrete and the abstract system is given by an abstraction relation α between the two state spaces. Since we consider only *path universally quantified* properties, it is sufficient that the abstract versions $\widetilde{S}_l$ exhibit more behavior than the original S_l with respect to the abstraction relation, i.e., the abstraction relation is a *simulation* relation. Formally, α is a simulation relation between both systems, if the following condition, called *safety of abstraction*, holds:

$$\forall c, c' \in \Sigma_C, a \in \Sigma_A. \tau_C(c, c') \wedge \alpha(c, a) \implies \exists a' \in \Sigma_A. \tau_A(a, a') \wedge \alpha(c', a') \ ,$$

where Σ_C is the concrete state space and τ_C is a concrete transition (respectively Σ_A and τ_A for the abstract system).

In the verification of the sliding window protocol, we prove safety of abstraction using the theorem prover PVS [ORSvH95]. The translation of the system transitions and the state space into a PVS theory is straightforward and omitted from the paper.

2.4 Verification Strategies

The techniques presented above can be applied in any suitable order and the application can be iterated. Having in mind that a property should be decomposed into more local properties, it is, however, advantageous to first apply decomposition. Indeed, it does not enlarge the state space but rather gives more possibilities for applying the two other abstraction techniques.

In the sequel, we present an iterative method which can be applied in order to decompose a given property into more local ones. To do so, assume we are given two processes S_1 and S_2 in parallel, and a property φ. Suppose we want to show $S_1 \parallel S_2 \models \varphi$ and let C denote the chaotic process which exhibits all possible behaviors. In Fig. 1, we describe an (semi-)algorithm given in pseudo-code which can be applied to decompose a property into more local properties. In the given description we tacitly identify processes and properties and denote by $\mathcal{R}(S)$ the set of reachable states of S.

Clearly, we can replace $\mathcal{R}(S_1 \parallel \psi_2)$ (resp. $\mathcal{R}(\psi_1 \parallel S_2)$) by any property which follows from $\mathcal{R}(S_1 \parallel \psi_2)$ (resp. $\mathcal{R}(\psi_1 \parallel S_2)$) and axioms which can be derived from the semantics such as the usual assumptions concerning the buffers.

We now illustrate this methodology by proving safety of a sliding window protocol used in *Mascara* [DPA$^+$98], a medium-access layer for wireless ATM-networks. We start with a description of the protocol.

$$\psi_1 := C;$$
$$\psi_2 := C;$$
Do
$$\psi_1 := \mathcal{R}(S_1 \| \psi_2)$$
$$[]$$
$$\psi_2 := \mathcal{R}(\psi_1 \| S_2)$$
Until $\psi_1 \wedge \psi_2 \Rightarrow \varphi$

Fig. 1. Property Decomposition

3   The Sliding Window Protocol

The sliding window protocol [Ste76] is a communication protocol to guarantee reliable data transmission over unreliable, buffered communication channels. Considering only unidirectional communication, the protocol consists of a sender and a receiver process, connected by two channels, one in each direction (cf. Fig. 2).

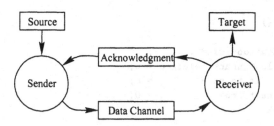

Fig. 2. Communication structure

The sender receives data from the source which has to be transmitted to the target. The data is sent to the receiver over the data channel, which may lose but not reorder messages. The sender stamps each data item with a sequence number such that the receiver can detect whether a message had been lost. The receiver acknowledges received data by sending the sequence number which it expects next over the lossy acknowledgment channel. The sender can retransmit unacknowledged messages, which are kept in the so-called *transmission window* until acknowledged. To hand out the data items to the target in the correct order, the receiver can temporarily store them in its *reception window.*

The protocol has three important parameters:

Transmission window size *tw*: This value specifies the maximal number of messages sent but not yet acknowledged together with those received from the source but not yet sent.

Reception window size *rw*: This is the maximum number of messages that can be kept at the receiver side without being delivered.

Cardinality of sequence numbers n: Since the transmission window is finite, a finite set of sequence numbers suffices to ensure unique identification of each message. The protocol works correctly with at least $n = tw + rw$ sequence numbers. In this case the numbers $\{0, \ldots, n-1\}$ are used cyclically modulo n.

Mascara's sliding window protocol uses a transmission window size of 15 and size 1 for the receiver, which means the receiver either delivers a message in case it fits into the output stream or it discards it. The protocol uses the minimal possible amount of sequence numbers, namely 16. Although in general, a sliding window protocol assures safety over unbounded lossy FIFO-channels, in Mascara the buffer is restricted to a size of 16.

In the following we give the Promela model (Promela is the input language of Spin) for sender and receiver.[1] In Sect. 4 we will refer to the transitions of sender and receiver using the names mentioned in the comments of the Promela code. The lossiness of communication is modeled using Promela communication channels of buffer size 16, where the receiving side may decide nondeterministically to lose the message.

```
proctype Sender()
{
  Data transmit_window[window_size];
  Window_index last_unacknowledged = 0;
  Window_index next_to_send      = 0;
  Window_index next_free         = 0;
  Seq_Number ack;

  do
  :: atomic{                                    /* receive_data */
     !(data_window_full) ->
       gen_to_send?(transmit_window[next_free]);
       next_free = ((next_free + 1) % window_size)
     }
  :: d_step{                                    /* send        */
     data_pending && nfull(send_to_rec) ->
       send_to_rec! transmit_window[next_to_send], next_to_send;
       next_to_send = (next_to_send + 1) % window_size
     }
  :: d_step{
     sliding_window_full ->                     /* timeout     */
       next_to_send = last_unacknowledged
     }
  :: d_step{                                    /* receive_ack */
     nempty(rec_to_send) -> rec_to_send?ack;
       if
       :: (ack == last_unacknowledged)   ->
```

---

[1] In the Promela code we leave out macro definitions for the data operations, which should be clear from the context.

```
proctype Receiver()
{
  byte next_expected = 0;
  Seq_Number received_number;

  do
  :: send_to_rec?(_,_)                                /* receive_lost */
  :: atomic{                                          /* receive      */
     send_to_rec?(data_item,received_number) ->
       if
       :: (received_number == next_expected) ->
            rec_to_upper!data_item;
            printf("Output %d\n", data_item);
            next_expected = (next_expected + 1) % window_size
       :: else  -> skip
       fi
     }
  :: rec_to_send!next_expected                        /* send_ack     */
  od
}
```

If the receiver gets a message with the expected sequence number, it delivers
the corresponding data item to the data target. The counter for the next expected
sequence number is increased cyclically by 1. Also, an acknowledgment may be
sent at any time, indicating the next expected sequence number (send_ack).

4   Verification of the Sliding Window Protocol

We want to prove a *safety property* of the sliding window protocol of Sect. 3,
namely that the protocol ensures reliable communication. This means no data
item is lost nor duplicated and the receiver delivers the data in the original order.
Relating the input stream at the sender to the output stream delivered by the
receiver, we say that the protocol is correct, if for all input sequences the output
sequence of each possible run of the protocol is a *prefix* of the input sequence.
Trying to establish the correctness of the protocol with the full window size of
16 directly will not succeed using Spin.

Observing that the protocol is *data independent*, we can start by considering
the stream of natural numbers as input, as opposed to arbitrary data, i.e., it is
enough to establish that if we have as input the stream of natural numbers, the
output is always a prefix thereof.

Before we formalize the properties, we introduce some useful notations. A
sequence of data items from a data domain D is a function $seq : \mathbb{N}_{<k} \to D$ for a
$k \in \mathbb{N} \cup \{\infty\}$, this k is the *length* of seq and is denoted as $\#seq$. We also denote a
sequence as $(seq_i)_{i<k}$, or $(seq_i)_{i \in \mathbb{N}}$ in case $\#seq = \infty$. If out is a possible output
sequence of the sliding window protocol for a given input sequence in, we denote
this with $out \in SW(in)$. Let $in_\mathbb{N} = (j)_{j \in \mathbb{N}}$. A *language* is a set of sequences.
For a language L, we denote with $out \in SW(L)$ that there is a word $in \in L$

```
                next_to_send = last_unacknowledged
        :: else -> last_unacknowledged = ack
        fi
   :: rec_to_send?_                                    /* ack_lost      */
      }
   od
}
```

As long as the transmission window is still capable of storing messages to be sent, the sender can read new data items from the data source. The new items are put in the open part of the window together with the already sent but yet unacknowledged messages. The position in the window corresponds with the sequence number given to the data items. Those messages are sent in the cyclic order of their sequence numbers (see Fig. 3) by the **send** transition.

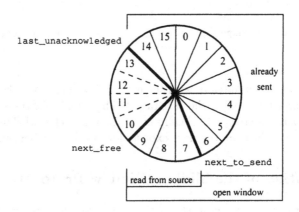

Fig. 3. Transmission window of the sender

A specific feature of Mascara's sliding window protocol is how the retransmission is triggered: in smooth operation of the protocol each acknowledgment will confirm one or more messages. The fact that twice the same acknowledgment is received is taken as indication by the sender that a transmission error has occurred and it start resending (by setting next_to_send back to last_unacknowledged). Another cause for resending in practice is a timeout occurring in case the acknowledgments are too late. This situation is modeled here in a simplified way where the timeout is bound to occur when the maximum number of 15 unacknowledged cells has been sent (sliding_window_full). An arriving acknowledgment causes the acknowledged message to fall out of the open window, the window 'slides' one message forward (receive_ack). The acknowledgment may also be lost which is modeled by ack_lost.

with $out \in SW(in)$. A run or a computation with a certain input is a sequence of consecutive states of the sliding window protocol.

Lemma 1. *If the protocol satisfies the property*

$$\text{For all } out \in SW(in_{\mathbb{N}}), k < \#out : out(k) = k \ , \qquad \text{(Prefix)}$$

then it is correct in the sense described above.

Proof. Assume that the protocol is erroneous, i.e., there exists an input sequence *in* and a trace of the protocol such that the output sequence *out* is no prefix of *in*. Then, we find a first error on a position $k < \#out$ such that

$$out(k) \neq in(k) \text{ and for all } j < k : out(j) = in(j) \ .$$

Since the protocol is data independent, we can adapt this trace with the input $in_{\mathbb{N}}$. Data independence ensures that exactly the same steps are possible. This yields to an output sequence $\widetilde{out}$ of the same length as *out*. Consider now position k of $\widetilde{out}$. Then, $\widetilde{out}(k) \neq in_{\mathbb{N}}(k)$. Thus, there exists $j \neq k$ with $in_{\mathbb{N}}(j) = \widetilde{out}(k)$. But by choice of $in_{\mathbb{N}}$ we are now able to derive $\widetilde{out}(k) \neq k$.

In the following, let *out* be an arbitrary output sequence of the sliding window protocol for the input sequence $in_{\mathbb{N}}$.

4.1 Decomposition of (Prefix)

After exploiting data independence to simplify the data domain, we continue by a first decomposition step, splitting the safety requirement into the following four properties.

Lemma 2. *The following properties are a decomposition of (Prefix):*

$$\forall i < \#out : out(i) \in \mathcal{M}_{16}(i) \qquad \text{(Mod16)}$$
$$\#out > 0 \implies out(0) = 0 \qquad \text{(Init)}$$
$$\forall i < \#out - 1 : out(i+1) > out(i) - 15 \qquad \text{(WSize)}$$
$$\forall i < \#out - 1 : out(i+1) \leq out(i) + 15 \qquad \text{(Lose)}$$

where $\mathcal{M}_{16}(i) = \{j \in \mathbb{N} \mid j \equiv_{16} i\} = \mathbb{N} \cap i + 16\mathbb{Z}$.

The induction principle motivates this decomposition. Property (Init) is the induction base, saying that the first output is correct. The other properties decompose the induction step, which states that $out(i) = i \implies out(i+1) = i + 1$.

One can observe that whatever happens between sender and receiver, the labeling of the input data items with the sequence numbers, and the receiving in just the right order of the sequence numbers done by the receiver, ensures Prop. (Mod16), restricting the positions on which input data elements can occur in the output sequence.

Properties (WSize) and (Lose) now give further restrictions to the output sequence positions, saying that the values of neighbored positions in the output sequence are not too far away.

Proof. We have to show that these properties together imply (`Prefix`), so assume they are valid. Let $i < \#out$. We prove $out(i) = i$ by induction on i.

Case: $i = 0$. In this case we have $out(0) = 0$ by (`Init`).

Case: $i \to i + 1$. Assume $out(i) = i$, $i + 1 < \#out$, and consider $out(i + 1)$. We know by (`Mod16`) that there exists a $k \in \mathbb{Z}$ such that $out(i + 1) = i + 1 + 16k$. Since $i = out(i)$ we have $out(i + 1) = out(i) + 1 + 16k$.

- If $k \geq 1$, we have $out(i + 1) \geq out(i) + 17$ in contradiction to (`Lose`).
- If $k \leq -1$, we have $out(i + 1) \leq out(i) - 15$ in contradiction to (`WSize`).

Consequently, $k = 0$ and $out(i + 1) = i + 1$.

We now establish Properties (`Mod16`), (`Init`), (`WSize`), and (`Lose`).

In the following sections we use the abbreviations R for the receiver and S for the sender process. The notion *send* means that the message has been put into the channel.

4.2 Property (`Mod16`)

First, we want to establish Prop. (`Mod16`): $\forall i < \#out : out(i) \in \mathcal{M}_{16}(i)$.

Data Independence By data independence, we can reduce the input language to the word $in_m = (0\,1\,2\,\ldots\,15)^\infty$. So we identify data items on positions $16k + i$ and $16k' + i$. We have to show the following:

(i) For all $out \in SW(in_m)$: out is a prefix of in_m.

Now we apply the decomposition principle explained in Sect. 2.4.

Considering a chaotic sender, we observe that R sends only acknowledgments n such that either $n = 0$, or $n > 0$ and R has received a message $(d, n - 1)$ before. Since the messages are exchanged via a buffer, one can derive that R sends only n if either $n = 0$, or $n > 0$ and S has sent a message $(d, n - 1)$ before.

If R behaves in this way, S can only send positions of the transmit window to which it has written before. Hence, we can derive a restriction for the messages standing in the buffer. With this restriction, we can construct an abstract system usable for verification of Prop. (i).

This decomposition is explained in detail below.

Abstractions Even with the reduced input language the system is far from being model-checkable. The main problem for the verification are the buffers from S to R and vice versa. A method often successful to overcome the state explosion caused by such a buffer is to restrict the possible messages which can occur in it, and to use two variables as the abstract buffer: one which holds the head value of the buffer, and one boolean which is true if and only if the buffer is empty, since these are the important informations for one system step.

The abstraction relation then says that the abstract variable holds exactly the head value of the buffer in the case it is non-empty. This relation must be restored after each read operation by assigning arbitrary values to the abstract variables. Here, restricting these values is often helpful.

As explained, we now apply the decomposition principle from Sect. 2.4 and start considering a chaotic sender. This leads to the following property:

(ii) In every run (with input in_m), each acknowledgment n sent by R is either 0, or $n > 0$ and R received a message $(d, n - 1)$ before.

Now we describe the abstraction used for the verification of this property. We abstract the buffer from S to R in the way described above, discard the acknowledgment buffer, and use a chaotic sender which is able to send any message. The receiver functionality is unchanged, except that R is not required to send, and that R changes the buffer variables arbitrarily after reading a message. Then we use Spin to establish that property.

Since every message occurring in the buffer is written to it by S, Prop. (ii) implies Prop. (iii).

(iii) In every run (with input in_m), each acknowledgment n sent by R is either 0, or $n > 0$ and S sent a message $(d, n - 1)$ before.

Relying on this Prop. (iii), we obtain by setting S in parallel with a receiver fulfilling Prop. (iii):

(iv) For all messages (d, n) occurring in the buffer from S to R (at any time in any run with input in_m), $d = n$.

The abstract system used to establish Prop. (iv) by model-checking is the following. The buffer from S to R is discarded, and the acknowledgment buffer is abstracted in a similar way as before. The abstract receiver non-deterministically sends arbitrary acknowledgments allowed by Prop. (iii). The abstract sender non-deterministically assigns values allowed by Prop. (iii) to the buffer variables after an acknowledgment reception, the rest of the sender is unchanged. For this abstract system, Prop. (iv) can be model-checked.

Now we describe the abstraction used for verifying Prop. (i) with Spin. The channel from S to R is abstracted to two variables as described above, the acknowledgment buffer is discarded. After each read operation of R, R restores the abstraction relation by assigning non-deterministically a value (n, n). These are the only possible values according to Prop. (iv). The abstract sender can assign arbitrary values (restricted by Prop. (iv)) to the buffer variables. Then, the property is easily model-checked using Spin.

The abstraction relation ensures that the receiver variables of the abstract and concrete systems coincide, and that the abstract channel variable holds the head value of the concrete channel in case it is non-empty.

4.3 Property (Init)

Following our approach we now prove $\#out > 0 \implies out(0) = 0$.

Decomposition Decomposing (Init) leads to the following requirements:

(v) For all runs with input $in_{\mathbb{N}}$, if a message with a data value $d \geq 16$ is sent by S, then the sender read an acknowledgment $\neq 0$ earlier.

(vi) R gives out only data items which R has received through the data channel.

We will show (v) by model-checking. For this property we use in the following sections data independence and abstractions to yield a suitable system. Property (vi) follows easily by data independence. Indeed, we can directly derive from the program text that R does not change received data nor introduces new data, that is, it only passes on the received data items.

The decomposition leads to a proof obligation, namely that the conjunction of Prop. (v) and (vi) implies Prop. (Init). This is shown next.

Proof. Consider a computation, a state in that computation, and assume $\#out > 0$ in that state. With Prop. (Mod16) we know that $out(0) = 16k$ for a suitable $k \in \mathbb{N}$. By (v) we know that before a data item $d \geq 16$ is sent by S, the sender receives an acknowledgment a different from 0. Consider the point in the computation when S receives an acknowledgment $a \neq 0$ for the first time. Then, a was sent by R, since the buffer does not invent data.

Consequently, R has changed the value of its variable next_expected which is initialized to 0, and therefore, R has received a message with sequence number 0.

Every message which R receives was sent by S earlier. Since $(0, 0)$ is the only message sent by S so far with sequence number 0, R has received this message.

If R changes next_expected, it also gives out the data item attached to the received message in the same atomic transition. Therefore, R starts the output sequence with the data item 0.

Data Independence By data independence we reduce the input language of the system for Prop. (v) to $0^{15} 0^* 1 0^\omega$. Adapting Prop. (v) to this new input language, we have to show the following:

(vii) For all runs with the input language $0^{15} 0^* 1 0^\omega$, whenever S sends data value "1", S received an acknowledgment $\neq 0$ before.

Now we use abstraction to construct an abstract system used to model-check this property.

Abstraction For Prop. (vii), we can use a very abstract receiver which non-deterministically is able to send every possible acknowledgment. The functionality of the sender is unchanged, except two modifications. First, the buffer between sender and receiver can be discarded. Second, the capacity of the acknowledgment channel still leads to state space explosion. Therefore, we abstract the buffer analogously to Sect. 4.2 to two variables rec_to_send (for the head element) and rec_to_send_empty. The abstract system can set these variables to arbitrary values after reading an acknowledgment.

After constructing this abstract system, one can observe that the functionality of the sender transition ack_lost is almost the same than the functionality of the whole receiver. Therefore, only little modifications must be made to abstract away the whole receiver. The concrete receiver steps are then simulated by the abstract ack_lost transition.

Furthermore, we introduce an auxiliary variable last_sent which holds the value of the last data item sent and is used to formulate the property, and which replaces the abstract channel from S to R with respect to Prop. (vii).

The abstraction relation which defines the relationship between the concrete and the abstract system is given in Fig. 4. Here, σ_C (resp. σ_A) is a concrete (resp.

$$\alpha(\sigma_C, \sigma_A) \stackrel{\text{def}}{=} \sigma_C(\text{transmit\_window}) = \sigma_A(\text{transmit\_window})$$
$$\wedge \, \sigma_C(\text{next\_to\_send}) = \sigma_A(\text{next\_to\_send})$$
$$\wedge \, \sigma_C(\text{next\_free}) = \sigma_A(\text{next\_free})$$
$$\wedge \, \sigma_C(\text{last\_unacknowledged}) = \sigma_A(\text{last\_unacknowledged})$$
$$\wedge \, \text{nonempty}(\sigma_C(\text{rec\_to\_send})) \implies$$
$$\text{head}(\sigma_C(\text{rec\_to\_send})) = \sigma_A(\text{rec\_to\_send})$$
$$\wedge \, \neg\sigma_A(\text{rec\_to\_send\_empty}) \iff$$
$$\text{nonempty}(\sigma_C(\text{rec\_to\_send}))$$
$$\wedge \, \text{nonempty}(\sigma_C(\text{send\_to\_rec})) \implies$$
$$\text{proj}_1(\text{last}(\sigma_C(\text{send\_to\_rec}))) = \sigma_A(\text{last\_sent})$$

Fig. 4. Property Decomposition

abstract) state, head of a FIFO queue gives the next element which will be read, last gives the last value appended, proj_i is the i'th projection, and nonempty of a FIFO queue holds whenever the queue is not empty.

With this abstract system, it is possible to establish the (adapted) property using model-checking. We made the abstraction proofs using PVS. The translation of the Promela-model into a PVS theory is straightforward, and the abstraction proofs were almost automatic.

4.4 Property (WSize)

To establish $\forall i < \#out - 1 : out(i+1) > out(i) - 15$, we use a similar approach as for Prop. (Init). Therefore, we do not go into every detail for this property. The property holds, since the transmit window is bounded, and since the sender fills the transmit window in cyclic order. After a data items falls out of the window, which happens if we read too many items from the upper layer, it can never be send again.

Decomposition We only mention one of the properties we got by decomposing (WSize):

(viii) For all runs with input $in_{\mathbb{N}}$, if the sender sends a value d, it will never send a value $d' \leq d - 15$ afterwards.

We will establish this property by model-checking and describe in the following sections how to apply data independence and abstraction to it. The decomposition further needs the fact that we have a FIFO buffer, and that R does not store, but directly delivers when it receives data.

Data Independence To verify Prop. (viii), we use data independence to reduce the input language of the system to $L = 0^* 1 0^{14} 0^* 2 0^\infty$. Then, we have to reformulate Prop. (viii) and obtain:

(ix) For all runs with input from L, after sending data item "2", the sender never sends a "1".

Abstractions To verify the reduced property, we again concentrate on the sender and use a very abstract receiver which only sends non-deterministically an arbitrary acknowledgment. In fact, the same abstract system (apart from the input language) can be used as given in Sect. 4.3.

4.5 Property (Lose)

To prove $\forall i < \#out - 1 : out(i + 1) \leq out(i) + 15$, let us start with the following lemma which is proven analogously to Lemma 2.

Lemma 3. *If Props. (Mod16)–(Lose) from page 9 hold for all states of a computation* $comp = s_0 \xrightarrow{t_0} s_1 \xrightarrow{t_1} \ldots$ *up to a state* s_n, *then* s_n *satisfies:* $\forall j \leq \#out - 1 : out(j) = j$.

For the proof of the next proposition, we introduce some new notions. A *non-empty position* of the *transmit window* in state s of the sender is a position i with $0 \leq i \leq 15$ such that

$$(i - s(\texttt{last\_unacknowledged})) \bmod 16$$
$$< (s(\texttt{next\_free}) - s(\texttt{last\_unacknowledged})) \bmod 16 .$$

In other words, it is a position in the open transmit window, one in the modulo interval $[s(\texttt{last\_unacknowledged}) \ldots \text{pred}_m(s(\texttt{next\_free}))]$, where $\text{pred}_m(i) = (i - 1) \bmod 16$. Analogously, an *empty position* is a position which is not nonempty. The notion that the sender *acknowledges* position i by taking transition t means that, in the original state, position i was a non-empty position, and after taking transition t, i has become an empty position. The sender *acknowledges erroneously* by executing a sequence of acknowledgment receptions, when after executing the sequence steps, there are more non-empty positions than before executing that sequence. This covers the case when the pointer last_unacknowledged jumps to an empty position by reading an acknowledgment, thus enlarging the open transmit window.

Proposition 1. *The sliding window protocol satisfies Prop. (Lose).*

Proof. Assume that Prop. (Lose) does not hold. Then we find a computation

$$comp = s_0 \xrightarrow{t_0} s_1 \xrightarrow{t_1} \dots \xrightarrow{t_{n-1}} s_n$$

such that Prop. (Lose) is violated. Each s_i is a state and each t_i is a transition of the system (for example a transition of the receiver). Let n be the first position such that s_n satisfies one of the following clauses:

(a) $out(i+1) > out(i) + 15$ for an i.
(b) By reading the acknowledgments from the acknowledgment buffer, S is able to acknowledge a data item d which has not been given out by R.
(c) S can acknowledge erroneously by executing a sequence of acknowledgment receptions.
(d) By reading the acknowledgments from the acknowledgment buffer, S can reach a state such that the value of next_expected is a bad acknowledgment in the sense of (b) or (c), i.e. S can reach a state, in which the value of next_expected would acknowledge a data item which has not yet been given out by R, or it would acknowledge erroneously.

It is obvious by initialization of the processes that $n > 0$.

Case: Property (a) holds in state s_n. Choose i such that (a) holds for that i. Since n is the minimal position such that (a) holds, the last transition t_{n-1} must have added $out(i+1)$ to the output sequence. Since n is the minimal position for which one of (a)–(d) holds, we know that in state s_{n-1} (a) does not hold, which implies that Prop. (Lose) holds together with the other Props. (Init)–(WSize). Lemma 3 then implies, that the output sequence of s_{n-1} is $0, 1, \dots, i$. Consequently, $out(i) = i$. Step t_{n-1} extends this sequence with $out(i+1)$. By (Mod16) we know that $out(i+1) = i + 1 + 16k$ for a suitable k. With Prop. (a) we then derive that $k \geq 1$. Consequently, $out(i+1) > (i+1) + 16$.

Then, the sender has already sent $i+1$ before. But this data item has never been given out by the receiver. On the other hand, the sender must have acknowledged data item $i+1$ in the past, otherwise it could not get data item $out(i+1)$ into its transmit window. Hence, on an earlier point in the computation, (b) must hold. Contradiction!

Case: Property (b) holds in s_n. Hence, by reading acknowledgments from the buffer, S can acknowledge a data item d which has not yet been given out by the receiver. Consider transition t_{n-1}.

- $t_{n-1} \in \{\text{send}, \text{timeout}, \text{receive\_lost}, \text{receive}\}$: In this case, the variables next_free, last_unacknowledged, and buffer rec_to_send are unchanged. Hence, (b) also holds in state s_{n-1}. Contradiction!

- $t_{n-1} = \text{receive\_data}$: Consider first the case that the new data item received by S and inserted in the transmit window on position $j = s_{n-1}(\text{next\_free})$ is the one falsely acknowledged. After step t_{n-1}, the sender is able to acknowledge d by reading acknowledgments. These transitions do not affect variable next_free. Hence, it is unchanged, and the only possibility to remove d from the transmit window, is to set the pointer last_unacknowledged to position $s_n(\text{next\_free})$.

  Now consider that the same sequence of acknowledgment receptions is done beginning in state s_{n-1}. With this sequence of steps we reach a state s such that $s(\text{next\_free}) = \text{pred}_m(s(\text{last\_unacknowledged}))$, which means the transmit window is maximally open.

  In case the open window had this size already in s_{n-1}, it is not possible to take t_{n-1} in state s_{n-1}. Contradiction. In the other case, (c) is already satisfied in s_{n-1}.

  Now consider the case, that d was already in position j in the transmit window in state s_{n-1}. After the same sequence of acknowledgment receptions starting in state s_{n-1}, a state s is reached.

  If $s(\text{last\_unacknowledged}) \neq s_n(\text{next\_free})$, then the open window in state s is a subset of the open window in the state in which d is falsely acknowledged. Consequently, d is acknowledged in s. Hence, (b) is valid in state s_{n-1}. Contradiction!

  In case $s(\text{last\_unacknowledged}) = s_n(\text{next\_free})$, the transmit window in state s is again maximal. This again leads to a contradiction (either t_{n-1} is not enabled, or (c) is already valid in s_{n-1}).

- $t_{n-1} \in \{\text{receive\_ack}, \text{ack\_lost}\}$: In this case, every state which can be reached by reading acknowledgments was also reachable before from s_{n-1} by reading acknowledgments. Hence, (b) must also hold in s_{n-1}. This holds also for all subsequent cases, they are therefore left out.

- $t_{n-1} = \text{send\_ack}$: In this case, (d) holds in state s_{n-1}, since the new acknowledgment appended to the acknowledgment channel by R is the value of its variable next_expected.

Case: Property (c) holds in s_n. By reading the acknowledgments in the acknowledgment buffer, S can acknowledge erroneously, which means it can enlarge its transmit window. Again, consider transition t_{n-1}.

- $t_{n-1} \in \{\text{send}, \text{timeout}, \text{receive\_lost}, \text{receive}\}$: (c) already holds in state s_{n-1}. Contradiction!

- $t_{n-1} = \text{receive\_data}$: The sender is able to enlarge the open transmit window by reading some acknowledgments . Consider again the same reception sequence of acknowledgments but starting in s_{n-1} reaching a state s.

  If $s(\text{last\_unacknowledged}) = s_{n-1}(\text{next\_free})$, then in the sequence starting from s_n enlarging the window, the resulting open window size is 1. But this is also the size in s_n, thus, the open window is not enlarged.

Also if $s(\texttt{last\_unacknowledged}) = s_n(\texttt{next\_free})$, the open window size is not enlarged.

Otherwise, in both sequences, starting either from s_n or s_{n-1}, the open window size is enlarged by the same amount. Thus, (c) is already valid in s_{n-1}.

- $t_{n-1} = \texttt{send\_ack}$: In this case, (d) holds in state s_{n-1}.

Case: Property (d) holds in s_n. Assume that (a) does not hold. Then we can derive (using Lemma 3) that the output sequence is $0, 1, \ldots, i$ for a suitable $i \geq 0$. Consider transition t_{n-1}.

- $t_{n-1} \in \{\texttt{send}, \texttt{timeout}, \texttt{receive\_lost}\}$: (d) also holds in state s_{n-1}. Contradiction!
- $t_{n-1} = \texttt{send\_ack}$: Since the value of the variable $\texttt{next\_expected}$ is appended to the acknowledgment channel, (d) is also valid in s_{n-1}.
- $t_{n-1} = \texttt{receive\_data}$: Basically the same argumentation can be used as in the cases (b) and (c). One can think of an acknowledgment channel extended by the value of $\texttt{next\_expected}$.
- $t_{n-1} = \texttt{receive}$: If the variable $\texttt{next\_expected}$ is unchanged by transition t_{n-1}, then (d) holds in s_{n-1}. Consequently, R must have received a message (d', n') with $n' = s_{n-1}(\texttt{next\_expected})$. Then, d' is given out by the receiver in this step, and there once was a state in which d' was in the transmit window on position n'.

  Assume first that (d) holds since the value of $\texttt{next\_expected}$ can be a bad acknowledgment in the sense of (b).

  Since (d) does not hold in s_{n-1}, the position in the transmit window in which the error occurs must be position n' (since t_{n-1} increases – modulo window size – the variable $\texttt{next\_expected}$ by 1). The output sequence (in state s_n) must be $0, 1, 2, \ldots, d'$.

  Hence, there is a data item $d'' > d'$ on position n'. Then, d' must have been acknowledged by the sender with a transition t_j with $j < n$. Since n is minimal, d' must already have been given out by R before step j. Consequently, d' is given out at least twice, once before transition t_j and once by taking transition t_{n-1}. Contradiction!

  Now assume that (d) holds since the value of $\texttt{next\_expected}$ would acknowledge erroneously, that means, enlarge the open transmit window. Thus, a state s is reachable by acknowledgment receptions such that an acknowledgment $n'' = s_n(\texttt{next\_expected})$ enlarges the open transmit window. Since $n' = \text{pred}_m(n'')$, n' would also enlarge it in case $n' \neq s_n(\texttt{next\_free})$. But then, (d) would be valid in s_{n-1}. Consequently, $s_{n-1}(\texttt{next\_expected}) = n' = s_n(\texttt{next\_free}) = s_{n-1}(\texttt{next\_free})$. But then, position n' in the transmit window of s_{n-1} is not in the open transmit window. Thus, d' is already acknowledged. But it has not yet been given out in state s_{n-1}. Hence, (b) is valid in s_{n-1}.

4.6 Verification Results

The following table shows the experimental results on a SUN Ultra Sparc with 1 GB of memory and 167 MHz processor. The last column shows whether we used the Spin option for compression in this particular case. We always used partial order reduction.

Property	time	max. depth	memory	compression
(Init)	3 h	1,000,000	516 MB	no
(WSize)	15 h	1,000,000	901 MB	yes
(i)	1 min	1,675	80 MB	no
(ii)	1 h	2,781	139 MB	no
(iv)	1.5 h	1,000,000	259 MB	no

5 Conclusion

In this paper we proposed a verification methodology that combines data independence, abstraction, and compositional reasoning. The essence of the approach is to exploit the added value of combining those techniques. Additionally it serves as a clean guideline to separate the properties amenable to automatic model-checking and those to be verified deductively.

We applied this methodology to analyze a realistic sliding window protocol taken from a wireless ATM protocol of window size of 16. To our knowledge, this is the largest size of a sliding window protocol verified with the help of model-checking techniques. In fact we applied the same methodology to prove a liveness property of the same protocol.

Related Work Various versions of the sliding window protocol have been studied in the literature. The treatment ranges from informal arguments [Knu81] [SL92] et. al. (and already in the original proposal [Ste76] of the protocol), to model-checking (e.g. in [RRSV87]), compositional reasoning (e.g. [Jon87]), proofs using theorem provers [Car89], or combinations of various techniques [Kai97]. Closest to our investigation is [Kai97], who also uses a combination of model-checking, abstraction and decomposition. Different from our work, [Kai97] does not use a theorem prover, but automatically checks safety of the abstraction using specific behavioral preorders. He succeeds in proving safety and liveness up to the window size of 7.

Acknowledgments We thank the anonymous referees for their helpful comments and suggestions.

References

[BBLS92] A. Bouajjani, S. Bensalem, C. Loiseaux, and J. Sifakis. Property preserving simulations. In G. v. Bochmann and D. K. Probst, editors, *CAV'92*, volume 663 of *LNCS*. Springer, 1992.

[Car89]   R. Cardell-Oliver. The specification and verification of sliding window protocols. Technical Report 183, University of Cambridge, 1989.

[CC77]   P. Cousot and R. Cousot. Abstract interpretation: A unified lattice model for static analysis of programs by construction or approximation of fixpoints. In *4th POPL, Los Angeles, CA*. ACM, 1977.

[CE81]   E. M. Clarke and E. A. Emerson. Synthesis of synchronisation skeletons for branching time temporal logic. In D. Kozen, editor, *Workshop on Logic of Programs 1981*, volume 131 of *LNCS*. Springer, 1981.

[CGL94]   E. Clarke, O. Grumberg, and D. Long. Model checking and abstraction. *TOPLAS*, 16(5):1512–1542, 1994.

[Dam96]   D. Dams. *Abstract interpretation and partition refinement for model che cking*. PhD thesis, Technical University of Eindhoven, 1996.

[DGG94]   D. Dams, R. Gerth, and O. Grumberg. Abstract interpretation of reactive systems: Abstractions preserving ACTL*, ECTL* and CTL*. In E.-R. Olderog, editor, *Proceedings of PROCOMET '94*. North-Holland, 1994.

[DPA+98] I. Dravapoulos, N. Pronios, A. Andritsou, I. Piveropoulos, N. Passas, D. Skyrianoglou, G. Awater, J. Kruys, N. Nikaein, A. Enout, S. Decrauzat, T. Kaltenschnee, T. Schumann, J. Meierhofer, S. Thömel, and J. Mikkonen. *The Magic WAND, Deliverable 3D5, Wireless ATM MAC, Final Report*, 1998.

[dRLP98] W.-P. de Roever, H. Langmaack, and A. Pnueli, editors. *Compos '97*, volume 1536 of *LNCS*. Springer, 1998.

[Hol91]   G. J. Holzmann. *Design and Validation of Computer Protocols*. Prentice Hall, 1991.

[Jon87]   B. Jonsson. *Compositional Verification of Distributed Systems*. PhD thesis, University of Uppsala, 1987. Technical Report DoCS 87/09.

[Kai97]   R. Kaivola. Using compositional preorders in the verification of sliding window protocol. In O. Grumberg, editor, *Proceedings of CAV '97*, volume 1256 of *LNCS*, pages 48–59. Springer, 1997.

[Kel95]   P. Kelb. *Abstraktionstechniken für Automatische Verifikationsmethoden*. PhD thesis, University of Oldenburg, 1995.

[Knu81]   D. E. Knuth. Verification of link-level protocols. *BIT*, 21:31–36, 1981.

[Kur94]   R. P. Kurshan. *Computer-Aided Verification of Coordinating Processes, the automata theoretic approach*. Princeton Series in Computer Science. Princeton University Press, 1994.

[LGS+95] C. Loiseaux, S. Graf, J. Sifakis, A. Bouajjani, and S. Bensalem. Property preserving abstractions for the verification of concurrent systems. *Formal Methods in System Design*, 6(1), 1995.

[Lon93]   D. E. Long. *Model Checking, Abstraction, and Compositional Reasoning*. PhD thesis, Carnegie Mellon, 1993.

[ORSvH95] S. Owre, J. Rushby, N. Shankar, and F. von Henke. Formal verification for fault-tolerant architectures: Prolegomena to the design of PVS. *IEEE Transactions on Software Engineering*, 21(2):107–125, 1995.

[QS81]   J. P. Queille and J. Sifakis. Specification and verification of concurrent systems in CESAR. In *Proceedings of the Fifth International Symposium on Programming*, 1981.

[RRSV87] J. L. Richier, C. Rodriguez, J. Sifakis, and J. Voiron. Verification in Xesar of the sliding window protocol. In *PSTV VII*. North-Holland, 1987.

[SL92]   A. U. Shankar and S. S. Lam. A stepwise refinement heuristics for protocol construction. *TOPLAS*, 14(3):417–461, 1992.

[Ste76]   N. V. Stenning. A data transfer protocol. *Computer Networks*, 11:99–110, 1976.

[Wol86]   P. Wolper. Expressing interesting properties of programs in propositional temporal logic. In *Thirteenth POPL (St. Peterburg Beach, FL)*, pages 184–193. ACM, 1986.

Formal Methods Adoption: What's Working, What's Not!

Dan Craigen

ORA Canada
1208 ONE Nicholas
Ottawa, Ontario, K1N 7B7
CANADA
dan@ora.on.ca
WWW home page: http://www.ora.on.ca

Abstract. Drawing from the author's twenty years of experience in formal methods research and development, and, particularly, with the EVES-based systems, this paper provides personal impressions on *what is* and *what is not* working with regards to the adoption and application of formal methods.

As both the community's understanding of technology transfer issues and formal methods technology improve, one is optimistic that formal methods will play an increasingly important role in industry. However, significant impediments continue to exist with, perhaps, the increasing complexity of systems being both a blessing and a curse.

1 Introduction

Drawing upon my twenty years of experience in formal methods R&D, I will discuss personal impressions on *what is* and *what is not* working with regards to the adoption and application of formal methods.[1] I will structure this paper primarily around a narrative of the history of my group's work on formal methods.[2] Some conclusions are drawn in 20-20 hindsight. I will generally eschew technical discussions of our own technology. The citations provide appropriate pointers and many of our technical reports are available through our web site.

2 Genesis: m-EVES

Our work on formal methods grew out of a mid- to late-70s DARPA motivated effort in developing a verifiable programming language, ultimately named Euclid.

---

[1] I am writing this paper as we introduce our newborn daughter (Cailin) into our family (which also includes Liz and Ailsa). Sleep deprivation and various distractions have taken their toll on what I had hoped to include herein.

[2] Currently, the formal methods group at ORA Canada consists of myself, Sentot Kromodimoeljo, Irwin Meisels and Mark Saaltink. Bill Pase (automated deduction) and Karen Summerskill (technical editor) are instrumental past members of the group.

Euclid was a Pascal derivative which was provided a Hoare-style axiomatization, extended Pascal in various ways to support larger-scale system programming, and even had a compiler written for much of the language. Initially, our R&D plans were to develop a Euclid Verification and Evaluation System (hence, the acronym, EVES[3]). However, circumstances would dictate otherwise.

In the early 80s, Bill Pase and the author were sponsored to review and assess U.S. efforts in developing program verification systems (Affirm, the Gypsy Verification Environment, the Stanford Pascal Verifier, and HDM [the Hierarchical Design Methodology]).[4] This was a great opportunity to come to terms with the then cutting-edge of technology in various disciplines, including automated deduction, software engineering and language design. One of our observations resulting from the survey and subsequent experimentation, was that the mathematical underpinnings of the program verification systems were suspect (actually, generally unsound). To be fair, however, it must be noted that the prime goals of the researchers were to show that such verification systems could be developed and applied. Consequently, it was prudent to ask whether these systems could or should be used to reason about security- or safety-critical applications. We felt that appropriate mathematical foundations were necessary.

As the survey came to conclusion, sponsorship for developing EVES was obtained. The initial intent was to use results from the U.S. program verification efforts (including the possible use of system components) and to enhance Euclid (resulting in a language called Ottawa Euclid) with a formal specification framework. To cut a long story short, we ended up rejecting Euclid (and Ottawa Euclid) because of language and logic pathologies and the inimical nature of the pathologies towards our goal of reasoning about security-critical applications. Furthermore, we were advised by our colleagues in the automated deduction community that it would be best to develop our own automated deduction facility (ultimately called Never). With these decisions, we launched into language design and prover development. A somewhat risk-adverse approach was taken in that we were to develop a proof-of-concept system for a reasonably simple programming language. Consequently, we developed the m-EVES system [1, 2] with its programming (somewhat akin to a cleaned up Pascal with libraries) and specification (essentially, first order type theory) language (m-Verdi) and prover (m-Never). As part of the language design, we developed the underlying semantics and proof theory. m-Never was a nifty integration and enhancement of ideas drawn from the Stanford Pascal Verifier, Affirm, Gypsy, and the Boyer-Moore prover). Subsequently, we demonstrated the use of m-EVES on (somewhat large) toy examples.

In retrospect, there were a number of observations and lessons that came out of the m-EVES exercise:

---

[3] Though we continue to use the EVES acronym, (for example, in Z/EVES) we have long ago jettisoned the underlying interpretation.

[4] From a technology transfer perspective, it is interesting to note that Bill and I became conduits for information flow between the research groups which, otherwise, had been working independently of each other.

Technology driven: The project was technology driven. We focused on engineering and R&D issues as it pertained to a proof-of-concept comprehensive and sound verification environment. Except for the consideration that our technology would be used for critical systems, we gave no real consideration of how clients might apply the technology. Be customer-centric. However, be wary, for sometimes the customer does not have it right!

Puritanical: As the overall project goals were to support the development of security- (later safety-) critical systems, we were serious about the mathematical underpinnings for the system. This has both positive and negative consequences, which were accentuated with EVES and are discussed in the next section. We were religious and inflexible in our certitude.

Controlled distribution: In the mid-80s, many North American systems were tightly controlled as to accessibility. This had the deleterious effect of constraining the development of user communities and of independent feedback.

Technology transfer: We gave only limited consideration of actual transfer of the technology. While we embodied what we viewed as good software development principles, we gave no real consideration to commercialization of m-EVES nor of how the technology might be adopted by other organizations. A few other organizations did successfully use the technology, but these generally were early adopters following technical interests. Be prepared to take the *whole product* perspective. A substantial amount of boring stuff needs to be developed to really provide a useful product.

The completion of m-EVES was a significant technical milestone and it led to the almost immediate effort in developing EVES. In retrospect, we should have delayed moving onwards with EVES until we had given m-EVES more substantial trials and considered its linkage into our sponsors' organizations.

3   Let's do it again!

In the mid-80s we got to do it all over again, both with respect to surveying technology and moving forwards with the EVES development.

3.1   Verification Assessment Study

Firstly, of some note, was the Verification Assessment Study [3] led by Dick Kemmerer (University of California at Santa Barbara). This study brought together representatives of Enhanced HDM (Karl Levitt, then at SRI International), the Gypsy Verification Environment (Don Good, then at UT-Austin), Affirm (Dave Musser, then at GE Schenectady) and FDM (Debbie Cooper, then at SDC, Santa Monica), along with myself as an independent participant. The primary idea for the Study was to allow for the sharing of technical details between the participants and help form the basis for future development. This experience allowed me to update my knowledge of these systems and provided some input into the ongoing EVES development.

Of some note, is the then view of what a mid-80s state-of-the-art verification system would look like, if only to consider how we have progressed since then. The VERkshop III proceedings [4] identified such a system as consisting of:

- a specification language based on first-order, typed predicate calculus.
- an imperative language derived from the Pascal/Algol 60 family of programming languages.
- a formal semantic characterization of the specification and implementation languages.
- a verification condition generator (itself a major research challenge of the mid-70s).
- a mechanical proof checker with some automated proof generation capabilities.
- a (small) supporting library of (reusable) theorems.
- a glass (as opposed to hard copy) user interface, possibly using bit mapped displays.
- a single system dedicated to one user at a time.
- the embedding of these components in a modest programming environment.

As it turned out, our work with EVES was aiming to achieve at least these requirements.

Technology transfer was discussed during the study and efforts were made by the sponsors to make the verification systems available for use on a Multics system through the ARPAnet. However, there was still contention between those who felt a more open distribution of technology was appropriate and those who did not. As noted above, the controlled distribution of many systems impeded adoption.

3.2 EVES

With the m-EVES proof of a concept deemed a success (at least in our minds and those of our sponsors), we moved forward (in the mid-80s) with the *production* EVES system [5, 6]. With EVES, we would not be making some of the simplifying assumptions of m-EVES. However, a key continuing tenet to our work was that EVES would be used for the specification and development of critical applications and, consequently, sound mathematical foundations were crucial.

Our first important decision was which mathematical framework to use. The expressiveness we wanted could be found in either untyped set theory or (our initial bias) higher-order logic. We chose set theory since, in part, we felt it would be an easier adoption channel and had better automated deduction support.

EVES was a technical success. We generally achieved all the goals that we set out for. We developed a language (Verdi) that supported the expression of general mathematical theories, specification of programs (pre/post form), sequential imperative constructs, and a reasonable library mechanism. The prover brought together ideas from across the automated deduction domain (Boyer-Moore style heuristics in a richer logic, decision procedures, good mix of automation and user direction). A solid mathematical basis in which the language semantics were described and the proof theory shown to be sound. The development of an independent proof checker mechanism that validated the proofs found by the prover.[5] The validation of putative proofs is an important requirement for critical applications. And a rigorously developed compiler, in which key passes of the compiler were rigorously specified and traceability from the compiler source to the compiler specification demonstrated. EVES has been successfully used (by both ourselves and external groups) on a number of applications including fielded safety- and security-critical applications.[6]

However, being able to demonstrate a successful project from a technical perspective is different from actually having the technology transition into general use. It must be admitted that EVES has not been successfully transfered. I believe there are a number of reasons; many of which generalize to other efforts in formal methods.

Language: Not many people (especially within industrial contexts) wish to learn yet another specification or programming language. Verdi was spare with respect to its notation (basically akin to Lisp s-expressions). Also, the programming component was restrictive. One interesting lesson was that our design was not usually restricted by formal semantics concerns, but by logic constraints. For example, we excluded global state because of the difficulties resulting in the Verdi inference rules. The typeless basis also seemed to be an impediment. The equivalent of type reasoning is usually a part of the proof effort. This meant that feedback on simple specification infelicities came a bit later than necessary. Finally, I generally concluded that language design was more trouble than it was worth. No matter what decisions one made, there were always critics!

Industry will consider adopting new languages if there are significant commercial reasons for doing so. The attributes of formal semantics and (support for mechanized) proof are very low on the priority list and languages designed with these latter attributes as their main characteristic just will not transfer.

Ambitious: We were highly ambitious in our language design goals and for the overall system. *I know of no system or research effort that has cast as wide a net as the EVES project.* By choosing such ambitious goals, we, in effect, delayed our "coming out party." It also meant that we were subject to derogation. By the 90s, if not earlier, the concept of "program verification" had engendered a pejorative tone. Though EVES supported the expression

---

[5] Hence, we separated issues pertaining to proof discovery (using the prover) and to proof validity. For proof discovery, we were free to use any mechanisms (including extra-logical mechanism) to help find proofs. The use of integer linear programming techniques in the decisions procedures is one example. The (comparatively) smaller proof checker was an embodiment of the EVES logic proof rules, was carefully scrutinized, and is reasonably reviewable by independent parties.

[6] Numerous technical reports on all these aspects of EVES are available at our web site.

and analysis of general mathematical concepts, competitors would sometimes deride our efforts as purely "program verification."

For ambitious projects, attempt to structure them in such a manner that useful products and results can be released throughout the project time frame.

Complexity: EVES is a complex system, as are most serious verification systems. The complexities of formal specification, heuristic proof, etc., make it a difficult system to come to terms with.

Industry does not need to add complex development and analytical technologies atop of already complex processes and products. While education will, in the long term, help the insertion of formal methods technology, crafty integration and hiding of complex technologies is likely to be more successful.

Isolated: As with most verification systems, EVES was a stand-alone system. This isolation (both physical and conceptually) makes it difficult to integrate into industrial processes.

Integrate, integrate, integrate! We have to bite the bullet and accept the realities of current hardware and software development processes. Aim to improve and evolve current processes. It is highly unlikely that we will succeed with discontinuous innovations, even though this is a hallmark trait of high-technology.

Publication: We did not actively publish our work. A substantial amount of quality R&D was performed and published in technical reports. However, for various reasons, we did not actively publish (publicize!) our efforts. Consequently, the broader community was not necessarily aware of our achievements.

Not open: EVES was a closed system. We gave no allowance for users to add functionality (except through the addition of reusable theories). This limited certain R&D opportunities.

Where possible, we need to open our systems; perhaps to the point of distributing open source software. At the very least, we need to define system APIs so as to support the integration process.

Distribution impediments: Though substantially eased by the early- to mid-90s, there were still some distribution impediments early on.

And we still see it today, where governmental security concerns are being replaced by corporate priority and market advantage issues.

4 Technology Transfer

4.1 Survey of Industrial Applications

In the early 90s we started to come to terms with technology transfer. In 1992/3, Susan Gerhart (then at Applied Formal Methods), Ted Ralston (then at Ralston Research Associates), and I embarked on what became a fairly influential survey of industrial applications of formal methods [7–9]. In this survey we looked at twelve formal methods projects in North America and Europe.[7] The objectives of the study were threefold:

- To better inform deliberations within industry and government on standards and regulations.
- To provide an authoritative record on the practical experience of formal methods to date.
- To suggest areas where future research and technology development are needed.

I will not rehash the conclusions of the survey, but one of the consequences of the effort was to apply an "innovation diffusion" model to the survey data [9]. As I believe the analytic framework is useful for understanding formal methods adoption, I will take a few moments to discuss the framework. Formal methods researchers would do worse than to consider their adoption trajectories in terms of these criteria (and of Chasm Model, discussed later). As of the mid-90s, we concluded that formal methods advocates were facing significant, though not unique, impediments in diffusing their technology to industry. The innovation diffusion model provides a framework for understanding the forces advancing and/or retarding the diffusion of formal methods. The framework is based on work by Rogers [10] and others.

As discussed in [9], we identified the following criteria:

Relative advantage: An analysis of the technical and business superiority of the innovation over technology it might replace. Until recently, formal methods did not compellingly pass the economic profitability test. However, especially with the use of model checking in Hardware verification, the balance is shifting. Achieving reliability levels through testing solely is running into problems with complexity and size.

The lack of a compelling economic argument often relegated formal methods to (a perceived ghetto of) security- and safety-critical systems, where the cost of system failure is inordinate. But, even here, adoption was minimal.

Compatibility: An analysis of how well the innovation meshes with existing practice. Typically, formal methods systems have not meshed well with existing practice. However, improved recognition of this issue is resulting in the insertion of formal methods-based technology into tools that are actually used by developers.

It is important to note that compatibility is not only at the tool level, but at a social level, in that the proposed innovations must fit well with *community values.* Regulatory environments can be particularly difficult to penetrate if only for the conservative view of change.

Complexity: An analysis of how easy the innovation is to use and understand. For large scale adoption, we have to hide some of the complexity of formal methods. Complexity can be mitigated by aggressive educational programs, push-button tools, and a formal methods taxonomy.

---

[7] A clear oversight of the survey was its lack of projects using model checking.

Trialability: An analysis of the type, scope and duration of feasibility experiments and pilot projects.

Observability: An analysis of how easily and widely the results and benefits of the innovation are communicated.

Transferability: An analysis of the economic, psychological and sociological factors influencing adoption and achieving critical mass. Principal factors are:

Prior technology drag. The presence of large and mature installed bases for prior technologies.

Irreversible investments. The cost of investing in the new technology.

Sponsorship. The presence of an individual or organization that promotes the new technology. Promotion includes subsidization of early adopters and the setting of standards.

Expectations. The benefits accruing from expectations that the technology will be extensively adopted.

Adoption of a superior innovation may still be negated by concerns, on the part of early adopters, arising from two early adoption risks: "transient incompatibility" and "risks of stranding." Transient incompatibility refers to risks accruing from delays in achieving a sufficiently large community interested in the new innovation. Stranding refers to the risks arising due to the failure to achieve critical mass.

We applied the above criteria to our survey data and concluded at that time, correctly I believe, that formal methods have a low adoption trajectory. See [9] for a detailed discussion of applying this framework to formal methods.

It is important to note that a low adoption trajectory is not necessarily inherent to formal methods. Changing perspectives on how to use the technology effectively, the development of new capabilities and the creation of new markets may all result in enhanced adoption for key technical facets.

4.2 Adopting Z

In addition to the survey, we were also looking for means to enhance the adoption rate of our EVES technology. This search was manifested by our efforts, for example, to remedy the syntax (resulting in s-Verdi) and to port EVES to Windows. However, the main manifestation was in our decision to link our EVES technology with Z, resulting in Z/EVES [11–13]. *This meshing of technologies has been particularly effective with Z/EVES now distributed to over forty countries.*

When we viewed the Z world we found a world in which there were an extensive number of consumers, a reasonable pedagogical literature, an incomplete language semantic definition and, generally, lousy tool support. If one negates the previous four conjuncts, one had a reasonable description of the EVES world. A union seemed to make sense! Furthermore, sponsorship was available to pursue the work. Though we were certain that technical difficulties would arise in linking Z with EVES, we were also certain of the benefits. We also noted that many of our North American colleagues derided Z as a language for which mechanical reasoning was impossible and showed absolutely no interest for tapping into a broader community. It is true that Z presents some challenges to mechanized proof support, but these are offset by Z's facilities for the concise and clear specifications. *Z/EVES shows that powerful proof support can, indeed, be provided for Z.* One does not necessarily have to design new languages that, arguably, have been designed for mechanized proof. Such efforts, while useful R&D, will not succeed in transitioning to a broad user community.

Z/EVES integrates a leading specification notation with a leading automated deduction capability. Z/EVES supports the entire Z notation. The Z/EVES prover provides powerful automated support (*e.g.*, conditional rewriting, heuristics, decision procedures) with user commands for directing the prover (*e.g.*, instantiate a specific variable, introduce a lemma, use a function definition). We have automated much of the Z Mathematical Toolkit and include this extended version with the Z/EVES release.

Z/EVES supports the analysis of Z specifications in several ways:

- syntax and type checking,
- schema expansion,
- precondition calculation,
- domain checking (*i.e.*, Are functions applied only on their domains?),
- refinement proofs, and
- general theorem proving.

The range of analysis supports an incremental adoption of Z/EVES capabilities. For example, very little knowledge of the theorem prover is required for syntax and type checking, and schema expansion. Even with domain checking, many of the proof obligations are easily proven; and for those that are not, often the generation of the proof obligation is a substantial aid in determining whether a meaningful specification has been written. It has been our experience that almost all Z specifications are materially improved through syntax and type checking conjoined with domain checking (even if only performed informally). Consequently, for very little effort on the part of the Z/EVES user, material returns accrue from analyses that fall short of the full use of the analytical capabilities of Z/EVES.

Z/EVES accepts its input in the markup format used by the LaTeX system and by Spivey's "fuzz" typechecker. Additionally, the Z/EVES interface is basically Emacs (or a Windows-related clone). While the use of LaTeX and Emacs are fine within the research community, both are impediments to a broader use by industry and by a next generation brought up in a PC-centric, Microsoft dominated world. John Knight's group at the University of Virginia have been working on a Framemaker-based tool for developing specifications in Z called

Zeus [14, 15]. Z specifications are written using all the publishing facilities of Framemaker, uses the Z character set, and interacts with Z/EVES via a graphical user interface. We are also focusing on GUI and word processor integration issues [16, 17]. A portable GUI for Z/EVES is due to be completed by the Fall of 1999. As part of this work, we have chosen XML as our markup language for Z and as the main means of communication between tools. We have opened up Z/EVES by formally specifying (in Z) the Z/EVES API [16]. This will allow others to integrate with Z/EVES in a seamless manner. We are also considering further how Z/EVES can be linked with Word [17]. A necessary evil!

Both our work on a Z/EVES GUI and the University of Virginia work on Zeus were discussed at the Z/EVES session of the FM'99 Z Users' Group meeting. We expect that these evolutionary changes to Z/EVES will further enhance its adoption trajectory. A current significant use of Z/EVES is in undergraduate and graduate courses. We expect that Z/EVES will play a significant role in formal methods training.

5 Applications

Over the years we have had a number of opportunities to use formal methods technology (primarily as embodied in EVES or Z/EVES). Some of these efforts have been clear technical successes. Others, a bit more marginal.

Recently, we have been analyzing authentication protocols and open source public key infrastructures (PKI). These efforts have been great learning experiences and helped to reinforce certain biases. While our work is generally hidden behind a veil of proprietary issues, some general observations can be reported.

Modeling and Analysis: Mathematically modeling key attributes of complex systems and analyzing such attributes can be highly cost effective. By focusing our analysis on certain design and implementation aspects of the PKI, we found significant infelicities. It's worth noting that modeling and analysis can be used in both a forward and reverse engineering manner. Either way, significant benefits can accrue. Obviously, one would prefer to engineer formal modeling and analysis into the development of systems; however, an industrial reality is that there is a huge base of legacy software that is becoming increasing difficult to manage and predict.

Complexity: The complexity of today's software and hardware artifacts is profound and, often, is a result of ill-discipline and reaction to market forces. (The mindset appears to be one along the lines of *best to get a product out with capability X, even though the implementation and design of X is suspect. There's always time to fix it later!*) My general view is that while formal methods has made outstanding progress over the last decade (or so), we are falling further behind industrial practice because of the rapid advances of hardware and software system requirements. At best, we must carefully slice out key aspects of such systems for modeling and analysis.

Open Source Software: Arguments have been made about the potential for achieving high reliability levels with open source software. Our review of important attributes of the PKI indicated important infelicities at both the conceptual and implementation levels. While there are definite benefits to the open source software movement, one must be very careful in attributing high reliability to such software. Many individuals involved with using and testing such software will have only fleeting commitments. I'm unsure that open source is a valid path to high reliability.

Limitations of Model Checking: In our work with PKI and authentication protocols we have used a number of tools in addition to EVES and Z/EVES. For example, we experimented with Murϕ, SMV, FDR2 and Dymna (a nice tool which identifies potential masquerade attacks in authentication protocols). The enhanced automation of the model checking tools certainly helped, but, in many cases, still required substantial setup. In fact, especially with Murϕ and SMV, I felt that I was in the midst of a programming exercise; in effect, writing abstract executable specifications. The latter statement is not necessarily a pejorative comment; such a view may aid adoption. But, what surprised us, in addition to the substantial setup, was that there were extreme difficulties in controlling state space explosion. In fact, we knew of one significant infelicity in the PKI that we tried to find using Murϕ. No matter how much we progressively abstracted our specification and pointed Murϕ to the problem area, we couldn't get the counterexample shown. There's obviously substantial R&D required in understanding how to abstract systems effectively, how to partition and/or control state space explosions, and on how to integrate (either through loose or tight coupling) the various modeling and analysis engines.

Benefits of Automation: Automated analysis of models has the significant potential benefits of generating accurate proofs (or calculations), extending our capabilities to complex artifacts that otherwise would be unmanageable, and doing so rapidly. Model checking has shown great promise in these regards. Theorem provers, much less so (because of the richer properties normally tackled).

Legacy Code: Formal methods can be highly effective in understanding legacy code. (I guess IBM learned this quite early with their use of Z to understand components of CICS.) One must be careful in selecting the important aspects of such systems, but there is a huge potential market here.

We are now much less puritanical in our use of formal methods; we are now making much better use of engineering judgment in choosing where and how to apply formal methods. In fact, in many respects, the perspective has changed from one in which one aims for total correctness and, instead, aims at exposing infelicities. It's almost become "design and formally debug," rather than "design and verify."

For years, our project resources were directed at evolving our technology base, *not* on applying the technology on artifacts of interest to the broader community within which our sponsorship resided. While such an approach has its benefits, it also has significant costs in that we were not able to demonstrate the utility of the technology to mission-oriented criteria, nor were we able to validate the applicability of the technology. We did not have the opportunity to evolve our work towards the realities of the sponsor's marketplace. There are substantial benefits that accrue from applying new technology on true industrial scale problems.

6 The Chasm

Geoffrey Moore's book *Crossing the Chasm* [18] focuses on high technology marketing. However, much of what he has to say relates to technology transfer and sets a useful model for formal methods adoption. While I cannot do full justice to his treatise, I feel it is worthwhile noting a few points, for they provide some indications on how formal methods must adapt to become truly successful.

Moore's view of the Technology Adoption Life Cycle is primarily based on the identification of five groups of potential adopters: Innovators, Early Adopters, Early Majority, Late Majority and Laggards. Understanding the differences and mindsets of these adopters is crucial for successful technology transfer.

Innovators: These folks pursue new technology products aggressively. Technology is the central purpose of their lives. One must win this group over as their endorsement of a new technology reassures other potential adopters.

Early Adopters: These folks are not techies, but individuals who find it easy to appreciate the benefits of a new technology and to relate the benefits to their concerns. They do not rely on well-established references in making buying decisions, preferring their intuition and vision. Early adopters are key to opening any high-tech market segment.

Early Majority: The early majority share the early adopter's ability to relate to technology, but are driven by a strong sense of practicality. They want to see well-established references before investing substantially. It is with the early majority the the opportunities for significant profits start to appear!

Late Majority: The late majority has the same concerns as the early majority plus one major additional fact: they are uncomfortable with technology products. They want a well-established standard, lots of support, and buy from large and well-established companies. If one succeeds in winning this group, profits can be substantial as most R&D costs have been amortized.

Laggards: Laggards don't want anything to do with new technology. It has to be buried deep inside another product.

Moore goes on to claim that the groups of adopters form a bell curve for technology adoption, except that there are gaps: between innovators and early adopters; between the early majority and the late majority; and, most significantly, between the early adopters and the early majority. In Moore's view, the last gap is, in fact, a chasm and therein lies the most significant danger for technology adoption. Early adopters are looking for a change agent. The early majority wants a productivity improvement for existing operations.

To cross the chasm, one must target a market segment defined around a *must-have* value proposition. There are three sources of a must-have condition:

- It enables a previously unavailable strategic capability that provides a dramatic competitive advantage in an area of prime operational focus.
- It radically improves productivity on an already well-understood critical success factor.
- It visibly, verifiably, and significantly reduces current total overall operating costs.

Basically, one must be able to argue that the new technology will radically improve productivity on an already well-understood critical success factor specific to the organization being targeted. Furthermore, there is no existing means by which comparable results can be achieved. Exercise for the reader: How does your technology meet these criteria?

From this perspective, one concludes that we chose some rather unfortunate value propositions for EVES. Perhaps the most unfortunate value proposition was that of mathematical soundness. Soundness (to a certain extent) is not a marketable proposition. Our efforts on code verification were also likely misplaced.

7 Discussion

Though our experiences and those of the general formal methods community has been mixed, I continue to believe that the technology will play a crucial role in the future.

One reason for my optimism is that we are increasing understanding key technology transfer issues. Models such as those of Rogers and Moore provide important insights. Moore's model seems to suggest that, on the most part, formal methods is still at the innovator or early adopter stage. Though, one can point to apparent successes at, for example, Siemens and Intel, suggesting incremental movement towards the early majority.[8] In both cases, it appears that the limitations of traditional validation processes (mainly simulation) were not up to the task for achieving the requisite reliability requirements. Reducing Q&A effort, wherein lies much of the development time, is the critical business requirement. Model checking and equivalence checking appear to have suitable business cases. Theorem proving does not (at least according to one senior Siemens individual)!

There have been failures at the innovator and early adopter stage as well, especially in the security-critical area. These failures are due to complex reasons, but amongst the reasons are (i) the lack of clear mission-oriented goals (rather than technical driven projects), (ii) intransigence and inflexibility on the part of formal methods researchers who refused to react positively to the real needs of their sponsors, (iii) the lack of research focus and clear evaluation criteria, and

---

[8] The perspective taken here is that the market for adoption is within Siemens, Intel or the like; not broad industrial acceptance. At Siemens and Intel, it appears that general development groups are using formal methods (as embodied in model checking).

(iv) the lack of a clear winning observable "product." In some organizations, a harsh "formal methods winter" has set in as current management view the lack of return on significant investments.

Positive results can come from surprising corners. One of the main achievements of NQTHM is the use of executable specifications to model hardware chips, sometimes at a speed that is faster than traditional hardware simulation tools.

We are also learning how to integrate our technology in a manner that potentially enhances existing engineering practices. For example, Prover Technology's integration of NP-Tools with STERNOL allowed for the automatic verification of safety properties of computerized railway interlocking systems. The actual analysis engine was completely hidden from the engineers, they had only to continue to use their own language and push the analysis buttons at the right time. According to Prover Technology, system verification was reduced by 90%. Numerous other current and planned efforts are looking at this type of integration (say, with more widely disseminated languages such as VHDL and UML).

The prime formal methods business case, at this point in time, is to enhance Q&A; to complement current testing resources. For those areas in which mechanized formal analysis can be effectively used, much of the limited testing resources can be reallocated to other parts of the assurance process. Formal modeling has obvious benefits, especially with regards to requirements elicitation and clarification. But, we are up against major challenges with the increasing complexity of systems and the changes of paradigm. Java is quite different from Algol 60. Heterogeneous distributed systems quite different from single processor systems. Out-of-order and speculative execution. Dynamic compilers. And so on.

8 Acknowledgements

My thanks to Mark Saaltink for his review of an earlier draft of this paper.

References

1. Dan Craigen, Sentot Kromodimoeljo, Irwin Meisels, Andy Nielson, Bill Pase and Mark Saaltink. m-EVES: A Tool for Verifying Software. In *Proceedings of the 11th International Conference on Software Engineering (ICSE'11)*, Singapore, April 1988.
2. Dan Craigen. An Application of the m-EVES Verification System. In *Proceedings of the 2nd Workshop on Software Testing, Verification and Analysis*, Banff, Alberta, July 1988.
3. Richard Kemmerer. Verification Assessment Study: Final Report. Volumes I-V, National Computer Security Center, 1986.
4. Proceedings of VERkshop III: A Formal Verification Workshop, Pajaro Dunes Conference Center, Watsonville, California, February 1985. Software Engineering Notes, Volume 10, Number 4, August 1985.
5. Dan Craigen, Sentot Kromodimoeljo, Irwin Meisels, Bill Pase and Mark Saaltink. EVES: An Overview. In *Proceedings of VDM'91: Formal Software Development Methods*. Volume 551, Lecture Notes in Computer Science, Springer-Verlag 1991.

6. Dan Craigen and Mark Saaltink. Simple Type Theory in EVES. In *Proceedings of the Fourth Banff Higher Order Workshop*. Graham Birtwistle (editor). Springer-Verlag, 1990.

7. Dan Craigen, Susan Gerhart and Ted Ralston. An International Survey of Industrial Applications of Formal Methods. NIST GCR 93/626 (Volumes 1 and 2), U.S. National Institute of Standards and Technology, March 1993. Also published by the U.S. Naval Research Laboratory (Formal Report 5546-93-9582, September 1993), and the Atomic Energy Control Board of Canada, January 1995.

8. Susan Gerhart, Dan Craigen and Ted Ralston. Observations on Industrial Practice Using Formal Methods. In *Proceedings of the 15th International Conference on Software Engineering (ICSE'15)*. Baltimore, Maryland, May 1993.

9. Dan Craigen, Susan Gerhart and Ted Ralston. Formal Methods Technology Transfer: Impediments and Innovation. In *Applications of Formal Methods*, M.G. Hinchey and J.P. Bowen (editors). Prentice-Hall International Series in Computer Science, September 1995.

10. Everett Rogers. Diffusion of Innovations. Free Press, New York 1983.

11. Mark Saaltink. The Z/EVES System. In *ZUM'97: The Z Formal Specification Notation (10th International Conference of Z Users*. Bowen, Hinchey, Till (editors). Lecture Notes in Computer Science, Volume 1212, Springer-Verlag.

12. Mark Saaltink and Irwin Meisels. The Z/EVES Reference Manual. ORA Canada Technical Report TR-97-5493-03d, December 1995.

13. Mark Saaltink. Domain Checking Z Specifications. Presented at the 4th NASA LaRC Formal Methods Workshop, Langley, Virginia, September 1997. ORA Canada conference paper CP-97-6018-65.

14. John Knight, Thomas Fletcher and Brian Hicks. Tools Support for Production Use of Formal Methods. Discussion paper in Proceedings of *FM'99: World Congress on Formal Methods*.

15. University of Virginia Software Engineering Group. Zeus: A Comprehensive Tool for Developing Formal Specifications. Version 1.3, March 1999.

16. Mark Saaltink, Sentot Kromodimoeljo and Irwin Meisels. The Z/EVES GUI Design and API. To appear.

17. Mark Saaltink. Integration of Z/EVES with Word Processors. To appear.

18. Geoffrey A. Moore. Crossing the Chasm. Harper Business, 1991.

Model Checking for Managers

Wil Janssen[1], Radu Mateescu[2], Sjouke Mauw[3,4], Peter Fennema[1] and
Petra van der Stappen[1]

[1]Telematica Instituut, P.O. Box 589, NL-7500 AN Enschede, the Netherlands
{Janssen,Stappen,Fennema}@telin.nl
[2]INRIA Rhone-Alpes, Montbonnot Saint-Martin, France
Radu.Mateescu@inrialpes.fr
[3]Eindhoven University of Technology, Department of Mathematics and Computing Science,
P.O. Box 513, NL-5600 MB Eindhoven, the Netherlands
sjouke@win.tue.nl
[4]CWI, P.O. Box 94079, NL-1090 GB Amsterdam, the Netherlands

Abstract. Model checking is traditionally applied to computer system design. It has proven to be a valuable technique. However, it requires detailed specifications of systems and requirements, and is therefore not very accessible. In this paper we show how model checking can be applied in the context of business modeling and analysis by people that are not trained in formal techniques. Spin is used as the model checker underlying a graphical modeling language, and requirements are specified using business requirements patterns, which are translated to LTL. We illustrate our approach using a business model of an insurance company.

1   Introduction

In the last few years model checking has proven to be a valuable tool in the development of correct systems. Applications range from software controlling storm surge barriers [Kars96], through space craft controllers [HaLP98] to integrated circuits. Tools like Spin [Hol97], SMV [SMV99] and CADP [CADP99,Gara98] have outgrown their infancy and are becoming professional tools that are applicable to real-life problems.

Model checking requires a number of steps. A correct abstraction from the problem must be defined in the input language of the model checker. Often this requires a translation from the problem domain to the concepts used in the model checker (such as message passing systems, process algebra or automata). This model must be validated in order to ensure that no mistakes are introduced by the abstraction. Thereafter, the correctness requirements must be formulated in the corresponding requirements language, such as never claims or temporal logic formulae. This again requires an abstraction from the informal requirements in the application domain.

Finally, the specification can be checked for satisfaction of the requirements. If the requirements are not satisfied, both the requirement specification as well as the system model must be checked: either the system does not satisfy the (informal) requirement, the requirement is not defined correctly or the model is an incorrect

abstraction of the system. To do so, the counter example must be translated back to the application domain.

All in all, this makes model checking complex and cumbersome: designing systems is not easy, developing specifications is a complex task and defining the right correctness requirements must be done carefully. Model checking is an activity for skilled computer scientists and engineers, isn't it?

Well, to a certain extent this is true. However, we argue that when given the appropriate tools and methods model checking can be made accessible to a large audience. Even for people that are not trained in formal techniques, model checking can be a valuable tool for developing correct systems. In the Testbed project [FrJa98] we have developed tools and methods for business process modeling and analysis, aiming at business analysts. Business analysts usually have a background in business administration and little or no knowledge of computer science. Testbed employs a graphical modeling language that closely corresponds to the concepts relevant to business modeling (activities, actors, co-operation, responsibilities, duration and so on). The tool Testbed Studio allows for easy modeling of business processes and provides a number of means of analysis, for both quantitative as well as functional properties (completion time, workloads, critical path, data flow, process type, multistep simulation and so on).

In [JMMS98] we showed that model checking can be applied in the context of Testbed and business modeling. On the basis of an operational semantics a translation from our business modeling language to Promela was defined. Model checking proved to help in validating and verifying business models. However, this was still performed by formalists outside the tool Testbed Studio. Model checking by managers requires a different approach.

Spin is "under the hood" of one of the analysis tools in Testbed Studio. Requirements are defined using a number of predefined patterns: traces of activities, combined occurrence, precedence and consequence. These requirements are translated to Linear Time Temporal Logic (LTL). The business process model is translated to Promela, using an operational semantics. The Promela model and LTL specification are checked using Spin and the outcome is visualized in the graphical environment of Testbed Studio.

Of course, such simplicity comes at a cost: using a fixed number of patterns restricts the expressivity to a large extent. Moreover, no data modeling language has been employed yet, allowing for full state space exploration, even for large models. Still, we carefully selected the patterns in the tool on the basis of a large number of practical applications. The coverage of questions that can be answered is substantial.

By complementing model checking with other means of analysis, especially for quantitative properties [JJVW98] the limitations of model checking in our set up, and the restriction to non-quantitative properties in general, are overcome.

The rest of this paper is organized as follows. We first discuss our graphical modeling language on the basis of an example. We then introduce the patterns used for functional analysis and their translation into LTL. These are illustrated using an

example. We conclude with a number of remarks on the implementation and our findings in using Spin in this context.

2 Functional analysis in Testbed

The Testbed project develops a systematic approach for business process engineering, particularly aimed at processes in the financial service sector [FrJa98]. A main objective is to give *insight* into the structure of business processes and the relations between them. This insight can be obtained by making *business process models* that clearly and precisely represent the *essence* of the business organisation. These models should encompass different levels of organisational detail, thus allowing the analyst to find bottlenecks and to assess the consequences of proposed changes for the customers and the organisation itself; see also, e.g. [JaEJ96].

Business modelling languages may be deployed for many different purposes. Not only do they supply a sound foundation for communicating and discussing business process designs, they may be used as well for, e.g.,
- *analysis* of business processes, that is, assessment of qualities and properties of business process designs, either in quantitative or qualitative terms;
- *export to implementation platforms*, such as workflow management and enterprise resource planning systems;
- *job design*, that is, designing detailed job specifications and generating job instructions.

Every specific purpose of a business modelling language brings about its own specific demands on the language. We first explain our business modeling language and illustrate its use with an example.

2.1 The Testbed modeling language AMBER

The core of the business modelling language contains concepts that enable basic reasoning about business processes. AMBER recognises three aspect domains:
- the *actor* domain, which allows for describing the resources deployed for carrying out business processes;
- the *behaviour* domain, which allows for describing what happens in a business process;
- the *item* domain, which allows for describing the items handled in business processes.

Here we restrict the discussion to the behaviour domain, as this is the relevant part for model checking. A detailed overview of the language can be found in [EJO+99].

The basic concept in the behaviour domain is the *action*. It models a unit of activity in business processes. An action can only happen when its *enabling condition* is satisfied. These conditions are formulated in terms of other actions having occurred yet, or not. Actions that are performed by more than one actor in co-operation are

called *interactions*. The contribution of an actor to an interaction is represented by a (stretched) semi-circle, e.g. *submit claim* and *receive claim* in figure 2.

Apart from the actions and their properties, causal or temporal relations between actions are important elements of a behaviour model. Figure 1 gives an overview of the main relations:

- The simplest situation is a single causality relation, which means that a certain action can only start when another (preceding) action has finished.
- We have two types of *splits*:
  1. an *or*-split, which means that after completion of the preceding action one of a number of possible actions is chosen.
  2. an *and*-split, which means that after completion of the preceding action several other actions can take place *in parallel*.
- Finally, we have two types of *joins*: an *or*-join (disjunction) indicates that *at least one* of the preceding actions must have been completed before an action can start, while an *and*-join (conjunction) indicates that *all* preceding actions must have been completed.

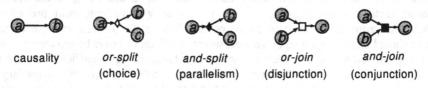

| causality | or-split (choice) | and-split (parallelism) | or-join (disjunction) | and-join (conjunction) |

Fig. 1. (Inter-) action relations.

The use of these relations is illustrated in the behavior model below.

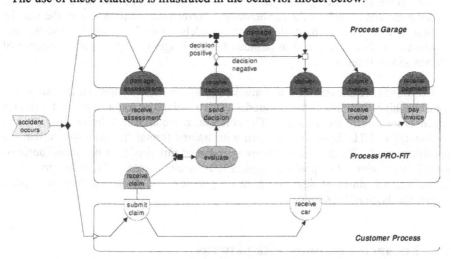

Fig. 2. The claim submission process

In figure 2 we model the claim submission process of an insurance company called *PRO-FIT*. After an accident occurs, the customer submits a claim to PRO-FIT. When the damage assessment has been submitted as well, the claim can be evaluated, leading either to a positive or a negative decision. In case of a positive decision the car is repaired and delivered, and the invoice is paid.

Data (the item domain) is not treated in this paper, as it is not yet taken into account in the functional analysis.

2.2 Analyzing AMBER models

Business models as described above function as a blueprint for the actual implementation. Procedures for people are derived from them and they may even function as a specification of the workflow implementations. Many business modeling environments have export possibilities to workflow. Therefore, the correctness of the business model becomes crucial to the company.

"Correctness" is a difficult property. It has quantitative elements (there are sufficient resources to do the work, completion time is according to the critical success factors of the organization and so on) as well as functional properties. Functional properties often concern the control flow in the process: every accepted claim should be accompanied by an assessment, no claim can ever be rejected as well as accepted, and so on. If models are small, simulation can give sufficient insight in the model to validate them. However, if processes –and thus their models- grow larger it becomes more difficult to check them. Model checking then becomes an interesting idea.

Unfortunately, the proper use of model checking techniques is not easy. It should be done at the abstraction level of the user: he or she should be able to define both the business models as well as the corresponding correctness requirements in the way he or she thinks. For Testbed this means models must be AMBER models, and requirements should be stated in (almost) natural language expressing occurrence of actions and their relations.

In [JMMS98] we showed how to translate AMBER models to Spin on the basis of a state machine description of the model. This resulted in highly compact Promela specifications of business models. The correctness requirements, however, were still formulated in LTL. Experiments, even with trained formalists, have shown that the specification of LTL queries was more a source of mistakes than the actual business models themselves. For practical applications in our context LTL is unacceptable. Therefore, we aimed at developing an easy to use and dedicated way to express requirements on AMBER models.

3   Enhancing usability with patterns

Hence, in this case we need an easy-to-use link to Spin, tailored to applying Spin to business models. We built such a link that offers the user a choice between a number of selected query types. The user can instantiate a query by setting a number of parameters. We call these query generators *patterns*.

3.1 Identifying patterns

Our approach to identifying patterns is a pragmatic one, starting from a business perspective. We studied a large number of business cases, for which process models were drawn. For each case relevant questions that might be answered using model checking were listed. The questions were divided into categories, after the complicating factors contained in the question. Each question was judged on solvability by model checking.

When looking for patterns, we found four types of questions that occur often. These are relatively simple questions. More complicated questions often concern the relation between two of these questions. The four patterns are:

1. Sequences of activities, e.g. "the sequence of activities *submit claim, receive payment* can (or can never) occur";
2. Consequences of activities, e.g. "every submitted claim will lead to *receive payment* and *receive car*";
3. Combined occurrence or exclusion, e.g. "*evaluate* and *pay invoice* always occur together";
4. Required precedence of activities, e.g. "*receive car* requires that *repair car* has happened".

These patterns are illustrated using a larger example in section 5.

We present our four patterns in table form. The tables contain both text fields and variable fields. A question is derived from the pattern by filling in the variable fields. Variable fields for (sets of / lists of) actions may be filled with any action from the current model (represented in bold and italicized). Other variable fields offer a choice between some predefined values. This choice is indicated in the table by a column with one italicized value in each entry. The first value listed is the chosen default. The meaning of the patterns is explained and examples are given. Two choices that often appear are that between an, each, and all, and that between ever, never, and always.

The word "an" acts as existential quantifier: the query *an action leads to...* should be read as *Does an action exist that leads to ....* Less trivial is the difference between *each* and *all*. If we ask whether *each* action leads to *y*, we mean to ask whether each individual *x* from *X* leads to *y*. If we ask if *all* actions lead to *y*, we mean to ask whether all actions $x \in X$ together lead to *y*. Thus if all $x \in X$ are executed, will *y* be executed?

The word "ever" can be viewed as existential quantifier: "property *p* ever" should be interpreted as: there is a run for which the property *p* holds. "Never" refers to the opposite: there is no run in which the property holds. The word "always" stands for the phrase "in all possible runs". For Spin this means to check the property (not *F*) in the case of never, and to check *F* in the case of always:

$$\text{never } F \quad = \quad \neg \exists \text{ path } p.\, p \models F$$
$$= \quad \forall \text{ paths } p.\, p \models \neg F$$

	=	$\neg F$ is true in Spin
ever F	=	$\exists$ path $p.\ p \models F$
	=	not ($\forall$ paths $p.\ p \models \neg F$)
	=	$\neg F$ is false in Spin
always F	=	$\forall$ paths $p.\ p \models F$
	=	F is true in Spin

Pattern 1: Tracing

The series of actions	*[a₁, a₂, ..., aₙ]*	occurs	*ever*
			always
			never

Queries derived from pattern 1 check whether actions a_1, a_2, through a_n occur in this order in the model. They need not occur consecutively: other actions may occur in between. This pattern is typically used to check a scenario. The pattern may also be used to check necessity of certain actions, for example by checking whether an action lies on the path that runs from customer to customer.

Pattern 2: Consequence

Each	action(s) from	*X*	lead(s) to	*an*	action(s) from	*Y*
All				*all*		
An						

This pattern is typically used to make sure that certain actions are executed, for example: after a decision concerning a damage claim, both the treasury department and the customer should be informed. It may also be used to check one property for two alternative paths, to see, for example, if both achieve the desired result. The query "each action from {expert judgement, standard judgement} leads to an action from {draw up rejection, draw up policy}" is an example.

Pattern 3: Combined occurrence

All actions from	*X*	*occur together always*
		occur together ever
		occur together never
		exclude one another always

The difference between "excluding one another" and "not occurring together" may need some clarification. The option "All actions of set X occur together never" should be interpreted as "There is no run in which all actions of set X occur together". The option "All actions of set X exclude one another always" should be interpreted as pairwise exclusion, that is "In each run, if one action of X occurs, the remaining actions in X do not occur". This difference is quite subtle, and not easy to explain to non-expert users. Explicit methodological guidance is a prerequisite.

Model checking is often used to rule out hazards and this pattern can be used for this purpose. An example is a complex process which includes a decision. The company wants to rule out that two different decisions are taken for one and the same case, which might happen because of splitting up the process or because of overlapping decision rules. We check whether a policy application can end up with two employees, who make different decisions using the query "all actions from {draw up rejection, draw up policy} exclude one another always".

The pattern can also be used to ensure the coupling of certain actions, like the case that both the treasury department and the customer are always informed.

Pattern 4: Precedence

Each	action(s) from	Y	require(s)	an	action(s) from	X
An				all		
All						

Pattern 4 ensures that all requirements for an activity to take place are fulfilled. A typical example is the fact that a customer should have a policy and have paid his contribution, before he can claim. The insurance company wants to make sure that if the customer does claim, without having paid his contribution, it is impossible for the claim to be settled anyway. This pattern can also be used to answer questions like what actions cause a certain customer contact and what functions are needed to create a certain product.

Of course, these patterns do not cover everything. One of the analysis questions asked for most is counting: "how often do the customer and PRO-FIT interact?". "How often is a claim checked for completeness?" Such patterns are difficult to implement without adapting the specification rigorously. Moreover, they require multiple analysis runs (can it occur once, then check if it can occur twice; if so, check for three et cetera). As yet, we have found no way to do this in an elegant way.

Furthermore, we would like to have a way to check for "model inclusion": is this AMBER model implemented by this process? We come back to this in the section on future work.

Dwyer et al. [DAC98] have worked on patterns for use in software development. Their basic elements are recognizable in our patterns:
- *Occurrence patterns*: the choice between ever, never, and always.
- *Ordering patterns*: precedence and response appearing in our patterns 4 and 2 respectively.
- *Compound patterns*: applying a pattern to more than one action at a time.

4   Implementation

In order to link a graphical tool such as Testbed Studio to Spin, including translation of queries, a number of steps must be taken in the tool. Besides that, good methodological support for the users is needed as well: a good tool without a carefully defined method still does not help; it just increases chaos instead of analyzing it. The methodological part, however, is beyond the scope of this paper.

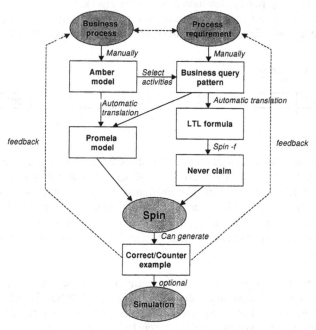

Fig. 3. The steps performed in Testbed Studio.

The approach taken in Testbed is shown in figure 3. Starting points are a business process plus the requirement that the business analyst would like to verify. The process is modeled using AMBER in Studio, and the requirement is defined in terms of the activities in the model. The model is then translated to Promela using the approach discussed in [JMMS98]. The translation uses the business query pattern to know what activities the user is interested in: the translation only generates activity occurrence information for those variables, in order to minimize the state space.

The business query itself is translated to LTL, and thereafter converted to a never-claim using the Spin LTL translator. The Promela specification and the never-claim together are then checked using Spin. If a trail is generated the outcome is translated back to Testbed Studio and visualized in the tool. The same information is also given to the simulator in Testbed Studio to simulate it, if the user wants to do so.

Not all AMBER models can be tackled by Spin. AMBER models can be non-finite state due to loops with unbounded parallelism. Models can be checked for finite-stateness before translating them to Promela (see [JMMS98]).

4.1 User interface

Model checking is only one of the analysis forms offered by Testbed Studio. The user can choose a pattern from a pull-down menu, as shown (in Dutch) in figure 4.

When a pattern is selected, the user can fill in the pattern parameters. Choices between predefined values, like between ever, never, and always, are offered in a pull-down menu. Actions and interactions are incorporated in the query by selecting them in the model, and then clicking the arrow below the input field.

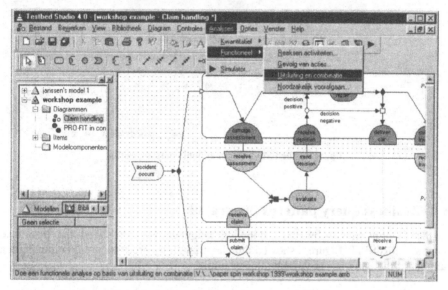

Fig. 4. Model checking in Testbed Studio (the current version of the tool is in Dutch).

The result of the query is returned in a new pop-up window. If an example is available, it is shown in the model. Testbed Studio's simulator can run the example. In figure 5 an example is shown of the question "does the series of activities *accident occurs, evaluate, pay invoice* ever occur?" Spin finds an example thereof, by using the LTL formula that states that the series is *impossible*, for which this positive example is a counter example. This trace can then be played in the Studio simulator.

Simulation can be done both using multisteps (maximal progress) or in an interleaving fashion. Interleaving is used for playback of Spin trails. By simulating the outcome of the analysis the user gets insight in why the model does not satisfy the requirement. Such a counterexample is very illustrative. In our approach we do not only give counterexamples, but also positive examples. For example, if the question is whether or not the sequence *accident occurs* followed by *pay invoice* can occur, we can show a positive example thereof. The reason for this is the fact that we can use the query stating that the sequence can *never* occur. For this query, any counterexample is a positive example to the user.

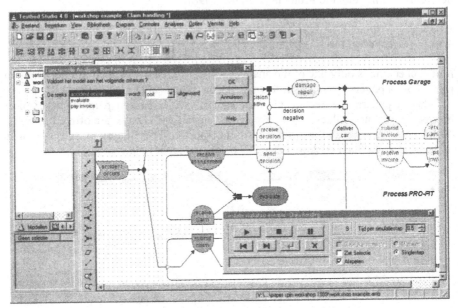

Fig. 5. Testbed Studio's functional analysis results.

5 Business query patterns illustrated

In the section on our business modeling language we introduced the insurance company PRO-FIT. Figure 2 showed the claim handling process. We now illustrate a number of the patterns above using this example.

Example of tracing pattern
Properties that the damage handling process clearly should satisfy are that a customer engaged in an accident always receives a fixed car in the end, and that the car should always be fixed before return. These properties can be checked by the queries "The series of actions [accident occurs, damage repair, receive car] occurs always" and "The series of actions [deliver car, damage repair] occurs never".

Testing the query "The series of actions [accident occurs, damage repair, receive car] occurs always" results in a negative answer. A counterexample is the result, visualizing the case of a negative decision. The query "The series of actions [deliver car, damage repair] occurs never" results in a positive answer, but without an example.

Example of consequence pattern
The option "each" can be used to check one property for two alternative paths, to see, for example, if both achieve the desired result. We might check the two possible decisions in the model with the query "each action from {receive decision} leads to an action from {deliver car}". The query results in a positive answer.

Example of combined occurrence pattern
We extend the model to demonstrate pattern 3 and assume that in case of a rejection by the insurer, the garage offers the customer to repair the car and charge the customer.

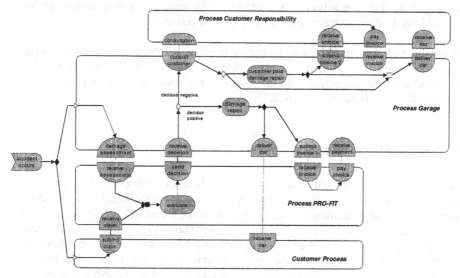

Fig. 6. PRO-FIT example extended.

We would like to make sure that the garage does not charge both the insurer and the customer for the same repair. The garage turns out to be reliable: the query "all actions from {submit invoice1, submit invoice2} exclude one another always" gives a positive result. In this case we could have asked the query "all actions from { submit invoice1, submit invoice2} occur together ever". Although the answer is the opposite, it offers the same knowledge.

6   Expressing patterns in LTL

We translated the queries derived from our patterns into LTL. In general, the answer to the query is "yes" if and only if the LTL expression evaluates to *true*. If not, the error trace given by Spin may serve as a counterexample.

In case of the patterns containing a choice between ever, never, and always, we only translated the "never" and "always" queries to LTL. The answer to an "ever" query is deduced from the answer to the corresponding "never" query. When a user asks an "ever" query, the "never" query is applied to the model. The resulting answer is negated to obtain the desired answer:

- if the "never" query results in a "no", the answer to the "ever" query is "yes". The counter example of the "never" query is an example for the "ever" query.
- if the "never" query results in a "yes", the answer to the "ever" query is "no".

Hence, in addition to the common counterexamples, we can return positive examples in some cases as well.

It is not possible to give an example (positive or negative) in all cases. For patterns with a choice between an, each, and all, no examples can be given when the option "an" is chosen. In that case the trace produced by Spin is no counterexample. One cannot show that "No action of X leads to ..." by means of a counterexample; one would have to show all traces from all actions. The full model is the example.

A selection of the translations of the queries is given in Table 1. In this table $X = \{ a_1, a_2, ..., a_n \}$ and $Y = \{ b_1, b_2, ..., b_m \}$. Arrows represent implication. In the LTL formulae a means that action a occurs. We use Spin syntax for LTL (e.g. <> denotes "eventually", ! is negation, and so on).

7   Evaluating the use of Spin

In general, Spin was well suited for this application. However, there are some practical limitations to the size of the query. The query is automatically translated to a never-claim. The translation has two steps: input to LTL and LTL to never-claim. The problems lie in the second part. When the query contains too many actions, the never claim becomes so large that it causes memory problems. The limitations are determined experimentally, and turn out to be very strong. For most fields the input must be limited to three or four actions. To prevent the system to crash, we allow only manageable inputs.

As for the general use of Spin, few problems were encountered. State space exploration was fast as the size of the state space was rather limited. We tested it with models with more than 150 nodes, leading to a state vector of 36 bytes, with 1500 states and 1700 transitions. This allowed searching for smallest examples without leading to unacceptable response times (always less than 10 seconds on a PC NT Workstation).

For the definition of our patterns in some cases CTL would have been easier. Especially when looking for possibilities in models this would have allowed for a direct translation instead of an encoding.

We also had problems with fairness: fairness in Spin is much too weak a notion to be of real help. When loops are part of a model this immediately leads to unwanted answers ("will this action always be reached? No it will not, as before it the model can loop forever..."). We experimented with counters to restrict the number of iterations in loops. This, however, leads to an immediate state space explosion.

Table 1. Translation of queries to LTL

Pattern 1: does the series of actions [a₁, a₂, ..., aₙ] never/ever/always occur		
1.1	never	$\texttt{neverafter[a_1 ... a_{n-1}; a_n] ||}$ $\texttt{neverafter[a_1 ... a_{n-2}; a_{n-1}] ||}$ $\texttt{...}$ $\texttt{neverafter[-;a_1]}$ **where** $\texttt{neverafter[a_1 ... a_{n-1}; a_n] =}$ $\texttt{([](a_1 -> neverafter[a_2 ... a_{n-1}; a_n]))}$ $\texttt{neverafter[-;a_1] = [] !a_1}$
1.2	always	$\texttt{<> (a_1 \&\& <>(! a_1 \&\& <>(a_2 \&\& <>(!a_{2 ...} <>(a_n)...))}$
Pattern 2: an/each/all action(s) from set X lead(s) to an/all action(s) from set Y		
2.1	an-an	$\texttt{[] (a_1 -> <> (b_1|| b_2 || ...|| b_m)) ||}$ $\texttt{[] (a_2 -> <> (b_1|| b_2 || ...|| b_m)) ||}$ $\texttt{...}$ $\texttt{[] (a_n -> <> (b_1|| b_2 || ...|| b_m))}$
2.2	an-all	$\texttt{[] (a_1 -> (<> b_1\&\& <> b_2 \&\& ...\&\& <> b_m)) ||}$ $\texttt{[] (a_2 -> (<> b_1\&\& <> b_2 \&\& ...\&\& <> b_m)) ||}$ $\texttt{...}$ $\texttt{[] (a_n -> (<> b_1\&\& <> b_2 \&\& ...\&\& <> b_m))}$
2.3	each-an	$\texttt{[] ((a_1 || ... || a_n) -> <>(b_1 || ... || b_m))}$
2.4	each-all	$\texttt{[] ((a_1 || ... || a_n) -> (<>b_1 \&\& ... \&\& <>b_m))}$
2.5	all-an	$\texttt{[] ((a_1 \&\& ... \&\& a_n) -> <> (b_1 || ... || b_m))}$
2.6	all-all	$\texttt{[] ((a_1 \&\& ... \&\& a_n) -> (<> b_1 \&\& ... \&\& <> b_m))}$
Pattern 3: do all actions from set X always/ever/never occur together **do all actions from set X exclude one another always**		
3.1	together always	$\texttt{<> a_1 \&\& ... \&\& <> a_n}$
3.2	together never	$\texttt{((<>a_1 \&\& <>a_2 \&\& ... \&\& <>a_{n-1}) → [] ! a_n) \&\&}$ $\texttt{((<>a_1 \&\& <>a_2 \&\& ... <>a_{n-2} \&\& <>a_n) → [] ! a_{n-1}) \&\&}$ $\texttt{...}$ $\texttt{((<>a_2 \&\& ... \&\& <>a_n) → [] ! a_1)}$
3.3	exclude one another always	$\texttt{(<> a_1 -> !<> (a_2 || a_3 || ... || a_n)) \&\&}$ $\texttt{(<> a_2 -> !<> (a_1 || a_3 || ... || a_n)) \&\&}$ $\texttt{...}$ $\texttt{(<> a_n -> !<> (a_1 || ... || a_{n-1}))}$
Pattern 4: an/each/all action(s) from set Y require(s) an/all action(s) from set X		
4.1	an-an	$\texttt{((!b_1 U (a_1 || ... ||a_n)) || [] !b_1) ||}$ $\texttt{((!b_2 U (a_1 || ... ||a_n)) || [] !b_2) ||}$ $\texttt{...}$ $\texttt{((!b_n U (a_1 || ... ||a_n)) || [] !b_m)}$
4.2	an-all	$\texttt{(!b_1Ua_1 \&\& !b_1Ua_2 \&\& ... \&\& !b_1Ua_n) ||}$ $\texttt{(!b_2Ua_1 \&\& !b_2Ua_2 \&\& ... \&\& !b_2Ua_n) ||}$ $\texttt{...}$ $\texttt{(!b_mUa_1 \&\& !b_mUa_2 \&\& ... \&\& !b_mUa_n) ||}$ $\texttt{[] !b_1 || [] !b_2 || ... || [] !b_m}$
4.3	each-an	$\texttt{((!b_1U(a_1|| ...|| a_n)) || []!b_1) \&\&}$ $\texttt{((!b_2U(a_1|| ...|| a_n)) || []!b_2) \&\&}$ $\texttt{...}$ $\texttt{((!b_mU(a_1|| ...|| a_n)) || []!b_m)}$
4.4	each-all	$\texttt{((!b_1Ua_1 \&\& !b_1Ua_2 \&\& ... \&\& !b_1Ua_n) || []!b_1) \&\&}$ $\texttt{((!b_2Ua_1 \&\& !b_2Ua_2 \&\& ... \&\& !b_2Ua_n) || []!b_2) \&\&}$ $\texttt{...}$ $\texttt{((!b_mUa_1 \&\& !b_mUa_2 \&\& ... \&\& !b_mUa_n) || []!b_m)}$

Finally, we had some problems in using bit-state hashing. For our models, bit-state hashing hardly ever lead to correct answers. The reason for this is still unclear. Using different hash functions was not of any help. As we plan to introduce data, which most certainly will lead to large state spaces, this problem needs to be looked at.

8 Conclusions and future extensions

We have shown how model checking can be made accessible to a large, not formally trained audience. Our approach has been validated in real-life situations and the first results are very promising. People are enthusiastic and find this type of analysis very appealing. It complements a number of other analysis techniques that have been traditionally been applied in business modeling, such as stochastic simulation.

A number of extensions are planned after careful validation of the current approach. One of these is to allow (logical) combinations of patterns, such as conjunction, implication and "unless". This is a straightforward extension of our implementation, where, however, the limitations of the Spin LTL translator will form a severe limitation.

Currently, our business modeling language is being extended with an object-oriented data modeling language. It would be desirable to add this language to the translation to Promela as well. However, its impact on business query patterns is still not clear and should be prepared together with end users of the tool.

Finally, we would like to use AMBER models as a requirements language as well, in order to be able to check correspondence between service specifications and implementations. This would support our business modeling approach, where often one starts with a service specification of the business model to be defined, which is then refined into a detailed business model.

In principle it is possible to translate AMBER models to LTL: and-joins roughly correspond to conjunction, or-joins to disjunction. However, it then becomes unclear what part of the model can be viewed as an assumption, and what is the consequence part. The AMBER model $a \rightarrow b$ can be read both as "if a occurs, then b will occur thereafter", or as "a and b will always occur, and a will precede b". To resolve those ambiguities additional graphical syntax or annotations in models are needed.

Acknowledgement

This paper results from the Testbed project, a 120 man-year research initiative that focuses on a virtual test environment for business processes. The Testbed consortium consists of ABP, the Dutch Tax Department, ING Group, IBM and the Telematica Instituut (The Netherlands) and co-operates with several Dutch universities and research institutes. The project is financially supported by the Dutch Ministry of Economic Affairs. We appreciate to acknowledge all Testbed contributors.

In the early stages of our work on functional analysis Jan Springintveld and Rob Gerth participated in the project as well. We gratefully acknowledge their

Xspin/Project - Integrated Validation Management for Xspin

Theo C. Ruys

Faculty of Computer Science, University of Twente.
P.O. Box 217, 7500 AE Enschede, The Netherlands.
ruys@cs.utwente.nl

Abstract. One of the difficulties of using model checkers "in the large" is the management of all (generated) data during the validation trajectory. It is important that the results obtained from the validation are always reproducible. Without tool support, the quality of the validation process depends on the accuracy of the persons who conduct the validation. This paper discusses Xspin/Project, an extension of Xspin, which automatically controls and manages the validation trajectory when using the model checker Spin.

1 Introduction

In the past years, we have been involved in several industrial projects concerning the modelling and validation of (communication) protocols [4, 19]. In these projects we used modelling languages and validation tools - like Promela and Spin [7, 9] - to specify and verify the protocols and their properties. During each of these projects we encountered the same practical problems of keeping track of various sorts of information and data, particularly:

- many documents, which describe parts of the system, often originating from different parties;
- many versions of the same document;
- many versions of validation models, not only revisions but also variants (different abstractions of the same system);
- validation data, including:
  - simulation traces;
  - directives and options to build particular verifiers;
  - verification results;
  - counterexamples; and
  - notes and remarks on the validation runs.

The first two sources of information are mainly related to the modelling of a system whereas the latter sources of information are prominent in the validation phase of a system. We experienced that apart from the inherent state space explosion of the model of the system under validation, the validation engineer contribution. We would like to thank the anonymous referees and Marc Lankhorst for their comments.

References

[CADP99]   *Caesar/Aldebaran Development Package homepage.* Available at: http://www.inrialpes.fr/vasy/cadp.html

[DAC98]   Property Specification Patterns for Finite-state Verification, Matthew B. Dwyer, George S. Avrunin and James C. Corbett. In: *Proceedings of the 2nd Workshop on Formal Methods in Software Practice*, March, 1998.

[EJO+99]   Eertink, H., W.P.M. Janssen, P.H.W.M. Oude Luttighuis, W. Teeuw, and C.A. Vissers, A Business Process Design Language. In: *Proceedings World Congress on Formal Methods.* Springer LNCS. Toulouse, September 1999.

[FrJa98]   Franken, H.M. and W. Janssen, Get a grip on changing business processes, *Knowledge & Process Management* (Wiley), Vol. 5, No. 4, pp. 208-215. December 1998.

[Gara98]   Garavel, H., *OPEN/CAESAR: An open software architecture for verification, simulation and testing.* INRIA Rapport de recherche n3352, January 1998.

[HALP98]   Havelund, K., M. Lowry and J. Penix. Formal analysis of a space craft controller using Spin. in G. Holzman, E. Najm and A. Serrhouchni (eds.), *Proceedings of the 4th International SPIN Workshop*, Paris, France, Nov. 1998, pp. 147167.

[Holz97]   Holzman, G.J., The model checker SPIN, *IEEE Transactions on Software Engineering*, Vol. 23, No. 5, May 1997, 279-295.

[JaEJ95]   Jacobson, I., M. Ericsson en A. Jacobson, *The Object Advantage - Business Process Reengineering with Object Technology*, ACM Books, 1995.

[JJVW98]   Jonkers, H., W. Janssen, A. Verschut and E. Wierstra, "A unified framework for design and performance analysis of distributed systems", in *Proceedings of the 3rd Annual IEEE International Computer Performance and Dependability Symposium* (IPDS"98), Durham, NC, USA, Sept. 1998, pp. 109-118.

[JMMS98]   Janssen, W., R. Mateescu, S.Mauw and J. Springintveld, Verifying business processes using SPIN, in G. Holzman, E. Najm and A. Serrhouchni (eds.), *Proceedings of the 4th International SPIN Workshop*, Paris, France, Nov. 1998, pp. 21-36. Also available at: http://netlib.bell-labs.com/netlib/spin/ws98/sjouke.ps.gz

[Kars96]   Kars, P., The application of Promela and Spin in the BOS project. In: *Proceedings Second Spin Workshop.* August 1996. Available at: http://netlib.bell-labs.com/netlib/spin/ws96/papers.html

[SMV99]   CMU Model Checking Home page. Available at: http://www.cs.cmu.edu/~modelcheck/smv.htm.

has to deal with the data and version explosion of the modelling phase and the validation phase as well.

In [18] we suggested to use literate programming techniques [12] to tackle the management problems in the modelling phase. We also suggested that Software Configuration Management [1, 11] tools are probably needed to manage the validation phase. This paper discusses Xspin/Project, an extension of Xspin, which manages and controls the validation trajectory when using the model checker Spin.

In Sect. 2 the management problems of the validation phase are discussed. Section 3 describes Xspin/Project and the paper is concluded with Sect. 4.

In the literature on formal methods, the terms validation and verification do not have a fixed meaning. In this paper both terms are used and the following interpretations are distinguished:

- With *verification* we identify the verification process using a model checker (e.g. Spin);
- We use the term *validation* to address the controlled, systematic analysis of systems. With respect to Spin, validation includes both the simulation and verification activities.

2 Validation Management

This section discusses the management of validation data. After briefly discussing the management problems of the validation phase, the current management support within Xspin is discussed. Software Configuration Management systems are proposed as the solution to the management problems.

2.1 Validation data

In current research on automatic verification tools, much effort is being put into efficient verification algorithms whereas control and management issues are - at best - supported in a limited way. As long as nasty errors are being exposed, this may be satisfactory enough. However, when one is aiming at the systematic verification of a system, one needs more than just a smart debugging tool.

One of the practical problems when using model checkers is the management of all (generated) data during the validation trajectory. It is important that the validation results obtained using a validation tool are always reproducible [8]. Without tool support, the validation engineer has to resort to general engineering practices and record all validation activities into a logbook. Consequently, the quality of the validation process depends on the accuracy of the validation engineer. This is clearly undesirable.

When an error is found in (one of) the model(s) of the system under validation, the model(s) should of course be corrected. Furthermore, all models which have been verified previously and which are affected by the error should be re-verified. It is tedious and errorprone to re-validate all previous models and properties manually. Both the logging and the re-verification activities should be automated and - ideally - be integrated into the validation tool.

2.2 Current management support in Xspin

Since version 3.1.2, Xspin includes a "LTL Property Manager", which stores the following information on a LTL verification run into a single file with extension .ltl:

- the **never** claim that is generated from the LTL property;
- definitions (**#defines**) of the propositions that are used in the LTL property (and in the corresponding **never** claim);
- user provided notes; and
- the output of the verification run.

The .ltl file uses **#ifdef** constructs[1] to isolate the **Promela** fragments from the user provided notes and the verification results. Consequently, the file is liable to being updated every time a verification run is executed: previous verification results will be overwritten unless the user saves each verification run in a different .ltl file.

Although the "LTL Property Manager" is clearly a step in the good direction with respect to a controlled verification trajectory, some essential ingredients of the verification run are not recorded:

- the options to come to the verification results:
  - options to Spin to generate the **pan** verifier;
  - options to the C compiler to compile the **pan** verifier; and
  - options to the **pan** verifier to steer the verification run.
- the **Promela** model on which the verification was performed;
- the trace (trail) to the counterexample, in case the property was violated.

The last aspect becomes even more apparent when the property that is being checked requires the existence of a counterexample to be satisfied. This is the case for all existential LTL properties of the type "does there exist an execution path where P becomes true?". The reason for this is that when checking a LTL property Q, Spin will implicitly check Q for *all* execution paths. Consequently, a property like "does there exist an execution path where P becomes true" is not expressible in LTL. Instead one has to resort to check that "for all execution paths, P is always *not* true" (i.e. in LTL: $\Box \, ! P$). If this transformed property is not valid, Spin will find a counterexample showing the execution path where P will become true. In this case the counterexample is the proof of the original property.

Spin is appraised most for its model checking capabilities. Besides these verification features, Spin includes a very helpful simulator, that can be used for debugging, sanity checks, rapid prototyping, simulation of generated counterexamples, etc. It is remarkable that Xspin has some limited support for verification management but has none for simulation.

---

[1] Promela source text is (by default) preprocessed by the standard C preprocessor, named cpp, before being parsed by Spin itself. The **#ifdef** directive is normally used for the conditional compilation of source text (i.e. C).

Although Xspin's "LTL Property Manager" is more than other validation tools have to offer, it is too primitive to use in an extensive validation project spanning more than a few days. Within such projects, we experienced that the validation process was seriously hampered by the fact that we had to record all our validation activities with Spin by hand. Instead of concentrating on the validation process, we had to invent schemes to keep track of the various validation models, the simulation traces, the verification results, etc. We also tried to use literate techniques to structure the validation process [18], but had to conclude that these techniques do not scale up for larger projects.

2.3 Software Configuration Management

The problems of managing the data that is generated during the validation phase relate to the maintenance problems found in software engineering [17]. This is not surprising as, in a sense, validation using a model checker involves the analysis of many successive versions of the model of a system. To tackle these maintenance problems within software engineering a lot of research has been carried out in the area of so called "Software Configuration Management".

Software Configuration Management (SCM) [1, 11] is the software engineering discipline of managing the evolution of large and complex software systems [21]. From the IEEE Standard Glossary of Software Engineering Terminology (Standard 729-1983 [10]):[2]

> Software Configuration Management is the process of identifying and defining the items in a system, controlling the release and change of these items throughout the life-cycle, recording and reporting the status of items and change requests, and verifying the completeness and correctness of items.

The items that comprise all information produced as part of the software engineering process are collectively called a *software configuration*. A general SCM system has the following operational aspects to manage the software engineering process [5, 10, 17]:

- *Identification.* An identification scheme reflects the structure of the product, identifies components and their type, making them unique and accessible in some form.
- *Version control.* Version control combines procedures and tools to manage different versions of configuration objects that are created during the software engineering process.
- *Change control.* Change control combines human procedures and automated tools to provide a mechanism for the control of change.

---

[2] SCM is a widely used term, with an equally wide range of meanings. See
http://www.enteract.com/~bradapp/acme/scm-defs.html for an extensive list of alternative SCM definitions.

- *Audit and review.* Validating the completeness of a product and maintaining consistency among the components by ensuring that the product is a well-defined collection of components.
- *Reporting.* Recording and reporting the status of components and change requests, and gathering vital statistics about components in the product.

Naturally, a SCM system should be supported by automated tools. Tools for version control and build management are essential. Furthermore, SCM tools should provide the developer with a "sandbox" environment: a consistent, flexible and reproducible environment to compile, edit and debug software [13]. SCM tools have greatly evolved over the last twenty years. Tools have gone from file oriented versioning utilities to full blown repository-based systems that manage projects and support team development environments, even across geographic locations. In this paper, a discussion on particular SCM tools is clearly out of scope. The interested reader, however, is invited to visit the "Configuration Management Yellow Pages" page on Internet [22] or consult the Proceedings of the Annual Workshops on Software Configuration Management. Conradi and Westfechtel [3] give an extensive overview of the current state of art of SCM and SCM systems.

Definitions Below we define the conceptual framework for the rest of this paper, borrowing terminology from the SCM community, in particular [3, 21].

- *object.* An object (or item) is any kind of identifiable entity put under SCM control.
- *version.* A version represents a state of an evolving object.
- *revision.* A version intended to supersede its predecessor is called a revision (historical versioning).
- *variants.* Versions intended to coexist are called variants (parallel versioning).
- *configuration.* A configuration is a consistent and complete version of a composite object, i.e. a set of object versions and their relationships.
- *product space.* The product space is composed of the objects and their relationships. The product space is organized by relationships between objects, e.g. composition relationships and (build) dependency relationships.
- *version space.* The version space is composed of the set of versions. The version space is often organized into a version graph or version grid.

2.4 SCM and Xspin

It is clear that the functionality of SCM systems and tools can be of considerable value to control and manage the validation phase. For the validation trajectory using Xspin we are mainly interested in the identification of validation objects, version control over these validation objects and reporting facilities on these objects. The change control functionality and the support for audit and review supported by SCM seem less applicable to validation.

During the validation phase, a *validation object* records the results of a validation activity. For validation using Xspin, three validation objects can be distinguished: the Promela model, the property and the validation result. Of these objects, several versions exist during the validation phase.

- *Model M.* M is the model of the system under validation. M_i denotes the i-th version of model M. A version can either be a variant or a revision. Within the validation framework, variants correspond to different abstractions of the same model M, whereas revisions are different versions of the same abstraction.
- *Property ϕ.* A property ϕ is a property which should hold for the model M under verification.
- *Validation results R.* R is a set of validation results. The set R_i denotes the set of validation results obtained by executing the validation tool on the model M_i. An element from the set R_i is denoted by $r_{i,j}$. Every element $r_{i,j}$ contains the outcome (e.g. a file) of the j-th validation on M_i and additional information that depends on the type of validation. For instance, when $r_{i,j}$ corresponds to a simulation run, the simulation goal and observations on the simulation should be added to $r_{i,j}$. Whereas for a verification run, apart from the verification goal (e.g. a LTL property), the directives and options to obtain the verifier should be added to $r_{i,j}$.

The *versioned product space* of the validation phase now consists of all versions of all validation objects during the validation of the model M.

3 Xspin/Project

In this section the Xspin/Project tool is discussed. Xspin/Project is an extension of Xspin using the version control system PRCS [15]. Xspin/Project controls and manages the validation activities when using Xspin. First the choice for the underlying version control system PRCS is motivated. Then the architecture and the functionality of Xspin/Project are discussed.

3.1 PRCS

To integrate management facilities into a validation tool like Xspin, the functionality of full-blown state-of-the-art SCM tools is not needed. For a controlled and reproducible validation phase, version control and build-management are most important. A file based version control tool like RCS [20] in combination with a basic build-management tool like make [6] appeared to be sufficient for a prototype version of Xspin/Project.

Concurrent Version System (CVS) [2] - the de-facto version control system among free systems - seemed to be unnecessarily complex with respect to operation, administration and user interface to be easily integrated into Xspin. The author was attracted by the simplicity of PRCS and decided to use this version control system for a first prototype version of Xspin/Project.

PRCS - the Project Revision Control System [15] - is a version-control system for collections of files with a simple operational model, a clean user interface and high performance. PRCS is freely available from [14]. The current version of PRCS is implemented using RCS [20] as its back-end storage mechanism.

PRCS has some additional features which makes it well suited for integration into Xspin:

- *Conceptually close to validation objects.* PRCS defines a project version as a labeled snapshot of a group of files, and provides operations on project versions as a whole. Thus a project version naturally relates to a specific validation model and all its validation results.
- *Version naming scheme.* PRCS' version naming scheme (see below) corresponds closely to the version concepts from the validation framework: abstraction and revisions of these abstractions.
- *Simple operational model.* In PRCS, each project version is identified by a single distinguished file, the version descriptor; this file contains a description of the files included in that particular version. Adding files (i.e. validation results) only involves adding the filename to this version descriptor file.

Terminology A *project* in PRCS is a collection of (project) versions.[3] A *version* is a snapshot of a set of files arranged into a directory tree. Every version has a name of the form $m.n$, where m is the major version name and n is the minor version name. A major version name m is a string chosen by the user, whereas the minor version name n is a positive integer, assigned consecutively by the system. A PRCS *repository* contains a group of projects. Two basic operations are available to save and load versions to and from the repository respectively:

- *checkin*: a complete version is put into the repository;
- *checkout*: reconstructs a complete version, identified by the project and version name.

The PRCS concepts correspond nicely with the concepts from the validation framework. A project corresponds with the complete validation trajectory of a system. Each version of the project is a Promela model M_i together with its validation results R_i. In a version $m.n$, the major version name m corresponds with the particular abstraction of the model M and the minor version name n corresponds with the n-th revision of the particular abstraction. The fact that the major version name m in PRCS is an arbitrary string can be used to give appropriate names to the different abstraction models.

3.2 Architecture

Figure 1 shows the architecture of Xspin/Project. Xspin/Project is an extension of Xspin. The Project-part of Xspin/Project is responsible for collecting the Promela

---

[3] A PRCS project corresponds to the term configuration of SCM.

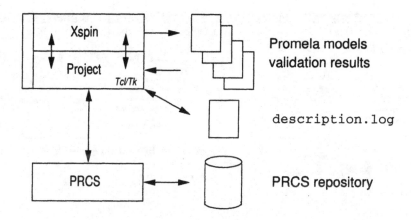

Fig. 1. Architecture of Xspin/Project.

models and validation results from Xspin and passing them to PRCS. Furthermore, the Project-part integrates a visual front end to PRCS into Xspin. The Project-extensions are written in Tcl/Tk [16].

Every Promela model M_i can be saved into the PRCS repository. Furthermore, the contents of any message box of Xspin which is the result of some validation run (i.e. $r_{i,j}$) can be saved into the PRCS repository. Xspin/Project uses a special file, i.e. description.log in which it stores additional information about the validation files (e.g. validation goals, options, directives, timestamps) into the current version of the project.

Xspin/Project needs PRCS version 1.2 [14] to be installed. PRCS on its turn needs RCS version 5.7 as its underlying version control system. Xspin/Project is available from http://www.cs.utwente.nl/~ruys/xspin-project.

3.3 Overview

In a nutshell the current version of Xspin/Project can be characterized as follows:

- Xspin/Project implements a visual front end to PRCS into Xspin. To the user, Xspin/Project is presented as a conceptual database of Promela models together with their validation results.
- The user of Xspin/Project can save all its validation activities into the PRCS database. Furthermore, the user is given the possibility to annotate these validation activities.
- All essential verification data such as directives and options to the C compiler and the pan verifier are automatically saved into the PRCS repository.
- Xspin/Project ensures the integrity of the Promela models and their validation models.

Xspin/Project uses plain PRCS as its underlying configuration management tool. This means that all additional powerful features (like diff and merge) of PRCS

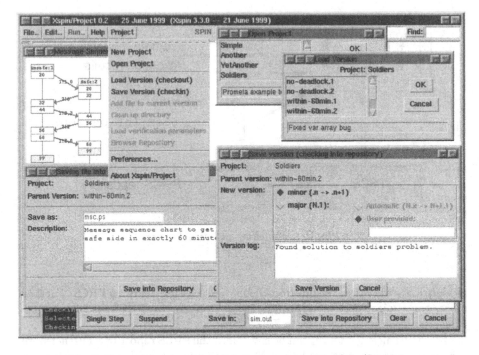

Fig. 2. Screen capture of a validation session with Xspin/Project.

are also available to the user. However, these advanced features of PRCS are not (yet) available from within Xspin/Project. To exploit these features, one should use PRCS' command-line options.

3.4 User awareness

Figure 2 captures a screenshot of a validation session with Xspin/Project. The added functionality of Xspin/Project provides the user with a "sandbox" environment: a consistent, flexible and reproducible environment to edit and validate Promela models. The user should not be unnecessarily hampered during the validation trajectory. Below we discuss the user awareness with respect to the features added by Xspin/Project on top of the original Xspin.

- *Accessing PRCS.* An extra toplevel menu has been added to Xspin: Project. This menu can be used to access most Xspin/Project functions, like:
  - Starting a new project.
  - Opening an existing project.
  - Loading (checking out) a particular Promela model (i.e. an explicit version of the project).
  - Saving (checking in) a particular Promela model and all its recorded validation results.

- Adding files explicitly to the current version. This may be useful when non-Xspin files are relevant to a validation run or when one has forgotten to save a Xspin file into the repository.
- Cleaning up the directory. Using this function all files that have been saved previously in the repository are removed from the current directory.

− *Saving validation results.* To every dialog box containing validation output (e.g. simulation traces, message sequence charts) an extra button has been added: "Save into Repository". When this button is pressed, Xspin/Project shows a dialog box where the user can annotate the particular file with some notes on the particular validation run. The file and the (optional) notes are subsequently saved into the repository. Furthermore, for verification runs, Xspin/Project saves all options that are needed to build and run the pan verifier into the `description.log` file.

− *Forcing version integrity.* When the user has saved the results of a validation run into the current version of the project, the corresponding Promela model will be locked: the user can only perform additional validation runs on the model. Only when the complete version has been saved (checked in) into the repository, the Promela model will be unlocked again for user edits. This strategy of Xspin/Project is necessary to keep all models and their validation results accurate.[4]

Software development vs. validation When using a SCM tool to control the software development process, a version of the 'product' consists of several files and rules to construct the product. Older versions correspond to inferior or less stable versions (containing bugs) or to versions of the product with fewer features.

In Xspin/Project, PRCS is used as a database to store and log all validation activities. Each different Promela model is stored together with the validation results on that particular model. In contrast with software development, earlier versions of the model are not inferior or less stable versions, but should be considered as different abstractions of the same model.

4 Conclusions

The success of model checking tools is mainly based on the bugs and errors that those verification tools have exposed in (existing) systems and standards. Now that model checking tools are becoming more widespread, the application of model checkers is slowly shifting from debugging to verification.

---

[4] This strict behaviour does not restrain the user when constructing a new Promela model. During the development of a Promela model, one usually performs several sanity checks (mostly simulation runs) on intermediate models before actual verification runs are tried. Naturally, these sanity runs do not have to end up in the validation repository. Therefore, the user is not forced to save all validation files but may only optionally do so.

This paper discusses the need for systematic control and management over the (generated) data when using an analysis tool like Spin for the validation of large systems. The strength of SCM systems and tools has briefly been discussed. We have concluded that the full power of SCM systems is not needed to manage the validation activities; a flexible version control mechanism is sufficient to manage the validation phase when using Xspin.

We have presented Xspin/Project, an integration of the version control system PRCS into Xspin. The current version of Xspin/Project presents the user with a conceptual database for Promela models and their validation results. To guide the verification engineer even further, we are currently working on the following extensions to Xspin/Project:

- *Reporting*: adding reporting facilities to generate a detailed overview of the complete validation trajectory.
- *Reverification*: when a Promela model has been altered, all previous verification runs on the model should be automatically re-verified.
- *Reuse*: reusing verification options of previous verification runs to verify new versions of Promela models.
- *Compare*: comparing different versions of Promela models (using PRCS' diff command) to get information on the abstractions and revisions made during the validation trajectory.

But even without these additions the current version of Xspin/Project already promises to be a great help in managing the version space explosion.

References

[1] Wayne A. Babich. *Software Configuration Management: Coordination for team productivity*. Addison-Wesley, Reading, MA, 1986.

[2] Brian Berliner. CVS II: Parallelizing Software Development. In *Proceedings of the Winter 1990 USENIX Conference, January 22-26, 1990, Washington DC, USA*, pages 341–352, Berkeley, CA, USA, January 1990. USENIX.

[3] Reidar Conradi and Bernhard Westfechtel. Version Models for Software Configuration Management. *ACM Computing Surveys*, 30(2):232–282, June 1998.

[4] Pedro R. D'Argenio, Joost-Pieter Katoen, Theo C. Ruys, and G. Jan Tretmans. The Bounded Retransmission Protocol must be on time! In Ed Brinksma, editor, *Proceedings of the Third International Workshop on Tools and Algorithms for the Construction and Analysis of Systems (TACAS'97)*, number 1217 in Lecture Notes in Computer Science (LNCS), pages 416–431, University of Twente, Enschede, The Netherlands, April 1997. Springer Verlag, Berlin.

[5] Susan Dart. Concepts in Configuration Management Systems. In P.H. Feiler, editor, *Proceedings of the Third International Workshop on Software Configuration Management (SCM'91)*, pages 1–18, Trondheim, Norway, June 1997. ACM SIGSOFT, ACM Press, New York.

[6] Stuart I. Feldman. Make – A Program for Maintaining Computer Programs. *Software – Practice and Experience*, 9(3):255–265, March 1979.

[7] Gerard J. Holzmann. *Design and Validation of Computer Protocols*. Prentice Hall, Englewood Cliffs, New Jersey, 1991.

Analyzing Mode Confusion via Model Checking*

Gerald Lüttgen[1] and Victor Carreño[2]

[1] Institute for Computer Applications in Science and Engineering, NASA Langley
Research Center, Hampton, Virginia 23681-2199, USA, luettgen@icase.edu
[2] Assessment Technology Branch, NASA Langley Research Center,
Hampton, Virginia 23681-2199, USA, v.a.carreno@larc.nasa.gov

Abstract. *Mode confusion* is a serious problem in aviation safety. Today's complex *avionics systems* make it difficult for pilots to maintain
awareness of the actual states, or *modes*, of the flight deck automation. NASA explores how formal methods, especially *theorem proving*,
can be used to discover mode confusion. The present paper investigates
whether *state-exploration techniques*, e.g., *model checking*, are better able
to achieve this task than theorem proving and also to compare the *verification tools* Murφ, SMV, and Spin for the specific application. While all
tools can handle the task well, their strengths are complementary.

1   Introduction

Digital system automation in the flight deck of aircraft has significantly contributed to aviation efficiency and safety. Unfortunately, the aviation community is also starting to experience some undesirable side effects as a result of
the high degree of automation. Incidents and accidents in aviation are increasingly attributed to *pilot-automation interaction*. Although automation has reduced the overall pilot workload, in some instances the workload has just been
re-distributed, causing short periods of very high workloads. In these periods,
pilots sometimes get confused about the actual states, or *modes*, of the flight
deck automation. *Mode confusion* may cause pilots to inappropriately interact
with the on-board automation, with possibly catastrophic consequences.

NASA Langley explores ways to minimize the impact of mode confusion on
aviation safety. One approach being studied is to identify the sources of mode
confusion by *formally modeling* and *analyzing* avionics systems. The *mode logic*
of a *flight guidance system* (FGS) was selected as a target system to develop
this approach and to determine its feasibility. The FGS offers a realistic avionics system and has been specified in many notations and languages including
CoRE [12], SCR [12], Z [6], ObjecTime [13], and PVS [2]. In the PVS [16] effort,
the FGS, which is characterized by its *synchronous*, *reactive*, and *deterministic*
behavior, was encoded as a finite state machine. Properties, which were identified

---

* This work was supported by the National Aeronautics and Space Administration
under NASA Contract No. NAS1-97046 while the first author was in residence at
the Institute for Computer Applications in Science and Engineering (ICASE), NASA
Langley Research Center, Hampton, Virginia 23681-2199, USA.

[8] Gerard J. Holzmann. The Theory and Practice of a Formal Method: NewCore. In *Proceedings of the IFIP World Congress*, Hamburg, Germany, August 1994. Also available from URL: http://cm.bell-labs.com/cm/cs/doc/94/index.html.

[9] Gerard J. Holzmann. The Model Checker SPIN. *IEEE Transactions on Software Engineering*, 23(5):279–295, May 1997. See also URL: http://netlib.bell-labs.com/netlib/spin/whatispin.html.

[10] IEEE. *IEEE Standard Glossary of Software Engineering Terminology: IEEE Standard 729-1983*. IEEE, New York, 1983.

[11] IEEE. *IEEE Guide to Software Configuration Management: ANSI/IEEE Std 1042-1987*. IEEE, New York, 1987.

[12] Donald E. Knuth. Literate Programming. *The Computer Journal*, 27(2):97–111, May 1984.

[13] David B. Leblang and Paul H. Levine. Software Configuration Management: Why is it needed and what should it do? In Jacky Estublier, editor, *ICSE SCM-4 and SCM-5 Workshops – Selected Papers*, number 1005 in Lecture Notes in Computer Science (LNCS), pages 53–60. Springer Verlag, Berlin, 1995.

[14] Josh MacDonald. PRCS – Project Revision Control System. Available from URL: http://www.xcf.berkeley.edu/~jmacd/prcs.html.

[15] Josh MacDonald, Paul N. Hilfinger, and Luigi Semenzato. PRCS: The Project Revision Control System. In B. Magnusson, editor, *Proceedings of the ECOOP'98 SCM-8 Symposium on Software Configuration Management (SCM'98)*, number 1439 in Lecture Notes in Computer Science (LNCS), pages 33–45, Brussels, Belgium, July 1998. Springer Verlag, Berlin.

[16] John K. Ousterhout. *Tcl and the Tk Toolkit*. Addison-Wesley Publishing Company, Reading, Massachusetts, 1994.

[17] Roger S. Pressman. *Software Engineering – A Practioner's Approach*. McGraw-Hill, New York, third edition, 1992.

[18] Theo C. Ruys and Ed Brinksma. Experience with Literate Programming in the Modelling and Validation of Systems. In Bernhard Steffen, editor, *Proceedings of the Fourth International Conference on Tools and Algorithms for the Construction and Analysis of Systems (TACAS'98)*, number 1384 in Lecture Notes in Computer Science (LNCS), pages 393–408, Lisbon, Portugal, April 1998. Springer Verlag, Berlin.

[19] Theo C. Ruys and Rom Langerak. Validation of Bosch' Mobile Communication Network Architecture with SPIN. In *Proceedings of SPIN97, the Third International Workshop on SPIN*, University of Twente, Enschede, The Netherlands, April 1997. Also available from URL: http://netlib.bell-labs.com/netlib/spin/ws97/ruys.ps.Z.

[20] Walter F. Tichy. RCS – A System for Version Control. *Software – Practice and Experience*, 15(7):637–654, July 1985.

[21] Walter F. Tichy. Tools for Software Configuration Management. In J.F.H. Winkler, editor, *Proceedings of the International Workshop on Software Version and Configuration Control*, pages 1–20, Grassau, Germany, January 1988. Teubner Verlag.

[22] André van der Hoek. Configuration Management Yellow Pages. Available from: http://www.cs.colorado.edu/users/andre/configuration_management.html, 1999.

as possible sources of mode confusion by experts in *human factors* [9], were also defined in the PVS language. These properties included *inconsistent behavior*, *ignored crew inputs*, and *indirect mode changes*. Proofs in the PVS model were undertaken to either show that a property holds or to discover conditions that preclude the property from being true. The employed style of theorem proving resembled a form of *state exploration*. Hence, the question arises whether state-exploration and *model-checking* techniques [3, 5] are better suited for the study of mode confusion.

In order to answer this question, we model and analyze the mode logic by applying three popular and publicly available *state-exploration/model-checking tools*, namely Murφ [4, 14], SMV [11, 17], and Spin [7, 18]. Although all three tools are appropriate for the task, each one has its own strengths and weaknesses. We compare the tools regarding (1) the suitability of their languages for *modeling* the mode logic, (2) their suitability for *specifying* and *verifying* the *mode confusion properties* of interest, and (3) their ability to generate and *animate diagnostic information*. The first aspect concerns the way in which we model the example system. The second aspect refers to the adequacy of the language in which properties are encoded and also to the degree of orthogonality between system and property specifications. The third aspect is perhaps the most important one for engineers since system designs are often incorrect in early design stages.

2 Flight Guidance Systems and Mode Logics

The *FGS* is a component of the *flight control system* (cf. Fig. 1). It continuously determines the difference between the actual state of an aircraft – its position, speed, and attitude as measured by its *sensors* – and its desired state as in-putted via the *crew interface* and/or the *flight management system*. In response, the FGS generates commands to minimize this difference, which the *autopilot* may translate into movements of the aircraft's *actuators*. These commands are calculated by *control law algorithms* that are selected by the *mode logic*.

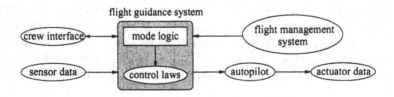

Fig. 1. Flight control system

In the following we focus on the mode-logic part of the FGS. Especially, we leave out the modeling of the control laws and, if no confusion arises, use interchangeably the terms FGS and mode logic. A mode logic essentially acts as a deterministic machine which is composed of several synchronous sub-machines.

It receives *events* from its *environment* and reacts to them by changing its state appropriately. This reaction may require several simultaneous mode changes. Fig. 2 shows a typical mode logic consisting of three interacting components: the *lateral guidance*, the *vertical guidance*, and the *flight director*. The mode of the flight director determines whether the FGS is used as a navigational aid. The lateral guidance subsumes the *roll* mode (Roll), the *heading* mode (HDG), the *navigation* mode (NAV), and the *lateral go-around* mode (LGA), whereas the vertical guidance subsumes the *pitch* mode (Pitch), the *vertical speed* mode (VS), and the *vertical go-around* mode (VGA). Each mode can be either *cleared* or *active*, with the NAV mode having additional sub-states in the *active* state.

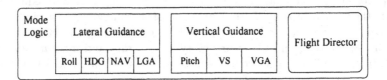

Fig. 2. Architecture of the model logic of the FGS

The properties of interest regarding the FGS can be classified as *mandatory properties* and *mode confusion properties*. Some of the mandatory properties are: (i) if the flight director is off, all lateral and vertical guidance modes must be cleared, (ii) if the flight director is on, then exactly one lateral and one vertical mode is active, and (iii) a default mode is activated when the flight director is on and other modes are cleared. Regarding mode confusion, several categories are identified in [9]. We have selected three categories to use in the analysis of our system: (1) *inconsistent behaviors*, i.e., a crew interface input has different functionality for different system states, (2) *ignored operator inputs*, i.e., a crew input does not result in a change of state, and (3) *indirect mode changes*, i.e., the system changes its state although no crew input is present. To discover sources of mode confusion, we formulate the negation of each property and try to prove it. Conditions that prevent us from successfully completing the proof – manifested by *unprovable subgoals* in a theorem prover and *error traces* in model-checking tools – are the ones we intend to uncover. This process is interactive and labor intensive when using theorem proving [13]. Thus, we investigate whether state-exploration/model-checking tools can perform the analysis more efficiently.

3 Modeling the Mode Logic in Murφ

Murφ [4, 14] is a state-exploration tool developed by David Dill's group at Stanford University and consists of a *compiler* and a *description language*. The compiler takes a system description and generates a C++ *special-purpose verifier* for it, which can then be used for checking *assertions* and *deadlock behavior*.

The Murϕ description language borrows many constructs found in imperative programming languages, such as Pascal. System descriptions may include declarations of *constants*, *finite data-types*, *global* and *local variables*, and unnested *procedures* and *functions*. Moreover, they contain *transition rules* for describing system behavior, a definition of the *initial states*, and a set of *state invariants* and *assertions*. Each transition rule may consist of a *guard* – which is never needed here – and an *action*, i.e., a statement which modifies global variables. A *state* in Murϕ's execution model is an assignment to all global variables in the considered description. A *transition* is determined by a rule which is chosen nondeterministically from those rules whose guards are true in the current state. The rule's execution updates some global variables according to its action.

Table 1. Specification of module *simple_guidance* in Murϕ

```
TYPE sg_modes   : ENUM { cleared, active };
TYPE sg_events  : ENUM { activate, deactivate, switch, clear };
TYPE sg_signals : ENUM { null, activated, deactivated };
PROCEDURE simple_guidance(VAR mode   : sg_modes;  event : sg_events;
                          VAR signal : sg_signals);
BEGIN
  IF mode=cleared THEN
    SWITCH event CASE activate   : signal:=activated;   mode:=active;
                 CASE deactivate : signal:=null;
                 CASE switch     : signal:=activated;   mode:=active;
                 CASE clear      : signal:=null;
    END;
  ELSE
    SWITCH event CASE activate   : signal:=null;
                 CASE deactivate : signal:=null;        mode:=cleared;
                 CASE switch     : signal:=deactivated; mode:=cleared;
                 CASE clear      : signal:=deactivated; mode:=cleared;
END; END; END;
```

The heart of the Murϕ model of the FGS is the deterministic procedure **fgs** which encodes the system's reaction to some event entering the mode logic. By declaring a transition rule for each event **env_ev** as RULE "rule_for_env_event" BEGIN **fgs(env_ev)**; END, we model the nondeterministic behavior of the environment which arbitrarily chooses the event entering the system at each synchronous step. Due to space constraints we do not completely present **fgs**, but concentrate on modeling the vertical-guidance component of the FGS [10]. Let us define the modes of this component as instantiations of an abstract datatype module **simple_guidance** which encodes each mode's behavior as a simple Mealy automaton (cf. Table 1). The module is parameterized by the mode **mode** under consideration, the input event **event**, and the output event **signal**. The parameters are of enumeration types **sg_mode**, **sg_events**, and **sg_signals**, respectively. The body of **simple_guidance** specifies the reaction of a mode to **event** with respect to **mode**. This reaction is described by an *if-statement*, two *case-selections*, and *assignments* to **mode** and **signal**. The vertical-guidance component is specified as a procedure, called **vertical_guidance** (cf. Table 2), and employs **simple_guidance** for describing the modes **pitch**, **vs**, and **vga**, which are defined as global variables. The task of **vertical_guidance** is firstly to recognize whether **env_ev** refers to mode Pitch, VS, or VGA. This is done by functions **pitch_event**, **vs_event**, and **vga_event**. Then **env_ev** is translated to an event of type **sg_events** via functions **pitch_conv**, **vs_conv**, and **vga_conv**, respectively, and passed to the mode to which it belongs. If this mode is activated by the event, i.e., **simple_guidance** returns value **activated** via local variable **sig**, then the other two modes must instantly be deactivated by invoking **simple_guidance** with the appropriate modes and event **deactivate**.

Table 2. Specification of module *vertical_guidance* in Murϕ

```
VAR pitch, vs, vga : sg_modes;
PROCEDURE vertical_guidance(env_ev:env_events);  VAR sig : sg_signals;
BEGIN CLEAR sig;
  IF  pitch_event(env_ev) THEN
    simple_guidance(pitch, pitch_conv(env_ev), sig);
    IF    sig=activated   THEN simple_guidance(vs,     deactivate, sig);
                               simple_guidance(vga,    deactivate, sig);
    END;
  ELSIF  vs_event(env_ev) THEN
    simple_guidance(vs, vs_conv(env_ev), sig);
    IF    sig=activated   THEN simple_guidance(pitch, deactivate, sig);
                               simple_guidance(vga,    deactivate, sig);
    ELSIF sig=deactivated THEN simple_guidance(pitch, activate,   sig);
    END;
  ELSIF vga_event(env_ev) THEN
    simple_guidance(vga, vga_conv(env_ev), sig);
    IF    sig=activated   THEN simple_guidance(pitch, deactivate, sig);
                               simple_guidance(vs,     deactivate, sig);
    ELSIF sig=deactivated THEN simple_guidance(pitch, activate,   sig);
END; END; END;
```

We now turn our focus to specifying mode confusion properties. As states are generated by Murϕ, **assert** statements, that were explicitly included in the action of a rule, are checked. If an assertion is violated – i.e., the **assert** statement is evaluated to false in some reachable system state – the Murϕ verifier halts and outputs diagnostic information which consists of a sequence of states leading from the initial state to the error state. The verifier also halts if the current state possesses no successor states, i.e., if it is deadlocked. Next, we show how an exemplary property of each category of the mode confusion properties mentioned in Section 2 can be stated as assertions. We encapsulate these assertions in procedure **mode_confusion_properties** which is invoked as the last

Table 3. Specification of some *mode confusion properties* in Murϕ

```
VAR old_pitch, old_vs, old_vga : sg_modes;
PROCEDURE mode_confusion_properties(env_ev:env_events);
BEGIN
  ALIAS mode_change : pitch!=old_pitch | vs!=old_vs | vga!=old_vga; DO
    -- check for response to pressing VS button
    IF env_ev=vs_switch_hit THEN
      assert (old_vs=cleared -> vs=active ) "vs_toggle_1";
      assert (old_vs=active  -> vs=cleared) "vs_toggle_2";
    END;
    -- search for ignored crew inputs (property violated)
    assert (crew_input(env_ev) -> mode_change)
           "search_for_ignored_crew_inputs";
    -- no unknown ignored crew inputs
    assert (crew_input(env_ev) & !ignored_crew_input(ev) -> mode_change)
           "no_unknown_ignored";
    -- search for indirect mode changes (property violated)
    assert (!crew_input(env_ev) -> !mode_change)
           "search_for_indirect_mode_changes";
    -- no unknown indirect mode changes
    assert (!crew_input(env_ev) & !indirect_mode_change(env_ev) ->
           !mode_change) "no_unknown_indirect_mode_changes";
  END;
  old_pitch:=pitch; old_vs:=vs; old_vga:=vga;
END;
```

statement in `fgs` (cf. Table 3). Here, "--" introduces a comment line, != denotes *inequality*, and |, &, !, and -> stand for *logical disjunction*, *conjunction*, *negation*, and *implication*, respectively. Since all properties of interest concern the transition from one system state to the next, we need to store the global variables' values of the previously visited state. For this purpose we introduce new global variables `old_pitch`, `old_vs`, and `old_vga`. The need for this overhead arises because Murϕ can only reason about simple *state invariants* and not about more general "*state transition invariants.*" Therefore, state transition invariants need to be encoded as state invariants, which doubles the size of the state vector for our system description. The first two assertions in Table 3, belonging to the first category of mode confusion properties, state that environment event `vs_switch_hit` acts like a toggle with respect to mode VS, i.e., if VS was in state `cleared` and `vs_switch_hit` arrived, then it is now in state `active`, and vice versa. Regarding the second category, we verify that no crew inputs are ignored, i.e., whenever an event that originated from the crew enters the mode logic, then at least one mode changes its value. We specify this property as `crew_input(env_ev) -> mode_change`, where `crew_input` is a function determining whether `env_ev` originates from the crew and where `mode_change` is a shortcut introduced as an `ALIAS` statement. As expected, this property does not always hold. The error trace returned by Murϕ helps us in identifying the cause, as is our objective. We filter out the cause by including a predicate `ignored_crew_input`, stating the negation of the cause, in the premise of the assertion (cf. Table 3). We then re-run Murφ and iterate this process until the assertion becomes true, thereby gradually capturing all crew-input scenarios responsible for mode confusion. Similarly, we approach the third category of mode confusion properties. The property we consider is *"no indirect mode changes"* which prohibits a system's state to change if `env_ev` is not originated by the crew. Using Murφ, we discover the conditions that invalidate this property and, subsequently, weaken it via predicate `indirect_mode_change`. The mandatory properties mentioned in Section 2 are formalized as `invariant` statements and proved. The difference between an `assert` and an `invariant` statement is that the former appears in the system description part of the model, while the latter does not. The reason for specifying mode confusion properties in the system description is their reference to `old_pitch`, `old_vs`, and `old_vga`. In order to keep the state space small, these variables must be re-assigned to the actual values of `pitch`, `vs`, and `vga`, respectively, before a step of the synchronous system is completed.

Summarizing, Murφ's description language turned out to be very convenient for our task since the PVS model of the FGS [13] could simply be carried over. Unfortunately, Murφ forces us to encode state transition invariants as state invariants, thereby doubling the number of global variables and Murφ's memory requirements. The full Murφ model subsumes about 30 assertions and leads to a finite automaton with 242 states and 3 388 transitions. In each state, any of the 14 environment events may enter the system ("242 × 14 = 3 388"). The state-space exploration took less than 2 seconds on a SUN SPARCstation 20.

4   Modeling the Mode Logic in SMV

The SMV system [11, 17], originally developed by Ken McMillan at Carnegie-Mellon University, is a model-checking tool for verifying finite-state systems against specifications in the *temporal logic* CTL [3, 5]. SMV implements a symbolic model-checking algorithm based on *Binary Decision Diagrams* (BDDs) [1].

SMV's description language is a very simple, yet elegant language for *modularly* specifying finite-state systems, which has the feel of a *hardware description language*. The language's data types are Booleans (where *false* and *true* are encoded as 0 and 1, respectively), enumeration types, and arrays. Its syntax resembles a style of *parallel assignments*, and its semantics is similar to single assignment *data flow languages*. In contrast to Murφ, SMV descriptions are *interpreted*. The interpreter makes sure that the specified system is implementable by checking for *multiple assignments* to the same variable, *circular assignments*, and *type errors*. The SMV language also includes constructs for stating system specifications in the temporal logic (fair)CTL [5], which allows one to express a rich class of temporal properties, including *safety*, *liveness*, and *fairness properties*. Here, we focus on safety properties to which invariants belong.

Table 4. Specification of module *simple_guidance* in SMV

```
MODULE  simple_guidance(activate, deactivate, switch, clear)
VAR     mode      : {cleared, active};
ASSIGN  init(mode) := cleared;
        next(mode) := case deactivated | deactivate : cleared;
                           activated                 : active;
                           1                         : mode;
                      esac;
DEFINE  activated   := (mode=cleared) & (activate | switch);
        deactivated := (mode=active ) & (clear    | switch);
```

A *module description* in SMV consists of four parts: (1) the MODULE clause, stating the module's name and its formal (call-by-reference) parameters, (2) the VAR clause, declaring variables needed for describing the module's behavior, (3) the ASSIGN clause, which specifies the initial value of all variables (cf. init) and how each variable is updated from state to state (cf. next), and (4) the DEFINE clause, which allows one to introduce abbreviations for more complex terms. The main module MAIN of our SMV specification encodes the environment of the FGS, which nondeterministically sends events to the mode logic. This is done by defining variable env_ev of enumeration type env_events, which contains all environment events, and by adding "init(env_ev):=env_events; next(env_ev):=env_events" to the ASSIGN clause. Similar to the Murϕ model, we specify a module simple_guidance (cf. Table 4) and, thereby, show how Mealy machines may be encoded in SMV. Module simple_guidance takes the input events activate, deactivate, switch, and clear – which can be either absent or present – as parameters. The state associated with simple_guidance is variable mode which may adopt values cleared and active. The initial value init(mode) of mode is cleared. The behavioral part of simple_guidance is described in the next(mode) statement consisting of a case expression. The value of this expression is determined by the first expression on the right hand side of the colon such that the condition on the left hand side is true. The symbols =, &, and | stand for *equality, logical conjunction,* and *logical disjunction,* respectively. The terms activated and deactivated, whose values are accessible from outside the module, are defined in the DEFINE clause.

Before we model module vertical_guidance, we comment on why we have encoded the input event of simple_guidance using four different signal lines instead of a single event of some enumeration type subsuming all four values. When activate, deactivate, switch, and clear are combined in an enumeration type, we need to identify the value of the input event via a SMV case construct. This induces a circularity which would be detected by the SMV interpreter, i.e., our description of the mode logic would be rejected. One difference between simple_guidance as a *module* in SMV and as an *abstract data-type* in Murϕ is that the mode variable is encapsulated within the SMV module and is not a call-by-reference parameter. The behavior of each mode of vertical_guidance, Pitch, VS, and VGA, can now be described by instantiating simple_guidance,

Table 5. Specification of module *vertical_guidance* in SMV

```
MODULE vertical_guidance(vs_pitch_wheel_changed, vs_switch_hit,
         ga_switch_hit, sync_switch_pressed,    ap_engaged_event)
VAR pitch : simple_guidance(pitch_activate, pitch_deactivate, 0, 0);
    vs    : simple_guidance(0, vs_deactivate, vs_switch_hit, 0);
    vga   : simple_guidance(0, vga_deactivate, ga_switch_hit, vga_clear);
DEFINE
  pitch_activate   := (vs_switch_hit & vs.deactivated) | (vga_event &
                       vga.deactivated) | vs_pitch_wheel_changed;
  pitch_deactivate := (vs_switch_hit & vs.activated) |
                       (vga_event & vga.activated);
  vs_deactivate    := (vs_pitch_wheel_changed & pitch.activated) |
                       (vga_event & vga.activated);
  vga_deactivate   := (vs_pitch_wheel_changed & pitch.activated) |
                       (vs_switch_hit & vs.activated);
  vga_clear   := ap_engaged_event | sync_switch_pressed;
  vga_event   := ap_engaged_event | sync_switch_pressed | ga_switch_hit;
```

as is done in the VAR clause in Table 5. Thereby, global variables pitch.mode, vs.mode, and vga.mode are created as part of the state vector of our SMV model. All actual parameters of each simple_guidance module can be specified as terms on the input parameters of vertical_guidance. Note that the functions pitch_event, vs_event, and vga_event used in the Murϕ description are encoded here in the DEFINE clause. Our modeling of vertical_guidance is self-explanatory and visualizes the differences between the SMV and the Murϕ languages. While in Murϕ each synchronous step of the FGS can be modeled by a *sequential algorithm*, it must be described by *parallel assignments* in SMV.

Table 6. Specification of some *mode confusion properties* in SMV

```
DEFINE mode_change :=
  !(vertical.pitch.mode=cleared <-> AX vertical.pitch.mode=cleared) |
  !(vertical.pitch.mode=active  <-> AX vertical.pitch.mode=active ) | ...
-- check for response to pressing VS button
SPEC AG (vertical.vs.mode=cleared & env_ev=vs_switch_hit ->
         AX vertical.vs.mode=active)
SPEC AG (vertical.vs.mode=active  & env_ev=vs_switch_hit ->
         AX vertical.vs.mode=cleared)
-- search for ignored crew inputs (property violated)
SPEC AG (crew_input -> mode_change)
-- no unknown ignored crew inputs
SPEC AG (crew_input & !ignored_crew_input -> mode_change)
-- search for indirect mode changes (property violated)
SPEC AG (!crew_input -> !mode_change)
-- no unknown indirect mode changes
SPEC AG ((!crew_input & !indirect_mode_change) -> !mode_change)
```

In SMV, temporal system properties are specified in the *Computational Tree Logic* (CTL) [3, 5] and may be introduced by the keyword SPEC within the same file as the system description. The properties of interest to us can be specified as CTL formulas of the form AGϕ, where AG stands for "always generally," i.e., every reachable state satisfies property ϕ. The formula AXϕ expresses that all successor states of the current state satisfy ϕ. In this light, the first formula in Table 6 states: "every reachable state satisfies that, if mode VS in vertical_guidance is currently cleared and event vs_switch_hit enters the system, then VS is active in every successor state of the current state." The symbols -> and <-> used in Table 6 stand for *logical implication* and *equivalence*, respectively. The identifiers mode_change, crew_input, indirect_mode_change, and ignored_crew_input are abbreviations of expressions defined in a DEFINE clause, as exemplary shown for mode_confusion. The presence of operator AX in CTL remedies the need to keep track of old values of mode variables. Thereby, the size of the associated state vector of the SMV model is cut in half when compared to the Murϕ model. Moreover, an orthogonal treatment of model and property specifications is achieved. The SMV system verified about thirty assertions in slightly more than half a second using 438 BDD nodes and allocated less than 1 MByte memory on a SUN SPARCstation 20. The properties "*search for ignored crew inputs*" and "*search for indirect mode changes*" were invalidated as in the Murϕ model. The returned error traces, including the assignments of each variable in every state of the traces, supported the identification of potential problems with the FGS model. SMV also includes an *interactive mode* which provides a very simple assistant for interactive debugging. The state space of the SMV model consists of 3 388 states, which corresponds to the 242 states of the Murϕ model since the actual environment event, out of 14 possible events, must be stored in a variable in SMV ("$242 \times 14 = 3\,388$").

Summarizing, SMV performed well for our example. CTL supports the convenient specification of mode confusion properties. However, SMV's system description language is not high-level when compared to Murϕ.

5 Modeling the Mode Logic in Spin

Last, but not least, we explore the utility of the verification tool Spin [7, 8, 18], which was developed by Gerard Holzmann at Bell Labs, for our case study. Spin is designed for analyzing the logical consistency of *concurrent systems*. It is especially targeted towards distributed systems, such as communication protocols. The system description language of Spin, called Promela, allows one to specify *nondeterministic processes*, *message channels*, and *variables* in a C-like syntax. Given a Promela description, whose semantics is again defined as a finite automaton, Spin can perform random or interactive *simulations* of the system's execution. Similar to Murϕ, it can also generate a special-purpose verifier in form of a C-program. This program performs an exhaustive exploration of the system's state space and may check for *deadlocks* and *unreachable code*, validate *invariants*, and verify properties specified in a *linear temporal logic* [5].

Table 7. Specification of the main process *init* in Spin

```
init{ env_ev=null; do :: atomic{
        if                              /* body encodes 1 synchr. step    */
        :: env_ev=vs_switch_hit         /* nondet. choice of env. event   */
        :: ...                          /* 14 cases, for each env. event  */
        fi; fgs(env_ev); env_ev=null    /* perform synchronous step       */
     od }
```

Since our FGS is a synchronous system, it falls out of the intended scope of Spin. Nevertheless, we show that Spin allows us to successfully carry out our case study. The Promela fragment depicted in Table 7 encodes the main process, referred to as init in Spin, which is the only process of our model. Here, the global variable env_ev is of type mtype which contains an enumeration of all event and signal names that occur in the mode logic. Promela's type system supports basic data types (such as bit, bool, and byte), as well as arrays, structures (i.e., records), and channels. Unfortunately, one may only introduce a single declaration of enumeration type, which must be named mtype. The statement atomic in init attempts to execute all statements in its body in one *indivisible* step. Especially, it prevents Spin from storing intermediate states which might arise when executing the body. Thus, we may use this construct for encoding the complex algorithm of the mode logic that performs a single synchronous step. The *repetition statement* do together with the *choice statement* if nondeterministically chooses which environment event to assign to env_ev. The reason that we have not simply spelled out fgs(vs_switch_hit), and so on for each environment event, is that fgs needs to be implemented as an *inline*. Expanding this long inline fourteen times turns out to be inefficient.

Table 8. Specification of module *simple_guidance* in Spin

```
inline simple_guidance(mode, event, signal)
{ if :: mode==cleared ->
         if :: event==activate   -> signal=activated;   mode=active
            :: event==deactivate -> signal=null
            :: event==switch     -> signal=activated;   mode=active
            :: event==clear      -> signal=null
         fi
    :: mode==active  ->
         if :: event==activate   -> signal=null
            :: event==deactivate -> signal=null;        mode=cleared
            :: event==switch     -> signal=deactivated; mode=cleared
            :: event==clear      -> signal=deactivated; mode=cleared
         fi
  fi }
```

Promela does not possess any kind of procedure construct other than the process declaration proctype. However, we may not introduce additional processes to the main process init, since then our model would not reflect a synchronous system any more. The only construct of Promela, which we can use for resembling the architecture of the FGS, is inline. This construct may take parameters, such as mode, event, and signal for component simple_guidance (cf. Table 8). When compiling a Promela description, each occurrence of simple_guidance in vertical_guidance is replaced with its body. The modes instantiating parameter mode are global variables of type bit, where cleared and active are defined as constants 0 and 1, respectively, using the preprocessor command #define. The body of simple_guidance contains the Promela statement if. Its behavior is defined by a nondeterministic selection of one of its executable options, which are separated by double colons, and by executing it. In our case, each option consists of a guarded expression which is executable if the expression on the left of -> evaluates to true in the current system state and which returns the result of evaluating the expression on the right hand side. The symbols == and = denote the *equality* and the *assignment* operator, respectively. Using simple_guidance, we can specify component vertical_guidance as another inline (cf. Table 9). The body of vertical_guidance is self-explanatory and similar to the one for Murϕ. It should only be noted that guard else is always executable and that expression skip leaves the current system state unchanged. Moreover, functions pitch_event, vs_event, and vga_event are spelled out as inlines here.

The verification technique we employed in Spin for reasoning about the FGS, namely *assertions*, is similar to the one we used in Murϕ. More precisely, Promela's assertion statement assert aborts the state exploration conducted by Spin's verifier whenever its argument expression evaluates to false in some system state associated with the assertion statement. Our specification of the mode confusion properties are depicted in Table 10, where '!', '&&', and '||' stand for the logical connectives *not*, *and*, and *or*, respectively. Moreover, the symbols /* and */ denote the begin and end of comments. In our specification, crew_input, mode_change, ignored_crew_input, and indirect_mode_change, which are defined as Boolean functions in Murϕ, are simply introduced via #defines. In order to encode expression mode_change, we have to keep a copy of the 'old' values of all global variables of interest, as in the Murϕ model. Stating the mode confusion properties in Spin's version of linear-time logic requires the re-compilation of Spin with compiler option -DNXT, such that the next-state operator, which is desired for specifying mode_change, becomes available. Although this would have allowed us to proceed as described for SMV, we preferred not to do so. The reason is that Spin does not support the definition of temporal formulas in a modular fashion, i.e., by composing complex formulas from more simpler ones, as SMV does. Thereby, temporal formulas related to mode confusion would be very lengthy and difficult to read. The verification results returned by the Spin verifier are similar to the ones for Murϕ. The Spin model of the FGS also possesses 242 states and 3 388 transitions (+ 1 "dummy" transition). Unfortunately, Spin crashes and core dumps when analyzing the invalid assertions *search for ig-*

Table 9. Specification of module *vertical_guidance* in Spin

```
inline pitch_event(env_ev) { env_ev==vs_pitch_wheel_changed }
inline vs_event(env_ev)    { env_ev==vs_switch_hit }
inline vga_event(env_ev)   { env_ev==ga_switch_hit || ... }
inline vertical_guidance(env_ev)
{ if :: pitch_event(env_ev) ->
      simple_guidance(activate, pitch_mode, pitch_signal);
      if :: pitch_signal==activated ->
              simple_guidance(deactivate,  vs_mode,  vs_signal);
              simple_guidance(deactivate, vga_mode, vga_signal)
         :: else                       -> skip
      fi
   :: vs_event(env_ev) ->
      simple_guidance(switch, vs_mode, vs_signal);
      if :: vs_signal==activated     ->
              simple_guidance(deactivate, pitch_mode, pitch_signal);
              simple_guidance(deactivate,  vga_mode,  vga_signal)
         :: vs_signal==deactivated   ->
              simple_guidance( activate, pitch_mode, pitch_signal)
         :: else                     -> skip
      fi
   :: vga_event(env_ev) ->
      if :: env_ev==ga_switch_hit    ->
              simple_guidance(switch, vga_mode, vga_signal)
         :: else                     ->
              simple_guidance( clear, vga_mode, vga_signal)
      fi;
      if :: vga_signal==activated    ->
              simple_guidance(deactivate, pitch_mode, pitch_signal);
              simple_guidance(deactivate,   vs_mode,    vs_signal)
         :: vga_signal==deactivated ->
              simple_guidance( activate, pitch_mode, pitch_signal)
         :: else                     -> skip
      fi
   :: else -> skip
 fi }
```

nored crew inputs and search for indirect mode changes. However, it still writes an error trace which can be fed into Spin's simulator. No other violated assertions were detected during the exhaustive state-space search which took under 2 seconds and required about 2.6 MBytes memory on a SUN SPARCstation 20. It should be mentioned that a previous effort to analyze a FGS using Spin suffered from an intractably large state space [15]. That model was then checked for invariants using Spin's *bitstate hashing algorithm*.

Summarizing, carrying out our case study in Spin was feasible but less elegant than in Murφ due to the lack of procedure and function constructs in Promela, which had to be encoded using inlines and #defines. We would like to see a

Table 10. Specification of some *mode confusion properties* in Spin

```
bit old_pitch_mode=cleared; bit old_vs_mode=cleared;
bit old_vga_mode =cleared;
/* check for response to pressing VS button            */
assert(!(old_vs_mode==cleared) || (vs_mode==active));
assert(!(old_vs_mode==active ) || (vs_mode==cleared));
/* search for ignored crew inputs (property violated)  */
assert(!(crew_input) || mode_change);
/* no unknown ignored crew inputs                      */
assert(!(crew_input && !(ignored_crew_input)) || mode_change);
/* search for indirect mode changes (property violated) */
assert(!(!(crew_input)) || !(mode_change));
/* no unknown indirect mode changes                    */
assert(!(!(crew_input) && !(indirect_mode_change)) || !(mode_change));
/* save the current mode values                        */
old_pitch_mode=pitch_mode;  old_vs_mode=vs_mode;  old_vga_mode=vga_mode;
```

richer type system in Spin, which can handle more than one mtype definition. Especially useful to us were Spin's capabilities to simulate Promela models and to feed back error traces into the simulator. Simulations helped us to quickly identify the causes of ignored crew inputs and indirect mode changes. Beside monitoring variables, we found it useful that Spin highlights the part of the Promela description corresponding to the system state under investigation.

6 Discussion

In this section we discuss the strengths and weaknesses of Murφ, SMV, and Spin regarding their system and property description languages and regarding their capabilities for generating and animating diagnostic information. We restrict our discussion to the observations we made on the FGS case study and refrain from a more general comparison or a comparison along the line of a "feature list." Not only is our experience with the tools limited, but a single case study will inevitably give a biased picture since tools are developed with different objectives and one will be more tailored for an application than another.

The system description languages of all three verification tools allow us to model the deterministic, synchronous behavior of the FGS, as well as the non-deterministic behavior of the system's environment. However, Murφ's language stands out since it (i) implements numerous language constructs and has a rich type system, as found in imperative programming languages, (ii) supports a modular programming style via parameterized procedures and functions, and (iii) permits one to easily adapt the existing PVS specification of the mode logic [13]. However, SMV's module concept is slightly more elegant than Murφ's procedure concept for our application since mode variables can be declared within the module to which they belong. A major difference between the tools' languages is that Murφ and Spin allow model encoding using sequential algorithms, whereas SMV requires an algorithm description by parallel assignments. Regarding Promela, one notices that it is designed to specify asynchronous systems. It only offers the process declaration construct proctype for encapsulating code fragments. We used inline declarations to work around this problem. However, an inline construct is no substitute for a procedure mechanism. Although, depending on the employed parameter mechanism, both constructs may semantically coincide, there is an important practical difference. Inlines may blow-up system descriptions, thereby making, e.g., syntax checks inefficient. We experienced durations of syntax checks well exceeding ten minutes for some variations of our Spin model. Finally, all three tools are missing the ability to organize events in a *taxonomy* via sub-typing. Such a concept would help us to divide all events into lateral-mode and vertical-mode events, and further into Pitch events, HDG events, etc.

Regarding the second issue, we also identified important differences among the tools. Since all mandatory and mode confusion properties of interest are invariants, they can be stated as assertions and verified in state-exploration tools, such as Murϕ, as well as more general model-checking tools, such as SMV and Spin. When specifying mode confusion properties, a temporal logic is most convenient since it allows one to implicitly refer to adjacent states in program paths using the next-state operator. This is important for describing property mode_change which requires one to access the mode variables of adjacent states. In contrast to Murϕ, the encoding of mode confusion properties in SMV does not require the storage of old values of mode variables. Thereby, the size of the associated state vector is cut in half. Spin can be employed both as an assertion checker, similar to Murϕ, and as a model checker, similar to SMV. Especially, SMV's BDD-based model checker performed very well in our case study since mode logics have the characteristics of Boolean terms which can be represented efficiently using BDDs. However, the small state space of our example system precludes us from fairly comparing the run times of Murϕ, SMV, and Spin.

Concerning the third issue, only Spin provides rich features for simulating and animating diagnostic information. Each tool returns an error trace whenever a desired system property is invalidated. Murϕ and SMV output a textual description of the error trace, which displays the global variables assignments at all states of the trace. Spin, however, is able to animate error traces using *message sequence charts*, *time sequence panels*, and *data value panels* which are integrated in its *graphical user interface*, known as Xspin. In our case study involving a synchronous system only the data value panel was of use. This feature and the ability to highlight the source code line corresponding to the current state in the simulation enabled us to detect sources of mode confusion quickly.

7 Conclusions and Future Work

This paper advocates the use of state-exploration techniques for analyzing mode confusion. Compared to theorem provers, model-checking tools are able to verify the properties of interest automatically. When weighing the strengths of Murϕ,

SMV, and Spin for our application, it turned out that these are complementary: Murϕ has the most pleasant system description language, including a rich type system; SMV's way of integrating temporal logics supports the convenient specification of mode confusion properties; Spin's capability of animating diagnostic information enables the fast detection of sources of mode confusion.

Regarding future work, our case study should be extended to include more components of today's digital flight decks and, subsequently, to explore other interesting properties related to mode confusion.

Acknowledgments. We thank Ricky Butler and Steve Miller for many enlightening discussions about mode confusion, as well as Ben Di Vito and the anonymous referees for their valuable comments and suggestions.

References

[1] R.E. Bryant. Graph-based algorithms for boolean function manipulation. *IEEE Transactions on Computers*, C-35(8), 1986.

[2] R.W. Butler, S.P. Miller, J.N. Potts, and V.A. Carreño. A formal methods approach to the analysis of mode confusion. In *DASC '98*, 1998. IEEE.

[3] E.M. Clarke, E.A. Emerson, and A.P. Sistla. Automatic verification of finite-state concurrent systems using temporal logic specifications. *ACM Transactions on Programming Languages and Systems*, 8(2):244–263, 1986.

[4] D.L. Dill. The Murphi verification system. In CAV '96, vol. 1102 of *LNCS*, pages 390–393, 1996. Springer-Verlag.

[5] E.A. Emerson. Temporal and modal logic. In *Handbook of Theoretical Computer Science*, vol. B, pages 995–1072, 1990. North-Holland.

[6] F. Fung and D. Jamsek. Formal specification of a flight guidance system. NASA Contractor Report NASA/CR-1998-206915, 1998.

[7] G. Holzmann. *Design and Validation of Computer Protocols*. Prentice Hall, 1991.

[8] G. Holzmann. The model checker Spin. *IEEE Transactions on Software Engineering*, 23(5):279–295, 1997.

[9] N.G. Leveson, L.D. Pinnel, S.D. Sandys, S. Koga, and J.D. Reese. Analyzing software specifications for mode confusion potential. In *Workshop on Human Error and System Development*, 1997.

[10] G. Lüttgen and V.A. Carreño. Murphi, SMV, and Spin models of the mode logic. See http://www.icase.edu/~luettgen/publications/publications.html.

[11] K.L. McMillan. *Symbolic Model Checking: An Approach to the State-Explosion Problem*. PhD thesis, Carnegie-Mellon University, 1992.

[12] S.P. Miller. Specifying the mode logic of a flight guidance system in CoRE and SCR. In *FMSP '98*, pages 44–53, 1998. ACM Press.

[13] S.P. Miller and J.N.Potts. Detecting mode confusion through formal modeling and analysis. NASA Contractor Report NASA/CR-1999-208971, 1999.

[14] Murϕ. Project Page at http://sprout.stanford.edu/dill/murphi.html.

[15] D. Naydich and J. Nowakowski. Flight guidance system validation using Spin. NASA Contractor Report NASA/CR-1998-208434, 1998.

[16] S. Owre, J. Rushby, N. Shankar, and F. von Henke. Formal verification for fault-tolerant systems: Prolegomena to the design of PVS. *IEEE Transactions on Software Engineering*, 21(2):107–125, 1995.

[17] SMV. Project Page at http://www.cs.cmu.edu/~modelcheck/smv.html.

[18] Spin. Project Page at http://netlib.bell-labs.com/netlib/spin/whatispin.html.

Detecting Feature Interactions in the Terrestrial Trunked Radio (TETRA) Network Using Promela and Xspin*

Carl B. Adekunle and Steve Schneider

Department of Computer Science,
Royal Holloway, University of London,
Egham Hill, Egham,
Surrey, TW20 0EX,
United Kingdom.
Tel: +44 (0)1784 443912
Fax: +44 (0)1784 439786
email: c.adekunle@dcs.rhbnc.ac.uk

Abstract. The problem caused by feature interactions serve to delay and increase the costs of introducing features to existing networks. We introduce a three stage technique that detects interactions in the TETRA network. Promela is used to model the network and features and its requirements are specified using linear temporal logic. The Xspin toolkit is used to verify and validate the model against its requirements.

1 Introduction

Telecommunications networks comprise numerous features that add extra functionalities on top of the basic services provided. With new features being incrementally added, it is unclear how they interact. For example, will the addition of a feature interfere with the behaviour of existing features? Or perhaps the new feature demonstrates unexpected behaviour as a result of integration with existing features. The problem caused by these feature interactions serve to delay and increase the costs of introducing features to existing networks. The problem is exacerbated because many features are designed and implemented by different companies across global networks. Assumptions are made about network implementations and consequently the behaviour of features differ. The feature interactions field [KK98] attempts to avoid, detect and resolve interactions at various stages of the features life cycle.

We research feature interactions in Terrestrial Trunked Radio [1] (TETRA)[TR95], which is a digital private mobile radio network specified by the European Telecommunications Standard Institute (ETSI). In TETRA, features are referred to as supplementary services though, for the purpose of this paper, we use the term features.

The TETRA network and features are modelled using the Protocol Meta language (Promela) [Hol90] and we specify requirements that the model should satisfy using

---

* Research funded by Motorola.
[1] Formally Trans-European Trunked Radio.

linear temporal logic [MP91]. The language of temporal logic is used to specify and reason about properties such as safety and liveness at an abstract level. We use the Xspin toolkit to verify the model for general properties such as deadlock and to validate the model against its requirements.

In this paper, we present and exploit a three stage technique to detect feature interactions. The technique is general enough to be applied to other languages and toolkits. It relies on the validation of requirements being completed for the first two stages to detect interactions in the final stage.

The rest of the paper is organised as follows: section 2 discusses feature interactions in more detail and outlines the three approaches used to tackle the problem. Section 3 introduces TETRA and highlights the areas of the network analysed for interactions. It also discusses the information extraction process used to decide what operations to model. In section 4 we summarise why we use Promela and Xspin to model the TETRA network and features. We also give an overview of temporal logic and the types of requirements it can be used to specify. The technique used to detect feature interactions is presented in section 5 and we demonstrate its effectiveness in section 6. Section 7 presents our conclusion.

2 Feature Interactions

Features in telecommunication networks add extra functionality on top of the basic services provided. Examples of features are Call Forwarding Unconditional (CFU) [Eura] and Barring of Incoming Calls (BIC) [Eurb]. Call Forwarding Unconditional allows its subscriber to divert all incoming setup requests to a designated mobile other than itself. Barring of Incoming Calls screens all incoming setup requests to the subscriber against a barred list. If the calling mobile is on that list, it is prevented from connecting to the subscriber. When both features are invoked by their subscriber, it is not clear what should happen to an incoming setup request from a calling mobile that is on the barred list. For example, mobile C subscribes to both features and has mobile B as its divert for the CFU and mobile A as barred on the BIC. Mobile A then makes a setup request to join C, should the CFU forward mobile A to B or should A be barred from not only connecting to C but also to B? Such uncertainty is a contributing factor in feature interactions.

The feature interactions field has arisen as a result of the need to detect and resolve interactions using three approaches, which are:

Avoidance - Involves using an architecture to prevent interaction by tackling issues such as resource contention. The features are specified, implemented and tested within the architecture [JP98].

Detection - Employs the use of model checking techniques such as simulation, verification and validation to detect interactions [LL94].

Resolution - Focuses on run time detection of interactions [TM98]. Feature interactions managers (FIM) are often used to resolve the interactions by prioritising the activation of features.

No single approach can detect all interactions, so a combination of all three provides the best possibility of detecting and resolving interactions during the software cycle of a feature.

A more generalised definition of interactions is: The behaviour of a feature is suppressed or modified by the existence of another feature. In our research, feature interactions is defined as the behaviour of a feature preventing another from satisfying its requirements. We use a detection approach to detect interactions using verification and validation model checking.

3 Terrestial Trunked Radio (TETRA)

TETRA is the next generation of digital private mobile radio (PMR) network. It allows the exchange of voice and data between mobile radios in a group and is currently scheduled to replace existing analog networks used by organisations like the police.

To connect to the network, a mobile radio requests call setup to another in its group via the Switching and Management Infrastructure (SwMI), which is made up of base stations, switches and controllers. The called mobile accepts or rejects the request by informing the SwMI which in turn informs the calling mobile of the response. Acceptance of a call setup request ensures both the calling and called mobiles are connected to the group. To transmit voice or data in the group, a mobile has to request permission from the SwMI, which grants or rejects the request. If granted, all mobiles in the group are informed of the identity of the mobile and all receive the transmission.

3.1 Circuit Mode Control Entity

In this section, we provide an overview of the areas related to mobile communication. The European Telecommunication Standard (ETS)[TR95] specifies the services and protocol used by the Circuit Mode Control Entity (CMCE), which lies in layer three of the International Organisation for Standardisation (ISO), Open Systems Interconnection (OSI) seven layer reference model.

Each hand held or vehicle based mobile has one CMCE that is responsible for connecting it to a group call. Figure 1 shows the four sub-entities that make up the CMCE. The dashed lines represent sub-entities and bi-directional channels that are not necessary to our research, so we focus only on the Call Control (CC) and Protocol Control (PC) sub-entities as they are essential to providing basic bearer services like call connections and transmission of voice and data.

The Call Control sub-entity is responsible for initiating, maintaining and releasing calls made by the mobile. It communicates via channel ra to user applications [2] (UA) that can be anything from a press to talk button to a liquid crystal display on the mobile. User applications are responsible for informing Call Control of activities such as call setup request to another mobile. Channel rd connects Call Control with the Protocol Control sub-entity, which is responsible for error correction and communicating with the SwMI using channel ri[3].

---

[2] User Applications are not defined by the ETS and therefore not shown in the figure.
[3] Via the Mobile Link Entity, which is not shown in the figure and is not modelled.

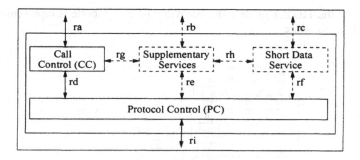

Fig. 1. Circuit Mode Control Entity

3.2 Information Extraction Process

In this section, we highlight the process we use to extract information from the ETS to model the TETRA network. The aim is to derive the minimum amount of information to successfully model the basic bearer services.

As mentioned in the previous section, only the Call Control and Protocol Control sub-entities from the CMCE need to be included in the model as processes. Though the Supplementary Services sub-entity is responsible for configuring and invoking features on behalf of the mobile, there is little need to model it as all its responsibility can be explicitly modelled in the SwMI process. The Short Data Services sub-entity has no bearing on the features, therefore it is not modelled. As the SwMI and user applications are outside the scope of the ETS, we model them as processes using cross referenced information from other sources.

All communication in TETRA is done using protocol data units (PDUs). The structure of each PDU varies according to its primitive type, which identifies the PDU. For example, the primitive *tncc_setup_request* has up to twenty four parameters. We simplify the structure of PDUs by requiring all primitives to have only four parameters as shown in figure 2. The front of the PDU is occupied by its primitive type. The four parameters identify the mobile (*Tsi*), its group (*GTsi*), the contact mobile (*DestTsi*) and any additional information about the PDU (*Msg*). To cut down on the number of PDUs in the model, we do not include call progress or query information. We also identify the variables that need to be included in the model.

Primitive type	Primitive parameters			
tncc_setup_request	Tsi	GTsi	DestTsi	Msg

Fig. 2. Protocol Data Unit Structure

We decided to model three mobiles, as this number is sufficient for our analysis. Figure 3 provides a diagrammatic view of the ten processes and bidirectional channels that make up the TETRA model. The behaviour of each mobile is represented by the *ua*, *cc* and *pc* processes.

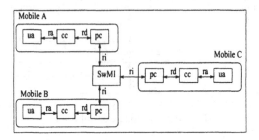

Fig. 3. Processes in the TETRA Model

4 Why Promela And Xspin?

The Specification and Description Language (SDL) was introduced in the late 1970's by the International Telecommunication Union (ITU)[4] and has found popular use in the telecommunications industry. Its graphical syntax and comprehensive toolkit support has contributed to it being the language of choice when implementing TETRA network. However, for our research it is unsuitable mainly because its semantics [SDL] allows processes to discard messages at the head of their FIFO queues [5], when they cannot remove messages due to absent corresponding input symbols[6]. The effect of this implicit consumption is to make it virtually impossible for an SDL system to deadlock due to processes being unable to remove messages from their queues.

As Promela uses a C like text syntax, we found engineers familiar with programming languages required little adjustment in understanding and using it. Promela's use of never claims to represent temporal formulae means that requirements could be specified and validated using the Xspin toolkit. Though we use Promela and Xspin, all results need to be applicable to SDL. How this is done is outside the scope of this paper.

4.1 Linear Temporal Logic

Using linear temporal logic, it is possible to specify and reason about temporal properties at an abstract level. A sequence of infinite states is regarded as a computation. The sequence represents a single path starting with an initial state s_0 and on execution of a transition, progresses to a successor state shown as $\sigma : s_0, s_1, s_2, \cdots$. Each state in the

---

[4] Formally CCITT.

[5] The SDL term is signal paths.

[6] SDL does have a SAVE symbol to store messages that can be handled in later states. If this operator is not used, the message is discarded.

sequence has an associated successor. First order temporal formulae are derived from combining state formulae with boolean connectives and future and past temporal operators. As the past operators do not add any expressibility to the language of temporal logic, we use only the future operators $\square$ (*always*), $\diamond$ (*eventually*), $\mathcal{U}$ (*until*) and $\mathcal{W}$ (*unless*). We do not cover the $\bigcirc$ (*next*) operator as it is the only operator able to detect stuttering (i.e. when a state is repeated in succession in a sequence). The definition of future operators is based on the temporal formula holding at states in the computation.

Specifying Requirement Properties. Using the temporal operators, we can specify properties of interest such as safety. For example, specifying the value of variable *count* is never less than zero $\square(count \geq 0)$. Liveness requires the system to eventually carry out a desirable behaviour such as system termination for a scheduled downtime $\diamond(terminate)$. A persistence property specifies that there are finitely many positions where a property does not hold, but when the property occurs it holds indefinitely. For example, on startup a system will reach a stable state and maintain the stability $\diamond \square(system\_stable)$. A response property allows the specification that an action has a corresponding reaction, either at the same position or in the future. For example, every request has a corresponding response $\square(request \rightarrow \diamond response)$. Other properties that can be specified as temporal formulae are obligation and reactivity.

5 A Technique to Detect Feature Interactions

Building and verifying the TETRA model is not sufficient to detect feature interactions. There is a need to apply the modelling language and toolkit in a manner that increases the likelihood of detecting interactions. We devised and use a three stage technique that is general enough to be used with any language and toolkit that allows validation of requirements. Each stage consists of iterative steps. The first two stages apply to most system development and do not involve the detection of feature interactions. However the two are essential to the final detection stage, which uses requirements to detect feature interactions. Verification and Validation is preferred over simulation because they explore more computations and check for general properties such as deadlock and livelock. The rest of this section, presents an overview of the stages involved in the technique.

5.1 Stage One

This stage is concerned with constructing the requirements for the base model, implementing, verifying and validating the base model against its requirements. The following steps are applied:

1. Constructing the base model requirements (REQ):
   REQ normally consists of a number of requirements, which are constructed using information from the information extraction process. This ensures the requirements are based on the intended behaviour of the model. For instance, there is no point in having a requirement about performance when the model is implemented without any performance operations.

2. Model the system (*Stage1 model*): Language dependent.
3. Verify *Stage1 model* for general properties:
   On discovery of an error, resolve it and repeat from this step. When all errors are resolved proceed to the next step.
4. Validate *Stage1 model* against *REQ*:
   If *Stage1 model* does not satisfy *REQ* and provided *REQ* is correctly constructed, resolve the error and repeat from step three. If *REQ* is incorrectly constructed, use the validation result to modify *REQ* and repeat this step. The aim of this step is to have the behaviour of the model satisfy all its requirements as shown below, where $\models$ represents "satisfies":
   $Stage1\ model \models REQ$

We make no attempt to specify how the requirements are constructed because it is dependent on the language and toolkit used. Nor are we concerned with how the model is implemented. In step four, if *stage1 model* does not satisfy the requirements, it is necessary to confirm that the requirements are correctly constructed. It may be that the behaviour of the model reveals an error in the requirements construction. When the model satisfies all requirements, stage one has produced a *Stage1 model* and *REQ* that will be used in the next two stages.

5.2 Stage Two

The aim of this stage is to detect any interactions between the *Stage1 model* and the integration of a single feature. It is not advisable to modify *REQ* as it would invalidate the results from stage one. We repeat this stage for each feature, resulting in multiple models containing only the integration of a feature with the base model. The integration of the feature requires modification to *Stage1 model* to derive *Stage2 model*.

1. Construct requirements for the feature (*P1*):
   This step is similar to that done in stage one.
2. Model the feature (*F1*): Language dependent.
3. Integrate *F1* with *Stage1 model* (*Stage2 model*): Language dependent.
4. Verify *Stage2 model* for general properties:
   On discovery of an error, resolve the error and repeat this step. When all errors are resolved, progress to the next step.
5. Validate *Stage2 model* against *REQ* and *P1* requirements:
   First *REQ* is validated. If *REQ* is not satisfied, the integration of the feature (including solutions to general property errors from the previous step) has modified the behaviour of the model to an **undesired** level, that it no longer satisfies its original requirements. What is done at this point is left to the model implementors. One solution is to review and modify resolutions to errors in step four and then to repeat that step before progressing to this one. When *REQ* is satisfied, then validate *P1*. If *P1* is not satisfied and providing it is correctly constructed, resolve the error and then repeat from step four (including validation of *REQ* in this step to ensure it is still satisfied). If *P1* is incorrectly specified, use the validation result to modify *P1* and repeat this step. The aim of this step is to ensure *Stage2 model* satisfies the conjunction of the original requirements and those of the feature's:
   $Stage2\ model \models REQ \wedge P1$

5.3 Stage Three

This is the feature interactions detection stage. This stage allows integration of more than one feature to an existing *Stage2 model*. Which features are integrated depend on issues such as what services are to be provided or analysis of combination of features. The integration of features requires modification to a *Stage2 model* to derive *Stage3 model*.

1. Integrating additional features to a *Stage2 model* (*Stage3 model*):
   Using one of the *Stage2 models* as a starting point, integrate features $F2 \ldots Fn$ to the model to derive *Stage3 model*. This must include all solutions to general property errors from *Stage2 model* for all the features integrated.
2. Verify *Stage3 model* for general properties:
   On detection of an error, resolve the error and then repeat this step.
3. Validate *Stage3 model* against $REQ \wedge P1 \wedge P2 \wedge Pn$ requirements:
   This step detects any interactions between the integrated features. The features requirement include only those integrated. If *Stage3 model* fails to satisfy any requirements, feature interaction has occurred:
   $Stage3\ model \models REQ \wedge P1 \wedge \ldots \wedge Pn$

Feature interactions is deemed to occur only if the behaviour of one feature prevents another feature from satisfying its requirement. Any errors such as deadlock that occur during step two should be resolved using guidelines applicable to the model. When all errors are resolved, it is the validation step that detects interactions. We know that completion of stage two for each feature in isolation satisfies all its requirements and those of the base model. Therefore, the validation step in stage three will detect any interactions, when a requirement is not satisfied. Any solutions applied to resolve feature interactions means returning to step two, where the cycle begins. Modifying any of the requirements at this stage invalidates the previous stages.

6 Applying the Technique Using Promela and Xspin

In this section, we show how each stage of the technique is applied to the TETRA basic bearer services and the CFU and BIC features. All requirements are constructed using linear temporal logic. We completed the information extraction process before starting this stage. It identified channel *ri*, as the one to include in any requirements containing messages. Consequently a mobile's call setup request is valid only when its *pc* process places a corresponding PDU in the channel.

6.1 Stage One - The Base Model

Constructing the base requirements. To construct a requirement, we apply the following steps:

1. An informal text description for each requirement is provided from the information extraction process.

2. The text description is turned into a temporal formula consisting of propositions and temporal operators.
3. The propositions are defined using messages and variables as parameters identified by the information extraction process.

For example, the text wording for a requirement concerned with all mobiles in the group call states that ,"All mobiles must join the group call and remain in the call." This is translated into the persistence temporal property $\diamondsuit \, \square \, (group\_setup)$. The proposition $group\_setup$ is defined as:

```
#define group_setup (IdleA == false && IdleB == false
                      && IdleC == false)
```

For the property to be satisfied all the variables must have the value false, which indicates they are in a call.

Modelling the TETRA basic bearer services. We first declare all global variables. To use a string reference for each mobile, we use the #*define* keyword. Each mobile is defined as a two character string [7], though in this paper we refer to the single character. We also define the group identity using the same keyword. The status of a mobile and other mobiles it can connect to, are declared as boolean variables and initialised with values. The example lists only declarations for mobile A:

```
#define  GROUP   0         /* Group ID */
#define  AA      100       /* mobile A */
bool     IdleA = true;     /* mobile is idle */
bool     ConnectAA_BB = false,
         ConnectAA_CC = false;
```

We declare the structure of each PDU to have four parameters using the *typedef* keyword. Primitive types are declared using *mtype* keyword. The channels used for communications between the processes are declared using the *chan* keyword:

```
typedef pdu {byte Tsi,   /* id for this mobile */
                  GTsi,  /* Group id for the mobiles */
                  DestTsi, /* Tsi for contact mobile */
                  Msg };   /* additional pdu data */

mtype = {tncc_setup_request, ...};

chan AAra = [1] of {mtype, pdu}; /* A's ra channel */
chan AArd = [1] of {mtype, pdu}; /* A's rd channel */
chan AAri = [1] of {mtype, pdu}; /* A's ri channel */
```

All channels are bounded to one. This allows earlier detection of deadlock [8] during verification and validation. After declaring the global variables, we declare the processes and define their behaviour as:

---

[7] To allow features like Short Number Addressing (SNA) to reduce it to one character.

[8] Caused by processes being unable to place a message in a full channel.

```
proctype SwMI()
{end_IDLE: atomic{...}}          /* SwMI's behaviour */

proctype pc(chan rd,             /* rd channel */
                 ri)             /* ri channel */
{...}                            /* pc's behaviour */

proctype cc(chan ra,             /* ra channel */
                 rd)             /* rd channel */
{...}                            /* cc's behaviour */

proctype ua(chan ra,             /* ra channel */
            byte UATsi;          /* mobile's identity */
            bit  AGTsi;          /* mobile group id */
            byte CanCall_1,      /* mobile to call */
            byte CanCall_2)      /* mobile to call */
{...}                            /* ua's behaviour */
```

As all processes in the base model do not terminate, we use the *end* keyword to indicate expected end states as shown for the SwMI. Since the SwMI coordinates communications between mobiles, we also use the *atomic* keyword to ensure it executes as many statements as possible without interleaving with the other processes. The behaviour of each mobile is constructed using the same pc, cc and ua processes. These processes are parameterised to identify the channels associated with each process upon instantiation. In addition, the ua process knows the identity of itself, its group and the other mobiles it can nondeterministically make a call setup request to. The ua passes these information to the other processes using the PDU parameters.

We use *init* and *run* keywords to instantiate all processes providing actual parameters for those that require them. As the SwMI process is the coordinating process, it is instantiated before any others to ensure it is ready for communication. For the same reason, the ua process for all mobiles is instantiated after its associated pc and cc processes, to prevent it requesting setup before the others are instantiated. We list only the SwMI and processes for mobile A, mobiles B and C follow the same format to create the environment in figure 3:

```
init{ run SwMI();
      run pc(AArd,AAri);         /* channels rd & ri */
      run cc(AAra,AArd);         /* channels ra & rd */
      run ua(AAra, AA,           /* channel ra & mobile id */
             GROUP, BB, CC);     /* Group Id & can calls */
} /* end of init */
```

Verifying the TETRA model for general properties. We use Xspin version 3.2.4 with the full queue option to block new messages. Use of this option leads to deadlock because of the way the processes are connected. For example, all pc processes fill their ri channels with a call setup request. The ua, cc and pc processes for all mobiles then block waiting for a response to their request. The SwMI non-deterministically removes one of the requests from a mobile's channel *ri* and blocks because it is unable to place a message on the called mobile's channel to inform it of an incoming request. The deadlock is reported by Xspin, which allows the use of the guided simulation to analyse its cause. All errors reported by Xspin were of similar nature and were resolved. Two error free models were implemented at the end of this step:

Tx model - On joining the group mobiles could request and be granted permission to transmit. During hash compact verification, it uses thirty one megabytes of memory.

Non Tx model - Mobiles cannot request transmit permission on joining the group call. They can non-deterministically reject or accept requests to join the group. During exhaustive verification, it uses seven megabytes of memory.

Validating the TETRA model against its requirements. The Tx model failed the persistence property requirement $\Diamond \Box (group\_setup)$. Its guided simulation revealed that transmission was (unintentionally!) assigned a higher priority than call setup. Thus, when two of the three mobiles joined the group call[9], their transmission activities prevent the SwMI from connecting the third mobile to either of the two. The Non Tx model on the other hand, satisfied all the requirements. Taking this into consideration and that it used considerably less memory than the Tx model, we used it for the next two stages. The alternative solution would be to correct the Tx model by assigning call setup a higher priority than transmission.

6.2 Stage Two - The CFU Feature

In this section, we show the steps used to integrate a feature with the Non Tx model. Though we use the Call Forwarding Unconditional feature as an example, the same procedures are followed for the Barring of Incoming Calls feature. We completed an information extraction process for each feature before starting this stage. It helped to identify the variables and messages required by the feature.

Constructing requirements for the CFU feature. This step follows the same step as for the base model requirements. We found that the feature's requirements should include the following amongst others:

- Activation and deactivation of the feature.
- All communications between the feature and mobiles.
- Global variables modified by the feature.

For example, the requirement, "The CFU informs the calling mobile of acceptance of its request by the called mobile," is translated into the response temporal property $\Box (cfu\_divert\_accept \rightarrow \Diamond cfu\_accept\_request\_ms)$. Proposition cfu_divert_accept defines the conditions that represents the called[10] mobile informing the CFU of acceptance. Proposition $cfu\_accept\_request\_ms$ represents the CFU informing the calling mobile of acceptance. They both are defined as:

---

[9] One accepting the request of the other.

[10] The mobile, the calling mobile was diverted to.

```
#define cfu_divert_accept
           (BBri?[pc_swmi_u_connect,BB,0,AA,255]
           && CfuActive_c == true)
#define cfu_accept_request_ms
           (AAri?[swmi_pc_d_connect,AA,0,BB,255]
           && ConnectAA_BB == true
           && ConnectAA_CC == false
           && CfuActive_c == false
           && IdleA == false && IdleB == false)
```

The response property [11] uses the implication symbol, therefore the only time the property is not satisfied is if proposition *cfu_divert_accept* occurs (i.e. the required parameter values occur in the same state) and *cfu_accept_request_ms* does not occur in future states . As we use Promela's conjunction operator (&&), a proposition is false if any one of its arguments does not match its required value when the others do in the same state. With this in mind, we intentionally use the minimum number of parameters in the definition for proposition *cfu_divert_accept*, so it has more of a chance of occurring. We also maximise the number of arguments for proposition *cfu_accept_request_ms* that allow it to occur. As the CFU is the only feature in the model, this is straight forward. We include only parameters that relate to the mobiles involved in the feature's task.

Using the parameters in this way contributes greatly towards detecting feature interactions in stage three. Minimising the arguments in the first proposition of the property reduces the likelihood of another feature falsifying it. Maximising the number of arguments in the second increase the possibility of it becoming false due to another feature in stage three, modifying one of its arguments.

When messages are used in propositions definition, we refer to specific channels , PDU primitive types and PDU parameters that are required. Being able to specify the PDU parameters in definitions allow us to ensure a response is a result of a previous action. For example, we know that the messages included in the above propositions are related because the first parameter (which identifies the mobile) and the third (its contact) match when reversed.

Modelling the CFU feature. All features are designed to terminate on completion of their task. It is necessary to introduce additional global variables [12] that specify the status of the feature, its subscriber, the calling and the divert to mobile. To allow flexibility, we use parameters in the definition of all features:

```
proctype cfu(byte SubscriberMs, /* mobile id */
                 CallingMs,      /* calling mobile */
                 DivertMs,       /* mobile to divert to */
                 GroupId,        /* group id */
                 Message)        /* additional pdu data */
{IDLE: atomic{...}}              /* cfu's behaviour */
```

---

[11] As the TETRA network is distributed, the response property is used for most of the requirements in the first two stages.

[12] Identified from the information extraction process for the feature.

We consider the CFU to be part of the SwMI and for this reason, it also uses the *atomic* keyword. Using the CallingMS and DivertMs parameters, the feature is able to dynamically decide which channel *ri* to use for communication with the mobiles.

Integrating the CFU with the base model. To integrate the CFU into the base model from stage one, we modify the SwMI process by using the *do. . .od* construct to instantiate the feature:

```
do /* activate features */
:: (CfuActive_c == false &&   /* not active for mobile */
   CfuAlreadyRan_c == false)-> /* not ran for C */
   CfuActive_c = true ;        /* to be activated */
   CfuAlreadyRan_c = true ;    /* cfu will be ran  */
   FeatureCounter_c++ ;        /* feature activated */
   run cfu(CalledTsi,          /* subscriber mobile */
           CallingTsi,         /* Calling mobile */
           BB,                 /* mobile to divert to */
           GTsi,               /* group id */
           Msg);               /* additional message */
:: /* termination of feature activation */
   (FeatureCounter_c == 1) -> /* total num. features */
   CfuAlreadyRan_c = false ;  /* cfu can run again */
   FeatureCounter_c = 0 ;     /* all features can run */
   goto end_IDLE ;            /* Swmi handle other calls */
od; /* activate features */
```

To run the CFU, the SwMI checks that the feature is not currently active and that it has not already run. If these conditions are met, the SwMI sets the status of the feature as active and marks the feature as already ran. The feature counter is then incremented, to show a feature has been activated. The CFU is then instantiated with parameters. To break out of the construct the SwMI uses the termination sequence. The feature counter must equal the total number of features activated for the subscriber. The feature is then marked as available to be ran. The feature counter is reset to zero and the SwMI is able to handle other calls. The CFU is responsible for reseting its status, to prevent the SwMI from instantiating two copies of the same feature. The SwMI blocks until the active CFU terminates before instantiating another copy of the feature. Providing actual parameters for the CFU, models the behaviour of the supplementary services sub-entity discussed in section 3.2.

Verifying the integrated model for general properties. Since both the CFU feature and the SwMI access channel *ri* to communicate with the mobiles, violation of an assert statement during verification revealed a race condition occurs with the SwMI consuming messages meant for the CFU and vice versa. We resolved this error by replacing the assert statement with additional code so that both SwMI and CFU, on retrieving a message, check whether the message is intended for itself. If this is not the case, the process puts the message back in the channel and blocks until it is removed by another.

Using the hash compact search, verification of the model used fourteen megabytes of memory.

Validating the base model and CFU requirements. This step revealed that propositions using messages parameters are influenced by removal of messages from channels. For example, the response property for the CFU in its original form was not satisfied. This is because the *cfu_accept_request_ms* proposition relied on the argument *CfuActive_c* equalling true (meaning the CFU feature is active). Analysis of its guided simulation revealed that when the message is placed in the channel by the CFU, the proposition is satisfied. However, by the time the calling mobile removes the message, the CFU is no longer active causing the requirement not to be satisfied. This is a case, where the acceptable behaviour of the model resulted in the requirement being modified to the form shown on page 11. Simply changing *CfuActive_c* to equal false resolved the error.

All base model requirements were satisfied provided they refer to mobiles that do not subscribe to the CFU feature [13]. This confirms that the requirements from stage one need to be included in the second and third stages, in order to ensure mobiles that do not subscribe to features are unaffected by feature integration. It is sufficient to validate requirements one at a time, as failure to satisfy an individual requirement will not satisfy their conjunction.

6.3 Stage Three - Feature Interactions Detection

Integrating the BIC with the CFU and base model. To answer the uncertainty raised in section 2, we integrated the BIC to the CFU's *Stage2 model*. As both the CFU and BIC are activated by the same message in the SwMI, we added the code required for the SwMI to instantiate the BIC in the same *do...od* construct used for the CFU. During instantiation, the BIC is supplied with actual parameters. In the listing below, modifications to the termination sequence is required to cater for integration of the BIC:

```
do
:: /* instantiate CFU  */
:: /* instantiate BIC  */
:: /* termination of feature activation */
   (FeatureCounter_c == 2) ->  /* total num. features */
   CfuAlreadyRan_c = false ;  /* cfu can run again */
   BicAlreadyRan_c = false ;  /* bic can run again */
   FeatureCounter_c = 0 ;     /* all features can run */
   goto end_IDLE ;            /* SwMI handles other calls */
od ; /* activate features */
```

All solutions required to resolve deadlock errors in stage two for the BIC were also included in the SwMI and pc processes. An interesting observation was that the BIC solutions were found to be a subset of the solutions required for the CFU. This is because when the features have carried out their specific function (e.g. the BIC screens the incoming request), they behave identically.

---

[13] This is because the CFU takes over parts of the SwMI's operations.

Verifying the model for general properties. The first deadlock error revealed that the CFU does forward a mobile that is on the subscriber's barred list to another, whilst the BIC bars the same mobile from contacting the subscriber. As far as we are concerned, both features are behaving as expected and this is not a case of feature interactions, so we continue with resolving all verification errors.

The final hash compact verification required two hundred and sixty nine megabytes of memory. Xspin also raised an "out of memory" message [14], indicating the state space exploration was not complete. Though the number of errors found was zero, we cannot conclude that the model is error free. However, we can conclude no errors were found in the state space explored. With this in mind, we progress to the next step.

Validating the base model, CFU and BIC requirement. Though the state space exploration was not completed in the previous step, we can still continue with the validation step. The aim is to see if the behaviour of the model violates any requirement, before memory constraints terminate the exploration.

We found two cases of feature interaction that did not exist in stage two for either feature in isolation.

— Though the BIC satisfied its requirements, its behaviour prevented the CFU from satisfying the requirement discussed on page 11. Feature interactions occurs because the BIC sets the status of the barred mobile as inactive, when it is rejected. However, the CFU continues to connect the barred mobile with the mobile it is diverted to. The CFU's requirement expects the status of the barred mobile to be active when connection is achieved. The behaviour of the BIC, causes the argument *IdleA == false* in proposition *cfu_accept_request_ms* to be false. As the proposition *cfu_divert_accept* has occurred, the requirement is not satisfied.
— The behaviour of the BIC in setting the status of the barred mobile as inactive also prevented the original requirement from stage one discussed on page 9 from being satisfied.

Discovering the interactions used only six megabytes of memory. This is because violation of the requirement was detected early during validation, therefore requiring less memory to store the generated state space.

7 Conclusion

We introduced a three stage technique that detects feature interactions. Each stage consists of iterative steps geared towards achieving specific objectives. The first stage produces a base model that satisfies its requirements. Stage two builds on the base model by integrating a single feature. Isolating the feature from others in this stage, allows correct construction and validation of its requirements. Successful completion of stage two results in a modified model that satisfies its original requirements and those of the

---

[14] Of all feature integrations the CFU and BIC prove to be the most complex and resource demanding to verify.

integrated feature. This stage is performed for all features. The final stage allows multiple features to be integrated to a model from stage two. Feature interactions is detected if the modified model does not satisfy any of its original requirements and those of the features integrated.

We demonstrated the effectiveness of the technique using Promela to model the TETRA network and two features. The Xspin toolkit was used to verify and validate the model in every stage. The most important benefit in using the Promela and Xspin combination is the ability to validate models against requirements using linear temporal logic. Since validation forms the heart of our technique, using Promela and Xspin in this manner allows proof of concept.

Acknowledgement

The authors would like to thank Neil Evans, Huma Lodhi and Helen Treharne for their comments on this paper. We also thank Motorola's Paul Baker and Clive Jervis for discussions about the TETRA network.

References

[Eura]   European Telecommunications Standards Institute. *Radio Equipment and Systems (RES); Trans-European Trunked Radio (TETRA); Voice plus Data (V+D); Part 10: Supplementary Services Stage 1; Part 10-04: Call Diversion.* ETS 300 392-10-04.

[Eurb]   European Telecommunications Standards Institute. *Radio Equipment and Systems (RES); Trans-European Trunked Radio (TETRA); Voice plus Data (V+D); Part 11: Supplementary Services (SS) Stage 2; Part 11-19: Barring of Incoming Calls (BIC).* ETS 300 392-11-19.

[Hol90] Gerard J. Holzmann. *Design and validation of computer protocols.* Prentice Hall, 1990. ISBN 0-13-539925-4.

[JP98]   M. Jackson and P.Zave. Distributed Feature Composition: A Virtual Architecture for Telecommunications Services. *IEEE Transactions on Software Engineering,* 24(10):831–847, October 1998.

[KK98]   D.O. Keck and P.J. Kuehn. The Feature and Service Interaction Problem in Telecommunications Systems:A Survey. *IEEE Transactions on Software Engineering,* 24(10):779–796, October 1998.

[LL94]   F. Joe Lin and Yow-Jian Lin. A Building Block Approach to Detecting and Resolving Feature Interaction. In W. Bouma and H. Velthuijsen, editors, *Feature Interactions in Telecommunication Systems,* chapter 6, pages 86–119. IOS Press, 1994.

[MP91]   Zohar Manna and Amir Pnueli. *The Temporal logic of Reactive and Concurrent Systems Specification.* Springer-Verlag, 1991. ISBN 0-387-97664-7 (v. 1).

[SDL]   *Annex F to Recommendation Z.100, (Formal Definition of SDL 92), Dynamic Semantics.*

[TM98]   S. Tsang and E.H. Magill. Learning To Detect and Avoid Run-Time Feature Interactions in Intelligent Networks. *IEEE Transactions on Software Engineering,* 24(10):818–830, October 1998.

[TR95]   ETSI TC-RES. *Radio Equipement and Systems (RES); Trans-European Trunked Radio (TETRA); Voice plus Data (V+D) Part 2: Air Interface (AI).* European Telecommunications Standard, 1995. ETS 300 392-2.

Java PathFinder
A Translator from Java to Promela

Klaus Havelund

NASA Ames Research Center
Recom Technologies
Moffett Field, CA, USA
havelund@ptolemy.arc.nasa.gov
http://ase.arc.nasa.gov/havelund

JAVA PATHFINDER [2], JPF, is a prototype translator from JAVA to PROMELA, the modeling language of the SPIN model checker [4]. JPF is a product of a major effort by the Automated Software Engineering group at NASA Ames to make model checking technology part of the software process. Experience has shown that severe bugs can be found in final code using this technique [1], and that automated translation from a programming language to a modeling language like PROMELA can help reducing the effort required.

JPF allows a programmer to annotate his JAVA program with assertions and verify them using the SPIN model checker. In addition, deadlocks can be identified. An assertion is written as a call to an `assert` method defined in a predefined JAVA class, the `Verify` class. The argument to the method is a boolean JAVA expression over the state variables. The `Verify` class contains additional temporal logic methods which allow to state temporal logic properties about static variables. Hence JAVA itself is used as the specification language. An application of JPF is described elsewhere in the proceedings [3].

A respectable subset of JAVA is covered by JPF, including dynamic object creation, object references as first class citizens, inheritance, exceptions, interrupts, and perhaps most importantly: thread operations. Among major concepts not translated are: packages, method overloading and overriding, method recursion, strings, and floating point numbers. Finally, the class library is not translated.

References

1. K. Havelund, M. Lowry, and J. Penix. Formal Analysis of a Space Craft Controller using SPIN. In G. Holzmann, E. Najm, and A. Serhrouchni, editors, *Proceedings of the 4th SPIN workshop, Paris, France*, November 1998. To appear in IEEE Transactions of Software Engineering.
2. K. Havelund and T. Pressburger. Model Checking Java Programs using Java PathFinder. Appearing in *International Journal on Software Tools for Technology Transfer* (STTT), 1999.
3. K. Havelund and J. Skakkebæk. Applying Model Checking in Java Verification. In R. Gerth, G. Holzmann, and S. Leue, editors, *Proceedings of the 6th SPIN workshop (these proceedings), Toulouse, France*, September 1999.
4. G. Holzmann. *The Design and Validation of Computer Protocols*. Prentice Hall, 1991.

VIP: A Visual Interface for Promela

Moataz Kamel and Stefan Leue

University of Waterloo, Waterloo, Ontario, Canada, N2L 3G1,
[M2Kamel|SLeue]@uwaterloo.ca,
WWW home page: http://www.fee.uwaterloo.ca/~[m2kamel|sleue]

The *Visual Interface to Promela* (VIP) tool is a Java based graphical front end to the Promela specification language and the SPIN model checker [2]. VIP supports a visual formalism called v-Promela [3] which extends the Promela language with a graphical notation to describe structural and behavioral aspects of a system. v-Promela also introduces hierarchical modeling and object-oriented concepts. The formalism is largely consistent with the UML-RT proposal [5] which evolved from the Real-Time Object-Oriented Modeling (ROOM) language [4] and the Unified Modeling Language (UML) [1]. The structural part of a v-Promela model consists of structural elements called *capsules* and describes their interconnection and hierarchical nesting using a variant of UML collaboration diagrams. The behavioral aspects of a v-Promela model are described by hierarchical communicating extended finite state machines and support such features as group transitions and optional return to history from group transitions.

The VIP tool provides a graphical v-Promela editor supporting point and click editing of v-Promela structure diagrams and hierarchically nested state machines. The editor incorporates syntax checking to warn the user about incorrect use of v-Promela graphical syntax. Storage and retrieval of models is made possible using Java serialization. The tool also has a fully integrated v-Promela compiler which generates Promela code. The resulting Promela models can be analyzed using existing SPIN technology. VIP requires the Java 1.2 Runtime Environment which is available for a variety of operating systems. VIP is not currently publicly available, but expected to be released in the near future.

References

1. Rational Software Corporation. UML notation guide. Research report, 1997. See also http://www.rational.com/uml. Also The Object Management Group, document number ad/07-08-05.
2. G.J. Holzmann. The model checker Spin. *IEEE Trans. on Software Engineering*, 23(5):279–295, May 1997. Special issue on Formal Methods in Software Practice.
3. S. Leue and G. Holzmann. v-Promela: A Visual, Object-Oriented Language for SPIN. In *Proceedings of the 2nd IEEE Symposium on Object-Oriented Real-Time Distributed Computing (ISORC'99), Saint Malo, France*, pages 14 – 23. IEEE Computer Society Press, May 1999.
4. B. Selic, G. Gullekson, and P.T. Ward. *Real-Time Object-Oriented Modelling*. John Wiley & Sons, Inc., 1994.
5. B. Selic and J. Rumbaugh. Using UML for modeling complex real-time systems. www.objectime.com/new/uml/index.html, March 1998.

Events in Property Patterns

Marsha Chechik and Dimitrie O. Păun

Department of Computer Science, University of Toronto,
Toronto, ON M5S 3G4, Canada.
Email: {chechik,dimi}@cs.toronto.edu

Abstract. A pattern-based approach to the presentation, codification and reuse of property specifications for finite-state verification was proposed by Dwyer and his colleagues in [4, 3]. The patterns enable non-experts to read and write formal specifications for realistic systems and facilitate easy conversion of specifications between formalisms, such as LTL, CTL, QRE. In this paper we extend the pattern system with *events* — changes of values of variables in the context of LTL.

1 Introduction

Temporal logics (TL) (e.g., [1], [5], [9], [16], [12]) have received a lot of attention in the research community. Not only are they useful for specifying properties of systems, recent advances in model-checking allow effective automatic checking of models of systems against such properties, e.g. using tools like SPIN [8] and SMV [13].

One important obstacle to using temporal logic is the ability to express complex properties correctly. To remedy this problem, Dwyer and his colleagues have proposed a pattern-based approach to the presentation, codification and reuse of property specifications. The system allows patterns like "P is absent between Q and S" or "S precedes P between Q and R" to be easily expressed in and translated between linear-time temporal logic (LTL) [11], computational tree logic (CTL) [2], quantified regular expressions (QRE) [15], and other state-based and event-based formalisms. Dwyer et. al. also performed a large-scale study in which specifications containing over 500 temporal properties were collected and analyzed. They noticed that over 90% of these could be classified under one of the proposed patterns [4].

In earlier work [20], we used the Promela/SPIN framework to model the Production Cell system. We attempted to use the pattern-base approach to help us formalize properties of this system in LTL. However, we found that the approach could not be applied directly, because our properties used *events* — changes of values of variables, e.g., "magnet should become deactivated", which we wanted to formalize as "magnet is active now and will be inactive in the next state". We called such events *edges*.

LTL is a temporal logic comprised of propositional formulas and temporal connectives □ ("always"), ◇ ("eventually"), ∘ ("next"), and $\mathcal{U}$ ("until"). The first three operators are unary, while the last one is binary. $\mathcal{U}$ is the *strong*

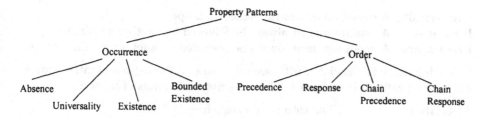

Fig. 1. A Pattern Hierarchy.

until; that is, it requires that B actually happen sometime in the future. In this context, we define edges as follows:

$$\uparrow A = \neg A \wedge \circ A \text{ — up or rising edge}$$
$$\downarrow A = A \wedge \circ \neg A \text{ — down or falling edge}$$
$$\updownarrow A = \uparrow A \vee \downarrow A \text{ — any edge}$$

LTL formulas containing events may have problems caused by the use of the "next" operator in the definition of edges. Temporal formulas that make use of "next" may not be *closed under stuttering*, i.e. their interpretation may be modified by transitions that leave the system in the same state ("stutter"). As we discuss later in the paper, this is an essential property for effective use of temporal formulas.

Model-checking allows relatively novice users to verify correctness of their systems quickly and effectively. However, it is essential that these users are able to specify correctness criteria in the appropriate temporal logic. For example, effective use of SPIN [8] depends critically on being able to express such criteria in LTL. Under the presence of events, it is often quite complex (see [19] for a thorough discussion). In this paper we extend the properties of Dwyer et. al. to include events in LTL properties. The rest of the paper is organized as follows: Section 2 overviews the pattern-based system. Section 3 presents our extension to the pattern-based system and discusses the extension process. Section 4 contains an informal summary of our treatment of closure under stuttering and presents a set of theorems that allow syntactic checking of formulas for this property. In addition, it shows how to use these theorems to prove that our extensions of the pattern-based system are closed under stuttering. Section 5 concludes the paper.

2 Overview of the Pattern-Based Approach

In this section we survey the pattern-based approach. For more information, please refer to [3, 4]. The patterns are organized hierarchically based on their semantics, as illustrated in Figure 1. Some of the patterns are described below:

Absence   A condition does not occur within a scope;
Existence A condition must occur within a scope;

Universality A condition occurs throughout a scope;
Response   A condition must always be followed by another within a scope;
Precedence A condition must always be preceded by another within a scope.

Each pattern is associated with several *scopes* — the regions of interest over which the condition is evaluated. There are five basic kinds of scopes:

A. Global   The entire state sequence;
B. Before R The state sequence up to condition R;
C. After Q The state sequence after condition Q;
D. Between Q **and** R The part of the state sequence between condition Q and condition R;
E. After Q **Until** R Similar to the previous one, except that the designated part of the state sequence continues even if the second condition does not occur.

These scopes are depicted in Figure 2. The scopes were initially defined in [4] to be closed-left, open-right intervals, although it is also possible to define other combinations, such as open-left, closed-right intervals.

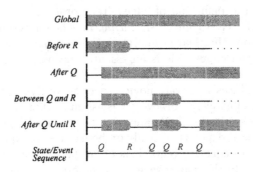

Fig. 2. Pattern Scopes.

For example, an LTL formulation of the property "S precedes P between Q and R" (**Precedence** pattern with "between Q and R" scope) is:

$$\Box((Q \wedge \Diamond R) \Rightarrow (\neg P \, \mathcal{U} \, (S \vee R)))$$

Even though the pattern system is formalism-independent [3], in this paper we are only concerned with the expression of properties in LTL.

S

3   Edges and the Pattern-Based System

LTL is a state-based formalism, and thus the original pattern system does not specify the expression of events in LTL. In this section we show how to include reasoning about events to the pattern system. These events can be used for specifying conditions as well as for defining the bounding scopes.

We start by introducing some notation that allows us a more compact representation of properties. We define the *weak* version of "until" as:

$$A \, W \, B = \Box A \vee (A \, \mathcal{U} \, B)$$

That is, we no longer require B to happen in the future; if it does not, than A should hold indefinitely. Another useful operator is "precedes":

$$A \, \mathcal{P} \, B = \neg(\neg A \, \mathcal{U} \, B)$$

That is, we want A to hold *before* B does. Note that in this case B may never happen. Also, we use $y \lhd x \rhd z$ to indicate **if** x **then** y **else** z, or $(x \wedge y) \vee (\neg x \wedge z)$. Finally, we write $\top$ and $\bot$ to indicate boolean values *true* and *false*, respectively.

Since our extension involves edges, we give a few relevant properties below:

$$\Box{\uparrow}A = \bot \tag{1}$$
$$\Box{\downarrow}A = \bot \tag{2}$$
$${\uparrow}A \, \mathcal{U} \, B = B \vee ({\uparrow}A \wedge \circ B) \tag{3}$$

Properties (1) and (2) indicate that edges of the same type cannot occur in every state of the system, whereas property (3) allows us to replace an "until" with a propositional expression.

We have explored the concept of edges in [19, 18], and list some of edge properties in the Appendix.

3.1 Extending the Pattern System

Introducing edges into the patterns generates an explosion in the number of formulas: conditions can be state-based or edge-based, inclusive or exclusive, and the interval ends can be either opened or closed. Our extension does not include all the possibilities, but rather a significant and representative set of them, as discussed below.

We were able to extend five of the nine patterns: **Absence** (Figure 3), **Existence** (Figure 4), **Universality** (Figure 5), **Response** (Figure 7), **Precedence** (Figure 6). For each of the five scopes, we list four formulas corresponding to the four combinations of state-based and edge-based conditions and interval bounds we have considered:

0. P, S — states, $\quad Q, R$ — states;
1. P, S — states, $\quad Q, R$ — up edges;
2. P, S — up edges, Q, R — states;
3. P, S — up edges, Q, R — up edges.

Combination 0 corresponds to the original formulation of [3], where all of P, S, Q and R are state-based. The remaining three combinations are our extensions

A. Globally	B. Before R	C. After Q
0. $\Box \neg P$	0. $\Diamond R \Rightarrow (\neg P\,\mathcal{U}\,R)$	0. $\Box(Q \Rightarrow \Box \neg P)$
1. $\Box \neg P$	1. $\Diamond \uparrow R \Rightarrow (\uparrow R\,\mathcal{P}\,P)$	1. $\Box(\uparrow Q \Rightarrow \circ \Box \neg P)$
2. $\Box \neg \uparrow P$	2. $\Diamond R \Rightarrow (\neg \uparrow P\,\mathcal{U}\,R)$	2. $\Box(Q \Rightarrow \Box \neg \uparrow P)$
3. $\Box \neg \uparrow P$	3. $\Diamond \uparrow R \Rightarrow (\neg \uparrow P\,\mathcal{U}\,\uparrow R)$	3. $\Box(\uparrow Q \Rightarrow \Box \neg \uparrow P)$

D. Between Q and R	E. After Q Until R
0. $\Box((Q \wedge \Diamond R) \Rightarrow (\neg P\,\mathcal{U}\,R))$	0. $\Box((Q \wedge \Diamond P) \Rightarrow (\neg P\,\mathcal{U}\,R))$
1. $\Box((\uparrow Q \wedge \Diamond \uparrow R \wedge \neg \uparrow R) \Rightarrow \circ(\uparrow R\,\mathcal{P}\,P))$	1. $\Box((\uparrow Q \wedge \neg \uparrow R \wedge \circ \Diamond P) \Rightarrow \circ(\uparrow R\,\mathcal{P}\,P))$
2. $\Box((Q \wedge \Diamond R) \Rightarrow (\neg \uparrow P\,\mathcal{U}\,R))$	2. $\Box(Q \Rightarrow (\neg \uparrow P\,\mathcal{W}\,R))$
3. $\Box((\uparrow Q \wedge \Diamond \uparrow R) \Rightarrow (\neg \uparrow P\,\mathcal{U}\,\uparrow R))$	3. $\Box(\uparrow Q \Rightarrow (\neg \uparrow P\,\mathcal{W}\,\uparrow R))$

Fig. 3. Formulations of the **Absence** Pattern

to the pattern system. We assume that multiple events can happen simultaneously, but only consider closed-left, open-right intervals, as in the original system. Also, we consider events P and S to be exclusive in the **Precedence** pattern and inclusive in the **Response** pattern[1]. We note, however, that it is perfectly possible to have formulas for all other combinations of interval bounds. Down edges can be substituted for up edges without changing the formulas. We have modified several of the 0-formulas (i.e. state-based conditions and intervals) from their original formulations of [3] to remove assumptions of interleaving and make them consistent with the closed-left, open-right intervals. Note that in the case of the **Universality** pattern, we do not list formulas for edge-based events as edges cannot be universally present (by (1) and (2)).

The four patterns that we did not extend are: **Bounded Existence**, **Precedence Chain**, **Response Chain**, **Constrained Chain**. While we considered the **Bounded Existence** pattern to be too convoluted to be useful in practice and thus not worth the effort of extending, the other three patterns were not extended for reasons that will become apparent in the next Section.

3.2 Discussion

What is involved in adding events to a property? Consider specifying the absence pattern under the "Between Q and R scope" where Q and R are (up) edges. The original formula is

$$\Box(Q \wedge \Diamond R \Rightarrow \neg P\,\mathcal{U}\,R)$$

This formula does not include P when Q and R occur simultaneously. This behavior is desired since the founding interval is half open and thus becomes empty when the two ends coincide. If we want to transform the condition and the interval bounds into edges, we may be tempted to use the formula:

$$\Box(\uparrow Q \wedge \Diamond \uparrow R \Rightarrow \neg P\,\mathcal{U}\,\uparrow R)$$

---

[1] Two events are considered exclusive if they are not allowed to happen at the same time, and inclusive otherwise.

A. Globally	B. Before R	C. After Q
0. $\Diamond P$	0. $\Diamond R \Rightarrow (P \mathcal{P} R)$	0. $\Diamond Q \Rightarrow \Diamond(Q \wedge \Diamond P)$
1. $\Diamond P$	1. $\Diamond \uparrow R \Rightarrow (\neg \uparrow R \, \mathcal{U} \, P)$	1. $\Diamond \uparrow Q \Rightarrow \Diamond(\uparrow Q \wedge \circ \Diamond P)$
2. $\Diamond \uparrow P$	2. $\Diamond R \Rightarrow (\uparrow P \, \mathcal{P} \, R)$	2. $\Diamond Q \Rightarrow \Diamond(Q \wedge \Diamond \uparrow P)$
3. $\Diamond \uparrow P$	3. $\Diamond \uparrow R \Rightarrow (\uparrow P \, \mathcal{P} \uparrow R)$	3. $\Diamond \uparrow Q \Rightarrow \Diamond(\uparrow Q \wedge \Diamond \uparrow P)$

D. Between Q and R

0. $\Box((Q \wedge \Diamond R) \Rightarrow ((P \mathcal{P} R) \wedge \neg R))$
1. $\Box((\uparrow Q \wedge \Diamond \uparrow R) \Rightarrow (\circ(\neg \uparrow R \, \mathcal{U} \, P) \wedge \neg \uparrow R))$
2. $\Box((Q \wedge \Diamond R) \Rightarrow ((\uparrow P \, \mathcal{P} \, R) \wedge \neg R))$
3. $\Box((\uparrow Q \wedge \Diamond \uparrow R) \Rightarrow ((\uparrow P \, \mathcal{P} \uparrow R) \wedge \neg \uparrow R))$

E. After Q Until R

0. $\Box(Q \Rightarrow (P \mathcal{P} R) \wedge \neg R \lhd \Diamond R \rhd \Diamond P)$
1. $\Box(\uparrow Q \Rightarrow \circ(\neg \uparrow R \, \mathcal{U} \, P) \wedge \neg \uparrow R)$
2. $\Box(Q \Rightarrow (\uparrow P \, \mathcal{P} \, R) \wedge \neg R \lhd \Diamond R \rhd \Diamond \uparrow P)$
3. $\Box(\uparrow Q \Rightarrow (\uparrow P \, \mathcal{P} \uparrow R) \wedge \neg \uparrow R \lhd \Diamond \uparrow R \rhd \Diamond \uparrow P)$

Fig. 4. Formulations of the **Existence** Pattern

A. Globally	B. Before R	C. After Q
0. $\Box P$	0. $\Diamond R \Rightarrow (P \, \mathcal{U} \, R)$	0. $\Box(Q \Rightarrow \Box P)$
1. $\Box P$	1. $\Diamond \uparrow R \Rightarrow (\uparrow R \, \mathcal{P} \, \neg P)$	1. $\Box(\uparrow Q \Rightarrow \circ \Box P)$

D. Between Q and R	E. After Q Until R
0. $\Box((Q \wedge \Diamond R) \Rightarrow (P \, \mathcal{U} \, R))$	0. $\Box(Q \Rightarrow P \, \mathcal{W} \, R)$
1. $\Box((\uparrow Q \wedge \Diamond \uparrow R \wedge \neg \uparrow R) \Rightarrow \circ(\uparrow R \, \mathcal{P} \, \neg P))$	1. $\Box(\uparrow Q \Rightarrow \circ(\uparrow R \, \mathcal{P} \, \neg P) \lhd \Diamond \uparrow R \rhd \Box P)$

Fig. 5. Formulations of the **Universality** Pattern

However, in order to effectively express properties containing edges, we need to realize that an edge is detected just *before* it occurs, as illustrated in Figure 8 That is, $\uparrow A$ becomes true in the state where A is false.

Thus, our formula has a problem: we start testing P *before* the edge in Q because this is when we detect $\uparrow Q$. We need to fix this by testing P *after* the edge in Q:

$$\Box(\uparrow Q \wedge \Diamond \uparrow R \Rightarrow \circ(\neg P \, \mathcal{U} \uparrow R))$$

We fixed the above problem but introduced another: the new formula does not work correctly when $\uparrow Q$ and $\uparrow P$ occur simultaneously. This happens because we make sure that $\uparrow R$ occurs one state too early. We need to fix the antecedent by making sure that the interval is non-empty:

$$\Box(\uparrow Q \wedge \neg \uparrow R \wedge \Diamond \uparrow R \Rightarrow \circ(\neg P \, \mathcal{U} \uparrow R))$$

Unfortunately, the resulting formula is still incorrect: if P and $\uparrow R$ occur simultaneously, then that occurrence of P will be ignored since $\uparrow R$ is detected in the

A. Globally	B. Before R
0. $\Diamond P \Rightarrow S \,\mathcal{P}\, P$	0. $\Diamond R \Rightarrow (\neg P \,\mathcal{U}\, ((S \wedge \neg P) \vee R))$
1. $\Diamond P \Rightarrow S \,\mathcal{P}\, P$	1. $\Diamond \uparrow R \Rightarrow ((\neg \uparrow R \,\mathcal{U}\, P) \Rightarrow (S \,\mathcal{P}\, P))$
2. $\Diamond \uparrow P \Rightarrow \uparrow S \,\mathcal{P}\, \uparrow P$	2. $\Diamond R \Rightarrow \neg \uparrow P \,\mathcal{U}\, ((\uparrow S \wedge \neg \uparrow P) \vee R)$
3. $\Diamond \uparrow P \Rightarrow \uparrow S \,\mathcal{P}\, \uparrow P$	3. $\Diamond \uparrow R \Rightarrow ((\uparrow P \,\mathcal{P}\, \uparrow R) \Rightarrow (\uparrow S \,\mathcal{P}\, \uparrow P))$

C. After Q

0. $\Diamond Q \Rightarrow \Diamond(Q \wedge (\Diamond P \Rightarrow (S \,\mathcal{P}\, P)))$
1. $\Diamond \uparrow Q \Rightarrow \Diamond(\uparrow Q \wedge \circ(\Diamond P \Rightarrow (S \,\mathcal{P}\, P)))$
2. $\Diamond Q \Rightarrow \Diamond(Q \wedge (\Diamond \uparrow P \Rightarrow (\uparrow S \,\mathcal{P}\, \uparrow P)))$
3. $\Diamond \uparrow Q \Rightarrow \Diamond(\uparrow Q \wedge (\Diamond \uparrow P \Rightarrow (\uparrow S \,\mathcal{P}\, \uparrow P)))$

D. Between Q and R

0. $\Box((Q \wedge \Diamond R) \Rightarrow (\neg P \,\mathcal{U}\, ((S \wedge \neg P) \vee R)))$
1. $\Box((\uparrow Q \wedge \neg \uparrow R \circ \Diamond \uparrow R) \Rightarrow \circ((\neg \uparrow R \,\mathcal{U}\, P) \Rightarrow (S \,\mathcal{P}\, P)))$
2. $\Box((Q \wedge \Diamond R) \Rightarrow (\neg \uparrow P \,\mathcal{U}\, ((\uparrow S \wedge \neg \uparrow P) \vee R)))$
3. $\Box((\uparrow Q \wedge \neg \uparrow R \circ \Diamond \uparrow R) \Rightarrow \circ((\uparrow P \,\mathcal{P}\, \uparrow R) \Rightarrow (\uparrow S \,\mathcal{P}\, \uparrow P)))$

E. After Q Until R

0. $\Box(Q \Rightarrow (\Diamond P \Rightarrow \neg P \,\mathcal{U}\, ((S \wedge \neg P) \vee R)))$
1. $\Box(\uparrow Q \Rightarrow \circ(\Diamond P \Rightarrow ((\neg \uparrow R \,\mathcal{U}\, P) \Rightarrow (S \,\mathcal{P}\, P))))$
2. $\Box(Q \Rightarrow (\Diamond P \Rightarrow \neg \uparrow P \,\mathcal{U}\, ((\uparrow S \wedge \neg \uparrow P) \vee R)))$
3. $\Box(\uparrow Q \Rightarrow \circ(\Diamond P \Rightarrow ((\uparrow P \,\mathcal{P}\, \uparrow R) \Rightarrow (\uparrow S \,\mathcal{P}\, \uparrow P))))$

Fig. 6. Formulations of the **Precedence** Pattern

state *before* the edge. This is not the intended behavior as the state before the edge is considered part of the interval. We need to fix it one more time:

$$\Box(\uparrow Q \wedge \neg \uparrow R \wedge \Diamond \uparrow R \Rightarrow \circ \neg(\neg \uparrow R \,\mathcal{U}\, P))$$

or better yet:

$$\Box(\uparrow Q \wedge \neg \uparrow R \wedge \Diamond \uparrow R \Rightarrow \circ(\uparrow R \,\mathcal{P}\, P))$$

Note that we can avoid many complications of the sort discussed above if we add the "previous" modality, Y. Using this new operator, we can detect edges just *after* they occur: $a \wedge \neg Y a$ (see Figure 8). Although having the "previous" operator can potentially simplify a number of properties, it is currently not supported by SPIN.

4 Closure Under Stuttering

The extension of the pattern system presented in Section 3, is an important development, and we hope that the resulting patterns provide real value to the end user. Still, can practitioners use our extensions directly, without worrying about any unexpected behavior?

A. Globally	B. Before R

0. $\Box(P \Rightarrow \Diamond S)$
1. $\Box(P \Rightarrow \Diamond S)$
2. $\Box(\uparrow P \Rightarrow \Diamond \uparrow S)$
3. $\Box(\uparrow P \Rightarrow \Diamond \uparrow S)$

0. $\Diamond R \Rightarrow (P \Rightarrow (\neg R\, \mathcal{U}\, S))\, \mathcal{U}\, R$
1. $\Diamond \uparrow R \Rightarrow ((P \Rightarrow (\neg \uparrow R\, \mathcal{U}\, S)) \wedge \neg \uparrow R)\, \mathcal{U}\, (\uparrow R \wedge (P \Rightarrow Q))$
2. $\Diamond R \Rightarrow (\uparrow P \Rightarrow (\neg R\, \mathcal{U}\, \uparrow S))\, \mathcal{U}\, R$
3. $\Diamond \uparrow R \Rightarrow (\uparrow P \Rightarrow (\neg \uparrow R\, \mathcal{U}\, \uparrow S))\, \mathcal{U}\, \uparrow R$

C. After Q

0. $\Box(Q \Rightarrow \Box(P \Rightarrow \Diamond S))$
1. $\Box(\uparrow Q \Rightarrow \circ\Box(P \Rightarrow \Diamond S))$
2. $\Box(Q \Rightarrow \Box(\uparrow P \Rightarrow \Diamond \uparrow S))$
3. $\Box(\uparrow Q \Rightarrow \Box(\uparrow P \Rightarrow \Diamond \uparrow S))$

D. Between Q and R

0. $\Box((Q \wedge \Diamond R) \Rightarrow ((P \Rightarrow (\neg R\, \mathcal{U}\, S))\, \mathcal{U}\, R))$
1. $\Box((\uparrow Q \wedge \Diamond \uparrow R \wedge \neg \uparrow R) \Rightarrow \circ(((P \Rightarrow (\neg \uparrow R\, \mathcal{U}\, S)) \wedge \neg \uparrow R)\, \mathcal{U}\, (\uparrow R \wedge (P \Rightarrow Q))))$
2. $\Box((Q \wedge \Diamond R) \Rightarrow ((\uparrow P \Rightarrow (\neg R\, \mathcal{U}\, \uparrow S))\, \mathcal{U}\, R))$
3. $\Box((\uparrow Q \wedge \Diamond \uparrow R) \Rightarrow ((\uparrow P \Rightarrow (\neg \uparrow R\, \mathcal{U}\, \uparrow S))\, \mathcal{U}\, \uparrow R))$

E. After Q Until R

0. $\Box(Q \Rightarrow (P \Rightarrow (\neg R\, \mathcal{U}\, S))\, \mathcal{W}\, R)$
1. $\Box(\uparrow Q \Rightarrow \circ(((P \Rightarrow (\neg \uparrow R\, \mathcal{U}\, S)) \wedge \neg \uparrow R)\, \mathcal{W}\, (\uparrow R \wedge (P \Rightarrow Q))))$
2. $\Box(\uparrow Q \Rightarrow (\uparrow P \Rightarrow (\neg R\, \mathcal{U}\, \uparrow S))\, \mathcal{W}\, R)$
3. $\Box(\uparrow Q \Rightarrow (\uparrow P \Rightarrow (\neg \uparrow R\, \mathcal{U}\, \uparrow S))\, \mathcal{W}\, \uparrow R)$

Fig. 7. Formulations of the **Response** Pattern

The patterns that we have created in the previous section contain the "next" operator. Thus, they may not be *closed under stuttering*. Intuitively, a formula is closed under stuttering when its interpretation is not modified by transitions that leave the system in the same state. For example, a formula $\Box a$ is closed under stuttering because no matter how much we repeat states, we cannot change the value of a. On the other hand, the formula $\circ a$ is not closed under stuttering. We can see that by considering a state sequence in which a is true in the first state and false in the second. Then $\circ a$ is false if we evaluate it on this sequence, and true if we repeat the first state.

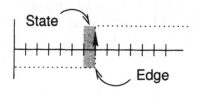

Fig. 8. Edge-detecting state

Closure under stuttering is an essential property of temporal formulas to ensure basic separation between abstraction levels and to enable powerful partial-order reduction algorithms utilized in mechanized checking, e.g. [8]. This property can be easily guaranteed for a subset of LTL that does not include the "next" operator [10]; however, events cannot be expressed in this subset. Determining whether an LTL formula is closed under stuttering is hard: the problem has been shown to be PSPACE-complete [17]. A computationally feasible algorithm which can identify a subclass of closed under stuttering formulas has been proposed in [7] but have not yet been implemented; without an implementation, one can not say how often the subclass of formulas identified by the algorithm is encountered in practice. Several temporal logics that try to solve the problem have been proposed. Such logics, e.g. TLA [10] and MTL [14], restrict the language so that all formulas expressed in it are, by definition, closed under stuttering. However, it is not clear if these languages are expressive enough for practical use.

In this section we briefly present a set of theorems that allow syntactic reasoning about closure under stuttering in LTL formulas and show how to apply them to our extensions of the pattern system. For a more complete treatment of closure under stuttering, please refer to [18, 19].

4.1 Formal Definition

The notation below is adopted from [6]. A sequence (or string) is a succession of elements joined by semicolons. For example, we write the sequence comprised of the first five natural numbers, in order, as $0; 1; 2; 3; 4$ or, more compactly, as $0; ..5$ (note the left-closed, right-open interval). We can obtain an item of the sequence by subscripting: $(0; 2; 4; 5)_2 = 4$. When the subscript is a sequence, we obtain a subsequence: $(0; 3; 1; 5; 8; 2)_{1;2;3} = (0; 3; 1; 5; 8; 2)_{1;..4} = 3; 1; 5$. A state is modeled by a function that maps variables to their values, so the value of variable a in state s_0 is $s_0(a)$. We denote the set of all infinite sequences of states as $stseq$, and the set of natural numbers as $\mathbb{N}$.

We say that an LTL formula F is closed under stuttering when its interpretation remains the same under state sequences that differ only by repeated states. We denote an interpretation of formula F in state sequence s as $s[\![F]\!]$, and a closed under stuttering formula as $\ll F \gg$. $\ll F \gg$ is formally defined as follows:

Definition 1. $\ll F \gg = \forall s \in stseq \cdot \forall i \in \mathbb{N} \cdot s[\![F]\!] = (s_{0;..i}; s_i; s_{i;..\infty})[\![F]\!]$

In other words, given any state sequence s, we can repeat any of its states without changing the interpretation of F. Note that $s_{0;..i}; s_i; s_{i;..\infty}$ is a sequence of states that differs from s only by repeating a state s_i.

4.2 Properties

Here we present several theorems that allow syntactic reasoning about closure under stuttering. First, we note that $\downarrow$ and $\uparrow$ can be used interchangeably when analyzing properties of the form

$$\ll A \gg \; \Rightarrow f(\uparrow A)$$

Thus, in what follows we will only discuss the $\uparrow$-edge.

We start with a few generic properties of closure under stuttering:

$$(const(a) \lor var(a)) \Rightarrow \; \ll a \gg \qquad (4)$$

$$\ll A \gg \; = \; \ll \neg A \gg \qquad (5)$$

$$(\ll A \gg \land \ll B \gg) \Rightarrow \; \ll A \land B \gg \qquad (6)$$

$$(\ll A \gg \land \ll B \gg) \Rightarrow \; \ll A \lor B \gg \qquad (7)$$

$$(\ll A \gg \land \ll B \gg) \Rightarrow \; \ll A \Rightarrow B \gg \qquad (8)$$

$$\ll A \gg \; \Rightarrow \; \ll \Box A \gg \qquad (9)$$

$$\ll A \gg \; \Rightarrow \; \ll \Diamond A \gg \qquad (10)$$

$$(\ll A \gg \land \ll B \gg) \Rightarrow \; \ll A \, \mathcal{U} \, B \gg \qquad (11)$$

For example, (4)-(8) indicate that all propositional formulas are closed under stuttering. The above properties do not include reasoning about formulas that contain the "next" operator. For those, we need the following theorem, proven in [18]:

Theorem 1 (cus-main-thm).

$$(\ll A \gg \land \ll B \gg \land \ll C \gg \land \ll D \gg \land \ll E \gg \land \ll F \gg)$$
$$\Rightarrow$$
$$\ll (\neg \uparrow A \lor \circ B \lor C) \, \mathcal{U} \, (\uparrow D \land \circ E \land F) \gg$$

This theorem establishes an important relationship between the "next" operator, edges, and closure under stuttering. It gives rise to a number of corollaries that we found to be useful in practice.

Property 1

$$(\ll A \gg \land \ll B \gg \land \ll C \gg) \Rightarrow \; \ll \Diamond(\uparrow A \land \circ B \land C) \gg$$

If we take $B = \top$ or $C = \top$ respectively, we obtain two simplified versions:

$$(\ll A \gg \land \ll B \gg) \Rightarrow \; \ll \Diamond(\uparrow A \land B) \gg$$

and

$$(\ll A \gg \land \ll B \gg) \Rightarrow \; \ll \Diamond(\uparrow A \land \circ B) \gg$$

These formulas represent an *existence* property: an event $\uparrow A$ must happen and then B, evaluated before or after the event, should hold.

Property 2

$$(\ll A \gg \land \ll B \gg \land \ll C \gg) \Rightarrow \; \ll \Box(\uparrow A \Rightarrow \circ B \lor C) \gg$$

is similar to Property 1. Its two simplified versions are

$$(\ll A\gg \wedge \ll B\gg) \Rightarrow \ll \Box(\uparrow A \Rightarrow B)\gg$$

and

$$(\ll A\gg \wedge \ll B\gg) \Rightarrow \ll \Box(\uparrow A \Rightarrow \circ B)\gg$$

They express a *universality* property: whenever an event $\uparrow A$ happens, B, evaluated right before or right after the event, will hold.

4.3 Closure Under Stuttering and the Pattern System

All properties of Figures 3-7 have been shown to be closed under stuttering. This was done using general rules of logic and properties identified above. For example, consider checking a property

$$\Box(\uparrow Q \wedge \neg\uparrow R \wedge \Diamond\uparrow R \Rightarrow \circ\neg(\neg\uparrow R \,\mathcal{U}\, P))$$

for closure under stuttering. The proof goes as follows:

$$\ll\Box(\uparrow Q \wedge \neg\uparrow R \wedge \circ\Diamond\uparrow R \Rightarrow \circ\neg(\neg\uparrow R \,\mathcal{U}\, P))\gg$$

by rules of logic and LTL
$$=\quad \ll\Box(\uparrow Q \wedge \neg\uparrow R \Rightarrow \circ(\neg(\neg\uparrow R \,\mathcal{U}\, P) \vee \neg\Diamond\uparrow R))\gg$$

by definition of $\uparrow$ and rules of logic
$$=\quad \ll\Box(\uparrow Q \wedge (R \vee \circ\neg R) \Rightarrow \circ(\neg(\neg\uparrow R \,\mathcal{U}\, P) \vee \neg\Diamond\uparrow R))\gg$$

again, by rules of logic and LTL
$$=\quad \ll\Box((\uparrow Q \wedge R \Rightarrow \circ(\neg(\neg\uparrow R \,\mathcal{U}\, P) \vee \neg\Diamond\uparrow R))) \wedge$$
$$\Box(\uparrow Q \Rightarrow \circ(\neg(\neg\uparrow R \,\mathcal{U}\, P) \vee \neg\Diamond\uparrow R \vee R))\gg$$

distribute $\ll\gg$ over the main conjunction
$$\Leftarrow\quad \ll\Box((\uparrow Q \wedge R \Rightarrow \circ(\neg(\neg\uparrow R \,\mathcal{U}\, P) \vee \neg\Diamond\uparrow R)))\gg \wedge$$
$$\ll\Box(\uparrow Q \Rightarrow \circ(\neg(\neg\uparrow R \,\mathcal{U}\, P) \vee \neg\Diamond\uparrow R \vee R))\gg$$

we can use now Property 2 on both conjuncts
$$\Leftarrow\quad \ll Q\gg \wedge \ll R\gg \wedge \ll\neg(\neg\uparrow R \,\mathcal{U}\, P) \vee \neg\Diamond\uparrow R\gg \wedge$$
$$\ll Q\gg \wedge \ll\neg(\neg\uparrow R \,\mathcal{U}\, P) \vee \neg\Diamond\uparrow R \vee R\gg$$

by rules of logic, (5) and (6)
$$\Leftarrow\quad \ll Q\gg \wedge \ll R\gg \wedge \ll\neg\uparrow R \,\mathcal{U}\, P\gg \wedge \ll\Diamond\uparrow R\gg \wedge$$
$$\ll Q\gg \wedge \ll\neg\uparrow R \,\mathcal{U}\, P\gg \wedge \ll\Diamond\uparrow R\gg \wedge \ll R\gg$$

by Theorem 1 and Property 1 we get
$$\Leftarrow\quad \ll Q\gg \wedge \ll R\gg \wedge \ll R\gg \wedge \ll P\gg \wedge \ll R\gg$$

We have thus proved that

$$(\ll P\gg \wedge \ll Q\gg \wedge \ll R\gg) \Rightarrow \ll\Box(\uparrow Q \wedge \neg\uparrow R \wedge \Diamond\uparrow R \Rightarrow \circ\neg(\neg\uparrow R \,\mathcal{U}\, P))\gg$$

Although the property is fairly complicated, the proof is not long, is completely syntactic, and each step in the proof is easy. Such a proof can potentially be performed by a theorem-prover with minimal help from the user.

As we noted earlier, we did not extend all patterns to include events. The reason is that **Precedence Chain**, **Response Chain** and **Constrained Chain** were not closed under stuttering even in their state-based formulations. Consider, for example, the **Response Chain** pattern under the Global scope, formalized as

$$\Box((S \wedge \circ \Diamond T) \Rightarrow \circ \Diamond (T \wedge \Diamond P))$$

When we evaluate this formula on the state sequence s:

$$
\begin{array}{llll}
 & s_0 & s_1 & s_2 \cdots \\
S & \top & \bot & \bot \cdots \\
T & \top & \bot & \bot \cdots \\
P & \bot & \bot & \bot \cdots
\end{array}
$$

we get $\top$ because the antecedent is always $\bot$. However, if we stutter the first state s_0, we get the sequence $s_0; s$:

$$
\begin{array}{lllll}
 & s_0 & s_0 & s_1 & s_2 \cdots \\
S & \top & \top & \bot & \bot \cdots \\
T & \top & \top & \bot & \bot \cdots \\
P & \bot & \bot & \bot & \bot \cdots
\end{array}
$$

The interpretation of the formula on this sequence is now $\bot$ because the antecedent is $\top$ and the consequent is $\bot$ (since $\Diamond P$ is always $\bot$). As stuttering causes a change in the interpretation of the formula, we can conclude that the formula is not closed under stuttering.

5 Conclusion

In this paper we developed a concept of edges and used it to extend the pattern-based system of Dwyer et. al. to reasoning about events. We have also presented a set of theorems that enable the syntax-based analysis of a large class of formulas for closure under stuttering. This class includes all LTL formulas of the patterns that appeared in this paper. Since research shows that patterns account for 90% of the temporal properties that have been specified so far [4], we believe that our approach is highly applicable to practical problems.

The goal of the pattern-based approach is to enable practitioners to easily codify complex properties into temporal logic. The extensions presented in this paper allow them to express events easily and effectively, without worrying about closure under stuttering. We hope that this work has moved us, as a community, one step closer to making automatic verification more widely usable.

166

References

1. A. Bernstein and P. K. Harter. Proving real time properties of programs with temporal logic. In *Proceedings of the Eight Symposium on Operating Systems Principles*, pages 1–11. ACM, 1981.
2. E.M. Clarke, E.A. Emerson, and A.P. Sistla. "Automatic Verification of Finite-State Concurrent Systems Using Temporal Logic Specifications". *ACM Transactions on Programming Languages and Systems*, 8(2):244–263, April 1986.
3. Matthew B. Dwyer, George S. Avrunin, and James C. Corbett. "Property Specification Patterns for Finite-state Verification". In *Proceedings of 2nd Workshop on Formal Methods in Software Practice*, March 1998.
4. Matthew B. Dwyer, George S. Avrunin, and James C. Corbett. "Patterns in Property Specifications for Finite-State Verification". In *Proceedings of 21st International Conference on Software Engineering*, May 1999.
5. B. T. Hailpern and S. S. Owicki. Modular verification of computer communication protocols. *IEEE Transactions on Communication*, 1(COM-31):56–68, 1983.
6. Eric C. R. Hehner. *A Practical Theory of Programming*. Texts and Monographs in Computer Science. Springer-Verlag, New York, 1993.
7. G. J. Holzmann and O. Kupferman. "Not Checking for Closure under Stuttering". In *Proceedings of SPIN'96*, 1996.
8. G.J. Holzmann. "The Model Checker SPIN". *IEEE Transactions on Software Engineering*, 23(5):279–295, May 1997.
9. Leslie Lamport. Specifying concurrent program modules. *ACM Transactions of Programming Languages and Systems*, 5:190–222, 1983.
10. Leslie Lamport. "The Temporal Logic of Actions". *ACM Transactions on Programming Languages and Systems*, 16:872–923, May 1994.
11. Z. Manna and A. Pnueli. "Tools and Rules for the Practicing Verifier". Technical Report STAN-CS-90-1321, Department of Computer Science, Stanford University, 1990. Appeared in *Carnegie Mellon Computer Science: A 25 year Commemorative*.
12. Z. Manna and A. Pnueli. *The Temporal Logic of Reactive and Concurrent Systems*. Springer-Verlag, 1992.
13. K.L. McMillan. *Symbolic Model Checking*. Kluwer Academic, 1993.
14. Abdelillah Mokkedem and Dominique Méry. A stuttering closed temporal logic for modular reasoning about concurrent programs. In *Temporal Logic: First International Conference, ICTL '94*, number 827 in Lecture Notes in Artificial Intelligence, Berlin, July 1994. Springer-Verlag.
15. Kurt M. Olender and Leon J. Osterweil. "Cecil: A Sequencing Constraint Language for Automatic Static Analysis Generation". *IEEE Transactions on Software Engineering*, 16(3):268–280, March 1990.
16. J. S. Ostroff. *Temporal Logic of Real-Time Systems*. Advanced Software Development Series. Research Studies Press (John Wiley & Sons), 1990.
17. Doron Peled, Thomas Wilke, and Pierre Wolper. "An Algorithmic Approach for Checking Closure Properties of ω-Regular Languages". In *Proceedings of CONCUR '96: 7th International Conference on Concurrency Theory*, August 1996.
18. Dimitrie O. Păun. Closure under stuttering in temporal formulas. Master's thesis, Department of Computer Science, University of Toronto, Toronto, Ontario M5S 3G4, CANADA, 1999. April.
19. Dimitrie O. Păun and Marsha Chechik. "Events in Linear-Time Properties". In *Proceedings of 4th International Conference on Requirements Engineering*, June 1999.

20. Dimitrie O. Păun, Marsha Chechik, and Bernd Biechelle. "Production Cell Revisited". In *Proceedings of SPIN'98*, November 1998.

A Properties of Edges

We list a few representative properties of edges here. Their proofs appear in [18]. [18] also contains a comprehensive study of the concept of edges.

Edges are related:

$$\uparrow \neg A = \downarrow A \tag{12}$$

$$\downarrow \neg A = \uparrow A \tag{13}$$

$$\updownarrow \neg A = \updownarrow A \tag{14}$$

Edges interact with the boolean operators as follows:

$$\uparrow(A \wedge B) = (\uparrow A \wedge \circ B) \vee (\uparrow B \wedge \circ A) \tag{15}$$

$$\uparrow(A \vee B) = (\uparrow A \wedge \neg B) \vee (\uparrow B \wedge \neg A) \tag{16}$$

$$\downarrow(A \wedge B) = (\downarrow A \wedge B) \vee (\downarrow B \wedge A) \tag{17}$$

$$\downarrow(A \vee B) = (\downarrow A \wedge \circ \neg B) \vee (\downarrow B \wedge \neg \circ A) \tag{18}$$

Edges interact with each other:

$$\downarrow\downarrow A = \downarrow A \tag{19}$$

$$\downarrow\uparrow A = \uparrow A \tag{20}$$

$$\uparrow\downarrow A = \circ\downarrow A \tag{21}$$

$$\uparrow\uparrow A = \circ\uparrow A \tag{22}$$

Edges interact with temporal operators as follows:

$$\uparrow\circ A = \circ\uparrow A \tag{23}$$

$$\downarrow\circ A = \circ\downarrow A \tag{24}$$

$$\uparrow\Box A = \uparrow A \wedge \circ\Box A \tag{25}$$

$$\downarrow\Box A = \bot \tag{26}$$

$$\uparrow\Diamond A = \bot \tag{27}$$

$$\downarrow\Diamond A = \downarrow A \wedge \circ\Box\neg A \tag{28}$$

$$\uparrow(A \, \mathcal{U} \, B) = \neg(A \vee B) \wedge \circ(A \, \mathcal{U} \, B) \tag{29}$$

$$\downarrow(A \, \mathcal{U} \, B) = B \wedge \neg\circ(A \, \mathcal{U} \, B) \tag{30}$$

Assume-Guarantee Model Checking of Software: A Comparative Case Study *

Corina S. Păsăreanu, Matthew B. Dwyer, and Michael Huth

Department of Computing and Information Sciences
Kansas State University, Manhattan, KS 66506, USA
{pcorina,dwyer,huth}@cis.ksu.edu

Abstract. A variety of assume-guarantee model checking approaches have been proposed in the literature. In this paper, we describe several possible implementations of those approaches for checking properties of software components (*units*) using SPIN and SMV model checkers. Model checking software units requires, in general, the definition of an environment which establishes the run-time context in which the unit executes. We describe how implementations of such environments can be synthesized from specifications of assumed environment behavior written in LTL. Those environments can then be used to check properties that the software unit must guarantee which can be written in LTL or ACTL. We report on several experiments that provide evidence about the relative performance of the different assume-guarantee approaches.

1 Introduction

Model checking is maturing into an effective technique for validating and verifying properties of complex systems and is beginning to be included as part of system quality assurance activities. While most of the practical impact of model checking has been in the domains of hardware and communication protocols, the techniques and tools that support model checking are beginning to see some application to software systems.

It is well-known that software defects are less costly the earlier they are removed in the development process. Towards this end, a number of researchers have worked on applying model checking to artifacts that appear throughout the software life-cycle, such as requirements [2], architectures [23], designs [16], and source code [7]. Source code, of course, is not a monolithic entity that is developed at one time. Source code evolves over time with different components, or *units*, reaching maturity at different points. Software units come in many different types. In well-designed software, a unit defines a layer of functionality with a narrow interface and a mechanism for hiding the details of its implementation from direct external access. Units may be invoked by other units through the operations of their interface and they may in turn invoke operations of other

---

* This work was supported in part by NSF and DARPA under grants CCR-9633388, CCR-9703094, and CCR-9708184 and by NASA under grant NAG-02-1209.

units; Java classes or Ada packages or tasks are examples of units. Testing units in isolation involves the definition of program components that invoke the operations of the unit, a *driver*, and that implement the operations used by the unit, a *stub*, in such a way that the behavior of the unit is exercised in some desired fashion. Stubs and drivers can be defined to also represent *parallel contexts*. Parallel contexts represent those portions of an application that execute in parallel with and engage in inter-task communication with the procedures and tasks of the software unit under test. Standard practice in modern software development is to begin the process of unit testing as soon as each unit is "code-complete". While testing will remain an important part of any software development process, model checking has the potential to serve as an effective complement to testing techniques by detecting defects relative to specific correctness properties and in some cases verifying properties of the software.

In this paper, we describe our adaptation and application of assume-guarantee style model checking to reasoning about correctness properties of software units, written in Ada. Units are fundamentally *open* systems and must be *closed* with a definition of the environment that they will execute in. The software components used to achieve this environment definition serve the role of stubs and drivers. The naive environment for properties stated in universal logics is the *universal* environment, which is capable of invoking any sequence of operations in the unit's interface. In many cases, one has behavioral information about unit interfaces, rather than just signatures, that can be exploited to refine the definition of the environment used to complete the unit's definition. In particular, we use linear-temporal logic (LTL) [20] as a means of specifying assumptions about interface behavior. When both the assumption ϕ and the guarantee property ψ are specified in LTL one can simply check the formula $\phi \rightarrow \psi$ with a model checker like SPIN [16]. LTL assumptions can also be used to synthesize refined environments, in which case ϕ can be eliminated from the formula to be checked. An additional benefit of synthesizing such environments is that it enables guarantee properties (ψ) specified in the universal fragment of computation tree logic (CTL) [6] to be checked with a model checker like SMV [22].

The theoretical foundations of this approach are not new. Several researchers have explored the efficacy and complexity of different styles of assume-guarantee reasoning with LTL and CTL specifications [27, 19]. The primary contributions of this paper are pragmatic (*i*) implementing a tool to synthesize stubs and drivers that encode given LTL assumptions, (*ii*) supporting local assumptions about the behavior of individual components of the environment, and (*iii*) providing initial experimental evidence of the performance tradeoffs involved with different styles of assume-guarantee reasoning for software units using SPIN and SMV. Secondary contributions of the work presented here include preliminary examination of several "real" programs, including specifications and a discussion on how to analyze components of these programs and some preliminary data on the kinds of properties for which CTL model checking exhibits a performance advantage over LTL model checking. The paper proceeds by surveying relevant background material in the next section. Section 3 presents our procedure for synthesizing Ada implementations of stubs and drivers from LTL assumptions. The Ada implementations are fed as input to an existing toolset for extracting finite-state models from source code which is described in Section 4. Section 5 then presents data on the performance of unit-level model checking based on synthesized environments. Section 6 describes related work and Section 7 concludes.

2 Background

Linear and Branching Temporal Logics. There are two principal types of temporal logics with discrete time: linear and branching. Linear temporal logic (LTL) is a language of assertions about computations. Its formulae are built from atomic propositions by means of Boolean connectives and the temporal connectives X ("next time") and U ("until"; pUq means that q holds at some point in the future, and that until that point, p is true). The formula $trueUp$, abbreviated Fp, says that p holds *eventually*, and $\neg F \neg p$, abbreviated Gp, says that p is *always* true. A program satisfies an LTL formula, if all its possible computations satisfy the formula. In contrast, computation tree logic (CTL) is a branching time logic about computation trees. Its temporal connectives consist of path quantifiers immediately followed by a single linear-temporal operator. The path quantifiers are A ("for all paths") and E ("for some path"). ACTL is the universal fragment of CTL. Using De Morgan's laws and dualities, any ACTL formula can be re-written to an equivalent CTL formula in which negations are applied only to atomic propositions, and that contains only A quantifiers; thus, in ACTL one can state properties of all computations of a program, but one can not state that certain computations exist.

Modular Verification. In modular verification, under the *assume-guarantee* paradigm [26], a specification consists of a pair $\langle \phi, \psi \rangle$, where ϕ and ψ are temporal logic formulae; ψ describes the guaranteed behavior of the module and ϕ describes the assumed behavior of the environment with which the module is interacting. For the linear temporal paradigm, both ϕ and ψ are LTL formulae. As observed in [26], in this case the assume-guarantee pair $\langle \phi, \psi \rangle$ can be combined to a single LTL formula $\phi \rightarrow \psi$. In the *linear branching modular model checking problem*, the assumption is an LTL formula, and the guarantee is a branching temporal logic formula (see e.g.[27]). Another approach is *branching modular model checking*, in which both assumption ϕ and guarantee ψ are branching temporal logic formulae. This case is considered in [14,19]. In these papers it is argued that, in the context of modular verification, it is advantageous to use only *universal* temporal logic (like LTL and ACTL). Universal temporal logic formulae have the helpful property that once they are satisfied in a module, they are also satisfied in any system that contains the module. We consider in this paper assumptions expressed in LTL and guarantees that can be expressed in both LTL and ACTL.

SPIN and SMV. We use two finite-state verification tools: SPIN, a reachability based model checker that explicitly enumerates the state space of the system being checked; and SMV, a "symbolic model checker", which uses Ordered Binary Decision Diagrams to encode subsets of the state space. These tools represent two of the major approaches to finite-state verification. SPIN accepts design specifications written in the Promela language and it accepts correctness properties written in LTL. SPIN can be used for assume-guarantee style verification by checking LTL specifications of the form $\phi \to \psi$ against "closed" modules. SMV checks properties written in CTL, with *fairness* constraints of the form GFf, for some CTL formula f. Modular verification can be performed in a very limited way, if ϕ can be expressed via such fairness constraints. A new version of SMV supports LTL model checking, in addition to CTL, and it is also especially designed for assume-guarantee style reasoning, where both the assumption and the guarantee are LTL formulae.

3 Synthesis of Environments from LTL Assumptions

Tableau Procedure. We close a software unit by generating source code that implements models of environments. To begin construction of any such model one must have a definition of the possible actions of the environment. For Ada programs, these actions include: interface actions (i.e. entry calls or accepts, calls to interface procedures of the software unit) or some other internal actions of the environment. Based on this definition, we construct *universal* stubs and drivers that represent all possible sequences of actions. When LTL local assumptions are available, we can synthesize refined models of environments, using tableau-like methods [21, 13]. A *local assumption* describes the temporal relations assumed to exist among the executions of the interface operations of the unit, invoked by one particular environment.

We assume that the parameters in unit calls have been abstracted to finite domains; Section 4 discusses how this is achieved. We then use the algorithm from [13] (the same algorithm is used in SPIN for generating never claims) together with the subset construction, justified in [24], to construct from an LTL formula ϕ a *deterministic* automaton that can be represented as a graph (and translated to Ada). The graph is a *maximal* model [14] of the environment assumption in that every computation which satisfies the assumption is a path in the graph, and that every finite path in the graph is the prefix of some computation that satisfies the assumption ([13]). If ϕ is a *safety* assumption, then all the paths in the graph satisfy ϕ. But if ϕ is a *liveness* specification, then there exists some path in the graph that does not satisfy ϕ. In the case studies presented in this paper, we used only safety assumptions, and hence the verification using synthesized environments can not yield false negatives (i.e. negative results produced as a consequence of considering paths that do not conform with the environment assumptions). Synthesized environments can be used in model checking of (stutter-closed [1]) guarantees ψ written in LTL or ACTL. Note that the LTL assumptions are not necessarily stutter-closed.

```
generic
   type Object_Type is private;

package Stack_Pt_Pt is

   type Stack_Type is limited private;

   type Process_Type is access
      procedure (object:in Object_Type;continue:in out boolean);

   procedure Pop(stack: in out Stack_Type;object:out Object_Type);
   procedure Push(object: in Object_Type;stack:in out Stack_Type);
   procedure Empty(stack: Stack_Type;result: out boolean);
   procedure Top_Down(stack:Stack_Type;Process: Process_Type);

   private
      type Stack_Type is
      record
         Top: integer :=0;
         Actual: array (1..Max_Size);
      end record;

end Stack_Pt_Pt;
```

(a) Stack Interface

```
-- no local assumption
      task body driver is
      state, choice: Integer;
      begin
      .......
      state:=0;
      loop
      case state is
         when 0 =>
         case choice is
            when 1 => Push(d1,stack); state:=0;
            when 2 => Push(d2,stack); state:=0;
            when 3 => Push(o,stack); state:=0;
            when 4 => Pop(stack,obj_out); state:=0;
            when 5 => Empty(stack,result); state:=0;
            when 6 => Top_Down(stack, stub ); state:=0;
            when 7 => null; state:=0;
            when others => exit;
         end case; end case;
      end loop;
      end driver;
```

(b) "Universal" driver

```
procedure stub(obj:in Object_Type;cont:in out boolean) is
      state, choice: Integer;
      begin -- stub for Process
      state:=0;
      loop
      case state is
         when 0 =>
         case choice is
            when 1 => null; state:=0;
            when others => exit;
         end case;
      end case;
      end loop;
      end stub;
```

(c) Stub for call-back procedure

(d) Graph generated from assumption

Fig. 1. Stack implementation

Our methodology for building maximal models of environments from local assumptions can be extended to handle global assumptions (i.e. assumptions that relate the behaviors of several local environments), as illustrated in the Replicated Workers Framework case study from Section 5.

An Example. To illustrate the techniques presented in this paper, we introduce a familiar software unit as an example. We consider the bounded stack implementation studied in [10] whose simplified interface is given in Figure 1(a). The implementation supports iteration in the stack-order (*Top_Down*), by invoking a user defined call-back routine (*Process*) for each datum stored in the stack. The universal driver is depicted in Figure 1(b); while the possible actions of the driver include all the interface operations of the stack package, we restrict the stub (presented in Figure 1(c)) to make no calls to the stack package. One property that is checked for this unit is that "If a pair of data are pushed then they must be popped in reverse order, provided that they are popped" (1s) (throughout the paper, we encode in the property names the systems they are referring to, e.g. (1s) means property 1 of the stack). Checking this order-related property requires the notion of data-independence [28]. We abstracted variables of *Object_Type* using a 2-ordered data abstraction [9]. This abstraction maps two distinct values in the concrete domain to the tokens d_1 and d_2 and all other concrete values to o. As stated in [28], in order to generalize the results of such a restricted model check to all pairs of values of *Object_type* one must assure that the tokens are input to the system at most once, which is specified as the LTL

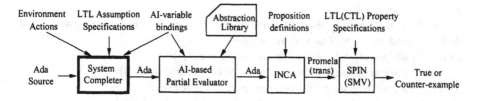

Fig. 2. Source Model Extraction Tools

assumption (about the driver):

$(G(\text{Push}(d_1,\text{stack}) \rightarrow XG\neg\text{Push}(d_1,\text{stack}))) \wedge G(\text{Push}(d_2,\text{stack}) \rightarrow XG\neg\text{Push}(d_2,\text{stack})).$

In Figure 1(d) we show the graph generated from the above assumption, where by $*$, we denote any other possible action of the driver: *Push(o,stack)*, *Pop(stack, obj_out)*, *Empty(stack,result)*, *Top_Down(stack,stub)* and *null*. In the Ada code, the internal non-observable actions of the environment are modeled by the *null* statement, internal choice in the environment is modeled by using the *choice* variable which will be abstracted to the *point* abstraction [9], and finally the abstracted parameter values are enumerated in specialized *Push* calls.

4 A Model Extraction Toolset

Toolset Components. For model checking properties of the Ada programs described in Section 5, we apply the methodology described in [9, 11] which is supported by the tool set illustrated in Figure 2. The first tool component constructs source code for drivers and stubs that complete the software unit, as discussed in Section 3. Incompletely defined Ada source code is fed to the System Completer, together with a description of the possible actions of the local environments and the LTL local assumptions written in terms of the environment actions; the names of the actions are uninterpreted strings and subsequent compile checks are performed for correctness. The completed program is abstracted and simplified using abstract interpretation [8] and partial evaluation [18] techniques. The resulting finite-state Ada program can be compiled by the INCA tool set [7] into the input languages of several verification tools. An important feature of INCA is its support for defining propositions for the observable states and actions of the system that the user is interested in reasoning about. These propositions have provided an advantage for interpreting counter examples, since the counter example will be rendered in terms of those states and actions.

The Stack Example. For the stack package presented in Section 3, we wrote the LTL and ACTL specifications derived from the English language description of the software package. After we closed the stack unit with a stub and a driver, we defined predicates *callPush_d1* and *callPush_d2* that are true immediately after the driver calls interface operation *Push* with the first parameter set to d_1 and d_2 respectively. Analogously, predicates *returnPop_d1* and *returnPop_d2* are true immediately after operation *Pop* called by the driver returns with *obj_out* set to d_1 and d_2 respectively. Using these predicates, property (1s) can be specified in the following way:

(1s) **If d_1 and d_2 are pushed in this order, then d_1 will not be popped until d_2 is popped or d_1 will never be popped.**

LTL: G((callPush_d_1 ∧ (¬returnPop_d_1 U callPush_d_2)) →

(¬returnPop_d_1 U (returnPop_d_2 ∨ G ¬returnPop_d_1)))

ACTL: ¬EF(callPush_d_1 ∧ (E(¬returnPop_d_1 U (callPush_d_2 ∧

E(¬returnPop_d_2 U (returnPop_d_1 ∧ ¬returnPop_d_2)))))))

Special control points can be added to the finite-state model of the Ada program; for example, we added such a control point immediately after procedure *Pop* returns d_1 and we defined the predicate *after_returnPop_d_1*, which is true just after predicate *returnPop_d_1* becomes false. We used this predicate for specifing a new stack property:

(2s) **Once d_1 is popped, it can not be popped again.**

LTL: G(after_returnPop_d_1 → G ¬returnPop_d_1)

ACTL: AG (after_returnPop_d_1 → AG ¬returnPop_d_1)

We can also use predicates that define the points at which selected program variables hold a given value. In the stack package, for example, we can define the predicate *TopEQzero* which holds in the states where variable *Top* is zero.

5 Experiments with Synthesized Environments

To assess the potential benefits of using synthesized environments in assume-guarantee model checking of software units, we analyzed several components of software systems. All of the properties we checked (a selection of which is given in Figure 3) are instances of property specification patterns [12]. In this section, we begin with brief descriptions of the software systems we analyzed. In Figure 4 depicting system architectures, lines with arrows represent either procedure invocations or calls to task entries; little shaded rectangles represent interface operations for software units. We then compare the times for SPIN and SMV model checking with universal and synthesized environments. Space limits prohibit the inclusion of all of the details of these studies, but, we have collected the original Ada source code, synthesized environment components, abstracted finite-state Ada code, proposition definitions, assumptions, properties, and Promela and SMV input descriptions on a web-site [25].

The Gas Station (g). The problem was analyzed in [4] using SPIN and SMV; it is a scalable concurrent simulation of an automated gas station. Its architecture is depicted in Figure 4(a). We analyzed the server subsystem, which consists of operator and pump processes that maintain a bounded length queue holding customers' requests. The environment consists of the customer tasks. We checked property (1g), for three versions of the gas station: with two (version g_2), three (version g_3) and four (version g_4) customers, respectively. Model checking the property on the server subsystem "closed" with the universal environment yields a counter example in which customer 1 makes a prepayment while using the pump, and thus it keeps using the pump indefinitely. We then assumed that a

(1g) **If customer 2 prepays while customer 1 is using the pump then the operator will activate the pump for customer 2 next.**
LTL: $G((\text{Start1} \wedge (\neg\text{Stop1 U Prepay2})) \rightarrow$
$(\neg\text{Activate1 U (Activate2} \vee G \neg\text{Activate1)))}$
ACTL: $\neg EF(\text{Start1} \wedge E(\neg\text{Stop1 U (Prepay2} \wedge$
$E(\neg\text{Activate2 U (Activate1} \wedge \neg\text{Activate2)))))}$

(4r) **The computation does not terminate unless the pool is empty (variable *workCount* is zero), or a worker signals work is *done*.**
LTL: $G(\text{callExecute} \rightarrow (\neg\text{returnExecute U}$
$(\text{done} \vee \text{workCountEQzero} \vee G \neg\text{returnExecute})))$
ACTL: $AG(\text{callExecute} \rightarrow \neg E(\neg(\text{done} \vee \text{workCountEQzero) U}$
$(\text{returnExecute} \wedge \neg(\text{done} \vee \text{workCountEQzero}))))$

(5r) **If a worker is ready to *Get* work, the workpool is not empty and the computation is not *done*, then eventually work is scheduled.**
LTL: $G((\text{workCountGRzero} \wedge \text{acceptPoolGet} \wedge \neg\text{done}) \rightarrow$
$F(\text{calldoWork1} \vee \text{calldoWork2} \vee \text{calldoWork3}))$
ACTL: $AG((\text{workCountGRzero} \wedge \text{acceptPoolGet} \wedge \neg\text{done}) \rightarrow$
$AF(\text{calldoWork1} \vee \text{calldoWork2} \vee \text{calldoWork3}))$

(6r) **The work pool schedules work in input order.**
LTL: $G((\text{returnInput\_}d_1 \wedge F \text{ returnInput\_}d_2) \rightarrow$
$(\neg\text{callGet\_}d_2 \text{ U (callGet\_}d_1 \vee G \neg\text{callGet\_}d_2)))$
ACTL: $\neg EF(\text{returnInput\_}d_1 \wedge E(\neg\text{callGet\_}d_1 \text{ U}$
$(\text{returnInput\_}d_2 \wedge E(\neg\text{callGet\_}d_1 \text{ U (callGet\_}d_2 \wedge \neg\text{callGet\_}d_1)))))$

(7r) **If stub *doWork* is invoked by worker task *i* on item d_1 then no other worker task *j* will invoke *doWork* on the same item d_1.**
LTL: $G(\text{calldoWorki\_}d_1 \rightarrow G \neg\text{calldoWorkj\_}d_1))$
ACTL: $AG(\text{calldoWorki\_}d_1 \rightarrow AG \neg\text{calldoWorkj\_}d_1)$

(8r) **If worker task *i* invokes *doWork* on d_1, that same worker task will not invoke *doWork* on d_1 again.**
LTL: $G(\text{returndoWorki\_}d_1 \rightarrow G \neg\text{calldoWorki\_}d_1)$
ACTL: $AG(\text{returndoWorki\_}d_1 \rightarrow AG \neg\text{calldoWorki\_}d_1)$

(7c) **If artist a_1 registers for event e_1 before artist a_2 does, then (until unregistration or termination) once dispatcher receives event e_1 from ADT it will not notify a_2 before notifying a_1.**
LTL: $G((\text{register\_}a_1e_1 \wedge (\neg(\text{unregister\_}a_1e_1 \vee \text{unregister\_}a_2e_1) \text{ U}$
$\text{register\_}a_2e_1) \wedge F(\text{term} \vee \text{unregister\_}a_1e_1 \vee \text{unregister\_}a_2e_1)) \rightarrow$
$((\text{notify\_artists\_}e_1 \rightarrow (\neg\text{notify\_client\_}a_2e_1 \text{ U(notify\_client\_}a_1e_1 \vee$
$G\neg\text{notify\_client\_}a_2e_1)))\text{U(term} \vee \text{unregister\_}a_1e_1 \vee \text{unregister\_}a_2e_1)))$
ACTL: $\neg EF(\text{register\_}a_1e_1 \wedge E((\neg\text{unregister\_}a_1e_1 \wedge \neg\text{notify\_client\_}a_1e_1) \text{ U}$
$(\text{register\_}a_2e_1 \wedge E((\neg\text{unregister\_}a_1e_1 \wedge \neg\text{unregister\_}a_2e_1 \wedge$
$\neg\text{notify\_client\_}a_1e_1) \text{ U notify\_client\_}a_2e_1))))$

(8c) **No artist attempts to register for event e_1 when the size of the array that stores artists registered for event e_1 is equal to the number of artists.**
LTL: $G(\text{e1szEQ2} \wedge (\text{after\_register\_}a_1e_1 \vee \text{after\_register\_}a_2e_1) \rightarrow$
$(\neg(\text{register\_}a_2e_1 \vee \text{register\_}a_1e_1) \text{ U}$
$(\text{e1szLT2} \vee G \neg(\text{register\_}a_2e_1 \vee \text{register\_}a_1e_1))))$
ACTL: $AG(\text{e1szEQ2} \wedge (\text{after\_register\_}a_1e_1 \vee \text{after\_register\_}a_2e_1) \rightarrow$
$\neg E(\neg\text{e1szLT2 U ((register\_}a_1e_1 \vee \text{register\_}a_2e_1) \wedge \neg\text{e1szLT2)))}$

Fig. 3. Specifications

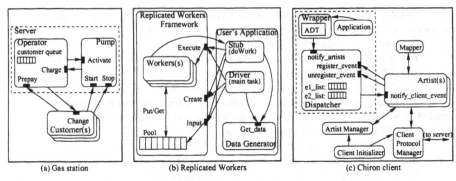

(a) Gas station   (b) Replicated Workers   (c) Chiron client

Fig. 4. Software architectures

customer does not prepay for subsequent pumping during current pumping. The LTL assumption for customer 1 is:

$G(Pump.Start \rightarrow (\neg Operator.Prepay(1)\ U\ (Pump.Stop \vee G\ \neg Operator.Prepay(1))))$.

Model checking property (1g) with the behavior of customer 1 restricted by the environment assumption yields true results.

The Replicated Workers Framework (r). This is a parameterizable job scheduler implemented as an Ada generic package which manages the startup, shutdown, and interaction of processes internally. The environment consists of a single driver (the main task) and two kinds of stub routines (*doWork* and *doResult*). Figure 4(b) illustrates a slightly simplified structure of the replicated workers framework and its interaction with the environment (the user's application). A variety of properties of this system (with three worker tasks) were model checked in [9], using SPIN. We reproduce here only the properties that needed some environment assumptions.

The environment assumptions used for checking both properties (4r) and (5r) restrict the stubs for the user-defined procedures to make no calls to the replicated workers framework: $G\ \neg(Create \vee Input \vee Execute)$.

For properties (6r), (7r) and (8r) we used the 2-ordered data abstraction described in Section 3. As discussed in Section 3, properties like (6r), (7r) and (8r) are true only under the environment assumption that d_1 and d_2 are input to the system only once. We observe that the latter assumption is global, rather than local, because work items can be input to the system from different tasks/environments (passed in from the main task and returned from calls to the *doWork* stubs). To enforce the necessary global assumption we created a new task, *Data_Generator*, that generates data items d_1, d_2 and o. The driver and the stubs (implemented as universal environments) communicate with the *Data_Generator* to *Get_data* to be input in the work pool. The LTL assumption used in the synthesis of *Data_Generator* is:

$(G(Get\_data(d_1) \rightarrow XG\neg Get\_data(d_1))) \wedge G(Get\_data(d_2) \rightarrow XG\neg Get\_data(d_2))$.

The Chiron Client (c). Chiron [29] is a user interface development system. The application for which an interface is to be constructed must be organized as abstract data types (ADTs). Chiron has a client-server architecture; Figure 4(c) gives a simplified view of the architecture of a client. The *Artists* maintain the graphical depictions of the ADTs. They indicate the events they are interested in by registering and de-registering with the *Dispatcher*, which notifies the artists of the events from the ADTs. We analyzed the dispatcher subsystem, which consists of the dispatcher, the wrapper and the application; while the environment consists of the artists and the other remaining components. We checked several properties for two versions of the dispatcher subsystem: with two artists registering for two events (version c_2) and with two artists registering for three events (version c_3), respectively. Only two properties required the use of environment assumptions: (7c) and (8c). Property (8c) can be written as a conjunction of two properties of the following form, that refer to only one artist a_i:

(8ic) **No artist a_i attempts to register for event e_1 when the size of the array that stores artists registered for event e_1 is equal to the number of artists.**
LTL:$G(\text{e1szEQ2} \wedge \text{after\_register\_}a_i e_1 \rightarrow (\neg \text{register\_}a_i e_1 \; U(\text{e1szLT2} \vee G \neg \text{register\_}a_i e_1)))$
ACTL:$AG(\text{e1szEQ2} \wedge \text{after\_register\_}a_i e_1 \rightarrow \neg E(\neg \text{e1szLT2} \; U(\text{register\_}a_i e_1 \wedge \neg \text{e1szLT2})))$

When model checking the properties on the dispatcher subsystem closed with universal environments, we obtained false results and counter examples in which one of the artists keeps registering for event e_1 while registered for event e_1. We used the assumption that an artist never registers for an event if it is already registered for that event, which is actually a specification of the Chiron system. The LTL assumption for artist a_1 is:
$G(\text{dispatcher.register}(a_1,e_1) \rightarrow X((\neg\text{dispatcher.register}(a_1,e_1)) \; U$
$(\text{dispatcher.unregister}(a_1,e_1) \vee G\neg\text{dispatcher.register}(a_1,e_1))))$.

We obtained true results when model checking with both artists a_1 and a_2 restricted by the environment assumptions.

Generic Containers Implementations. In [10] a large collection of properties were checked of implementations of bounded **stack (s)**, **queue (q)** and **priority queue (p)**. These are sequential software units that were completed with a single driver environment component and with stubs for user-defined procedures. We already described the stack implementation in Section 3. Similar properties were checked for queue and priority queue.

Results. In each of these studies, several of the properties required environment assumptions for successful model checking. These model checks were performed with synthesized environments and, alternatively, with assumptions in the formulae (for LTL); we used SPIN, version 3.09 and SMV (Cadence version), on a SUN ULTRA5 with a 270Mhz UltraSparc IIi and 128Meg of RAM.

Figure 5 gives the data for each of the model checking runs using SPIN. The names in the first column encode the systems and property that are checked; a subscript denotes the version of the system being analyzed. For model checking specifications of the form $\phi \rightarrow \psi$ using universal environments, we report the total of user and system time in seconds to convert LTL to the SPIN input format, i.e. never claim, (t_{never}) and to execute the model checker (t_{MC}). We also report the memory used in verification in Mbytes (mem) and the total time to construct Promela code from the initial Ada program (t_{build}). For the

Prop.	t_{never}	t_{MC}	mem	t_{build}	t'_{never}	t'_{MC}	mem'	t'_{build}
$1g_2$	655.5	3.8	2.005	1.6	0.1	0.5	1.698	1.6
$1g_3$	655.5	149.4	11.938	1.7	0.1	18.4	4.565	1.8
$1g_4$	655.5	5604.7	268.348	2.6	0.1	606.5	101.436	2.7
$4r$	0.3	7.4	5.385	11.9	0.1	3.1	2.620	7.6
$5r$	0.1	21.1	2.313	11.9	0.1	12.4	2.005	7.6
$6r$	539.5	486.4	77.372	36.8	0.1	330.1	66.415	47.2
$7r$	0.1	567.2	78.089	36.8	0.1	242.7	51.669	47.2
$8r$	0.1	548.4	73.481	36.8	0.1	227.1	48.495	47.2
$7c_2$	-				25.1	30.4	4.975	6.5
$81c_2$	63.0	223.1	9.788	6.1	0.1	21.6	3.746	6.5
$82c_2$	62.6	236.9	10.095	6.1	0.1	22.1	3.746	6.5
$7c_3$	-				25.1	132.8	16.137	11.8
$81c_3$	63.0	700.3	29.551	7.4	0.1	114.6	10.812	11.8
$82c_3$	62.6	1348.1	33.033	7.4	0.1	119.9	10.812	11.8
$1s$	367.5	0.2	2.108	27.1	0.2	0.1	2.005	15.5
$2s$	0.1	0.2	2.005	27.1	0.1	0.1	2.005	15.5
$1p$	338.2	0.2	2.517	35.3	0.1	0.1	2.108	25.6
$2p$	365.6	0.3	2.517	35.3	0.1	0.1	2.108	25.6
$3p$	0.1	0.3	2.313	35.3	0.1	0.1	2.108	25.6
$1q$	513.9	0.1	2.005	27.8	0.1	0.1	1.801	22.4
$2q$	0.1	0.1	1.903	27.8	0.1	0.1	1.801	22.4

Fig. 5. SPIN results

verification using synthesized environments we report measurements of the same times and sizes; a ' denotes the synthesized measure. SPIN ran out of memory, when we tried to generate never claims for properties (7c) and (8c), with the assumptions encoded in the formulae of the form $\phi_{a1} \wedge \phi_{a2} \rightarrow property$, where ϕ_{a1} and ϕ_{a2} are the local assumptions about artists a_1 and a_2. However, we were able to generate never claims for properties (81c) and (82c).

Figure 6 gives the data for each of the model checking runs using SMV. For verifying specifications using universal environments when both ϕ and ψ are LTL formulae, we report the total of user and system time in seconds to model check specifications (t_{MC_LTL}), the memory used in Mbyte (mem_{LTL}) and the total time to construct SMV input files from the Ada program (t_{build}). For model checks using synthesized environments, we report the measurements of the same times and sizes (denoted by '). In addition, synthesized environments can be used in CTL model checking, for which we give the total model checking time (t'_{MC_CTL}) and the memory used (mem'_{CTL}).

Discussion. Our data indicate that synthesized environments enable faster model-checking. Figure 7 plots the ratio of model check time (memory) for a property ψ relative to checks of $\phi \rightarrow \psi$ with SPIN using the universal environment (i.e t'_{MC}/t_{MC} and mem'/mem). In all cases, the synthesized environments enabled reductions in model check times and memory. The performance advantage arises from the fact that while the universal environment is smaller than the synthesized environment in most cases, the assumption must be encoded in the formulae to be checked and this contributes, in general, as many states to the never claim as to the synthesized environment. This leads to larger state spaces to be searched. We note that in two cases it was impossible to generate never claims from LTL formulae (of the form $\phi \rightarrow \psi$), while the synthesized environments made model checking possible.

Prop.	t_{MC_LTL}	mem_{LTL}	t_{build}	t'_{MC_LTL}	mem'_{LTL}	t'_{MC_CTL}	mem'_{CTL}	t'_{build}
$1g_2$	5.56	4.898	3.9	2.34	4.505	0.78	4.071	5.1
$1g_3$	23.05	6.913	8.9	8.03	6.274	2.77	5.488	11.5
$1g_4$	127.49	18.136	31.8	52.00	13.844	16.13	11.517	39.6
$4r$	67.23	23.478	158.14	16.3	9.379	11.03	8.339	55.69
$5r$	95.31	32.112	158.14	26.10	12.574	25.98	12.631	55.69
$6r$	611.09	28.442	130.4	430.73	30.113	63.27	20.922	114.12
$7r$	74.44	20.160	130.4	60.18	20.922	62.66	20.922	114.12
$8r$	74.16	20.160	130.4	60.53	20.922	62.39	20.922	114.12
$7c_2$	266.91	18.751	9.3	90.66	28.122	56.06	24.674	15.41
$8c_2$	51.6	13.475	9.3	59.81	24.870	55.69	24.543	15.41
$7c_3$	593.74	43.704	19.1	382.71	73.449	283.6	67.346	44.8
$8c_3$	191.18	32.235	19.1	161.14	47.054	157.28	45.907	44.8
$1s$	3.42	5.627	40.5	2.14	4.939	0.88	3.399	25.5
$2s$	2.21	5.332	40.5	0.8	3.399	0.85	3.399	25.5
$1p$	11.49	8.724	1:01.8	4.1	6.274	4.18	6.045	41.2
$2p$	11.16	8.716	1:01.8	4.80	6.266	4.13	6.045	41.2
$3p$	9.72	8.421	1:01.8	4.05	6.045	4.10	6.045	41.2
$1q$	3.09	5.398	40.2	2.10	4.874	1.60	4.792	41.2
$2q$	2.23	5.250	40.2	1.63	4.792	1.64	4.792	41.2

Fig. 6. SMV results

CTL model checking these systems with SMV was not feasible, previously, due to the difficulty of expressing assumptions in CTL. With synthesized environments, however, we can compare performances of LTL versus CTL model checking using SMV. Figure 8 plots the ratio of model check time (memory) for SMV using synthesized environments relative to universal environments. For each problem, the first bar gives the ratio for LTL model checking using SMV with the synthesized environment versus the universal SMV baseline (i.e. t'_{MC_LTL}/t_{MC_LTL} and mem'_{LTL}/mem_{LTL}) and the second bar gives the ratio for CTL model checking using SMV with the synthesized environment versus the universal SMV baseline (i.e. t'_{MC_CTL}/t_{MC_LTL} and mem'_{CTL}/mem_{LTL}). As in the case of SPIN, synthesized environments seem to enable faster model checking with SMV. In terms of memory requirements, it is not clear that synthesized environments are better. Further empirical study is needed to determine the kinds of assumptions to which the use of synthesized environments is suited to. The present data suggest to synthesize environments from assumptions that reduce the state space of the model (e.g. the assumption about the environment of the stack unit: "d_1 and d_2 are input to the stack only once").

The universal environment approach has the advantage of generality. In particular, the model generated with the universal environment can be reused with different assumptions, whereas synthesized environments encode a single set of assumptions. Thus for the universal case, model construction time could be amortized across a number of model checks. The data indicates, however, that model construction time is not the dominant factor in the overall analysis time and that the time to regenerate synthesized environments appears to be more than recovered by reduced model check times. This observation, however, is based on studying systems with relatively few external calls and a small interface action set. Also, we used relatively simple assumptions for which the synthesized environments were small (maximum 5 nodes in the generated graphs).

It is well-known that the complexity of model checking varies with the logic used, for example CTL model checking is linear in the size of the formula and

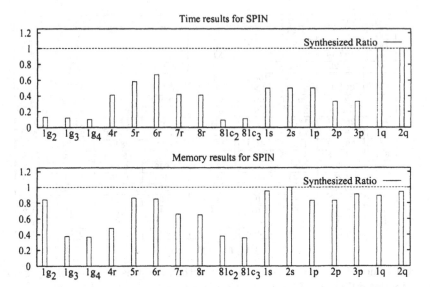

Fig. 7. Performance comparisons for SPIN model checking

LTL model checking is exponential. For practitioners, the relevant question is whether this distinction occurs in practice and if so how much more costly LTL model checking is. Since SMV supports both LTL and CTL model checking the data in Figure 6 (in columns t'_{MC_LTL} and t'_{MC_CTL}) can shed some light on the kinds of properties for which LTL model checking is more expensive than CTL model checking. One of the main problems in such a comparison is ensuring that the property specifications in the two logics are the same; we minimized this bias by using the predefined specification templates provided with the specification patterns system [12]. Ignoring scaling of systems and variations of encoded assumptions, there were a total of 15 properties checked. Of these, eight were faster to check in the CTL case, five were faster in the LTL case, and the other two took essentially the same time. In only four cases (1g,6r,7c,1s), was there a significant difference in model check time; each of these cases favored CTL. These four specifications are instances of the *global response-chain* pattern [12]. While it is tempting to conclude that CTL is advantageous for this class of specifications we observe that the LTL specifications for response-chains are not claimed to be "optimal" in any sense. A much broader study of the relationship between model check time, property being checked, and formulation of the property in temporal logics is needed to characterize the practical differences between LTL and CTL model checking. Our current results suggest that in most cases the difference is negligible but that certain forms of specifications may lend themselves to more efficient CTL model checking.

While not explicit in the data reported in this paper, it is interesting to note that in many cases, properties of the systems we studied could be model checked without any assumptions and, when necessary, relatively few assumptions were sufficient to achieve the level of precision necessary for property verification (out of 39 properties, only 18 properties needed assumptions).

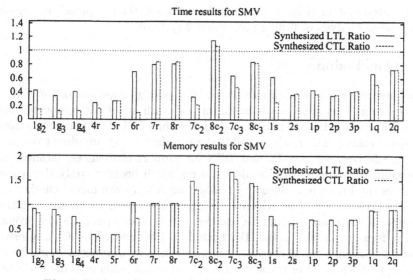

Fig. 8. Performance comparisons for SMV model checking

6 Related Work

The work described in this paper touches on model checking software systems and model checking open systems.

Much of the related work was described in Section 2. There has been some recent work on developing translation tools to convert software written in high-level programming languages to the input languages of model checkers. In addition to the INCA tools, which support Ada, there are two toolsets for translating Java programs to Promela, the input language of SPIN. JCAT [17] handles a significantly restricted subset of the Java language and Java Path Finder [15] handles a much larger portion of the language, including exceptions and inheritance. Neither of these tools provides any support for abstracting the control and data states of the program. We are working to port the environment synthesis tool described in this paper to generate environments in Java.

Our use of assumptions to synthesize a model of the environment is similar to work on compositional analysis. These divide-and-conquer approaches decompose a system into sub-systems, derive interfaces that summarize the behavior of each subsystem (e.g. [5]), then perform analyses using interfaces in place of the details of the sub-systems. This notion of capturing environment behavior with interfaces also appears in recent developments on theoretical issues related to modular verification (e.g. [20, 19]). There has been considerably less work on the practical issues involved with finite-state verification of partial software systems. Aside from our work reported in [9, 10], there is another recent related practical effort. Avrunin, Dillon and Corbett [3] have developed a technique that allows partial systems to be described in a mixture of source code and specifications. In their work, specifications can be thought of as assumptions on a naive completion of a partial system given in code. Unlike our work, their approach is targeted to automated analysis of timing properties of systems.

7 Conclusion

We have presented an approach to model checking properties of software units *in isolation*. This approach is based on the synthesis of environments that encode LTL assumptions. The approach also enables LTL-ACTL assume-guarantee model checking. The reader should take care in making any direct comparison of the effectiveness of SMV and SPIN for support of assume-guarantee model checking. Such comparison would require a much broader study that carefully assesses the biases introduced by translating Ada to the model checker inputs as was done in [7]. The evidence seems to be conclusive on the question of whether assumptions should be encoded in the state space, i.e., environment, or the formula to be checked. For both LTL-LTL and LTL-ACTL approaches assume-guarantee model checking is more efficient with respect to time for safety assumptions encoded in the state space. This result holds regardless of whether the model checks are performed with SMV or SPIN.

References

1. M. Abadi and L. Lamport. Composing specifications. *ACM Transactions on Programming Languages and Systems*, 15(1):73-132, January 1993.
2. J. Atlee and J. Gannon. State-based model checking of event-driven system requirements. *IEEE Transactions on Software Engineering*, 19(1):24-40, June 1993.
3. G.S. Avrunin, J.C. Corbett, and L.K. Dillon. Analyzing partially-implemented real-time systems. In *Proceedings of the 19th International Conference on Software Engineering*, May 1997.
4. A.T. Chamillard. *An Empirical Comparison of Static Concurrency Analysis Techniques*. PhD thesis, University of Massachusetts at Amherst, May 1996.
5. S.C. Cheung and J. Kramer. Checking subsystem safety properties in compositional reachability analysis. In *Proceedings of the 18th International Conference on Software Engineering*, Berlin, March 1996.
6. E.M. Clarke, E.A. Emerson, and A.P. Sistla. Automatic verification of finite-state concurrent systems using temporal logic specifications. *ACM Transactions on Programming Languages and Systems*, 8(2):244-263, April 1986.
7. J.C. Corbett. Evaluating deadlock detection methods for concurrent software. *IEEE Transactions on Software Engineering*, 22(3), March 1996.
8. P. Cousot and R. Cousot. Abstract interpretation: A unified lattice model for static analysis of programs by construction or approximation of fixpoints. In *Conference Record of the Fourth Annual ACM Symposium on Principles of Programming Languages*, pages 238-252, 1977.
9. M.B. Dwyer and C.S. Păsăreanu. Filter-based model checking of partial systems. In *Proceedings of the Sixth ACM SIGSOFT Symposium on Foundations of Software Engineering*, November 1998.
10. M.B. Dwyer and C.S. Păsăreanu. Model checking generic container implementations. In *Generic Programing: Proceedings of a Dagstuhl Seminar*, Lecture Notes in Computer Science, Dagstuhl Castle, Germany, 1998. to appear.

11. M.B. Dwyer, C.S. Păsăreanu, and J.C. Corbett. Translating ada programs for model checking : A tutorial. Technical Report 98-12, Kansas State University, Department of Computing and Information Sciences, 1998.

12. M.B. Dwyer, G.S. Avrunin, and J.C. Corbett. Patterns in property specifications for finite-state verification. In *Proceedings of the 21st International Conference on Software Engineering*, May 1999.

13. R. Gerth, D. Peled, M.Y. Vardi, and P. Wolper. Simple On-the-fly Automatic Verification of Linear Temporal Logic. In *Proceedings of PSTV'95*, 1995.

14. O. Grumberg and D.E. Long. Model Checking and Modular Verification. *ACM Transactions on Programming Languages and Systems*, 16(3):843-871, May 1994.

15. K. Havelund and T. Pressburger. Model checking java programs using java pathfinder. *International Journal on Software Tools for Technology Transfer*, 1999. to appear.

16. G.J. Holzmann. The model checker SPIN. *IEEE Transactions on Software Engineering*, 23(5):279-294, May 1997.

17. R. Iosef. A concurrency analysis tool for java programs. Master's thesis, Polytechnic University of Turin, August 1997.

18. N.D. Jones, C.K. Gomard, and P. Sestoft. *Partial Evaluation and Automatic Program Generation*. Prentice-Hall International, 1993.

19. O. Kupferman and M.Y. Vardi. On the complexity of branching modular model checking (extended abstract). In Insup Lee and Scott A. Smolka, editors, *CONCUR '95: Concurrency Theory, 6th International Conference*, volume 962 of *Lecture Notes in Computer Science*, pages 408-422, Philadelphia, Pennsylvania, 21-24 August 1995. Springer-Verlag.

20. Z. Manna and A. Pnueli. *The Temporal Logic of Reactive and Concurrent Systems: Specification*. Springer-Verlag, 1991.

21. Z. Manna and P. Wolper. Synthesis of communicating processes from temporal logic. *ACM Transactions on Programming Languages and Systems (TOPLAS)*, 6(1):68-93, 1984.

22. K.L. McMillan. *Symbolic Model Checking*. Kluwer Academic Publishers, 1993.

23. G.N. Naumovich, G.S. Avrunin, L.A. Clarke, and L.J. Osterweil. Applying static analysis to software architectures. In *LNCS 1301*. The 6th European Software Engineering Conference held jointly with the 5th ACM SIGSOFT Symposium on the Foundations of Software Engineering, September 1997.

24. C.S. Păsăreanu, M.B. Dwyer, and M. Huth. Modular Verification of Software Units. Technical Report 98-15, Kansas State University, Department of Computing and Information Sciences, 1998.

25. C.S. Păsăreanu and M.B. Dwyer. Software Model Checking Case Studies. http://www.cis.ksu.edu/santos/bandera/index.html#case-studies, 1998.

26. A. Pnueli. In transition from global to modular temporal reasoning about programs. In K. Apt, editor, *Logics and Models of Concurrent Systems*, pages 123-144. Springer-Verlag, 1985.

27. M.Y. Vardi. On the complexity of modular model checking. In *Proceedings, Tenth Annual IEEE Symposium on Logic in Computer Science*, pages 101-111, San Diego, California, 26-29 June 1995. IEEE Computer Society Press.

28. P. Wolper. Specifying interesting properties of programs in propositional temporal logics. In *Proceedings of the 13th ACM Symposium on Principles of Programming Languages*, pages 184-193, St. Petersburg, Fla., January 1986.

29. M. Young, R.N. Taylor, D.L. Levine, K.A. Nies, and D. Brodbeck. A concurrency analysis tool suite: Rationale, design, and preliminary experience. *ACM Transactions on Software Engineering and Methodology*, 4(1):64-106, January 1995.

A Framework for Automatic Construction of Abstract Promela Models

Maria-del-Mar Gallardo and Pedro Merino
{gallardo,pedro}@lcc.uma.es

Dpto. de Lenguajes y Ciencias de la Computacion
University of Malaga, 29071 Malaga, Spain

Abstract. One of the current trends in model checking for the verification of concurrent systems is to reduce the state space produced by the model, and one of the more promising ways to achieve this objective is to support some kind of automatic construction of more abstract models. This paper presents a proposal in this direction. The main contribution of the paper is the definition of a semantics framework which allows us to relate different models of the system, each one with a particular abstraction level. Automatic source-to-source transformation is supported by this formal basis. The method is applied to Promela models.

1 Introduction

Formal verification is a powerful method to ensure confidence regarding the correctness of many complex and critical systems [5, 8]. This technique is currently supported by many commercial and non-commercial tools such as SPIN [11, 12]. However, verification is only possible and fruitful if *useful formal models* of these systems are available. A useful model is an abstract representation of the real system, with exactly the details necessary to ensure that satisfaction of interesting properties in the model implies satisfaction in the real system. Excessive model detail may produce the well-known state explosion problem, which could prevent its analysis with current tools. Whereas research in recent years has mainly focussed on algorithms to improve automatic verification, mainly based on model checking [3, 15], it is now necessary to conduct research into methods for the automatic construction of useful abstract models (as defended by Amir Pnueli in the 4th SPIN workshop).

One technique recently exploited to obtain more abstract models is abstract interpretation [2], which allows us to employ the new models in order to analyze specific properties using less time or memory [4, 6]. Abstract interpretation (A.I.) is an automatic analysis technique to statically deduce dynamic program properties, which is based on the idea of approximation. Every program data is approximated, by means of the so-called abstraction function α, by a higher level description (abstract denotation) which represents the data property of interest. Analysis is carried out by executing programs with the abstract data instead of the actual data. To do this, it is necessary to redefine the meaning of the program instructions so that they can be applied to abstract data. In both [4, 6], transition systems are used to construct models and the abstraction is oriented to the verification of universal safety temporal properties, i.e., properties that hold in all states along every possible execution path. Both works also extend their proposal to existential properties. In [4], properties are expressed with CTL formulas, while in [6] the modal μ-calculus is used.

This paper reports work in progress towards the construction of an environment for automatic verification based on transforming Promela models using abstract interpretation as a formal basis. The main components of the environment are shown in Figure 1. The key concept is that given a model M, the user must supply an abstraction function α to transform this model into a new abstract model M_i^*. The function can be provided from a library, and it can be refined for this particular model using the property to be analyzed. The properties must also be transformed when the model is transformed. Our aim is to keep all the formal descriptions (models and properties) as related as possible to the results, by using a specific management tool.

We present a semantics framework to support the transformations mentioned above based on A.I. This analysis technique basically defines a relation between two semantic levels, the concrete and the abstract one. Given a language L and $Sem : L \rightarrow (Det, \leq)$ a semantics of L which associates each program $M \in L$ with a denotation d belonging to the poset $(Det, \leq)$, the objective of A.I. is to automatically construct an abstract program M^* in which the program characteristics to be analyzed are preserved while the rest of the program characteristics are abstracted. The meaning of the new program M^* is given by an abstract semantics $Sem^* : L \rightarrow (Det^*, \leq^*)$. Correctness of the analysis is proved by means of the abstraction function $\alpha : (Det, \leq) \rightarrow (Det^*, \leq^*)$ and the concretization function $\gamma : (Det^*, \leq^*) \rightarrow (Det, \leq)$ which relate these two semantic levels. $((Det, \leq), (Det^*, \leq^*), \alpha, \gamma)$ usually forms a Galois connection and the correctness is formalized using any of the two following equivalent expressions:

$$\alpha(Sem(M)) \leq^* Sem^*(M^*) \tag{1}$$
$$Sem(M) \leq \gamma(Sem^*(M^*)). \tag{2}$$

$\leq$ and $\leq^*$ represent the precision given by the two respective semantics, i.e., $d_1^* \leq^* d_2^*$ indicates that the semantics value d_1^* is more precise than d_2^*, or from another point of view, that d_2^* approximates d_1^*. Following this, $\alpha(d) \leq^* d^*$ means that d^* is an abstract approximation of d, and $d \leq \gamma(d^*)$ indicates that $\gamma(d^*)$ is more general than d. Considering this, (1) and (2) represent that $Sem^*(M^*)$ is a correct approximation of $Sem(M)$.

Many program aspects of the concrete semantics construction are not affected by the abstraction process, and therefore it is possible to define a semantics parameterized by the language aspects which are influenced by the process of abstraction. This idea was used in [13] for the A.I. of Prolog and more recently in [7] who defined the generalized semantics of constraint logic languages. We follow this idea to define a generalized semantics of a subset of Promela. This semantics will allow us to define, in a common semantics framework, different levels of abstraction from an initial model and to easily compare them for precision. The key issue here is that all models, the abstract ones and the initial, are instances of the same semantic framework. Compared to other related works, our proposal is based on the automatic source-to-source transformation of Promela models, thus allowing the use of SPIN for verification of both concrete and abstract models. In [9] we presented previous results on the use of A.I. for verifying abstract properties of programs.

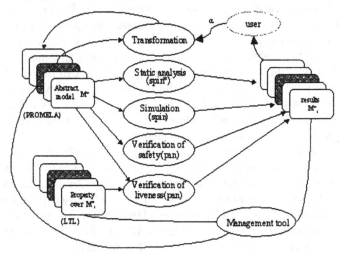

Fig. 1. Overview of an environment for verifying by transformation

The organization of the paper is as follows. Section 2 describes the generalized semantics of Promela and Section 3 explains the transformation method proposed and presents some correctness results. Section 4 contains an example which illustrates how to combine our method with the SPIN tool. In Section 5, we present conclusions and future work.

2 Promela generalized semantics

The objective of this section is to define the generalized semantics of a significant subset of the Promela language. As explained above, the generalized semantics describes the operational behavior of a program making explicit the domain-dependent model characteristics which are influenced by the abstraction as data and instructions. We first define the subset of Promela considered in the paper. We do not try to precisely explain the syntax or the meaning of each Promela instruction. Instead, some knowledge of the language is assumed.

Every model $M \in Promela$ is a sequence of processes $M = P_1 || \ldots || P_n$ which run in parallel. Let $Inst$ be the set of basic instructions from which the processes are constructed. $Inst$ includes the assignment instruction $=$, the Boolean and arithmetic operators, the if and $goto$ instructions, and the instructions for sending (receiving) messages to (from) channels represented by the sets $Input$ and

Output, respectively. Let us define *Label* as a set of labels and *Decl* as the declarative part of the model. Using these definitions, every process is described as:

$$P = Decl; \{Label : Tran\}$$

where

$$Tran = \{(Input|Output|null); Inst\},$$

null being the empty instruction.

We intentionally omit the instruction *run* that creates the processes from the main program in order to make the description clearer. Also, we assume that *init* is one of the model's processes.

Every label is intended to represent an internal process state defined by the programmer. In each one of these logical states, the process will carry out a transition which will usually begin reading or sending a message through a channel and will follow this with a sequence of arbitrary instructions. The transition may end with a *goto* instruction which will provoke the process into jumping to another logical state. The example in Figure 4 follows the syntax defined above. We now present the generalized semantics of Promela, introducing the definition gradually in order to be clear.

1. Let *State* be the set of tuples which represent the internal state of the model, that is, every tuple, which is written as $(g, l_1, \ldots, l_n, c_1, \ldots, c_m, i_1, \ldots, i_n)$ contains the value of global variables of the model, local variables for each process, the messages stored in the model channels, and the instruction just executed by every process P_j $(j = 1, \ldots, n)$. g and l_j are also tuples, each one representing the actual value of a global or local variable at a point during the execution.

2. Let *Sequence* be the set of finite or infinite sequences of states.

3. Let $Inst_M$ and $Inst_j$ be the set of instructions of all the model processes and P_j, respectively.

4. Let $Initial : Promela \rightarrow State$ be the function which, given a model, returns its initial state, i.e., that in which its variables have been initialized, all channels are empty and each just-executed process instruction is a special one which precedes the first instruction in every process.

5. Let $next\_inst_j : Inst_j \rightarrow Inst_j$ be the function which given a process P_j and an instruction i of P_j returns the instruction which follows i in the code of P_j. If i is the last instruction of P_j then $next\_inst_j(i) = end$.

6. Let $just\_exe_j : State \rightarrow Inst_j$ be the just-executed function which, given a process and a state, returns the last instruction of the process executed, i.e., $just\_exe_j((g, l_1, \ldots, l_n, c_1, \ldots, c_m, i_1, \ldots, i_j, \ldots, i_n)) = i_j$.

7. Given $eval : BoolExp \times State \rightarrow \{false, true\}$, $eval(exp, s)$ returns the evaluation of the Boolean expression exp in the state s.

8. Let $exec_j : Inst_j \times State \rightarrow \{false, true\}$ be the executable function defined as
   - $exec_j(i, s) = eval(i, s)$, if i is a Boolean expression.
   - $exec_j(i, s) = false$, if i implies reading from an empty channel, reading a specified message from the channel which does not match with the first channel message, or writing on a full channel.

- $exec_j(i,s) = false$, if i is a non-deterministic instruction such as $if ::$ $exp_1- > i_1; \ldots :: exp_k- > i_k fi$ and $exec_j(exp_r, s) = false$, for all $1 \leq r \leq k$.
- $exec_j(i,s) = true$, otherwise.

In short, $exec_j(i,s)$ returns $true$ if the instruction i of process P_j does not suspend in the state s and returns $false$, otherwise.

9. Let $next_j : Inst_j \times State \rightarrow \wp(Inst_j) \cup \{delay, end\}$ be the function which given a process instruction returns the next instruction to be executed, i. e.,
   - $next_j(i,s) = delay$, if $exec_j(next\_inst_j(i), s) = false$,
   - $next_j(i,s) = end$, if $next\_inst_j(i) = end$.
   - $next_j(i,s) = \{exp_{r1}, \ldots, exp_{rs}\}$, if $next\_inst_j(i)$ is a non-deterministic instruction such as $if :: exp_1- > i_1; \ldots :: exp_k- > i_k fi$ and some instructions $exp_{r1}, \ldots, exp_{rs}$ exist such that $exec_j(exp_{rm}, s) = true$ ($1 \leq m \leq s$).
   - $next_j(i,s) = next\_inst_j(i)$, otherwise.

10. Let $S : (Inst_1 \cup \ldots \cup Inst_n) \times State \rightarrow State$ be a semantics function which gives meaning to each Promela instruction. $S(i, ((g, l_1, \ldots, l_j, \ldots, l_n, c, i_1, \ldots, i_j, \ldots, i_n)) = s' = (g', l_1, \ldots, l'_j, \ldots, l_n, c', i_1, \ldots, i, \ldots, i_n)$ means that executing the instruction i belonging to a given process P_j, when the model is in the state s, produces the evolution of the model towards the state s'. S is a generic function, that is, it is unspecified; we only substitute i_j by i in the state to indicate that i is the last instruction executed in the process P_j. The high level behavior of the model is not dependent on this function and this is why we do not define it. In [14], the meaning of every Promela instruction can be found.

11. Let $Trans : State \rightarrow \wp(State) \cup \{end, deadlock\}$ be the transition function which, given a model state s, returns the set of next states to which it can evolve from s. $Trans$ is defined as:
   - $Trans(s) = \cup_{j=1\ldots n}(\cup_{i \in (next_j(just\_exec_j(s),s) \cap Inst_j)}\{S(i,s)\})$, if $j \in \{1, \ldots, n\}$ exists such that $next_j(just\_exec_j(s), s) \notin \{delay, end\}$
   - $Trans(s) = end$, if $\forall j = 1, \ldots, n$, $next_j(just\_exec_j(s), s) = end$, and
   - $Trans(s) = deadlock$, otherwise.

Next, we define the generalized semantics $Gen : Promela \rightarrow \wp(Sequence)$ using the function $Trans$.

$Gen(M) = \{s_0 \rightarrow s_1 \rightarrow \ldots \rightarrow s_k \rightarrow \ldots \in Sequence/Initial(M) = s_0,$
$\forall j > 0.(Trans(s_{j-1}) \notin \{deadlock, end\}, s_j \in Trans(s_{j-1}))\} \cup$
$\{s_0 \rightarrow s_1 \rightarrow \ldots \rightarrow s_k \nrightarrow \in Sequences/Initial(M) = s_0,$
$Trans(s_k) \in \{deadlock, end\}, \forall 0 < j \leq k.(Trans(s_{j-1}) \notin \{deadlock, end\},$
$s_j \in Trans(s_{j-1}))\}$

Gen associates each $Promela$ model M with the set of all possible state sequences that M can display in different model executions. This semantics is useful for our purposes due to each sequence corresponding to a possible model execution that we must analyze when we are carrying out model checking. In addition, since the meaning of the model operations is unspecified, it is possible to change this without modifying the operational behavior of the model. As the operational behavior of a given model $M \in Promela$, represented by $Gen(M)$, depends on the functions $eval$ and S, we denote it with $Gen(M, eval, S)$, $eval$ and S being the parameters of the generalized semantics.

3 Abstract generalized semantics

In this section, we explain how to obtain an abstract model from an original model. The meaning of the abstract model is given by the generalized semantics defined above to which we have added two conditions to guarantee correctness. To do the abstraction, we assume the existence of an abstraction function which transforms actual data and operations into abstract ones. An automatic source-to-source transformation will result in an abstract model. The object model of the transformation will be obtained from the correct implementation of the abstract instructions produced by the data abstraction. The benefit of this method is that the abstract model obtained is a Promela model which can be analyzed by the SPIN tool.

We first explain the initial step to obtain abstract models given the concrete ones, then present the abstract semantics (generalized semantics + correctness conditions), prove some correctness results, and finally present how to obtain correct abstract models in Promela.

3.1 Automatic transformation from concrete models to abstract models

Next, we use the following definitions. As before, let $M = P_1 || \ldots || P_n$ be a Promela model involving the concurrent execution of n processes.

- Let us suppose that M contains s global and local variables $v_1, \ldots, v_s$, each one ranging over a (non-empty) set of values D_i. Let D be $D_1 \times \ldots \times D_s$.
- Let us suppose that M contains m channels $c_1, \ldots, c_m$, and let C_j be the domain of all possible values that c_j may store. Let C be $C_1 \times \ldots \times C_m$.
- Finally, let $Inst$ be $Inst_1 \times \ldots \times Inst_n$, $Inst_j$ being the set of instructions which form P_j.

From these definitions, we have $State = D \times C \times Inst$. Let $\alpha = \alpha_d \times \alpha_c : D \times C \rightarrow D^* \times C^*$ be an abstraction function which transforms each concrete state into an abstracted one. Note that temporarily the instructions are not being taken into account. We assume that $(D^*, \leq_d^*)$ and $(C^*, \leq_c^*)$ are posets, where the partial order represents the relative precision of the approximation of every abstract data, as is classic in abstract interpretation. Sometimes, we will use α_d and α_c over simple variables and channels instead of tuples. We allow this abuse of notation for clarity in the exposition.

From α_d and α_c, we define an approximation of the instructions. α_{inst} denotes the function which transforms every concrete instruction into an abstract one, by renaming the original instruction and changing data and messages by the corresponding abstract ones using α. Let $Inst^*$ be $Inst_1^* \times \ldots \times Inst_n^*$, each $Inst_j^*$ being the set of abstract instructions of the process P_j. Finally, let M^* be the abstract model obtained by substituting each instruction i of P_j by $\alpha_{inst}(i)$.

$\alpha = \alpha_d \times \alpha_c$ and α_{inst} define an abstraction of the model states, denoted by α_s, in the following way:

$$\alpha_s((g, l, c, i_1, \ldots, i_n)) = (\alpha_d((g, l)), \alpha_c(c), \alpha_{inst}(i_1), \ldots, \alpha_{inst}(i_n))$$

Given two abstract states $s_1^* = (g_1^*, l_1^*, c_1^*, inst_1^*)$ and $s_2^* = (g_2^*, l_2^*, c_2^*, inst_2^*)$, we say that $s_1^* \leq_s^* s_2^*$ (s_1^* is more precise than s_2^*) iff the following conditions hold: (1) $(g_1^*, l_1^*) \leq_d^* (g_2^*, l_2^*)$, (2) $c_1^* \leq_c^* c_2^*$ and (3) $Inst_1^* = Inst_2^*$.

Figure 2 illustrates the first part of the transformation method guided by an abstraction presented above. Model M has only one process ($init$) and one global variable i ranging over the integer numbers. We consider the classic abstraction $\alpha : int \rightarrow \{\bot, even, odd, evenodd\}$ defined as $\alpha(2n) = even$, and $\alpha(2n+1) = odd$, for all $n \geq 0$. $\bot$ and $evenodd$ are the bottom and top of the domain, respectively. The partial order defined on this domain is $\forall x \in \{\bot, even, odd, evenodd\}.(\bot \leq x \leq evenodd)$.

```
init { int i;                          #define even 0
    start: if                          #define odd 1
            :: i = i + 1; goto start;  #define evenodd 2
            :: goto end;               init { int i =* even;
          fi                               start: if
    end:skip }                                     :: i =* i +* odd;goto start;
                                                   :: goto end
                                               fi;
                                           end:skip }

       Model M                         Model M*
```

Fig. 2. Concrete and abstract models

In the transformed model M^*, the constants 0 and 1 have been substituted by $even$ and odd, respectively. In addition, the operation $+$ and the instruction $=$ have been replaced by $+^*$ and $=^*$, though they are not yet defined. The automatic transformation from M to M^* can be easily made, and only the definition of the abstract operations and instructions have been left out. In Section 3.4, we complete the transformation by substituting each abstract operator and each abstract instruction by a Promela code, which is a correct approximation, with respect to the semantics defined in the following section, of the respective concrete operation and instruction.

3.2 Abstract semantics

Now we define the abstract semantics of a Promela model. Given a model M whose semantics is given by $Gen(M, eval, S)$ and an abstraction function α defined as in Section 3.1, we construct the abstract model M^* using α as exposed above. The abstract generalized semantics $Gen^*(M^*, eval^*, S^*)$ of M^* is defined as Gen. Next we use the superindex * to refer to the abstract states, abstract sequences, and other elements of the generalized semantics of the abstract model M^*. We impose the following conditions on the meaning of the abstract operations and instructions ($eval^*$ and S^*), to assure the correctness of the transformation $M \rightarrow M^*$:

1. Let us suppose that $eval^*$: $BoolExp^* \times State^* \rightarrow \{false, true\}$ verifies the following correctness relation: $\forall s^* \in State^*.(\forall s \in State.\alpha_s(s) \leq_s^* s^* \Rightarrow eval(exp, s) \leq_b^* eval^*(\alpha_{inst}(exp), s^*)))$.
The partial order used in the set $\{false, true\}$ is $false \leq_b^* true$, which in our context means that if $eval^*$ returns $false$ then the evaluation of $\alpha_{inst}(exp)$ in each concretization of the abstract state s^* is $false$; otherwise $eval^*$ will return $true$. Thus $eval(exp, s) = false \not\Rightarrow eval^*(\alpha_{inst}(exp), \alpha_s(s)) = false$, however $eval^*(exp^*, s^*) = false \Rightarrow eval(exp, s) = false$, for all Boolean expressions exp and states s such that $\alpha_{inst}(exp) = exp^*$ and $\alpha_s(s) \leq_s^* s^*$.
2. Let S^* : $(Inst_1^* \cup \ldots \cup Inst_n^*) \times State^* \rightarrow State^*$ be an abstract function verifying the relation: $\forall s^* \in State^*.(\forall s \in State.(\alpha(s) \leq_s^* s^* \Rightarrow \alpha(S(i, s)) \leq_s^* S^*(\alpha_{inst}(i), s^*)))$.
S^* gives abstract and correct meaning to the instructions of the abstract model M^*. As before, S^* is not specified, we have only declared its correctness relation with S.

3.3 Correctness

In this section, we prove a correctness result of the abstraction. We impose the condition that every state in each concrete execution path corresponds to an abstract state in an abstract execution path. This is a strong result as we need the whole concrete computation to be simulated step-by-step by the abstraction. Weaker correctness conditions can be defined by imposing the condition that the approximation holds at some specified points of the concrete model (and not in all states) in a similar way to the collecting semantics used in abstract interpretation [2].

In the following, let us suppose that $\alpha = \alpha_d \times \alpha_c : D \times C \rightarrow D^* \times C^*$ is an abstraction function of a concrete Promela model $M = P_1 || \ldots || P_n$, in the same conditions as the previous discussion, $Gen(M, eval, S)$ and $Gen^*(M^*, eval^*, S^*)$ being the semantics of M and its transformation M^*.

Given $seq = s_0 \rightarrow s_1 \rightarrow \ldots \rightarrow s_k \rightarrow \ldots \in Sequence$, we define $\alpha_{seq}(seq)$ as $\alpha_s(s_0) \rightarrow \alpha_s(s_1) \rightarrow \ldots \rightarrow \alpha_s(s_k) \rightarrow \ldots \in Sequence^*$.

Given a channel c, let $|c| \in N$ denote the number of messages stored by c in a particular state s. In addition, if $|c| = n$ and $1 \leq j \leq n$, c_j represents the j-th message.

Definition 1. *Given* $seq^*, seq^{*'} \in Sequence^*$, *then* $seq^* \leq_{seq}^* seq^{*'}$, *iff for all* $i \geq 0, s_i^* \leq_s^* s_i^{*'}$.

Definition 2. *An abstraction* α *preserves the length of the channels iff for each channel* c, $|c| = |\alpha_c(c)|$.

Lemma 1. *If* α *is an abstraction which preserves the length of the channels, then* $\forall i \in Inst.(\forall s^* \in State^*.(\forall s \in State.(\alpha_s(s) \leq_s^* s^*, exec_j^*(\alpha_{inst}(i), s^*) = false \Rightarrow exec_j(i, s) = false)))$.

Proof. Let us consider $s \in State$ and $s^* \in State^*$ such that $\alpha_s(s) \leq_s^* s^*$.

1. If i is a Boolean expression then, by hypothesis $eval^*(\alpha_{inst}(i), s^*) = false$, and since $eval^*$ verifies $eval(i, s) \leq_b^* eval^*(\alpha_{inst}(i), s^*)$, then we deduce that $eval(i, s) = false$, that is, $exec_j(i, s) = false$.
2. If $i = c?msg$ then we consider two cases:
   (a) i imposes no condition over the message read. In this case, as α preserves the length of the channels $|c| = |\alpha_c(c)|$, and as $exec_j^*(\alpha_{inst}(i), s^*) = false$, we have $|c| = |\alpha_c(c)| = 0$, and hence $exec_j(i, s) = false$.
   (b) i imposes some matching condition over the message read from c. The case $|c| = 0$ has been proved in (a). Therefore, let us assume that $|c| > 0$. As $exec_j^*(a_{inst}(i), s^*) = false$, the first abstract message of $\alpha_c(c)$, $\alpha_c(c)_1$, does not verify this condition, which really is the Boolean test $\alpha_c(c)_1 ==^* \alpha_d(msg)$. Thus, by 1, as $eval^*(\alpha_c(c)_1 ==^* \alpha_d(msg), s^*) = false$, we deduce that $eval(c_1 == msg, s) = false$ or equivalently that $exec_j(i, s) = false$.
3. If $i = c!msg$ as before, if α preserves the length of the channels then $exec_j^*(\alpha_{inst}(i), s^*) = false \Rightarrow exec_j(i, s) = false$.
4. No other instruction suspends in the concrete model or in the abstract one. The instruction if is analyzed using cases 1, 2 and 3. [1]

In the rest of the section, we always assume that α preserves the length of the channels.

Lemma 2. *If $s_1, s_2 \in State$ and $s_1^* \in State^*$ verify that $s_2 \in Trans(s_1)$ and $\alpha_s(s_1) \leq_s^* s_1^*$ then an abstract state $s_2^* \in State^*$ exists such that $s_2^* \in Trans^*(s_1^*)$ and $\alpha_s(s_2) \leq_s^* s_2^*$.*

Proof. $s_2 \in Trans(s_1)$ implies that $j \in \{1, \ldots, n\}$ and $i \in Inst_j$ exist such $s_2 = S(i, s_1)$. This means that $exec_j(i, s_1) = true$, and applying Lemma 1 we have that $exec_j^*(\alpha_{inst}(i), s_1^*) = true$. So, we can choose the instruction $\alpha_{inst}(i) \in Inst_j^*$ to evolve from s_1^* to $S^*(\alpha_{inst}(i), s_1^*)$. Let s_2^* be $S^*(\alpha_{inst}(i), s_1^*)$. By definition, $s_2^* \in Trans^*(s_1^*)$, and also by the correctness condition (point 2) we have $\alpha(S(i, s_1)) \leq_s^* S^*(\alpha_{inst}(i), s_1^*)$, that is, $\alpha(s_2) \leq_s^* s_2^*$.

Lemma 3. $\forall s \in State.(\forall s^* \in State^*.(\alpha_s(s) \leq_s^* s^*, Trans(s) = end \Rightarrow Trans^*(s^*) = end)).$

Proof. If $\alpha(s) \leq_s^* s^*$ then the process counters of both states (s and s^*) are pointing to the same concrete or abstract instructions. So, $Trans(s) = end$ means that all the counters in s are pointing to the end of each model process and the same for s^*.

Theorem 1. *Let $Gen(M, eval, S)$ and $Gen^*(M^*, eval^*, S^*)$ be the semantics of the models M and M^* verifying the conditions presented in Section 3.2, then for each deadlock-free sequence $seq \in Gen(M, eval, S)$, an abstract deadlock-free sequence $seq^* \in Gen^*(M^*, eval^*, S^*)$ exists, such that $\alpha_{seq}(seq) \leq_{seq}^* seq^*$.*

---

[1] We assume that there is not rendezvous in the model M. It is possible to include it but this would unnecessarily complicate the presentation.

Proof. Let *seq* be $s_0 \to s_1 \to s_2 \to \ldots \in Gen(M, eval, S)$, using Lemma 2 we build *seq** as follows:

1. Let s_0^* be $\alpha_s(s_0)$ the initial state of every execution path of M^*.
2. Let s_1^* be the abstract state given by Lemma 2 using $s_0^* \in State^*$, and s_0, $s_1 \in State$. $s_1^* \in State^*$ verifies that $s_1^* \in Trans^*(s_0^*)$ and $\alpha(s_1) \leq_s^* s_1^*$.
3. Applying Lemma 2, we successively obtain the abstract states s_2^*, s_3^*, etc.
4. By Lemma 3, if *seq* is a finite sequence, we have that *seq** is also finite.

Definition 3. *Given two Promela models* M, $M^* \in Promela$, *then we say that* M^* α-*approximates* M, *and we denote it with* $M \sqsubseteq_\alpha M^*$, *if* $Gen(M, eval, S)$ *and* $Gen^*(M^*, eval^*, S^*)$ *are related as explained in Section 3.2, and verify the hypotesis of Theorem 1. In particular,* α *preserves the length of the channels and* M *is deadlock-free.*

The next propositions explain the relationship between the concrete and abstract models when proving temporal properties. One property F over one model M is built with the usual temporal operators, Boolean connectives and propositions. Propositions are tests over data, channels or labels. For convenience, we assume that all formulas are in negation normal form, that is, negations only appear in propositions. In the following, we call abstract properties to those which are defined over abstract models (propositions evaluated over abstract states). Given a concrete property F (or proposition P) over a model M, we can obtain its abstract version, denoted by $\alpha_f(F)$ ($\alpha_f(P)$), by preserving the formula structure (Boolean and temporal operators) and abstracting data.

Definition 4. *Let us assume that* $M \sqsubseteq_\alpha M^*$. *Let* P^* *be an abstract proposition,* G^*, H^* *and* F^* *abstract temporal formulas and* $seq = s_0 \to s_1 \to \ldots \to \in Gen(M, eval, S)$, *then*

1. $s \in State$ *satisfies* P^* *(s* $\models P^*$*) iff an abstract state* $s^* \in State^*$ *exists such* $\alpha_s(s) \leq_s^* s^*$ *and* $s^* \models P^*$.
2. $seq \models []G^*$ *iff for each* $i \geq 0$, $s_i \models G^*$.
3. $seq \models \diamond G^*$ *iff* $i \geq 0$ *exists such that* $s_i \models G^*$.
4. $seq \models G^* U H^*$ *iff* $i \geq 0$ *exists such that* $s_i \models H^*$ *and for all* $0 \leq j \leq i - 1, s_j \models G^*$.
5. $seq \models G^* \wedge H^*$ *iff* $seq \models G^*$ *and* $seq \models H^*$.
6. $seq \models G^* \vee H^*$ *iff* $seq \models G^*$ *or* $seq \models H^*$.
7. $M \models F^*$ *iff for all execution paths* $seq \in Gen(M, eval, S)$, $seq \models F^*$.

Proposition 1. *Let* F^* *be a universal abstract property over* M^* *(which must hold on all execution paths). If* $M \sqsubseteq_\alpha M^*$ *and* $M^* \models F^*$ *then* $M \models F^*$.

Proof. By induction over the formula structure using Theorem 1 (see [10]).

This proposition proves that if the abstract model M^* verifies an abstract property F^*, the concrete model M also verifies F^*. If the abstraction function α and the abstract domain $D^* \times C^*$ define useful information for the user, this result can be a powerful means for debugging the model. For instance, with the typical abstraction $\alpha : int \rightarrow \{\bot, even, odd, evenodd\}$ defined in Section 3.1, it could be interesting to verify $F^* = [](x == even)$, assuming that x is a global variable of a model M. However, the user could also be interested in proving a concrete formula F (over the concrete domain) by proving $\alpha_f(F)$ (or other abstract version F^* of F) over M^*. Next, we discuss how to relate F^* and F.

Definition 5. *Given P_1^*, P_2^*, F_1^* and F_2^* abstract propositions and formulas*

1. $P_1^* \Rightarrow^* P_2^*$ *iff* $\forall s \in State.(s \models P_1^* \Rightarrow s \models P_2^*)$.
2. $F_1^* \Rightarrow^* F_2^*$ *iff* $\forall seq \in Gen(M, eval, S). \ (seq \models F_1^* \Rightarrow seq \models F_2^*)$.

Proposition 2. *Given an abstract proposition P^* and a state $s \in State$, if $s \models P^*$ then a concrete proposition P exists such that $s \models P$ and $\alpha_f(P) \Rightarrow^* P^*$.*

Proof. If $s \models P^*$ then $\exists s^* \in State^*.(\alpha_s(s) \leq_s^* s^*$ and $s^* \models P^*)$. This means that $\alpha_s(s)$ verifies a stronger version Q^* of P^* (the data and the contents of channels of $\alpha_s(s)$ are more precise than the ones of s^*). So, s verifies the proposition P obtained by substituting the abstract values of Q^* in $\alpha_s(s)$ by the corresponding concrete data in s. By construction, $\alpha_f(P) = Q^*$ and $\alpha_f(P) \Rightarrow^* P^*$.

Proposition 3. *Given a model M and an abstract property F^*, if $M \models F^*$ then $M \models \vee\{F : \alpha_f(F) \Rightarrow^* F^*\}$.*

Proof. By induction over the formula structure using Proposition 2 (see [10]).

This proposition gives us the relationship between the abstract formula proved in the abstract model and the concrete formulas which hold in the concrete model. This result is very useful when the set $\{F : \alpha_f(F) \Rightarrow^* F^*\}$ has only one element, this is, when there is only one concrete formula F, such that $\alpha_f(F) \Rightarrow^* F^*$. Under this condition, the user knows that F holds in M. So, when the objective of one abstraction is to prove a concrete formula F over the concrete model M, we must define the abstraction function α in such a way that only one concretization of $\alpha_f(F)$ exists. If this happens and the system proves that $M^* \models \alpha_f(F)$, Proposition 3 guarantees that $M \models F$, as was expected by the user. One example of this situation is shown in [4]. The user wants to prove the formula $F = [](a = 42 \rightarrow b = 42)$ over a model M (with only two global variables a and b) and chooses the abstraction function $\alpha : Int \rightarrow \{0, 1\}$ defined as $\alpha(42) = 0$, $\alpha(i) = 1$, if $i \neq 42$ to build the abstract model M^*. With this definition if $\alpha_f(F) = F^* = [](a = 0 \rightarrow b = 0)$ and $M^* \models \alpha_f(F)$ we have that $M \models F$, as expected by the user.

In the previous discussions, we have assumed that the concrete model M is deadlock-free. The next Proposition studies how to analyze deadlock in M. For this purpose we need to impose some conditions which are presented in the following definition.

Definition 6. *Given an abstraction function α, we say that α verifies the executability conditions iff $exec_j(i, s) = exec_j^*(\alpha_{inst}(i), s^*)$, for each pair of states $s^* \in State^*$, $s \in State$, such that $\alpha_s(s) \leq_s^* s^*$, and for each $i \in Inst_j$.*

Proposition 4. *Let M^* be an abstraction of M obtained by means of the function α, verifying the conditions presented in Section 3.2. Let us assume that α also verifies the executability conditions presented above. If $Gen^*(M^*, eval^*, S^*)$ has no execution sequence which deadlocks then $Gen(M, eval, S)$ has no deadlock either.*

Proof. Given $seq = s_0 \rightarrow \ldots \rightarrow s_k \rightarrow deadlock \in Gen(M, eval, S)$ by Theorem 1, we can construct an abstract sequence $s_0^* \rightarrow \ldots \rightarrow s_k^*$ such that $\forall 0 \leq i \leq k.(\alpha_s(s_i) \leq_s^* s_i^*)$. Let us consider the states s_k and s_k^*. By hypothesis, $Trans(s_k) = deadlock$, this is, $\forall j = 1, \ldots, n$, if $i_j = just\_exec_j(s)$ then $exec_j(next\_inst_j(i_j), s_k) = false$, and by Definition 6 we have $(exec_j^*(next\_inst_j^*(\alpha_{inst}(i_j), s_k^*)) = false)$, that is, $Trans^*(s_k^*) = deadlock$.

3.4 Model transformation based on abstract interpretation

Proposition 5. *Let $M = P_1 || \ldots || P_n$ be a Promela model and $\alpha = \alpha_d \times \alpha_c$: $D \times C \rightarrow D^* \times C^*$ an abstraction function verifying the conditions of Section 3.1 (α preserves the length of the channels). Let $Inst^*$ be the set of abstract instructions derived from α. Let M^* be the model obtained by abstracting all the constants and instructions of M. Let us suppose that for each instruction $i^* \in Inst^*$ a Promela implementation exists verifying the correctness conditions imposed in Section 3.2. Under these conditions, the model MI^*, obtained by atomically substituting each model instruction by its implementation, verifies Theorem 1.*

Example in Figure 2 (continuing): The model obtained by substituting $+^*$ and $=^*$ by its implementation is:

```
#define even 0
#define odd 1
#define evenodd 2
init {  byte i = even;
start:     if
           :: d_step { if
                       ::i == evenodd -> i=evenodd
                       ::i==even -> i=odd
                       ::i==odd -> i=even
                       fi };goto start;
           :: goto end;
           fi;
end:skip;
}               Model MI*
```

4   Example

We illustrate the concepts presented above by verifying the version of the ABP protocol given in Figures 3 and 4. This version of the protocol enables the transmission of data from process A to process B over an unreliable channel. The error-free behavior of the protocol consists in A sending data message with a control bit equal to 1 and receiving a reply message also with bit 1 (states S1 and S2 in A). In this error-free scenario, B waits for data messages with bit 1 and replies with the same bit (states S2 and S1 in B). Other states in A and B are used to recover the transmission from an error in the channel. Figure 3 shows the state machines for every process in the protocol (extracted from SPIN documentation). Our version for this protocol also contains the process C to model an unreliable channel between A and B. This process controls the maximum number of errors in the line in order to preserve the correct behavior of the protocol.

In order to ensure the correctness of the protocol, the user can use SPIN to analyze at least the two following properties.

Invalid end states. The intended behavior of process A is to send data messages infinitely often, so there are no end labels in the model to specify legal end states in process A or B, and every deadlock should be reported as an invalid end state.

Temporal property. As suggested in SPIN documentation, the designer of the protocol would like to know if it has the following property: "In all computations, every message sent by A is received error-free at least once and accepted at most once by B." Following the idea of Holzmann's assertion, this property can be written with the temporal formula

$$F = \texttt{[] (B\_accept -> B\_accept\_ok)}$$

where the informal meaning of the propositions B_accept is that process B will immediately accept the data received in mr, and B_accept_ok means that the expected value in mr follows the value stored in lmr.

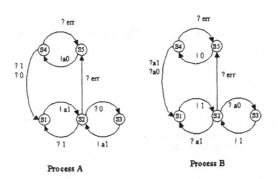

Process A   Process B

Fig. 3. State machines for the ABP protocol

The state-space of the model in Figure 4 (with 4 data to be sent) has 955 states. This space state can be obviously explored with current computers in order to ensure the desired correctness requirements. But let us assume that we do not have enough memory in the computer. Then, the use of abstractions could simplify our work.

As explained in the previous section, the construction of a (more) abstract model for a given model must be driven by the property to be verified. If we examine the meaning of the propositions in F, we see that the evaluation of

B_accept does not depend directly on data values. So we choose an abstraction function that makes easier the evaluation B_accept_ok. The model $M1^*$ is an abstraction of *M1* replacing the real data value in the message with only two abstract values: *even* and *odd*. This means that the global variables mt, mr and lmr and the variable m in process C will range over $\{\perp, even, odd, evenodd\}$. The abstract model Promela $M1^*$ is obtained by transforming the assignment sentence and the sum operations in processes A and B (in a similar way that in Section 3.4).

```
#define MAX 4
byte mt, mr, lmr;
proctype A(chan in, out)                  proctype B(chan in, out)
{      byte vr;                            {      byte ar;
S1:    mt = (mt+1)%MAX;                           goto S2;
       out!mt,1;                          S1:    lmr = mr;
       goto S2;                                  out!1;
S2:    in?vr;                                     goto S2;
       if                                 S2:    in?mr,ar;
       :: (vr == 1) -> goto S1                   if
       :: (vr == 0) -> goto S3                   :: (ar == 1) -> goto S1
       :: (vr == error) -> goto S5              :: (ar == 0) -> goto S3
       fi;                                       :: (ar == error)-> goto S5
S3:    out!mt,1;                                 fi;
       goto S4;                            S3:    out!1;
S4:    in?vr;                                     goto S2;
       if                                 S4:    in?mr,ar;
       :: goto S1                                if
       :: (vr == error)-> goto S5               :: goto S1
       fi;                                       :: (ar == error)-> goto S5
S5:    out!mt,0;                                 fi;
       goto S4                            S5: out!0;
}                                               goto S4
                                          }

proctype C(chan a2c, c2b, b2c, c2a)
{ byte m, v,errors_a = 0, errors_b = 0;
S1:if
   :: a2c ? m,v -> if
                   :: atomic{errors_b=0; c2b ! m, v }-> goto S1
                   :: errors_b < 1 -> atomic{errors_b++; c2b ! m, error }-> goto S1
                   fi
   :: b2c ? v ->    if
                   :: atomic{errors_a=0; c2a ! v}-> goto S1
                   :: errors_a < 1 -> atomic{errors_a++; c2a ! error }-> goto S1
                   fi
   fi }

init { chan b2c = [2] of {byte}, c2a = [2] of {byte},
        a2c = [2] of {byte, byte}, c2b = [2] of { byte, byte };
     atomic {run A(c2a, a2c);run C(a2c, c2b, b2c, c2a); run B(c2b, b2c) } }
```

Fig. 4. Promela model of ABP (M1)

This abstraction verifies the hypothesis of Proposition 4, because we do not abstract any sentence that can suspend in *M1*, and the abstraction preserves the length of the channels. So we can employ $M1^*$ to verify the absence of deadlock in the model *M1*. This property is proved by inspecting 232 states in $M1^*$.

The verification of *M1* requires 448 states. The abstract propositions in F^* are defined as: `#define B_accept B[3]@S1` and `#define B_accept_ok mr != lmr`

We can easily prove that $M1 \sqsubseteq_\alpha M1^*$, and by Proposition 1, if $M1^* \models F^*$ then $M1 \models F^*$. So we only have to prove $M1 \models F^*$. Fortunately, SPIN checks that F^* is valid in all computations of $M1^*$ exploring only 106 states.

If we want to verify a concrete formula with a similar meaning over *M1*, such as

$$F' = \quad [] \ ((B[3]@S1 \ \text{->} \ mr \ \text{==} \ (lmr \ +1) \ \% \ \text{MAX})$$

`MAX` being the real number of different data messages, then we have to explore 448 states in *M1*. So we have saved memory using the abstract model.

	M1	*M1**	*M2*	*M2**
State space	448	232	952	297
Deadlock ? Explored States	No 448	No 232	No 952	No 297
Valid F ? Explored States	Yes 448	Yes 106	No 281	No 149

Table 1. Verification results

Table 1 shows all these results with *M1* and *M1**. The table also shows the verification of the models *M2* and *M2**. The model *M2* is similar to the original in the SPIN documentation (any number of errors), but with an intermediate process to model the channel. *M2** is obtained with the same abstraction as *M1**. Results for *M2* and *M2** show that violation of F^* over *M2** does not provide a definitive result about its violation over *M2*. But deadlock can be directly analyzed in the abstract model.

5   Conclusions and further work

We have presented a generalized semantics of Promela which is suitable for justifying the use of abstract interpretation to automatically transform Promela models into more abstract versions. The transformed (abstracted) models can be employed to reduce the state space for the verification using SPIN. The same framework can be used to define the semantics of the original (concrete) Promela model as well as the new (abstracted) models, therefore, it allows us to relate different abstractions of the same system. The way of using abstract interpretation enables the verification of universal temporal properties of the original system by verifying a more abstract version, as in other related works. We also are working on the use of program specialization (partial evaluation) in order to prove existential properties, i.e., properties that hold along one execution path.

We are currently working on tools to integrate the abstract interpretation technique into XSPIN. Our aim is to put this technique into everyday use by constructing a user-friendly environment that provides a library of standard abstraction functions.

Acknowledgement. We would like to thanks the anonymous referees for their useful comments and suggestions on this and earlier versions of the paper.

References

1. Barlett A., Scantlebury R.A., Wilkinson P.T.: A note on reliable full-duplex transmission over half-duplex lines. Communications of the ACM, 12 (5)(1969) 260–265
2. Cousot P., Cousot R.: Abstract Interpretation: A Unified Lattice Model for Static Analysis of Programs by Construction or Approximation of Fixpoints. Conference Record of the 4th ACM Symposium on Principles of Programming Languages (1977)
3. Clarke E.M., Emerson E. A., Sistla A.P.: Automatic Verification of Finite-State Concurrent Systems Using Temporal Logic Specifications. ACM Trans. on Programming Languages and Systems, 8 (2), (1986) 244–263
4. Clarke E.M., Grumberg O., Long D.E.: Model Checking and Abstraction. ACM Transaction on Languages and Systems, 16(5) (1994) 1512–1542
5. Clarke E.M., Wing J.M.: Formal Methods: State of the Art and Future Directions. ACM Computing Surveys, ACM 50TH Anniversary Issue Workshop on Strategic Directions in Computing Research, 28(4) (1996)626–643
6. Dams D., Gerth R., Grumberg O.: Abstract Interpretation of Reactive Systems. ACM Transactions on Programming Languages and Systems, 19(2) March (1997) 253–291
7. Giacobazzi R., Debray S.K., Levi G.: A Generalized Semantics for Constraint Logic Programs. Proceedings of the International Conference on Fifth Generation Computer Systems (1992) 581–591
8. Gunter C., Mitchell J.: Strategic Directions in Software Engineering and Programming Languages. ACM Workshop on Strategic Directions in Computing Research, ACM Computing Surveys, 28(4)(1996) 727–737
9. Gallardo M.M., Merino P., Troya J.M.: Relating Abstract Interpretation with Logic Program Verification. Proceedings of the International Workshop on Verification, Model Cheking and Abstract Interpretation, Port Jefferson, USA, (1997)
10. Gallardo M.M., Merino P.: A Formal basis to Improve the Automatic Verification of Concurrent Systems. Technical Report LCC IT 99/10. Dpto. de Lenguajes y Ciencias de la Computacion. University of Malaga.(1999)
11. Holzmann G.J.: Design and Validation of Computer Protocols. Prentice-Hall, New Jersey (1991)
12. Holzmann G.J.: Designing Bug-Free Protocols with SPIN. Computer Communications, 20(2) (1997) 97–105
13. Jones, N.D., Søndergaard, H.: A Semantics-based framework for the abstract interpretation of Prolog. Abstract Interpretation of Declarative Languages. S. Abramsky and C. Hankin, Eds. Ellis Horwood, Chichester, U.K. (1987) 123–142
14. Natarajan V., Holzmann G.J.: Outline for an Operational Semantics of Promela. The SPIN Verification Systems. DIMACS Series in Discrete Mathematics and Theoretical Computer Science. AMS Vol. 32 (1997) 133–152
15. Vardi M., Wolper P.: An Automata-Theoretic Approach to Automatic Program Verification. Proc. of the Symp. on Logic in Computer Science, Cambridge (1986)

Model Checking Operator Procedures

Wenhui Zhang

Institute for Energy Technology, P.O.Box 173, N-1751 Halden, Norway
Wenhui.Zhang@hrp.no

Abstract. Operator procedures are documents telling operators what to do in various situations. They are widely used in process industries including the nuclear power industry. The correctness of such procedures is of great importance. We describe how model checking can be used to detect potential errors and to verify properties of operator procedures. As there could be problems with modelling and model checking large systems, incremental modelling and verification is proposed as a strategy to help overcome these problems. A case study is presented to show how model checking (with the model checker Spin [5]) and the incremental strategy work in practise.

1 Introduction

Operator procedures are documents telling operators what to do in various situations. There are procedures to be used in normal operation situations, in case of disturbances and in case of emergencies. Operator procedures are widely used in process industries including the nuclear power industry. The correctness of such procedures is of great importance. The following is a quote from the report on the accident at the Three Mile Island [6]: "A series of events - compounded by equipment failures, inappropriate procedures, and human errors and ignorance - escalated into the worst crisis yet experienced by the nation's nuclear power industry." Such inappropriate procedures included procedures for loss of coolant accident and for pressurizer operations [7].

To assess the correctness of operator procedures, we need correctness requirements. The correctness requirements of an operator procedure include goals that must be achieved upon completion of an execution of the procedure, safety constraints that must be maintained during an execution of the procedure and general structural requirements. For achieving goals, necessary and effective instructions must be explicitly specified in the procedure. In addition, time and resource constraints for carrying out the instructions must be satisfiable. For maintaining safety constraints, preparation steps for the goal-oriented instructions must be included in the procedure. It is also important that instructions are specified in the correct order and time and resource constraints for carrying out the preparation steps are satisfiable. Structural requirements make a procedure simple and easy to understand. They include no undefined references and unreachable instructions.

Violation of the correctness requirements could result in many types of errors. Although all types of violations are important with respect to correctness, formal verification techniques only offer a partial solution to the verification of procedures. Problems related to time and resource constraints are more complicated and are not considered for verification in this paper. We divide the types of errors to be considered for verification into three categories: structural errors, execution errors and consistency errors. *Structural errors* include undefined references and unreachable instructions as mentioned earlier. A reference is undefined, if it refers to no instruction in the procedure. The cause of an undefined reference could be that the reference is wrong or the instruction to which it refers is missing. An instruction is unreachable, if it cannot be reached from any potential execution of the procedure. For instance, if there is a block of instructions without any reference from outside of the block, the instructions in the block will be unreachable (unless one of the instructions in the block is the starting point of the procedure). A more complicate situation is that there are instructions refer to this block, but the conditions for using the references never become true in all potential executions of the procedure. *Execution errors* are errors that prevent an execution to be completed. They include deadlocks and infinite loops. There is a deadlock, if the operator stops at some point and is not able to do anything in order to complete the procedure. For instance, the operator may be waiting for a condition which never becomes true. There is an infinite loop, if the operator is captured by a loop and cannot jump out of the loop by following the instructions of the procedure. The causes for infinite loops could be wrong actions, wrong conditions or wrong references in goto instructions, and other types of problems. *Consistency errors* indicate inconsistency between the set of instructions of the procedure and given specifications. They include violation of assertions (representing conditions for performing actions), violation of invariants and unreached goals. The basic question is how to detect potential errors in operator procedures. In this paper, we discuss using model checking for this purpose.

2 Verification Approach

To begin with, we have a procedure that needs to be verified. It is however not sufficient to analyse the procedure alone. We have to take into consideration the environment in which the procedure is used. As our work is related to procedure correctness in power plants, in the following, we refer to a power plant as the environment of the procedure.

2.1 Model Checking

The idea of using model checking is as follows. When we design a procedure, we do so in a natural or semi-formal language. When the procedure is executed, the operator (in the following, the meaning of an operator is defined as a person or a robot that strictly follows the procedure) gets responses from the plant as the procedure is being carried out. Such a procedure, the set of the possible initial states of the plant, the plant processes and the interaction between these processes determine a logical structure. On the other hand, there could be correctness conditions for the plant and the interaction between the operator and the plant. For instance, we may want to express the following: "Pump-A" must not be running at the time one starts repairing "Valve-A" (an assertion at a point of an execution of the procedure), "Valve-B" is closed unless "Valve-C" is closed (an invariant in an execution of the procedure), and the state of the plant will become "Normal" after starting the procedure (a liveness property of the procedure). These conditions can be verified against the logical structure.

2.2 Verification and Error Detection

As explained above, in order to be able to verify a procedure, there are two main tasks: modelling the logical structure and verification with respect to correctness conditions. The modelling task is to create the following processes:

- A model-procedure process, which is used to model the procedure (or the operator in a process of executing the procedure).
- A set of plant processes, which are used to model the physical processes of the plant (or assumptions on the physical processes).
- A set of interaction processes, which are used to model the interaction between the model-procedure process and the plant processes.
- An initialisation process, which is a process for choosing an initial state from the set of possible initial states of the plant.

The following are the principles for modelling:

- The model-procedure process communicates only with the interaction processes and does not directly read or update variables representing the system state. We impose these restrictions to the model-procedure process because it is very helpful with a clear separation of the consequences of the actions of the model-procedure process and the consequences of the actions of other processes.
- The interaction processes communicate with the model-procedure process and the plant processes. They may read and update the system state and may also initiate and activate some of the plant processes.
- The plant processes communicate with the interaction processes and may read and update the system state. Sometimes synchronisation mechanism is necessary in order to ensure the ability of the interaction processes to take appropriate actions immediately after changes are made to the system state by the plant processes.
- The initialisation process updates the system state before other processes read or update the system state.

After these processes are created, we can use a model checker to check errors of the types described in the previous section. The techniques for checking errors are as follows:

- For detecting undefined references, we check syntactic errors.
- For detecting deadlocks and infinite loops, we check execution errors of the procedure (using an auxiliary variable to indicate the completion of an execution of the procedure).
- For detecting unreachable instructions, it is not necessary to use any special technique, since such problems can also be reported by checking execution errors (unreachable instructions can be detected in cases where no execution errors are found).
- For detecting violation of conditions for performing actions, we need assertions describing conditions for relevant actions and we check whether the procedure is consistent with respect to the assertions.
- For detecting violation of invariants, we need invariants and we check whether the procedure is consistent with respect to the invariants (i.e. whether they hold in all reachable states of the model).
- For detecting unreached goals, we need goals and we check whether the procedure is consistent with respect to the goals (i.e. whether they can be reached in all reachable paths of the model).

As the verification can be carried out by using fully automated model checking tools, the verification task is simple. *The major problems* of model checking operator procedures are the complexity of the modelling of the relevant processes of the power plant and the complexity of the models. Because there are many processes that interfere with each other in the power plant, a model of the relevant processes of the power plant can be very complicated. On the other hand, it is not necessary to have a complete model for using model checking. The necessary and optimal complexity depends on the properties to be verified. In order to limit the complexity, one has to make a decision on how complicated the plant process model should be. This is a difficult decision, because a complicated model may not be suitable (too large) for automated model checking and a too much simplified model may not be sufficient for model checking of certain properties. There has been a lot work on how to overcome the complexity of model checking by using algorithmic techniques (e.g. as in [2] and [12]) to minimise the size of the internal representation of the models and the transition relations and by using rule based methods (e.g. as in [1] and [3]) for decomposing the verification tasks. In the following, we take a practical approach and propose an incremental strategy for modelling and verification.

2.3 Incremental Modelling and Verification

The motivation for incremental modelling and verification is to overcome the complexity of modelling and the problem of deciding how complicated the plant process model should be. The basic idea is to divide the modelling process in different phases and perform model checking within each phase.

Phase 1 We create a model of the procedure (or an operator in a process of executing the procedure) and check syntactic errors in order to detect undefined references.

Phase 2 We derive assumptions on the interaction between the operator and the power plant from the procedure text and create an interaction model. In this phase, we check whether there are execution errors, in order to detect deadlocks and infinite loops, and to detect unreachable instructions in case there are no deadlocks and infinite loops.

Phase 3 We add an initialisation process and refine the interaction model by revising the set of relevant values for each of the variables representing involved plant units and other relevant aspects. We check whether there are execution errors and whether there are consistency errors with respect to given specifications (assertions, invariants and goals).

Phase 4 We add a plant process model and refine the interaction model accordingly. The plant process model should capture essential aspects of relevant physical processes and should be modelled as simple as possible. If the number of relevant processes is large, some of the (possibly less important) processes may be left to later phases. In this phase, we also check whether there are execution errors and consistency errors.

Phase 5, 6, ... In phase 5, we refine the plant process model and check the same categories of errors as in phase 4. The refinement may include two aspects, to add details into existing plant processes and to extend the model with new processes. In the latter case, we also need to modify the interaction processes. We may continue to refine the plant process model in phase 6, 7 and so on, until we are satisfied with the plant process model or until the model is too complicated for model checking.

2.4 Process Knowledge

Process knowledge is very important for verification of procedures. We need process knowledge for formulating correctness requirements such as safety constraints and goals. In addition, there are different needs of process knowledge for modelling procedures and for modelling relevant plant processes in the different phases.

- Phase 1: The need for process knowledge is relatively moderate (some knowledge for understanding terminologies is needed). The need may depend on how well procedures are structured and whether the terminologies used in the procedures are standardised.
- Phase 2: The need for process knowledge is basically the same as in phase 1.
- Phase 3: The need for process knowledge is increasing. One needs to know under what conditions the procedure are assumed to be applied. One also needs to know how many different values are necessary for the states of certain plant objects.
- Phase 4: One needs to know how the states of different plant objects change and must be able to catch the essence of these changes with simple models.
- Phase 5, 6, ...: The need for process knowledge is basically the same as in phase 4.

2.5 Summary

The tasks of modelling in the different phases of the incremental modelling and verification are as follows:

- Phase 1: Create a model of the procedure.
- Phase 2: Add an interaction model.
- Phase 3: Add an initialisation process and refine the interaction model.
- Phase 4: Add a model of the physical processes.
- Phase 5,6,...: Refine the previously created plant and interaction models.

The verification sub-tasks to be performed in the different phases are summarised in the following table:

	phase 1	phase 2	phase 3	phase 4	phase 5,6,...
check syntactic errors	x				
check execution errors		x	x	x	x
check assertion violations			x	x	x
check invariant violations			x	x	x
check unreached goals			x	x	x

Remark The model of the procedure remains the same in all phases (unless an error is detected and the procedure has to be changed). Only the models of physical processes and the interaction processes are modified in the different phases. The sub-steps (verification sub-tasks) within each phase are ordered according to increasing difficulty of correctness specifications. It is possible to rearrange the sub-steps or to combine all or some sub-steps into one big step, if it is desirable.

Discussion Theoretically, if the model in phase 4 is accurate enough and there is no limitation on computational resources, all errors of the considered types could be detected. However, it is difficult to decide how accurate a model should be. Therefore we create a simple model (or make simple assumptions) to begin with and increase the accuracy of the model step by step and detect potential errors at the same time. The following arguments explain why it is sensible to divide the modelling and verification in so many phases.

- There is a clear distinction between the verification sub-tasks in phase 1 and that in phase 2.
- There is a clear distinction between the need for process knowledge in phase 2 and that in phase 3. In addition, depending on how many plant states are possible initial states and how many values are relevant for each of the involved plant units, the verification sub-tasks in phase 3 can be much more time consuming than that in phase 2.
- The modelling task is much more complicated in phase 4 than that in phase 3 and it also requires much more process knowledge in phase 4. In addition, the verification sub-tasks in phase 4 are usually much more time consuming than that in phase 3.

– Phases 5, 6 and so forth are meant to be additional phases for refining the previously created plant process model and performing model checking in order to increase confidence on the correctness and to detect potential errors that might have escaped the previous analysis.

This strategy is especially helpful in early phases of procedure evaluation when there could be many errors and a large portion of these errors can be detected and removed at early phases of the strategy (with simple models and short model checking time).

3   A Case Study

The case study is verification of an operator procedure with seeded errors. The purpose of this case study is to show the general usefulness of model checking and the incremental strategy of modelling and verification. The operator procedure considered here is "PROCEDURE D-YB-001 — The steam generator control valve opens and remains open" [11]. It is a disturbance procedure to be applied when one of the steam generator control valves (located on the feed water side) opens and remains open.

3.1   The Procedure

The primary goal of the procedure is to repair a defected control valve (there are 4 control valves) that has a problem (i.e. opens and remains open). The basic action sequence of the operator is as follows:

– Start isolating the steam generator.
– Manipulate the primary loop.
– Continue isolation of the steam generator.
– Repair the steam generator control valve and prepare to increase the power.
– Increase the power.

The description of the development of the disturbance is as follows:

– Trouble signal is initiated on steam generator level rise > 3.30m.
– Valve RL33/35/72/74S003 closes automatically.
– After manual disconnection of the main circulation pump, the reactor limiting system automatically reduces the reactor power to a power level permissible with the number of main circulation pumps still in operation.
– When the main circulation pump is disconnected, the plant controller reduces the turbine output to a power level permissible by the number of pumps still in operation. The primary and secondary circuit parameters stabilise within permissible limits. Similarly the disconnected loop's steam generator water level stabilises.
– If the steam generator level rises > 3.54m, an emergency shut-down of both turbines will take place.

The size of the procedure is at 14 pages and 1139 lines (according to the textual version of the procedure from the Computerized Operation Manuals System [11]). There are 93 instructions (each of the instructions consists of one or several actions) involving around 40 plant units such as valves, steam level meters, pumps, pump speed meters and protection signals.

3.2 Correctness Specifications

Correctness specifications include goals, invariants and assertions. For the case study, we have formulated one goal, one invariant and one assertion for performing open-valve actions.

The Goal: "Every execution of the procedure terminates and upon the completion of the execution, all control valves (RL33S002, RL35S002, RL72S002 and RL74S002) are normal or the supervisor is notified (in case the power level at a certain check-point is not normal)".

The Invariant: "During an execution of the procedure, the valve YA13S002 must be open, unless the pump YD13D001 is stopped".

The Assertion: "Before performing an open-valve action to a valve, the state of the valve must be different from open".

3.3 Seeded Errors

We have seeded the following 10 errors into the procedure. The errors cover all types (7 types, 3 categories) of errors described in section 1.

1. A wrong reference - leading to an undefined reference.
   Problem: the instruction "gosub 7" is mistakenly written as "gosub 8".
2. A missing case - leading to a deadlock.
   Problem: the case "if RESULT is None then goto ..." is missing in a list of such goto-instructions.
3. A wrong condition in a wait-instruction (or an action that does not achieve its intended function, depending on interpretation) - leading to a deadlock.
   Problem: the condition "YD13Y013 $\geq$ 1400" in a wait-instruction is written as "YD13Y013 $\geq$ 2000".
4. A wrong condition in a goto-instruction - leading to an infinite loop.
   Problem: the condition "not (RL13S001 is Opening or RL13S001 is Open)" is written as "RL13S001 is Opening or RL13S001 is Open".
5. A missing instruction (or an action that does not achieve its intended function) - leading to an infinite loop.
   Problem: the instruction "if the valve is not opening, address the YZ63 (reset protection) signal ..." is missing (this instruction is specified as a comment in the original procedure).

6. A wrong reference - leading to an unreachable instruction.
   Problem: the instruction "goto 7 2" is written as "goto 7 3".
7. A wrong action - leading to violation of the condition for the action.
   Problem: the action "open RL13S001" is written as "close RL13S001".
8. A wrong sequence of actions - leading to violation of the invariant.
   Problem: the two actions in the sequence "stop YD13D001; ...; close YA13S002" are swapped.
9. A missing instruction - leading to an unreached goal.
   Problem: the action "notify Supervisor" is missing.
10. An action that does not achieve its intended function - leading to an unreached goal.
    In this case, we assume that the action "notify Supervisor" is implemented by using an unreliable message system which may not achieve the intended function of the action. Although it may not be a problem of the procedure design, it is interesting with respect to the correctness of the procedure whose execution is an integrated part of the physical processes of the plant.

3.4 Model Checking with Spin

The model checking tool used in the verification is Spin developed by the formal methods and verification group at Bell Laboratories [5]. For modelling, the language Promela is used. Promela is a process meta-language provided by the model checker Spin. With respect to modelling operator procedures, it has the advantage that it can easily be used to describe actions, sequences of actions, waiting for given conditions, and conditional and unconditional jumps. In addition, we can define a set of macros to represent actions, so that the model of a procedure would have the same structure and similar contents as the original procedure. For instance, an instruction to open the valve "RL33S001" can be modelled as openValve(RL33S001) with the macro openValve(id) defined as a sequence of statements that send a message to an interaction process and wait until receiving a proceed-signal from the interaction process. Upon receiving a message, the interaction process interprets the message in order to take appropriate actions (for instance to change the state of the system and to activate or initiate plant processes) and provides appropriate feedback to the model-procedure process. Plant processes could run by themselves or could be activated or initiated by interaction processes. Assuming that opening (respectively closing) a valve takes time and makes the state of the valve evolve from Closed to Opening and Open (respectively from Open to Closing and Closed), and that valves have protection signals such that they cannot be opened before their associated protection signals are switched off, a simple plant process for opening and closing valves could be as follows:

```
proctype OpenCloseValve(byte id,action)
{
    if
    :: action==Close;
```

```
        do
        :: Valve[id]==Open; Valve[id]=Closing;
        :: Valve[id]==Closing; Valve[id]=Closed; break;
        :: Valve[id]==Closed; break;
        od;
  :: action==Open && Protection[ValveToProtection[id]]==On; skip;
  :: action==Open && Protection[ValveToProtection[id]]==Off;
        do
        :: Valve[id]==Closed; Valve[id]=Opening;
        :: Valve[id]==Opening; Valve[id]=Open; break;
        :: Valve[id]==Open; break;
        od;
    fi;
}
```

where ValveToProtection[] is an array (a function) that maps a valve identifier
to its protection signal identifier, Valve[] is an array that maps a valve identifier
to its current state and Protection[] is an array that maps a protection signal
identifier to its current state. This process can be initiated by an interaction
process when the latter receives a message from the model-procedure process for
opening or closing a valve. The statements "Valve[id]==Closed; break;" in the
process seem to be redundant. However these statements are useful if instructions
for closing a valve are allowed in situations where the valve is already closed.
This example illustrates how one might model a process in Promela. In the case
study, we have made assumptions and simplifications in order to minimise the
number of processes.

Formalising Correctness Specifications

For correctness specifications, we use propositional linear temporal logic formulas
(translated to never-claims) to represent goals, monitoring processes to represent invariants and assertions to represent conditions for performing actions. We
outline our approach to express properties of operator procedures as follows.

Structural Errors No formula is needed for checking structural errors. Undefined
references can be detected by checking syntax and unreachable instructions can
be detected by checking execution errors (described below).

Execution Errors Presence of deadlocks or infinite loops can be checked by
asking whether the instruction indicating the end of an execution is reachable in
all potential executions of the procedure. For verification, we add an auxiliary
statement "ProcedureCompleted=Yes" right before finishing an execution and
the formula representing the fact that there are no deadlocks and infinite loops
is as follows:

$$\diamondsuit \text{ (ProcedureCompleted==Yes)}$$

Conditions for Performing Actions Conditions for performing actions can be specified as local safety properties related to specific instructions. Let the macro openValve(id) represent open-valve actions. The condition for performing open-valve actions in section 3.2 is added by replacing the statement openValve(id) with the following statements:

$$\text{assert(Valve[id]!=Open); openValve(id)}$$

Invariants Invariants can be specified as global safety properties (not related to any specific instruction). The invariant in section 3.2 is specified as follows:

```
proctype monitor()
{
        assert(Valve[YA13S002]==Open || Pump[YD13D001]==Stopped);
}
```

Goals Goals can be specified as liveness properties using propositional linear temporal logic formulas. The goal in section 3.2 is specified as follows:

> ◇   (ProcedureCompleted==Yes && (
> (CheckPointPowerLevel !=NOTnormal ->
> Valve[RL33S002]==Normal && Valve[RL35S002]==Normal &&
> Valve[RL72S002]==Normal && Valve[RL74S002]==Normal) ||
> (CheckPointPowerLevel==NOTnormal -> Supervisor==Notified)))

Detecting the Errors

We first created a model of the procedure (with some modifications to the original procedure in order to avoid errors not caused by the seeded errors) and then created abstract models of the relevant plant processes (for simplicity, we had assumed that there was at most one defected control valve at the beginning of an application of the procedure) and used the model checker Spin to verify the models. The seeded errors were detected as follows:

Phase 1 A model of the procedure (with the seeded errors) was created and error 1 was detected by performing syntactic check.

Phase 2 A set of assumptions on the environment was identified and 3 interaction processes modelling the assumptions were created. Errors 4 and 6 were detected. Error 4 was detected by checking execution errors. Error 6 was an unreachable instruction which was detected by re-checking execution errors after error 4 was corrected.

Phase 3 A process for modelling the possible initial states of the plant was added and modification to the set of relevant values for a variable was made. Error 2 was detected by checking execution errors. Error 7 was detected by checking the assertion. Error 8 was detected by checking the invariant. Error 9 was detected by checking the goal.

Remark Error 2 (a missing case) could not be detected as a deadlock in the previous phases, because it depends on a correct set of relevant values of the variable involved in the case analysis. Violation of assertions (error 7), violation of invariants (error 8) and unreached goals (error 9) were not checked in the previous phase.

Phase 4 A simple model of plant processes (consisting of 13 processes, one for each steam level meter, one for each pump speed meter, one for each cycling valve, and one for opening and closing of valves with protection signals) was created and errors 5 and 3 were detected by checking execution errors.

Remark Error 5 (a missing instruction) could not be detected in the previous phases, because the missing instruction is an instruction used to correct an action that in some executions of the procedure do not achieve its intended function and to detect this kind of problems requires a model of the consequences of the action. Error 3 (a wrong condition) could not be detected in the previous phases, because it depends on a process that controls the value of the variable in the condition.

Phase 5 One process for sending messages to the supervisor with an unreliable communication method (the consequence is that a message could be lost) was added and error 10 was detected by checking execution errors.

Remark Error 10 (an action that does not achieve its intended function) could not be detected in the previous phases, because lack of a model of the action causes the purpose of the action to be achieved by default.

Summary The following table shows the phases and the verification sub-tasks in which the errors were detected:

	phase 1	phase 2	phase 3	phase 4	phase 5
check syntactic errors	error 1				
check execution errors		errors 4,6	error 2	errors 5,3	
check assertion violations			error 7		
check invariant violations			error 8		
check unreached goals			error 9		error 10

Computation Times and Memory Usages

The verification was carried out by using Spin (version 3.2.4) on an HP-computer (machine and model numbers 9000/778) with an HP-UX operating system (release B.10.20). The times for syntactic check varied from 3 to 5 seconds in the different phases depending on the complexity of the models. The times for compilation varied from 10 to 15 seconds in the different phases. In the following, we present times used for model checking.

Error Detection The following table shows the model checking times (in seconds, exclude times for syntactic check and compilation) for detecting the errors in the different verification phases. The table is sorted by the order in which the errors were detected.

	phase 1	phase 2	phase 3	phase 4	phase 5
error 1	-				
error 4		0.3			
error 6		0.4			
error 2			0.6		
error 7			0.3		
error 8			0.4		
error 9			0.5		
error 5				27	
error 3				10	
error 10					4612

There were respectively 1, 4, 5, 18 and 19 processes (excluding monitoring processes and never-claims) in the 5 phases. The table shows that in the early phases the model checker was very fast and in the later phases it needed significantly more time to run model checking.

Verification Errors were removed as detected. In order to be sure that there were no more errors, one had to re-run the model checker. The following table shows the model checking times (in seconds) for the re-running of the model checker (with no error reports) in the different tasks and phases:

	phase 1	phase 2	phase 3	phase 4	phase 5
check syntactic errors	-				
check execution errors		0.4	0.5	13145	13974
check assertion violations			0.3	146	157
check invariant violations			0.3	433	496
check unreached goals			0.5	13125	13692

The verification in the later phases took much more time than that in the early phases (the interesting aspect is the relative model checking times, not the absolute values, since the latter depends on many factors such as the computer on which the model checker was running). There were also big differences between verification times for different types of tasks. Generally, it takes more time to verify liveness properties than to verify safety properties. The table also shows that the verification took much more time than the error detection when the number of processes was relatively large.

Memory Usage for Verification The following table shows the associated memory usages (in megabytes) for carrying out the verification of the procedure in the different phases and for the different tasks:

	phase 1	phase 2	phase 3	phase 4	phase 5
check syntactic errors	-				
check execution errors		3	3	13	13
check assertion violations			3	23	25
check invariant violations			3	59	63
check unreached goals			3	13	13

Discussion As time and memory usage are considered, the tables show that the differences could be very large in different phases. Therefore incremental modelling and verification is practical, since many errors can be detected when the models are simple and model checking times are short, so that the need for detecting errors and re-running model checking for large models is reduced.

3.5 Limitations

As the example shows, model checking can be used to check errors of the considered types. In fact, we have found all of the seeded problems with the help of model checking. However, there are limitations of model checking. One of which is that the set of detectable problems depends on the accuracy of the model of the plant. We have already seen that many of the seeded problems are not detectable with a too much simplified model. On the other hand, the complexity of useful models with respect to model checking is limited by the capacity of model checking tools and computational resources. Another limitation is that the set of detectable problems depends on the set of correctness specifications consisting of safety constraints and goals. In the example, there are one assertion, one invariant and one goal. This set of correctness specifications is of course not complete. Assuming that there was a wrong sequence of actions where the two actions in the sequence "stop YD15D001; ...; close YA15S002" were swapped, and that the models of the plant were the same, additional correctness specifications would be needed for detecting the problem. Generally, there is no guarantee that the set of correctness specifications to be used in model checking is sufficient to detect all problems.

4   Related Work

In the recent years, procedures have been computerised in order to reduce operator stress and to enhance safety [9] [8] [4]. Computerised procedures provide a better opportunity for formal verification as they are written in formal or semi-formal languages with better structure and formality. Earlier work on using formal methods for verification of operator procedures includes investigating techniques based on algebraic specifications and related theorem proving tools [10] [13]. Generally, the weakness with theorem proving is that the verification process is basically interactive. One of the disadvantages is that the user has to find a strategy for proving theorems. It is a time-consuming process. Another disadvantage is that if the user fails to prove a theorem, we cannot be sure whether the theorem is not provable or the strategy is not correct. Model checking has the advantage that it could utilise fully automated tools, although there are other limitations with model checking as explained earlier.

5 Concluding Remarks

This paper has discussed potential for applying model checking to the verification of operator procedures and to detect potential problems in such procedures. The result of the research has shown that model checking can be used to check errors of many types, including deadlocks, infinite loops, unreachable instructions, violation of conditions for performing actions, violation of invariants, and unreached goals. By analysing detected errors, we could find and remove different types of potential problems in such procedures.

The major problems for model checking operator procedures are the complexity of the modelling of the relevant processes of the power plant and the complexity of the models. As it is not easy to find the right complexity level for modelling and model checking, incremental modelling and verification was proposed. It is worth emphasizing that the practical interest of verification is to find errors that could otherwise be hard to detect and not necessary to prove the absolute correctness of procedures. Incremental modelling and verification is a practical strategy focussing on error detection and helps overcome the complexity of modelling and the problem of deciding how complicated the plant process model should be.

For many reasons, model checking (in general, formal methods) does not provide an absolute guarantee of perfection. First, model checking cannot guarantee that the set of correctness specifications is correct and complete. Second, model checking cannot guarantee that the process model of a physical device such as a pump speed meter is accurate with respect to the physics of the device. In addition, there are limitations on computational resources and the capacity of model checking tools, and there may be errors in the model checking tools themselves. Nevertheless, model checking provides a significant capability for discovering large portions of the design errors as demonstrated in the case study.

Further Work: The incremental strategy divides the process of modelling and verification into several phases with increasing complexity of plant process models. One advantage of the strategy is that it avoids full verification versus no verification approach and allows verification to be performed to a certain degree. The degree depends on the size of procedures and plant process models. With respect to scalability, it is important to push the limit as far away as possible. As the case study is considered, the processes were created with emphasis on readability, uniformity of instruction representations and clean interfaces between processes, and not on optimal model checking times. Directions for further research include investigating techniques that can be used to reduce model checking times without sacrificing too much of the mentioned desirable properties of procedure models and plant process models and investigating other approaches for verification and error detection.

ACKNOWLEDGEMENTS

The research described in this paper was carried out at the OECD Halden Reactor Project at the Institute for Energy Technology. The author thanks G. Dahll, T. Sivertsen, K. Stølen and other members of the project for helpful comments and discussions. The author also thanks anonymous referees for their comments.

References

1. M. Abadi and L. Lamport. Conjoining specifications. ACM Transactions on Programming Languages and Systems 17(3):507-534. May 1995.
2. J. R. Burch, E. M. Clarke and D. E. Long. Symbolic Model Checking with Partitioned Transition Relations. International Conference on Very Large Scale Integration, pp. 49-58. North-Holland, August 1991.
3. O. Grumberg and D. E. Long. Model Checking and Modular Verification. ACM Transactions on Programming Languages and Systems 16(3):843-871. May 1994.
4. D. G. Hoecker, K. M. Corker, E. M. Roth, M. H. Lipner and M. S. Bunzo. Man-Machine Design and Analysis System (MIDAS) Applied to a Computer-Based Procedure-Aiding System. Proceedings of the Human Factors and Ergonomics Society 38th Annual Meeting 1: 195-199. 1994.
5. G. J. Holzmann. The Model Checker Spin. IEEE Transaction on Software Engineering 23(5): 279-295. 1997.
6. J. G. Kemeny. Report of the President's Commission on the Accident at Three Mile Island. U.S. Government Accounting Office. 1979.
7. N. G. Leveson. Software System Safety and Computers. Addison-Wesley Publishing Company. 1995.
8. M. H. Lipner and S. P. Kerch. Operational Benefits of an Advanced Computerised Procedure System. 1994 IEEE Conference Record: Nuclear Science Symposium and Medical Imaging Conference:(1068-1072). 1995.
9. L. Reynes and G. Beltranda. A Computerised Control Room to Improve Nuclear Power Plant Operation and Safety. Nuclear Safety 31(4):504-511. 1990.
10. T. Sivertsen and H. Valisuo. Algebraic Specification and Theorem Proving used in Formal Verification of Discrete Event Control Systems. OECD Halden Reactor Project Report: HWR-260, Institute for Energy Technology, Norway. 1989.
11. J. Teigen and J. E. Hulsund. COPMA-III - Software Design and Implementation Issues. OECD Halden Reactor Project Report: HWR-509, Institute for Energy Technology, Norway. 1998.
12. H. J. Touati, H. Savoj, B. Lin, R. K. Brayton and A. Sangiovanni-Vincentelli. Implicit State Enumeration of Finite State Machines Using BDDs. IEEE International Conference on Computer-Aided Design, pp. 130-133. IEEE Computer Society Press, November 1990.
13. K. Ylikoski and G. Dahll. Verification of Procedures. OECD Halden Reactor Project Report: HWR-318, Institute for Energy Technology, Norway. 1992.

Applying Model Checking in Java Verification

Klaus Havelund[1] and Jens Ulrik Skakkebæk[2]

[1] NASA Ames Research Center, Recom Technologies, Moffett Field, CA, USA
havelund@ptolemy.arc.nasa.gov, http://ase.arc.nasa.gov/havelund
[2] Computer Systems Laboratory, Stanford University, Stanford, CA 94305, USA
jus@cs.stanford.edu, http://verify.stanford.edu/jus

Abstract. This paper presents our experiences in applying the JAVA PATHFINDER (JPF), a recently developed JAVA to PROMELA translator, in the search for synchronization bugs in a Chinese Chess game server application written in JAVA. We give an overview of JPF and the subset of JAVA that it supports and describe an initial effort to abstract and analyze the game server. Finally, we evaluate the results of the effort.

1 Introduction

Model checking has increasingly gained acceptance within hardware [15, 1] and protocol verification [13] as an additional means to discovering bugs. However, verifying programs is different from verifying hardware or protocols: the state space is often much bigger and the relationships harder to understand because of asynchronous behavior and a more complicated underlying semantics. The size and complexity of software pushes current formal verification technology beyond its limits. It is therefore likely that effective application of model checking to software verification will be a debugging process where smaller, selected parts of the software is model checked. The process will draw on multiple abstraction and verification techniques under user guidance, and is currently not well understood.

In order to investigate the challenges that software poses for model checking, we have applied the JAVA PATHFINDER (JPF) [12], a recently developed JAVA to PROMELA translator, in the analysis of a game server application written in JAVA [8]. PROMELA is the modeling language of the SPIN model checker [13]. We performed the abstractions by hand and translated the simplified JAVA program to PROMELA using JPF. Although the example is not big (16 classes and about 1400 LOC), it is still non-trivial and is not written with formal verification in mind. In the process, we developed a suspicion of a deadlock bug in the software which was confirmed using SPIN. SPIN also produced an even simpler error scenario than we had found ourselves.

Few attempts have been made to automatically model check programs written in real programming languages. The most recent attempt to model check software that we are aware of is the one reported in [2], which also tries to model check JAVA programs by mapping into PROMELA. This work does, however, not handle exceptions, nor polymorphism (passing, e.g., an object of a subclass of a class C to a method requiring a C object as parameter). The work in [3] defines a translator from a concurrent extension of a very limited subset of C++ to PROMELA. The drawback of this solution is that the concurrency extensions are not broadly used by C++ programmers. Corbett [4] describes a theory of translating JAVA to a transition model, making use of static pointer analysis to aid *virtual coarsening*, which reduces the size of the model.

The VeriSoft tool [7] is a an exhaustive state-space exploration tool for detecting synchronization errors between processes. As a major advantage, it also verifies the actual code. However, since the visited states are not stored in the verification process, each time a new branch of possible execution is verified it has to rerun from the beginning, making it less efficient. Furthermore, each process is treated as a black box and properties have to be specified at the process interfaces. In contrast, model checking allows for more efficient verification (since states are saved along the way) and for specifying internal process properties, but requires more abstraction. It is still unclear which has the most advantages.

Data flow analysis has been applied to verify limited properties of concurrent programs, including JAVA [16]. These methods are useful for ruling out certain behaviors of the concurrent system but are much less precise than model checking. However, as we will argue later, they can potentially be useful in identifying problem areas for verification by state space exploration methods.

The JPF tool is introduced in Section 2 and the application to the game server is described in Section 3. We evaluate the results in Section 4 and conclude with a discussion in Section 5.

2 The JAVA PATHFINDER

JPF [12] is a translator that automatically translates a non-trivial subset of JAVA into PROMELA, the modeling language of the SPIN verification system [13]. JPF allows a programmer to annotate his JAVA program with assertions and verify them using the SPIN model checker. In addition, deadlocks can be identified. Assertions are specified as calls of methods defined in a special class (the Verify class), all of whose methods are static.

A significant subset of JAVA is supported by JPF: dynamic creation of objects with data and methods, static variables and static methods, class inheritance, threads and synchronization primitives for modeling monitors (synchronized statements, and the wait and notify methods), exceptions, thread interrupts, and most of the standard programming language constructs such as assignment statements, conditional statements and loops. However, the translator is still a prototype and misses some features, such as packages, overloading, method overriding, recursion, strings, floating point numbers, some thread operations like suspend and resume, and some control constructs, such as the continue statement. In addition, arrays are not objects as they are in JAVA, but are modeled using PROMELA's own arrays to obtain efficient verification. Finally, the libraries are not translated. Note that many of these features can be avoided by small modifications to the input code, and we expect the current version of JPF to be useful on a large class of software. The game server application described in Section 3 fits in the currently translated subset of JAVA with a few modifications.

We shall illustrate JPF with a small, but non-trivial, example. The example is inspired by one of five concurrency bugs that were found in an effort by NASA Ames to verify, using SPIN, an operating system implemented in a multi-threaded version of COMMON LISP for the DEEP–SPACE 1 spacecraft [11]. The operating system is one component of NASA's Remote Agent [17], an experimental artificial intelligence based spacecraft control system architecture. The bug, found before launch, is concerned with lock releasing on a data structure shared between several threads.

2.1 The Lock Releasing Problem Cast into JAVA

The Main Code The operating system is responsible for executing *tasks* on board the space craft. A task may for example be to run a camera. A task may *lock* properties (states to be maintained) in a *lock table* before executing, *releasing* these locks after execution. For example, one such property may be to "keep the thrusting low" during camera operation. For various reasons tasks may, however, get *interrupted* during their execution, and the particular focus here will be on whether all locks always get released in that case.

Figure 1 shows the Task class. Its constructor (the method with the same name as the class) takes three arguments: a *lock table* t which contains the locks, a property p (here just an integer) to be locked before the activity is executed, and the *activity* a to be executed by the task. An Activity object is required to provide an activity() method which when executed will perform a given task. Note that this is the way that JAVA supports higher order methods taking methods as arguments, and that JPF handles this.

The run method of the Task class specifies the behavior of the task; this method has to be part of any Thread subclass. The behavior is programmed using JAVA's try-catch-finally exception construct, which executes the locking and then the activity, unless an exception is thrown. This exception will be *caught* locally if it is a LockException, or thrown further out. In any case, the finally clause is always executed, releasing the lock.

Figure 1 furthermore shows the JAVA class LockTable, which models the table of all locks. It provides an array mapping each property (here a number between 0 and 2) into the task that locks it, or null otherwise. The method lock locks a property to a particular task, throwing an exception if the property has already been locked. The release method releases the lock again. These methods are defined as *synchronized* to obtain mutual safe access to the table when executed. A LockTable object will then work as a monitor, only allowing one thread to operate in it, that is: call its methods, at any time.

A Test Environment Typically an exception is thrown explicitly within a thread using the throw(e) statement, where e is an exception object (a normal

```
class Task extends Thread{
  LockTable t; int p; Activity a;

  public Task(LockTable t,int p,Activity a){
    this.t = t; this.p = p; this.a = a;
    this.start();
  }

  public void run(){
    try {t.lock(p,this);a.activity();}
    catch (LockException e) {}
    finally {t.release(p);};
  }
}

class LockTable{
  Task[] table = new Task[3];

  public synchronized void lock(int property,Task task)
  throws LockException{
    if (table[property] != null){
      LockException e = new LockException();
      throw(e);
    };
    table[property] = task;
  }

  public synchronized void release(int property){
    table[property] = null;
  }
}
```

Fig. 1. Task Execution and Lock Table

object of an exception class which may include data and methods). Alternatively, one thread S may throw a *ThreadDeath* exception in another thread T by executing T.stop(). This is exactly what the Daemon task shown in Figure 2 does. The daemon together with the Main class with the main method, that starts all threads, constitute an *environment* that we set up to *debug* the task releasing. The daemon will be started to run in parallel with the task, and will eventually stop the task, but at an unspecified point in time. The task is started with the property 1 and some activity not detailed here. The assert statement is "executed" after the termination of the task (the join method waits for the termination). The assertion states that the property is no longer locked. The assert statement is expressed as a call to the static method assert in the Verify class:

```
class Verify{
  public static void assert(boolean b){}
}
```

Since this method is static it can be called directly on the class without making an object instance first. It takes a Boolean argument, the validity of which will be checked. The body of this method is of no real importance for the verification since only the call of this method will be translated into a corresponding PROMELA assert statement. A meaningful body, like raising an exception for example, could be useful during normal testing though, but it would not be translated into PROMELA.

One can consider other kinds of Verify methods, in general methods corresponding to the operators in LTL, the linear temporal logic of SPIN. Since these methods can be called wherever statements can occur, this kind of logic represents what could be called an *embedded temporal logic*. As an example, one could consider statements of the form: Verify.eventually(year == 2000) occurring in the code. The major advantage of this approach is that we do not need to change the JAVA language, and we do not need to parse special comments. JAVA itself is used as the specification language. Note, that at this point, only the assert method is supported.

```
class Daemon extends Thread{        class Main{
  Task task;                          public static void main(String[] args){
                                        LockTable table   = new LockTable();
  public Daemon(Task task){             Activity activity = new Activity();
    this.task = task;                   Task task = new Task(table,1,activity);
    this.start();                       Daemon daemon   = new Daemon(task);
  }                                     try {task.join();}
                                        catch (InterruptedException e) {};
  public void run(){                    Verify.assert(table.table[1] == null);
    task.stop();                      }
  }                                 }
}
```

Fig. 2. Environment

The Error Trace When running the SPIN model checker on the generated PROMELA program, the assertion is found to be violated, and the error trace illustrates the kind of bug that was identified in the Remote Agent. The error highlighted is the following. Although the main activity of the task is protected by a try ... finally construct such that the lock releasing will occur in case of an interrupt (stop), the finally construct itself is not protected the same way. That is, if the task is stopped when within the finally construct, e.g. just before the lock releasing, the releasing never gets executed. The generated error trace exhibits exactly this behavior. This has been called the "unwind-protect" problem in LISP, obviously also present in JAVA, and is causing a real bug as illustrated here.

2.2 Translation to PROMELA

This section shortly describes the translation of JAVA into PROMELA. A more detailed description of the translation can be found in [12].

Classes and Objects Each class definition in JAVA introduces data variables and methods. When an object of that class is created with the **new** method, the Java Virtual Machine lays out a new data area on the heap for the data variables. Since PROMELA does not have a dynamic heap, a different solution has to be adopted. For each class an integer indexed array of some fixed static size is declared, where each entry is a record (*typedef* in PROMELA) containing the variables of the class. Hence, each entry represents one object of that class. A pointer always points to the next free "object" in the array. An object reference is a pair (c, i), where c is the class and i is the index of the object in the corresponding array (the pair is represented as the integer $c * 100 + i$). Inheritance is simply modeled by text inclusion: if a class B extends (inherits from) a class A, then each entry in the B array will contain A's variables as well as B's variables.

Methods JAVA method definitions are simply translated into macro definitions parameterized with an object reference – the object on which the method is called. That is, a PROMELA program is allowed to contain macro definitions, which are expanded out where called. For example, when a thread calls a method on an object, it "calls" the macro with the object identifier as parameter. The drawback with macros is their lack of local variables. Hence, JAVA method local variables have to be translated to global variables (within the calling thread), prefixed with their origin (class and method). PROMELA has recently been extended with inline procedures (motivated by some of our work presented in [11]), and these could be used instead, although it would not make a difference in the principles.

Threads Threads in JAVA are naturally translated to PROMELA processes. That is, any class being defined as extending the **Thread** class, such as **Task** and **Daemon** in the example, is translated to a **proctype**. The body of the process is the translation of the body of the **run** method. The main program (the **main** method) will be translated into an **init** clause in PROMELA, which itself is a special process.

Object Synchronization JAVA supports mutually exclusive access to objects via synchronized methods. That is, if a thread calls a synchronized method on an object, then no other thread can call synchronized methods on the same object as long as the first thread has not terminated its call. We model this by introducing a **LOCK** field in the data area of each object, hence in particular in each entry of the array representing the **LockTable** objects. This field will either be **null** if no thread has locked the object, or it will be equal to the process identification of the thread (PROMELA process) that locks it (via a call to a synchronized method). Some of the macros generated from our example, modeling locking, unlocking and synchronization, are shown in Figure 3.

The macro **LockTable_release** is the translation of the **release** method in the **LockTable** class. It executes the body of the method (a statement) with

```
#define LockTable_release(obj,property)
  synchronized(obj,LockTable_set_table(obj,property,null))

#define synchronized(obj,stmt)
  if
  :: get_LOCK(obj) == this -> stmt
  :: else ->
      lock(obj);
      try(stmt) unless {d_finally(unlock(obj))}
  fi

#define lock(obj)                    #define unlock(obj)
  atomic{                              set_LOCK(obj,null)
    get_LOCK(obj) == null ->
      set_LOCK(obj,this)}
```

Fig. 3. Synchronization Macros

synchronized access to the object. The **synchronized** macro executes the statement directly if the lock is already owned by the thread (equal to **this**), and
otherwise it locks the object and executes the statement, finally releasing the
lock after use. The **lock** macro sets the lock to **this** as soon as it gets available
(equals **null** – note that expressions in PROMELA are blocking as long as they
evaluate to false).

Exceptions One of the major capabilities of the translator is that it handles
exceptions. Java exceptions are complicated when considering all the situations
that may arise, such as method returns in the middle of **try** constructs, the
finally construct, interrupts (which are exceptions thrown from one thread to
another) of threads that have called the **wait** method, and the fact that objects
have to be unlocked when an exception is thrown out of a synchronized method.
PROMELA's **unless** construct seems related to an exception construct, except
for the fact that it works "outside in" instead of "inside out", the latter being
the case for JAVA's **try** construct. That is, suppose a JAVA program contains
two nested **try** constructs as indicated in the left part of Figure 4.

```
try{                          {
  try{S1} catch (E x){S2}        S1 unless {catch(exn_E,x,S2)}
}                             }
catch (E y){S3}               unless {catch(exn_E,x,S3}
```

Fig. 4. Exceptions in JAVA (left) and PROMELA (right)

If S1 throws an exception object of class E, then this exception should be
caught by the inner **catch** statement, and S2 should be executed. On the right
hand side of the figure is a simplified version of how we model exceptions in
PROMELA. However, with the traditional PROMELA semantics of the **unless**

construct, the outermost `catch` would be matched, and S3 would be executed. Gerard Holzmann, the designer of SPIN, implemented a `-J` (J for JAVA) option giving the needed "inside out" semantics. Now, in the data area for a thread, in addition to the LOCK variable mentioned earlier, there is also an exception variable EXN. Throwing an exception, which is itself an object, is now modeled by setting the EXN variable to contain the exception object reference. and this will then trigger the `unless` statements. Even with addition of the `-J` option to SPIN, the translation is quite elaborate.

3 A Game Server Application

To investigate the practical usefulness of JPF, we have applied JPF in partial verification of a game server for Chinese Chess, developed by An Nguyen at Stanford University. The code is an older and simpler version of the code that is currently running. It was used for 3 weeks and was not written with formal verification in mind. The code was later rewritten because it was unstable and deadlocked too frequently.

Compared to industrial applications, the server code is fairly small: it consists of 11 JAVA classes of about 800 LOC in total. The client code is another 5 classes and 600 LOC. The code of each thread and method in the game server is not very complicated. The complexity stems from the communication interaction between multiple types of threads.

As expected, even though it is relatively small, the state size still drastically exceeds the limits of any model checker. It is possible that the example is manageable by tools like Verisoft [7]. This is, however, besides the point: we are using the application to investigate the limits and trade-offs for model checking, as well as studying viable approaches to abstraction.

3.1 Overview of the Code

The overall code is divided into server side code and client side code. The client code consists of JAVA Applets that are used to display the game boards, the game pieces, and to relay the user commands to the game server. There is no direct communication between players. All communication between players is done via the server.

The multiple players and game boards are naturally handled by a multi-threaded JAVA architecture in the server code. Although the client side code in effect is also multi-threaded to handle multiple requests from the user, the multi-threading is hidden in the browser application and each individual Applet is written as sequential code. We focus on the server code and leave verification of the multi-threaded user-interface code to future work.

Threads The thread structure is illustrated in Figure 5. At any point in time several game boards can be active, each served by a `ServerBoard` thread. For each participant of a game there is a `Connection` thread to handle the communication between the `ServerBoard` and the network connection associated with the player. Each `ServerBoard` can have multiple `Connections` associated with it (2 players and multiple observers). Inter-board communication messages are stored in a FIFO queue `ServerObjectQueue` and handled by the `ServerObjectHandler` thread. `ServerBoard` threads are the only producers of messages, and `ServerObjectHandler` is the only consumer.

Server is the main thread. It handles initialization and contains the main data structures of the server. Finally, there are two kinds of "vulture" threads for cleaning up global data structures that become obsolete when players log out: `Server` has an associated `ServerVulture` thread, and each `ServerBoard` thread has an associated `ConnectionVulture`.

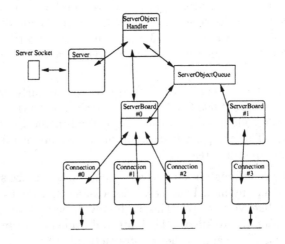

Fig. 5. A simplified illustration of the system. The boxes with rounded edges denote threads, the square boxes denote non-thread objects. For simplicity, we have not shown the vulture threads. In this example, `ServerBoard` 0 has three players associated with it, `ServerBoard` 1 has one. The arrows indicate the communication patterns between the different threads.

Commands A player has a predefined set of commands that can be sent via the network to the server. When a command arrives, it is stored in a separate FIFO queue in the associated `ServerBoard`. The `ServerBoard` thread then processes the commands one at a time.

The commands can be grouped into three classes: game commands, administration commands, and communication commands. Game commands are used to move the pieces around the board and to stop a game. Administration commands are used to create new boards, move between them, and log out. Finally, communication commands are used to communicate between the players, either to a few ("whisper") or to a larger crowd ("broadcast"). There are 12 different commands.

Each time a move is made, the other players in the game are notified by the `ServerBoard` broadcasting the information to its `Connections`.

When a player creates boards, moves between boards, leaves the game, or sends out a global broadcast, the command is read by the `ServerBoard` and then stored in `ServerObjectQueue` for processing by `ServerObjectHandler`, which processes the commands one at a time. `ServerObjectHandler` handles global broadcasts by calling local broadcast commands in each of the `ServerBoard` threads.

3.2 Abstraction

We focussed on abstracting out a synchronization and communication "skeleton" and removed game code that was not important for detecting synchronization errors. In the process, we formed an idea of a potential deadlock in the code by studying the order in which threads obtained locks and accessed shared data. However, we were not positive that the deadlock was present until it was demonstrated by the model checker. Subsequently, we therefore targeted the abstractions at demonstrating this bug.

Focused on demonstrating the potential deadlock, we manually cut away big chunks of the program by interleaved application of static slicing and over- and under-approximations, known as the "meat-axe" technique in [11].

Static Slicing Given a marking of a statement in the program, static slicing techniques [18] will produce the subset of the program that corresponds to the *cone-of-influence*. In *forward* slicing, the output is the part of the program that is potentially influenced by the marked statement. In *backward* slicing, the output is the part of the program that potentially can influence the values of the variables at the statement of interest.

We used forward slicing to remove the part of code that was potentially irrelevant to the verification task. The relevant code was all the code that was not directly game related. We marked irrelevant variables, methods, and classes, and used this as a guidance to (manually) forward-slice the program from the unmarked variables. For example, the `Board` class contains the data structures related to the Chinese Chess board and the positions of the pieces and was removed; methods related to communication with the player process were also removed; and fields containing a player's role in the game were likewise removed. Of the 11 server code classes, two of them could be removed fully.

We did not use backward slicing in the abstraction. The deadlock scenario that we were interested in was caused by thread interaction. Marking a particular statement involved in the deadlock scenario would clearly have given a slice that was too large/imprecise for our purpose.

Over-Approximations Over-approximations are obtained from the original program by introduction of non-determinism in the control flow such that the abstracted model will exhibit more behaviors than the original program. Over-approximations are sound in the sense that when checking safety properties, if no bugs are found in the abstracted model, no bugs exist in the original program. Counter examples, on the other hand, are not necessarily true counter examples in the original model.

Over-approximations were used many times in the abstraction of the game server code. We illustrate this with two examples. First, it was useful to abstract the control conditions marked in the slicing process. For instance:

```
if (...something game related...) then {...server.broadcast(...);...}
```

was changed to

```
if (nondet.flag) then {...server.broadcast(...);...}
```

where nondet.flag is a flag in a new class NonDet that is non-deterministically set and reset by the model checker in all possible interleavings with other threads.

Second, we abstracted the types of messages that the threads pass around to a few. The messages are encoded in strings, where the first characters of the string contains the command, e.g., "/broadcast", "/open", and "/join". ServerBoard and ServerObjectHandler determine the type of messages by looking at this string prefix. Typically, this is done in a nested if-then-else structure:

```
if (line.startswith("/broadcast") then {...}
else if (line.startswith("/talk") then {...board.processCommand(...);...}
else if (line.startswith("/whisper") then {...board.broadcast(...);...}
else {...}
```

We abstracted the message strings into a record with a type and a value. From code inspection, we found 3 commands that were related to the concurrency behavior we were interested in pursuing and mapped the message type into something equivalent to an enumerated type with values broadcast, open, join, and other. The latter was introduced by us to capture the remaining types of commands. The nested control structure was then modified to be

```
if (line.type=broadcast) then {...}
else if (line.type=other) then {...
        if (nondet.flag) then board.processCommand(...);
        else board.broadcast(...);
        }
else {...}
```

where non-determinism was introduced to model all possible behaviors of external events associated with the commands mapping to other.

This last abstraction is a form of abstract interpretation [5] where the user decides which behavior to keep in the collapsed code.

Under-Approximations Under-approximations are obtained by removing code (and state that it depends on) from the program, with the effect of reducing the possible behaviors of the original program. Under-approximations may not be sound for safety properties, since the code that is removed could be causing bugs in the original program – bugs that are not caught when verifying the abstract model. However, when checking safety properties, if a bug is found in the under-approximation, it will also be present in the original model. Under-approximation is a very useful technique when narrowing the search space to a particular part of the code.

We used under-approximations many times in the game server verification. First, we ignored some exceptions of the program, including the exception handling. In the part of the server code that we were interested in, the exception handling was of little importance. Second, initially we limited the number of threads to two `ServerBoard` threads and two `Connection` threads; and the number of messages from the players to consider were limited to 3. Third, we inserted 3-4 extra synchronization points to sequentialize the thread behaviors. This limited the number of possible interleavings that SPIN had to consider and more quickly guided it towards the deadlock scenario.

3.3 Verification

We combined the abstracted JAVA classes into a file, translated it using the JPF, and tried to run it through SPIN. It took several more cycles of abstraction before the model was sufficiently manageable for SPIN to find the deadlock bug. We inserted JPF print statements in appropriate places in the JAVA code. This information made it easy to interpret SPIN's Message Sequence Chart [13] description of the counter example scenario.

The bug we confirmed was a deadlock caused by cyclic waits between a number of threads. It involved only three threads to cause the deadlock. Using SPIN we were able to find an unknown and significantly simpler deadlock scenario with two threads. We will present this simpler example below.

The deadlock may occur when the `ServerObjectQueue` becomes full. It happens when a `ServerBoard` processes incoming messages from its `Connections`, while the `ServerObjectHandler` wants to broadcast a message to the same connections.

The deadlock, illustrated in Figure 6, may arise as follows: The `ServerBoard` thread has obtained exclusive access to its connections by locking the `connections` vector, which stores references to the connections. Next, it goes through a loop where it processes the incoming connection messages, one at a time. Some of the messages must be processed by `ServerObjectHandler` and the `ServerBoard` thread will therefore want to put these messages in the `ServerObjectQueue`. However, if the queue runs full in this process it will busy-wait on the queue, while holding the lock on `connections`.

If the `ServerObjectHandler` is simultaneously processing a command that causes a broadcast of a message to the connections of the `ServerBoard` thread, it

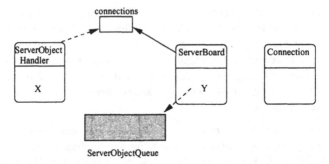

Fig. 6. Deadlock scenario: `ServerBoard` waits for a free slot in the queue, and `ServerObjectHandler` waits for the lock on `connections` to be released. Dashed lines indicates wait, the solid line indicates the lock that has been obtained. X and Y are the messages waiting to be processed.

will try to obtain the lock on `connections` by a **synchronize**. However, the lock will never be released by `ServerBoard` and a cyclic wait has been established.

Note that the deadlock is caused by a simultaneous wait on a JAVA lock, using the **synchronized** statement, and a busy wait on the queue. The code for enqueueing and dequeueing was written by the developer himself and is not part of the Java Virtual Machine (JVM).

4 Evaluation

The analysis itself took a month till the bug was confirmed. However, during this period much time was used on understanding the code and improving JPF to translate the subset of JAVA that the game server covers. In future applications of the JPF, this will be reduced significantly. At present, we have not yet completed the verification of all parts of the code. More effort would be required to fully verify the code.

Static slicing and abstract interpretation [5] turned out to be useful, but did not produce sufficiently small models. Under-approximations were necessary to narrow down the search space to focus on the bugs that we were interested in finding. This confirms the experiences from the Remote Agent analysis [11]. In general, user guidance was crucial for identifying parts of the code were the techniques could be applied.

Concerning the JPF technology itself, current model checkers, including SPIN, have been constructed with hardware and protocols in mind and require static memory allocation. That is, they do not support the dynamic nature of object oriented software, more specifically the **new** C(...) construct which generates an object from a class C. JPF currently generates statically sized global PROMELA arrays that hold the state of the objects, causing wasted memory when only few objects are allocated while the arrays are initialized to hold a larger number. In addition to wasted memory, a second problem with this array solution is the intricate name resolution machinery required to search for the right array when looking up variables. This is caused by the class subtyping in JAVA (*polymorphism*), where the class of an object cannot be statically decided. Consider for example a method taking a C object as parameter. It can be applied to any object of any subclass of C. As a consequence, variable lookups consist of conditional expressions searching through the subclasses. In an early version of JPF this in fact caused a code blow up that made the C compiler gcc fail on the C code that SPIN generates from the resulting PROMELA program. A related issue is the lack of variables local to "methods" in PROMELA. Macros have no concept of locality, leading to further machinery in the translation of variables local to JAVA methods.

JPF does not handle all of JAVA, major substantial omissions being recursion, strings and floating point numbers, and perhaps most importantly: the JAVA libraries. Recursion requires more elaborated modeling of the Java Virtual Machine, for example in terms of a call stack, which however will be costly. Alternatively PROMELA's process concept can be used to model recursive methods, but this solution appears to be time inefficient. It was tried, but undocumented, in the work described in [11]. The translation of JAVA exceptions is quite sophisticated, handling all the special circumstances possible. Gerard Holzmann helped in providing a new semantics of PROMELA's unless construct, but even in that case the translation is "clever". JPF is currently being improved to translate a bigger subset of JAVA, and to handle an extension of the Verify class with linear temporal logic operators.

The translation does not cater for garbage collection. Normally garbage collection (or the lack thereof) is hidden from the programmer, and should not effect the functionality of a program. However, the effectiveness of the verification may be improved by regarding states with garbage equivalent to states without garbage. Garbage collection seems absolutely non-trivial to handle.

5 Discussion and Future Work

Successful application of model checking in program verification will involve an iterative process of abstraction and verification and will draw on multiple techniques for abstracting manageable models from the original program. The sheer size and complexity of the software-under-verification pushes current verification technology to its limits and the goal of the abstraction process is to fit parts of the verification problem within boundaries of feasible verification. In order to make model checking of programs scalable, program abstraction needs to be better understood, and supported with automated tools. Below we will briefly discuss issues relevant to a future verification environment.

Static Analysis Static analysis such as data flow analysis [16] can be used to identify potential problem areas. The techniques must be able to recognize complex dependencies such as deadlocks involving cyclic wait on data as well as locks (as our example illustrated). In general, automated guidance is crucial to guide the effort to certain parts of the software that is potentially buggy. Under-approximations (such as partial evaluation [14] and other program specialization techniques [10]) remove behaviors from the original model. The verification engineer must apply these cautiously in order not to remove behavior that could lead to bug scenarios.

User Guided Abstractions by Code Annotation User-interaction, potentially aided by heuristics, is crucial for effective application of the abstraction techniques. Code annotations are a potential means of capturing the higher-level understanding of the programmer at the time of development and could provide hints to the abstraction tool. For instance, the game server code could contain information that would guide an abstraction tool to understand the strings that are being passed around as actual message types. Alternatively, predefined coding styles in the form of design patterns could be recognized by an abstraction tool. It is also possible that automatic abstraction techniques suggested by Graf and Saidi [9], extended with string pattern matching, could be applied to determine the enumeration type.

Libraries One of the decisions to make in the abstraction process is deciding the boundaries of the program to be verified and how to model its environment. For the game server, the obvious boundaries were the network interface. However, in other cases the correctness properties may be specified in terms of the client applications. In this case, the network needs to be modeled also. An effective verification environment needs pre-written environment models of commonly used libraries. The game server code, for instance, uses the JAVA Vector class. By studying the JVM specification we were able to write simple stubs that modeled the class sufficiently for our use. In general, such environment modules must be predefined to save the verification engineer time and effort.

Compositional Approaches An alternative solution to dealing with scalability is compositional model checking [6], where only smaller portions of code are verified at a time, assuming properties about the "rest of the code", and where the results are then composed to deduce the correctness of larger portions of code. This approach is not problem free though since composing proofs is non-trivial and often requires iteration as does induction proofs (no silver bullet around). A practical solution is so-called *unit testing* where a class or a small collection of classes are tested by putting them in parallel with an aggressive *environment*. The Remote Agent analysis presented in Section 3 is an example of this. It's likely that model checking at least can play an important role in program verification at this level.

Acknowledgments The authors wish to acknowledge the following persons at NASA Ames for their contributions in terms of ideas and support: Tom Pressburger, Mike Lowry, John Penix and Willem Visser. At Stanford we would like to thank David Dill for discussions and comments. The second author is sponsored by NASA contract number NAG2-891: An Integrated Environment for Efficient Formal Design and Verification.

References

1. J. R. Burch, E. M. Clarke, K. L. McMillan, and D. L. Dill. Sequential circuit verification using symbolic model checking. In *27th ACM/IEEE Design Automation Conference*, 1990.

2. R. Iosif C. Demartini and R. Sisto. Modeling and Validation of Java Multithreading Applications using SPIN. In G. Holzmann, E. Najm, and A. Serhrouchni, editors, *Proceedings of the 4th SPIN workshop, Paris, France*, November 1998.

3. T. Cattel. Modeling and Verification of sC++ Applications. In *Proceedings of the Tools and Algorithms for the Construction and Analysis of Systems, Lisbon, Portugal, LNCS 1384*, April 1998.

4. J. C. Corbett. Constructing Compact Models of Concurrent Java Programs. In *Proceedings of the ACM Sigsoft Symposium on Software Testing and Analysis, Clearwater Beach, Florida.*, March 1998.

5. P. Cousot and R. Cousot. Abstract interpretation: A unified lattice model for static analysis of programs by construction or approximation of fixpoints. *ACM Symposium on Principles of Programming Languages*, pages 238–252, 1977.

6. W. de Roever, H. Langmaack, and A. Pnueli (Eds.). *Compositionality: The Significant Difference, International Symposium, COMPOS'97, Bad Malente, Germany. LNCS 1536.* Springer-Verlag, September 1997.

7. P. Godefroid. Model checking for programming languages using Verisoft. In *ACM Symposium on Principles of Programming Languages*, pages 174–186, Paris, January 1997.

8. J. Gosling, B. Joy, and G. Steele. *The Java Language Specification.* The Java Series. A-W, 1996.

9. S. Graf and H. Saidi. Construction of abstract state graphs with PVS. In O. Grumberg, editor, *CAV.* Springer-Verlag, June 1997.

10. J. Hatcliff, M. Dwyer, S. Laubach, and D. Schmidt. Stating static analysis using abstraction-based program specialization, 1998.

11. K. Havelund, M. Lowry, and J. Penix. Formal Analysis of a Space Craft Controller using SPIN. In G. Holzmann, E. Najm, and A. Serhrouchni, editors, *Proceedings of the 4th SPIN workshop, Paris, France*, November 1998.

12. K. Havelund and T. Pressburger. Model Checking Java Programs using Java PathFinder. NASA Ames Research Center. To appear in the *International Journal on Software Tools for Technology Transfer* (STTT), 1999.

13. Gerard Holzmann. *The Design and Validation of Computer Protocols.* Prentice Hall, 1991.

14. N. D. Jones, editor. *Special Issue on Partial Evaluation, 1993 (Journal of Functional Programming, vol. 3, no. 4).* Cambridge University Press, 1993.

15. K.L. McMillan. *Symbolic Model Checking: An Approach to the State Explosion Problem.* Kluwer Academic Publishers, 1993.

16. G. Naumovich, G.S. Avrunin, and L.A. Clarke. Data flow analysis for checking properties of concurrent java programs. Technical Report 98-22, Computer Science Department, University of Massachusetts at Amherst, April 1998.

17. B. Pell, E. Gat, R. Keesing, N. Muscettola, and B. Smith. Plan Execution for Autonomous Spacecrafts. In *Proceedings of the 1997 International Joint Conference on Artificial Intelligence*, 1997.

18. F. Tip. A survey of program slicing techniques. *Journal of Programming Languages*, 3(3):121–189, 1995.

The Engineering of a Model Checker: The Gnu i-Protocol Case Study Revisited

Gerard J. Holzmann

Bell Laboratories, Lucent Technologies,
600 Mountain Avenue, Murray Hill, NJ 07974, USA
gerard@research.bell-labs.com

Abstract. In a recent study a series of model checkers, among which Spin [5], SMV [9], and a newer system called XMC [10], were compared on performance. The measurements used for this comparison focused on a model of the i-protocol from GNU uucp version 1.04. Eight versions of this i-protocol model were obtained by varying window size, assumptions about the transmission channel, and the presence or absence of a patch for a known livelock error. The results as published in [1] show the XMC system to outperform the other model checking systems on most of the tests. It also contains a challenge to the builders of the other model checkers to match the results. This paper answers that challenge for the Spin model checker. We show that with either default Spin verification runs, or a reasonable choice of parameter settings, the version of Spin that was used for the tests in [1] (Spin 2.9.7) can outperform the results obtained with XMC in six out of eight tests. Inspired by the comparisons, and the description in of the optimizations used in XMC, we also extended Spin with some of the same optimizations, leading to a new Spin version 3.3.0. We show that with these changes Spin can outperform XMC on all eight tests.

Introduction

The details of the i-protocol, and the various versions of the model that were built to verify it, are given in [1] and need not be repeated here. We focus on the tests as reported in [1], specifically as they relate to Spin. The three main parameters that were modified to obtain the eight testcases for the i-protocol model are as follows:

1. A window size of either one or two is used. We distinguish these two cases here as 1-- and 2--.
2. The possibility of message distortions is either included or excluded. We distinguish these two cases as -f- (*full*) and -m- (*mini*) respectively).
3. A patch to prevent the known livelock error is enabled or disabled. We distinguish these two cases as --f (*fixed*) and --n (*non-fixed*) respectively.

The eight testcases can then be identified as 1mf, 1mn, 2mn, 2mf, 1ff, 1fn, 2fn, and 2ff. Within these eight cases, we should distinguish two groups. In the first group we place all the *non-fixed* versions of the model: 1mn, 2mn, 1fn, and 2fn. All *fixed* versions are in the second group: 1mf, 2mf, 1ff, and 2ff.

The reason for the distinction is the way in which the tests in [1] were performed. For all non-fixed versions of the model the verification run was halted as soon as the livelock error had been reported. Because of unpredictable and uncontrollable variations in search order, the amount of work done up to that point is not a reliable indicator of the overall performance of the model checkers. The measurement can serve only as a soft heuristic. For completeness only, we have included these measurements also in the new tests that we have performed. As we shall see in this case, the results for the first group and the second group of models are not inconsistent, but this should be considered a coincidence.

Overview of Paper

For most of the measurements performed here we adopt the Promela model of the i-protocol as it was developed for the original study in [1], unmodified. We must observe, though, that when the runs of Spin are compared with runs of XMC, or other model checkers, we are not just comparing the *tools* but also the relative quality of the *models*.

The most striking observations in [1] are differences between the tools in the use of basic resources such as memory and runtime, but also differences in the number of reachable states that are searched to solve the model checking problem. In principle, for explicit state model checkers, for a given problem specification, the size of the reachable statespace *before* reduction should match. In all versions of Spin the reduction algorithms can be disabled to perform a reference measurement for this purpose, giving the size of the original state space before reduction. The model checker XMC does not support such an option, which makes it harder to verify that the models used are equivalent.

In what follows we will try to address these problems separately. We first review the measurements reported in [1] (reported below as S297), while adopting the model from [1] unchanged, and restrict ourselves to making some small corrections in the use of Spin alone. Two types of corrections are made separately: the removal of faulty parameter setting (reported as S297*) and the addition of a useful compile time directive (reported as S297+).

Next we consider what portion of the differences in the statespace sizes searched by the two tools (XMC and Spin) can be attributed to differences in reduction strategies. Several of the strategies that have been used in XMC can beneficially be added to Spin. We have done so, leading to a new release of Spin numbered Version 3.3.0. The new measurements show considerable gains in performance for Spin. Differences in statespace sizes searched by XMC and Spin remain, however, which leads to a closer consideration of the models that were used. We conclude the paper with a final set of measurements for an equivalent, but slightly rewritten, Promela model of the i-protocol. The results are illuminating.

First Results

Tables 1 and 2 reproduce the results from [1] as they relate to XMC and Spin. The results show a disproportionate amount of memory used for the Spin runs, even for very small statespaces (e.g. for model 1mn). Dividing the reported 749 Mbytes of memory used for model 1mn by the 425 reported reachable states corresponds to an excessive amount of memory use of 1.76 Mbytes per state. Each state-vector in this model is no more than about 100 bytes long, so something is wrong.

The cause is not hard to find. The default stacksize used in the experiments in [1] was increased well beyond what was necessary to perform the runs. Using the default settings from Spin already produces more competitive numbers. In these tables we have included the results for the version of Spin that matches the on used in [1] with the stacksize set to a size that suffices to solve the problem, which is typically somewhat smaller than the default. These entries are labeled S297*, to distinguish them from the test results reported in [1]. Also added are entries labeled S297+ for the same runs with the loss-less COLLAPSE compression option [4] enabled, to reduce memory requirements some more for an additional runtime cost. The memory requirements can be reduced still further, at a higher run time penalty, by using the minimized automaton option [6], but we have not pursued this here.

The results for XMC and Spin are for different types of models, so a direct comparison of the results is not necessarily meaningful. We take a closer look at this issue towards the end of the paper, but meanwhile adopt the models precisely as they were used in the original study [1].

Table 1. Test Results First Group, from [1] for XMC and Spin Version 2.9.7 (S297)

Model	Tool	Reachable States	Memory (Mb)	Time (m:s)
1mn	XMC	341	5.0	0:01
	S297	425	749.0	0:10
	S297*	14K	1.8	0:01
	S297+	14K	1.5	0:01
2mn	XMC	1K	11.0	0:02
	S297	35K	751.0	0:12
	S297*	46K	7.6	0:03
	S297+	46K	5.1	0:04
1fn	XMC	961	9.0	0:01
	S297	5.2K	749.0	0:11
	S297*	5.2K	1.9	0:01
	S297+	5.2K	1.7	0:01
2fn	XMC	4K	35.0	0:05
	S297	17K	750.0	0:17
	S297*	68K	12.0	0:03
	S297+	68K	8.6	0:06

Table 2. Test Results Second Group, from [1] for XMC and Spin Version 2.9.7 (S297)

Model	Tool	Reachable States	Memory (Mb)	Time (m:s)
1mf	XMC	3K	78.0	0:17
	S297	322K	774.0	0:31
	S297*	322K	29.9	0:13
	S297+	322K	14.5	0:21
2mf	XMC	20K	475.0	1:49
	S297	1.9M	905.0	2:28
	S297*	1.9M	181.0	1:34
	S297+	1.9M	82.0	2:20
1ff	XMC	36K	1051.0	3:36
	S297	12.6M	1713.0	17:50
	S297*	12.6M	1088.0	17:38
	S297+	12.6M	497.0	31:06
2ff	XMC	315K	4708.0	47:15
	S297	-	-	-
	S297+	>28M	>1600.0	>89:00

All C programs were compiled with standard optimization enabled. All new measurements reported in this paper were made on an SGI IP27 Challenge MIPS R1000 computer with 1.6 Gigabytes of available memory. The performance of this machine matches the SGI IP25 Challenge MIPS R1000 used in [1], which makes a direct comparison of runtimes and memory use possible. All runtimes in the last column of Tables 1 and 2 are calculated as user time plus system time, as measured by the Unix® time command. The last test (for model 2ff) is clearly the most challenging one. It could not be completed with the model as given within the available 1.6 Gigabytes of memory on our machine.

The precise measurements from [1] could not be reproduced in three of the eight cases, curiously leading to larger problem sizes in the new tests. Nonetheless, the final results are substantially different from those reported in [1]. Spin version 2.9.7 outperforms XMC in six of the eight testcases. In each of these cases Spin used fewer resources, despite searching considerably larger statespaces. The difference is statespace size is most likely due to a more aggressive use of reductions, as outlined in [2], and as we shall investigate below. For models 1ff and 2ff, XMC is the winner in statespace size, memory use, and runtime requirements.

The difference in the statespace sizes explored, illustrated in Tables 1 and 2, does point to the potential importance of the optimization techniques that were employed in the design of XMC. In the next section we describe the implementation in Spin Version 3.3.0 of these and similar reduction techniques, and we repeat the experiments for Spin with these optimizations added.

Spin Version 3.3.0

In [2] several optimization techniques are mentioned that are likely in part responsible for the small statespace sizes that are constructed with the XMC model checker. Among these techniques are:

1. The merging of internal transitions into single internal steps to avoid redundant interleavings during the model checking process and to avoid the performance of extra work at run-time.
2. Dead variable elimination based on a standard control-flow analysis.
3. Aggressive optimization of the control structure, e.g., to eliminate dead branches.

We discuss each of these points in more detail below.

Statement Merging

The principle of the statement merging technique is well established. Statement merging is a special case of partial order reduction. The partial order reduction method that is implemented in Spin version 2 was described in [3]. This method suppresses redundant interleavings of process actions wherever safely possible, but it does not attempt to perform compile-time optimizations when non-interleaved sequences of process actions can be merged into a single step. A proposal to add this capability was made earlier in [11], but not pursued at the time. In terms of Spin semantics, the change that has now been made in Spin version 3.3.0 amounts to the automatic assignment of **d_step** constructs to all pieces of code where this can safely be done under the partial order reduction rules from [3]. The implementation is conservative by not including selection or iteration statements into these merge sequences. The reason for this is as follows. A condition for the safety of the transformation we have applied is that no non-deterministic constructs be included in the merge sequences. It is, however, not possible to reliably determine at compile time whether the evaluation of the guards in a selection or iteration construct may produce non-determinism at run time.

Figure 1 illustrates the context in which statement merging can be applied. In the current implementation of Spin, we determine at compile time (statically) whether the conditions are satisfied for the creation of states with indegree and outdegree necessarily equal to one. This implementation is conservative, and might be improved upon to increase the amount of reduction obtained. Our implementation can, for instance, be extended by including also sub-sets of selection and iteration construct that *can* statically be determined to be deterministic. Such an extension can translate immediately into additional run time reductions.

Dead Variable Elimination

The second technique can similarly be done statically at compile-time in the model checker. Spin 3.3.0 recognizes globally dead, write-only variables and eliminates them from the state-vector. These types of variables can, for instance, appear in models that are parameterized to yield different interpretation of a single general specification, as we see in the current set of testcases. Eliminating these variables translates into memory savings by globally shrinking all state descriptors, without loss of information. It can reduce search spaces as well, by avoiding the storage of write-only values that provably can have no bearing on the correctness properties of a model. (An often seen case is the use of a write-only counter variable that, unless it is eliminated, can multiply the search space by the full range of the counter Cases such as this are discussed in more detail in [7].)

Fig. 1. Fragment of a graph reduced under standard partial order reduction rules. Transitions with both indegree and outdegree equal to one are merged with the new statement merging technique. Merging these statements avoids the creation at runtime of the shaded states.

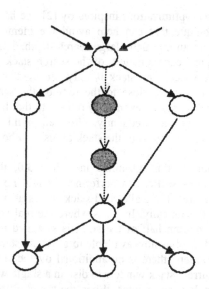

Based on similar observations, Spin 3.3.0 performs a data-flow analysis at compile-time to also avoid the storage of values for *temporarily* dead variables. A variable is temporarily dead if it cannot be read until *after* the variable has been assigned a new value. Our implementation is again conservative by resetting temporarily dead variables to a fixed value of zero, instead of temporarily stripping these variables from the state descriptor itself. The motivation for the latter is efficiency: the model checker would be slowed down too by having to assemble and reassemble the state descriptor on the fly from a varying collection of elements at each step.

Automata Pruning

The third technique will eliminate dead parts of the control structure. Parts of the model can become unreachable, as with globally dead variables, for specific parameter settings that are used to specialize the behavior of a general model specification. The savings will be in avoiding the evaluation of guard conditions at run time in cases where a static evaluation at compile time can predict that the conditions are necessarily false for the given parameter settings. Especially for larger models than considered here (e.g., [8]), this option can prove to be beneficial. For the i-protocol, however, this reduction method does not appear to contribute significant extra savings.

Stack Cycling

In addition to the three optimizations inspired by [2], we have also implemented a new stack cycling technique that can help avoid the memory expense of model checking runs that require an unusually large search depth. This method exploits the observation that the typical access pattern of the search stack is very different from that of the regular state space. The stack is only accessed in a strictly predictable order: frames high on the stack, close to the root of the search tree, will not be accessed until the depth-first search eventually returns to that level, while frames low on the stack will be accessed frequently. We can build an effective caching mechanism that swaps large portions of the stack to disk, without significant run-time overhead.

In the implementation of this discipline in Spin 3.3.0, the default stack size, predefined by Spin, always suffices to perform a search, no matter how deep the search stack grows. The predefined allocated stack serves as a 'window' into the real stack, which can grow dynamically. In cases where the real stack grows larger than the allocated stack, the bottom half of the stack is swapped to disk, and the search continues with the freed up slots now available to grow the stack further. Because the stack is accessed via pointers, there is no additional overhead beyond the writing of the bottom half of the current stack window to disk in a single write operation, and the reassignment of one single stack pointer. When the search retreats, and stack frames are needed that are currently on disk, the reverse happens. Half the stack window is read back in from disk in a single read operation, and the stack pointer is adjusted. There is remarkably little overhead involved, and the process is fully transparent to the model checking process itself.

New Measurements

The first three optimizations are part of the new default search strategy in Spin 3.3.0. Stack cycling is kept as a compile-time option, since the need for it is still relatively rare. We have used it on just one of the tests for the i-protocol, shown in Table 3. For the most challenging model, 2ff, this option can shave an extra 160

Mbytes from the memory requirements, reducing it to 606 Mbytes, in return for an increase of runtime of approximately 5 percent.

Table 3. Test Results first group, comparing XMC and Spin Version 3.3.0 (S330)

Model	Tool	Reachable States	Memory (MB)	Time (m:s)
1mn	XMC	341	5.0	0:01
	S330	3K	1.6	0:01
	S330+	3K	1.5	0:01
2mn	XMC	1K	11.0	0:02
	S330	15K	3.0	0:01
	S330+	15K	2.2	0:01
1fn	XMC	961	9.0	0:01
	S330	851	1.3	0:01
	S330+	851	1.3	0:01
2fn	XMC	4K	35.0	0:05
	S330	20K	3.8	0:02
	S330+	20K	2.8	0:01

Table 3 lists all test results, comparing the performance of XMC as reported in [1] with the results for Spin 3.3.0. For the test results marked S330, we only used parameter settings that were sufficient to solve the problem. On the results marked S330+ we added the optional COLLAPSE compression mode [4] to reduce the memory requirements without affecting coverage, but while sacrificing some speed.

Curiously, the numbers of states searched by Spin, with one exception (1fn) remains larger than reported for XMC, yet the resource requirements are considerably smaller in all cases. We return to this issue in the last section of this paper.

Table 4. Test Results second group, comparing XMC and Spin Version 3.3.0 (S330)

Model	Tool	Reachable States	Memory (MB)	Time (m:s)
1mf	XMC	3K	78.0	0:17
	S330	148K	14.0	0:05
	S330+	148K	6.8	0:09
2mf	XMC	20K	475	1:49
	S330	965K	87.0	0:39
	S330+	965K	37.7	1:01
1ff	XMC	36K	1051.0	3:36
	S330	2.5M	214.0	2:15
	S330+	2.5M	90.7	3:12
2ff	XMC	315K	4708.0	47:15
	S330+	21.9M	606.0	62:00

Based on the measurements for SMV as reported in [1], for the given model in Promela and the given model in SMV, the Spin verification appears to outperform

SMV on these tests in seven out of eight cases. According to [1], in four cases SMV ran out of memory, in three cases it used substantially more memory, and in only one case (1ff) it used less. Unfortunately, in the absence of a more focused series of experiments comparing SMV and Spin directly, and in the absence of a more careful examination of differences and similarities between the SMV model and the Spin model used in these tests, no conclusions can be drawn from these observations.

The Effect of Each Optimization

To get a better indication of the effect that is contributed by the optimizations separately, we measured the performance of the model checker for one of the testcases with the individual optimizations enabled or disabled. We used the 2mf model for these measurements. Automata pruning and the elimination of globally dead variables were not a factor in the measurements for this specific set of models, so we have omitted these from Table 5.

For reference, the first row in the table matches the result for 2mf in Table 4, and the last matches the result for 2mf in Table 2 for Spin version 2.9.7. As an additional checkpoint, we also include the results for version 3.3.0 with all new optimizations turned off, in the fourth row of Table 5. It turns out to use slightly less memory and slightly more runtime than version 2.9.7, due to small and otherwise unrelated, changes in the code. Statement merging appears to contribute almost all the benefits that are observed in this experiment. The dataflow analysis appears to carry a small penalty in this case, unless it is combined with statement merging.

Table 5. Test results for Spin Versions 3.3.0 and 2.9.7 on model version 2mf.

Version	States	Memory (Mb)	Time (m:s)
All optimizations enabled	965K	87	0:58
Statement merging only	970K	100	0:59
Dataflow analysis only	1.9M	179	2:17
No optimizations (Version 3.3.0)	1.9M	173	2:12
No optimizations (Version 2.9.7)	1.9M	181	1:59

The Accuracy of the Model

If we review the results tabulated in [1], a few things stand out. The first we mentioned earlier in this paper: the large divergence in the sizes of the statespaces searched by each of the tools, despite the fact that all tools attempt to solve the same problem. Part of this divergence can be attributed to differences in reduction techniques employed, but not all. A second item is the difference in the sizes of the state-descriptors that are used in the *explicit-state* model checkers. We can obtain this number nominally by dividing overall memory use reported by the number of states that was stored. For the Murφ tool, for instance, the size of a state descriptor comes out at roughly 60 bytes. For Spin, however, the number is roughly 128: twice as large. A comparison of the two models used for these tests, the one for the Murφ tool and the one built for the Spin tool, shows important differences. The Spin model, as constructed for these experiments, uses more processes, more types of data, fewer cases of atomicity, etc. etc. It is not hard to improve upon the Spin model, without affecting its functionality though. The author spent 1 hour of editing time to make mostly straightforward changes to the Spin version of the i-protocol model, following the recommendations documented in [7]. Sink and source processes, as defined in [7], were removed. The revised Spin model is a better match to the competing models. The results of the measurements with this revised model, for both Spin version 2.9.7 and Spin version 3.3.0, are tabulated in Tables 6 and 7, again compared against the original XMC measurements from [1].

Table 6. Final Results, first group, revised model, XMC and Spin Versions 2.9.7 and 3.3.0

Model	Tool	Reachable States	Memory (MB)	Time (m:s)
1mn	XMC	341	5.0	0:01
	2.9.7	86	1.8	0:01
	3.3.0	77	1.8	0:01
2mn	XMC	1K	11.0	0:02
	2.9.7	111	1.8	0:01
	3.3.0	101	1.8	0:01
1fn	XMC	961	9.0	0:01
	2.9.7	86	1.8	0:01
	3.3.0	77	1.8	0:01
2fn	XMC	4K	35	0:05
	2.9.7	111	1.8	0:01
	3.3.0	101	1.8	0:01

In these final measurements, all Spin tests were run with compression enabled, with a search stack limit set to a level that accommodated the most complex version of the model (2ff). The numbers for XMC are again taken from [1], measured on hardware with identical performance. As before, all runs in the first group stop when the livelock error is detected (and all runs successfully detect this error). All results for the second group of models, shown in Table 7, are for exhaustive verification runs, that stop when the full state space of the model has been explored, and the absence of liveness and safety errors was proven.

In the first group of tests, Spin explores a smaller state space in all 4 cases, by a comfortable margin. But, as noted before, the tests in this first group are not necessarily indicative of overall tool performance. The tests in the second group are a better indicator for this (since the verifications are run to completion in all cases).

Table 7. Final Results, second group, revised model, XMC and Spin Versions 2.9.7 and 3.3.0

Model	Tool	Reachable States	Memory (MB)	Time (m:s)
1mf	XMC	3K	78.0	0:17
	2.9.7	17K	2.1	0:07
	3.3.0	13K	1.9	0:05
2mf	XMC	20K	475.0	1:49
	2.9.7	75K	3.4	0:03
	3.3.0	55K	2.9	0:02
1ff	XMC	36K	1051.0	3:36
	2.9.7	35K	2.5	0:01
	3.3.0	25K	2.3	0:01
2ff	XMC	315K	4708.0	47:15
	2.9.7	208K	6.5	0:08
	3.3.0	161K	5.2	0:06

For the second group of tests Spin explores more states than XMC in 2 out of 4 cases, and fewer states than XMC in the other 2 of the 4. The numbers are close enough, though to give some reassurance that the models are comparable. In all cases in this group Spin uses fewer resources, by a very comfortable margin.

Comparing the results from Tables 6 and 7 to those presented in Table 3 and 4 emphasizes the importance of model construction. The effect on complexity of a well-designed [7] or a poorly designed model can easily overpower the effect of the search algorithm used, or the choice of model checking tool. With these observations we do not intend to underestimate the significance of what was achieved in [1]. Testing and comparing model checkers in a scientifically meaningful way is hard. It is perhaps an art form that none of us have quite mastered yet.

Conclusion

The suggestions for optimization from the report on the XMC model checker [2] are sufficiently general that they can readily be included in other model checking systems. We have implemented three of the optimization techniques in the Spin model checker, and confirmed that these optimizations can reduce its resource requirements. The remaining discrepancies in the numbers of states searched during the model checking process between XMC and Spin Version 3.3.0 are only partly due to further opportunities for reduction that may exist in the Spin model checker. The data in Tables 6 and 7, however, shows that the remaining differences can be attributed to differences in the way that the models were constructed.

In the measurements from Tables 6 and 7, Spin outperforms XMC on memory use and time consumption by one to three orders of magnitude. In the implementation of most model checking algorithms there is a delicate trade-off to be made between time and space. It is almost always the case that reducing the memory requirements further can be achieved only at the expense of the time requirements, and vice versa. All memory requirement figures reported here for Spin can be reduced further, in some cases significantly, by using more aggressive memory compression options (e.g., as the minimized automaton representation detailed in [6]). We have resisted the temptation to do so here.

Figure 2 summarizes the results we have obtained for the original Spin models from [1] by plotting the relative memory use for the three most significant series of measurements for all eight test cases. The vertical axis shows memory use in Megabytes. The horizontal axis lists the various testcases and versions of the tool. We have omitted the result from Table 6 in this Figure. If plotted, it would show a very considerable advantage for the Spin verifications in all tests.

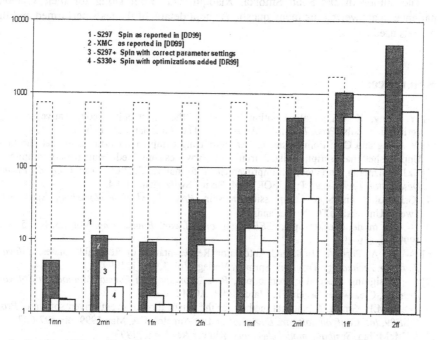

Fig. 2. Graphical View of Relative Performance of XMC, and Spin Versions 2.9.7 and 3.3.0.

The reference performance is the one given for XMC in [1], shown here in dark grey, and labeled with the number 2. Dotted, and labeled by 1, is the performance of Spin 2.9.7 as reported in [1]. In light grey, labeled 3, we give the corrected measurements performed here, for the same tests with Spin 2.9.7, as listed in Tables 1 and 2. Next to that, in white, and labeled 4, we give the performance on the same problem when Spin 3.3.0 is used.

The Promela source for the i-protocol as it is tested here and in [1] is available online from: http://www.cs.sunysb.edu/~lmc/papers/tacas99/proti.spin.1fn.

The revised Spin model for 2ff, represented in Table 6, is available from the current author. Also available from the website shown above is the C source for both version 1.04 and version 1.06.1 of the GNU uucp i-protocol. The source is approx. 1500 lines of C. It should be feasible to produce a version on which we can directly perform Spin model checking without first manually constructing a Promela model. We have earlier applied such a method in the verification of a commercial telephone call processing system. The method we have developed is detailed in [8]. At the time of writing we are extending this method to tackle C implementations of general protocols, such as the one discussed here.

Acknowledgements

The author thanks Scott Smolka, Xiaoqun Du, Yifei Dong for their gracious patience in answering the many questions about details of the tests performed and the models used in [1].

References

[1] Y. Dong, X. Du, et al., Fighting livelock in the i-protocol: a comparative study of verification tools. *Proc. TACAS99*, Amsterdam, The Netherlands, March 1999.

[2] Y. Dong and C.R. Ramakrishnan. An optimizing compiler for efficient model checking. Unpublished manuscript, available from: http://www.cs.sunysb.edu/~lmc/papers/compiler/.

[3] G.J. Holzmann, D. Peled, An improvement in formal verification, *Proc. Conf. on Formal Description Techniques*, Proc. FORTE94, Berne, Switzerland, 1994.

[4] G.J. Holzmann, State Compression in Spin, *Proc. Third Spin Workshop*, April 1997, Twente University, The Netherlands.

[5] --, The model checker Spin, *IEEE Trans. on Software Engineering*, Vol. 23, No. 5, May 1997, pp. 279-295.

[6] -- and A. Puri, A Minimized Automaton Representation of Reachable States, *Software Tools for Technology Transfer*, Springer Verlag, Vol. 3, No. 1, 1999.

[7] --, Designing executable abstractions, *Proc. Workshop on Formal Methods in Software Practice*, Clearwater Beach, Fl., March 1998, ACM Press.

[8] -- and M.H. Smith, A practical method for the verification of event driven software. *Proc. ICSE99, Int. Conf. on Software Engineering*, Los Angeles, CA, May 1999, pp. 597-607.

[9] K. McMillan, *Symbolic model checking*. Kluwer Academic, 1993.

[10] Y.S. Ramakrishna, C.R. Ramakrishnan, et al., Efficient model checking using tabled resolution. *Proc. CAV97, LNCS 1254*, pp. 143-154, Springer Verlag.

[11] H. van der Schoot and H. Ural, An improvement on partial order model checking with ample sets. *Computer Science Technical Report*, TR-96-11, Univ. of Ottawa, Canada, Sept. 1996.

Embedding a Dialect of SDL in PROMELA

Heikki Tuominen

Nokia Telecommunications,
P.O. Box 372, FIN-00045 Nokia Group, Finland
heikki.j.tuominen@nokia.com

Abstract. We describe a translation from a dialect of SDL-88 to PRO-
MELA, the input language of the SPIN model checker. The fairly straightforward translation covers data types as well as processes, procedures,
and services. Together with SPIN the translation provides a simulation
and verification environment for most SDL features.

1 Introduction

TNSDL, Nokia Telecommunications SDL, is a dialect of SDL-88 [6] used for
developing switching system software. As one possibility to construct a simulation and verification environment for TNSDL an embedding in—or a translation
to—PROMELA [1] has been investigated. The defined and mostly implemented
translation provides an SDL front-end to the SPIN model checker [3] with properties similar to those of commercial SDL tools.

Using an existing tool, SPIN in this case, as the basis of an SDL verification
environment might bring some compromises but certainly saves a lot of development effort when compared with implementing everything from scratch. Among
the types of languages with advanced tool support, e.g. Petri nets and process
algebras, PROMELA seems to be an ideal choice for SDL because of the close
relationship between the languages. PROMELA being conceptually extremely
close to SDL makes the translation fairly simple and allows preserving the structure of the system in the translation thus perhaps providing some advantage in
the verification phase.

The close relation between SDL and PROMELA is no accident: the first version of PROMELA was designed as an extension to another language in order to
support analysis of SDL descriptions [4]. Most SDL concepts have direct counterparts in PROMELA and the translation is very straightforward. The most
notable examples are the processes, their dynamic creation, and communication
through message passing. Some other features, like passing parameters to SDL
procedures, require a slightly more complicated translation and for very few SDL
aspects there seems to be no feasible representation in current PROMELA. The
TNSDL pointer data type—not present in SDL-88—might serve as an example
of this last category.

TNSDL differs from the SDL-88 recommendation in various details, including both simplifications and extensions. With respect to the translation to PRO-
MELA the definition of data types and routing of signals are perhaps the two

most remarkable differences. Instead of the algebraic specifications in SDL-88 TNSDL has a C-like type system and instead of the channels and signal routes TNSDL includes a routing file which defines the destination processes for signals sent without an explicit process address. Translating the corresponding aspects of SDL-88 to PROMELA would probably be more complicated than the presented translation of TNSDL.

Essentially the same approach to SDL verification has earlier been applied at AT&T [2, 4]. The translation described in this paper attempts to cover more SDL features by making use of the recent extensions in the PROMELA language but unfortunately we cannot currently report on any practical applications of the method. There also exists an experimental verification system for TNSDL based on a translation to Petri nets [5] but for the above reasons we feel PROMELA to be a more natural target language.

The rest of the paper describes the translation from TNSDL to PROMELA organized as follows. Section 2 describes the translation of data types, the declarative part of SDL. The communication part, i.e. signal queues, and the operational part, i.e. processes and other similar entities, are covered in Sections 3 and 4, respectively. Finally, the implementation is touched on in Section 5 and the concluding Section 6 enumerates some limitations found in PROMELA and SPIN during the study. Overall, no formal definition of the translation is attempted, the description is based solely on examples and prose. Also, various technical details are ignored in the presentation, e.g. names of data types, processes, and procedures are assumed to be unique over the whole system to be translated.

2 Declarative SDL

The declarative part of SDL covers the definition of data types which are then used in variable declarations. In contrast to the algebraic specifications in the SDL-88 recommendation, TNSDL has a more implementation-oriented C-like type system with arrays, unions, pointers etc. As PROMELA has a similar, although more restricted, C-based type system the translation of data types is quite simple.

Like normal programming languages TNSDL provides a set of predefined data types and ways to construct new types on top of the existing ones. The PROMELA representation of these two faces of the type system is described in the two subsequent sections.

2.1 Predefined types

Predefined types are the basic ways to represent data. TNSDL has a set of normal integer types of various sizes and some types corresponding to fundamental SDL concepts. The representation of these types in PROMELA is defined in Table 1, the dashes indicate the currently missing counterparts of the marginal floating point number types. Constants of the predefined types are declared in

PROMELA using **define** directives as indicated in Table 2 for the **bool** and **condition** types.

TNSDL	PROMELA
bool	bool
byte	byte
word	unsigned : 16
dword	unsigned : 32
shortint	short
integer	short
longint	int
real	–
doublereal	–
character	byte
pid	chan
duration	unsigned : 32
condition	bool

Table 1. Translation of predefined types.

TNSDL	PROMELA
	#define T true
	#define F false
	#define SUCCESS true
	#define FAILURE false

Table 2. Translation of constants in predefined types.

2.2 Type expressions

Type expressions are ways to build new data types based on the existing ones. TNSDL includes seven kinds of them: type names, arrays, integer subranges, enumerations, structures, unions, and pointers. In this terminology PROMELA has only arrays and structures, even them in a restricted form, but they turn out to be sufficient for representing all TNSDL types except pointers.

PROMELA representations of some TNSDL type definitions are given in Table 3. Auxiliary types are used to overcome the limitations of PROMELA, mainly the lack of nested type expressions. Constants of the user-defined types, enumeration constants among them, are directly replaced by their values in the translation and no **define** directives are thus needed for them.

3 Communication

Asynchronous communication through message passing is one of the characteristic features of SDL. An infinite queue for storing the received messages, or signals, is implicitly associated with each process. With some minor limitations the same mechanism is available also in PROMELA and the translation is again rather obvious.

The signal queues are not visible in SDL code but in PROMELA they have to be defined like variables: queues, or channels, have finite length and are typed. A typed channel can only carry signals whose parameters match its definition and since it is not known at translation time which signals will be sent to which processes all the channels are made "wide" enough to carry any signal present in the system. Each channel has thus appropriate fields for storing any signal with its parameters in a single slot. Actually the type of the channels is defined as a data type, a structure with proper fields for the parameters of the SDL signals. In addition, the structure contains fields for the signal name and the identifier of the sending process.

As an example, Table 4 contains the channel type for an SDL system with two signals, sig1_s and sig2_s. mtype is an enumeration type defining constants for all the signals in the system and _sig_t is the data type used to represent signals outside the channels. Unfortunately SPIN does not allow a channel with type _sig_t to be defined because certain data types are forbidden on channels. These include at least arrays whose base type is defined with a **typedef** and types containing the **unsigned** construct. For this reason the signals are on the channels represented using another type, _csig_t, which contains the same information as _sig_t but in a slightly different form. In _csig_t the critical arrays are represented as structures and the unsigned integers as signed ones. Signals are converted between these two representations using the generated PROMELA inline procedures, Table 5.

The mechanism used for routing signals which are sent without an explicit target process is simpler in TNSDL than in SDL-88. Instead of signal lists associated with signal routes and channels TNSDL contains specific syntax for defining the "default" target for a signal. The target is specified as one of the master processes of the system, which are created at system start-up and limited to have only one instance. The signal queue of such a master process is global in the PROMELA representation and it is directly used as the target in these cases.

4 Operational SDL

The behavior of an SDL system is produced by its processes, i.e. entities which receive and send signals as well as perform calculations. This section describes

TNSDL	PROMELA

```
TYPE name_t                      #define name_t byte
  REPRESENTATION byte;
ENDTYPE name_t;


TYPE array_t                     typedef array_t {
  REPRESENTATION                    struct_t item[2];
    ARRAY (2) OF struct_t;       }
ENDTYPE array_t;


TYPE range_t                     #define range_t byte
  REPRESENTATION (1:100);
ENDTYPE range_t;


TYPE enum_t                      #define enum_t byte
  REPRESENTATION ENUM
    a,b,c
  ENDENUM;
ENDTYPE enum_t;


TYPE struct_t                    typedef struct_t_aux_1 {
  REPRESENTATION STRUCT             enum_t f11;
    f1 STRUCT                    }
        f11 enum_t;              typedef struct_t {
      ENDSTRUCT;                    struct_t_aux_1 f1;
    f2 byte;                       byte f2;
  ENDSTRUCT;                     }
ENDTYPE struct_t;


TYPE union_t                     typedef union_t {
  REPRESENTATION UNION              array_t f1;
    f1 array_t;                     struct_t f2;
    f2 struct_t;                 }
  ENDUNION;
ENDTYPE union_t;


TYPE pointer_t                   -
  REPRESENTATION
    POINTER(union_t);
ENDTYPE pointer_t;
```

Table 3. Translation of type expressions.

TNSDL	PROMELA

SIGNAL
  sig1_s
  (
    par1 byte;
  );
  sig2_s
  (
    p1 array_t;
    p2 word;
  );
	mtype = {sig1_s,sig2_s}
	typedef _sig_t {
	  mtype f1;
	  chan f2; /* sender */
	  byte f3;
	  array_t f4;
	  unsigned f5 : 32;
	}
	typedef _carray_t {
	  struct_t item_0;
	  struct_t item_1;
	}
	typedef _csig_t {
	  mtype f1;
	  chan f2;
	  byte f3;
	  _carray_t f4;
	  int f5;
	}

Table 4. Translation of signal declarations.

the representation of SDL processes in PROMELA. Also procedures and services, which can be considered as variations of the same theme, are discussed.

4.1 Processes

An SDL process is an extended finite state automaton which upon reading a signal from its queue carries out the associated computation and then enters the next state. The read, or received, signal is indicated in an INPUT statement which is followed by a sequence of action statements, called a transition. Each process also contains a START transition which is executed when a process instance is created. Furthermore, an instance can terminate itself using the STOP statement.

TNSDL processes are translated to PROMELA processes. The master processes correspond to **active** processes with global queues and the others to normal PROMELA processes with local queues. The translation is illustrated with an example containing both a master and a regular process in Table 6. The example also indicates the general structure of the generated processes, i.e. a sequence of variable declarations, state descriptions, and transitions. SDL transitions are sequences of statements which are translated to PROMELA statement by statement as illustrated in Table 7.

TNSDL	PROMELA

```
                              _csig_t _cs;
                              inline _receive_sig(ch,sig) {
                                ch?_cs;
                                sig.f1 = _cs.f1;
                                sig.f2 = _cs.f2;
                                sig.f3 = _cs.f3;
                                sig.f4.item[0] = _cs.f4.item_0;
                                sig.f4.item[1] = _cs.f4.item_1;
                                sig.f5 = _cs.f5 + 32768;
                              }
                              inline _send_sig1_s(t,s,p1) {
                                _cs.f1 = sig1_s;
                                _cs.f2 = s;
                                _cs.f3 = p1;
                                t!_cs;
                              }
                              inline _send_sig2_s(t,s,p1,p2) {
                                _cs.f1 = sig2_s;
                                _cs.f2 = s;
                                _cs.f4.item_0 = p1[0];
                                _cs.f4.item_1 = p1[1];
                                _cs.f5 = p2 - 32768;
                                t!_cs;
                              }
                              inline _send_sig(ch,sig) {
                                _cs.f1 = sig.f1;
                                _cs.f2 = sig.f2;
                                _cs.f3 = sig.f3;
                                _cs.f4.item_0 = sig.f4.item[0];
                                _cs.f4.item_1 = sig.f4.item[1];
                                _cs.f5 = sig.f5 - 32768;
                                ch!_cs;
                              }
```

Table 5. Translation of signal declarations, continued.

TNSDL	PROMELA

```
PROCESS tail;                          proctype tail (chan PARENT;
  FPAR p1 byte;                                       chan __offspring;
                                                      byte p1) {
  START;                                 chan SELF = [N] of {_csig_t}
  STOP;                                  __offspring!SELF;
ENDPROCESS tail;                         goto _transition0;
                                         _transition0:
                                         goto end;
                                         end:
                                         skip;
                                       }


                                       chan _head = [N] of {_csig_t}
MASTER PROCESS head;                   active proctype head () {
  DCL x byte;                            chan SELF= _head;
                                         chan SENDER, OFFPSRING;
  START;                                 chan _offspring = [0] of {chan}
  CREATE tail(3);                        byte x;
  NEXTSTATE idle;
                                         goto _transition0;

  STATE idle;
    INPUT sig1_s(x);                     idle:
      TASK x := x + 1;                   do
      NEXTSTATE idle;                    ::  _receive_sig(SELF,_sig) ->
  ENDSTATE idle;                             if
ENDPROCESS head;                           ::  sig1_s == _sig.f1 ->
                                               SENDER = _sig.f2;
                                               x = _sig.f3;
                                               goto _transition1;
                                           :: else ->
                                               skip;
                                           fi;
                                       od;

                                         _transition0:
                                         run tail(SELF,_offspring,3);
                                         _offspring?OFFSPRING;
                                         goto idle;

                                         _transition1:
                                         x = x + 1;
                                         goto idle;
                                       }
```

Table 6. Translation of processes.

TNSDL	PROMELA
`OUTPUT sig1_s(100) TO SENDER;`	`_send_sig1(SENDER,SELF,100);`
`STOP;`	`goto end;`
	`...`
	`end:`
	`skip;`
`TASK a := b + 2;`	`a = b + 2;`
`CREATE client(1,2);`	`chan _offspring = [0] of {chan};`
	`run client(SELF,_offspring,1,2);`
	`_offspring?OFFSPRING;`
`DECISION x;`	`if`
`  (<3)  TASK y := y + 1;`	`:: (x<3) -> y = y + 1;`
`  (4,5) TASK y := y + 2;`	`:: (x==4 || x==5) -> y = y + 2;`
`  ELSE  TASK y := y + 3;`	`:: else -> y = y + 3;`
`ENDDECISION;`	`fi`
`WHILE counter > 0;`	`do`
`  TASK counter := counter - 1;`	`:: counter > 0 ->`
`ENDWHILE;`	`   counter = counter - 1;`
	`:: else -> break;`
	`od`
`NEXTSTATE idle;`	`goto idle;`
`JOIN spaghetti;`	`goto spaghetti;`
`SET(NOW+b,timer_a);`	`_rnd_rcv_timer_a(_timer,SELF);`
	`_rnd_rcv_timer_a(SELF,_timer);`
	`_send_timer_a(_timer,SELF);`
`RESET(timer_a);`	`_rnd_rcv_timer_a(_timer,SELF);`
	`_rnd_rcv_timer_a(SELF,_timer);`

Table 7. Translation of action statements.

Unexpected signals, i.e. ones without a matching INPUT statement in the current state, are normally "consumed implicitly" in SDL. This silent deletion can, however, be prevented using SAVE statements which preserve the indicated signals for later processing. SAVE statements are translated to PROMELA using additional local save queues to which the saved signals are sent. Always when the SDL state of the process changes the signal queue is prefixed with the contents of the save queue.

4.2   Timers

Timers are ways to incorporate real-time features in SDL descriptions. A process can set a timer to fire after a wanted period of time and the firing timer then sends an appropriate signal to the activating process.

As PROMELA has no real time related features the representation of timers is forced to be an approximation. Timers are in the translation represented by a process which receives all the requests corresponding to SET statements and simply sends the proper timer signal immediately back to the activating process. The translation of SET statements and their opposites, RESET statements, is sketched in Table 7; the _rnd_rcv_timer_a procedure is used to remove the possible earlier activation signal of the timer both from the signal queue of the timer process and the activating process.

4.3   Procedures

Procedures provide in SDL, like in normal programming languages, a mechanism for grouping certain behavior together. They are subroutines which can be called in processes, other procedures, and even in the procedures themselves. A procedure is defined very much like a process—it can contain states, inputs, transitions etc.—but is naturally less independent. For example, a procedure does not have a signal queue of its own, it relies on the queue of the calling process.

PROMELA inline procedures provide a useful mechanism for representing SDL procedures but they cannot be used alone because they are based on macro expansion and cannot represent cyclic recursive procedures. Thus, each SDL procedure is translated to a PROMELA inline procedure mostly following the rules defined for processes but in addition a simple PROMELA process is generated for each procedure invocation, i.e. a CALL statement. The additional process takes mainly care of calling the inline procedure with proper parameters.

SDL procedures can have two kinds of parameters: value and reference ones, also called IN and IN/OUT parameters. Value parameters represent the native mechanism in PROMELA and pose thus no problems in the translation but the reference ones implement a kind of remote referencing and require somewhat more effort. Roughly speaking, the values of the reference parameters are passed to the PROMELA process implementing the SDL procedure in the beginning and sent back to the calling process at the end of the execution. The same mechanism is used to make the process-level variables visible within the procedure when required. As an example, Table 8 includes the translation of a simple TNSDL procedure.

4.4 Services

SDL services, or subautomata as they are called in TNSDL, are another way to create structure within a process. A process defined using services is internally like a set of processes but seen from the outside it behaves like a single process, i.e. it has only one signal queue and process identifier.

Each SDL service is translated to a PROMELA process and an additional main process is generated for controlling the aggregate. The main process takes care of first creating the service processes and then relaying the received signals to proper services as well as synchronizing the services. Each signal can be received only by one service and services within a process are not allowed to execute truly concurrently with each other. In addition to the normal communication mechanism services can use another one, called priority signals in SDL-88 and internal signals in TNSDL. These signals, always exchanged within an SDL process, have a higher priority than the normal ones and are in the PROMELA translation transferred through an additional internal signal queue.

Table 9 provides an example of the generated main process and Table 10 outlines the translation of a single service. In order to make the process-level variables visible to all the services they are in the beginning of the main process as well as after the transitions in the services sent to specific channels and received from them in the beginning of the transitions.

4.5 Modules

TNSDL modules, an extension to SDL-88, bring a possibility to share data among processes. Modules can contain procedures which can be called in any process of the system and variables which are visible to all procedures in the module. In the PROMELA representation the module variables are made global and the procedures are translated much like normal procedures.

5 Implementation

The described central parts of the translation have been implemented in an experimental tool called TNPRO. Actually TNPRO is an alternative back-end in a TNSDL to Petri net translator [5] which moreover uses the front-end of a TNSDL to C translator for parsing TNSDL. The functionality of TNPRO has so far been demonstrated only with small—a few hundred lines each—artificial TNSDL descriptions.

TNSDL	PROMELA

```
PROCESS dummy;                    inline proc (a,b) {
  DCL x byte;                       goto _transition0;

  PROCEDURE proc;                   _transition0:
  FPAR IN a byte,                   b = a;
       IN/OUT b byte;               goto _return;
                                  }
    START;                        proctype dummy () {
    TASK b := a;                    chan _ret1 = [0] of {bool};
    RETURN;                         byte x;
  ENDPROCEDURE proc;                chan _x = [1] of {byte}
                                    goto _transition0;
  START;
  CALL proc(3,x);                   _transition0:
  STOP;                             _x!x;
ENDPROCESS dummy;                   run proc_1(_ret1,SELF,
                                               SENDER,3,_x);
                                    _ret1?true;
                                    _x?x;
                                    goto end;

                                    end:
                                    skip;
                                  }
                                  proctype proc_1(chan _ret2;
                                              chan SELF;
                                              chan SENDER;
                                              byte a;
                                              chan _b) {
                                    byte b;
                                    _b?b;
                                    proc(a,b);
                                    _return:
                                    _b!b;
                                    _ret2!true;
                                  }
```

Table 8. Translation of procedures.

TNSDL	PROMELA

```
PROCESS auto;
  DCL x byte;

  SUBAUTOMATON auto1;
  ...
  ENDSUBAUTOMATON auto1;

  SUBAUTOMATON auto2;
  ...
  ENDSUBAUTOMATON auto2;
ENDPROCESS auto;
```

```
proctype auto () {
  byte x;
  chan _x = [1] of {byte};
  chan _int = [N] of {_csig_t};
  chan _sync = [1] of {byte};
  chan _auto1 = [0] of {_csig_t};
  chan _auto2 = [0] of {_csig_t};
  chan _iauto1 =[0] of {_csig_t};
  chan _iauto2 =[0] of {_csig_t};

  _sync!2;
  _x!x;
  run auto1(SELF,_auto1,_iauto1,
            _int,_sync,_x);
  run auto2(SELF,_auto2,_iauto2,
            _int,_sync,_x);
  do
  ::_sync?0 ->
    if
    ::_receive_sig(_int,_sig) ->
      if
      ::sig1_s == _sig.f1 ->
        _send_sig(_iauto1,_sig);
      :: sig2_s == _sig.f1 ->
        _send_sig(_iauto2,_sig);
      :: else -> _sync!0;
      fi;
    ::empty(_int) &&
      nempty(SELF) ->
      _receive_sig(SELF,_sig);
      if
      ::sig1_s == _sig.f1 ->
        _send_sig(_iauto1,_sig);
      :: sig2_s == _sig.f1 ->
        _send_sig(_iauto2,_sig);
      :: else -> _sync!0;
      fi;
    fi;
  od;
}
```

Table 9. Translation of services (subautomata).

TNSDL	PROMELA

```
SUBAUTOMATON auto1;          proctype auto1 (chan SELF;
  START;                                  chan _auto;
  NEXTSTATE idle;                         chan _iauto;
                                          chan _internal;
  STATE idle;                             chan _sync;
    INPUT INTERNAL sig1_s(x);             chan _x) {
      STOP;                  byte _cntr;
  ENDSTATE idle;             _sync?_cntr;
ENDSUBAUTOMATON auto1;       _cntr = _cntr - 1;
                             byte x;
                             _x?x;
                             goto _transition0;

                             idle:
                             _x!x;
                             _sync!_cntr;
                             _cntr = 0;
                             do
                             :: _receive_sig(_auto,_sig) ->
                                _x?x;
                                if
                                :: else -> _sync!_cntr;
                                fi
                             :: _receive_sig(_iauto,_sig) ->
                                _x?x;
                                if
                                :: sig1_s == _sig.f1 ->
                                   x = _sig.f3;
                                   goto _transition1;
                                :: else -> _sync!_cntr;
                                fi
                             od

                             _transition0:
                             goto idle;
                             _transition1;
                             goto end;

                             end:
                             skip;
                             }
```

Table 10. Translation of a single service (subautomaton).

6 Conclusions

A translation from TNSDL, a dialect of SDL-88, to PROMELA was outlined. PROMELA turned out to be an ideal target language for such a translation which in most places is very straightforward. PROMELA has, however, some restrictions and limitations whose elimination would further simplify the translation and make it feasible for industrial applications.

First, there are some TNSDL features which seem to have no proper counterpart in PROMELA and cannot be translated.

- PROMELA does not have a data type for real numbers. Fortunately these are very seldom used in the TNSDL world and when used could probably be approximated by integers.
- PROMELA has no pointers. Unfortunately they are widely used in switching software and in order to analyze real applications some representation for them should be found. Pointers could perhaps to some extent be simulated using channels in PROMELA: the channel variable could stand for the pointer and the contents of the channel for the pointed item.

Secondly, there are some constructs which are not allowed in PROMELA although they perhaps could be without any major redesign in SPIN.

- The type system could be more liberal, ideally the typedef construct could be as flexible as in C.
- The range of data types allowed on channels could be wider.
- The data type chan could be treated more consistently with other types. E.g. chan typed fields of structures cannot currently be assigned to variables in the following way.

```
typedef chan_t {
  chan f;
}
chan_t x;
chan y;
y = x.f;
```

For this reason TNSDL process identifiers are actually represented as bytes in PROMELA. This works because bytes seem to be the C representation of chan types in the code generated by SPIN.

- The assignment statement could work directly also for types defined with the typedef construct. E.g. the following assignment is currently forbidden.

```
typedef assign_t {
  byte f;
}
assign_t x,y;
x = y;
```

- In the current form of the TNSDL to PROMELA translation remote referencing of variables would be very useful even if it would ruin some of the
partial order reduction capabilities.

References

1. Gerard J. Holzmann. *Design and Validation of Computer Protocols*. Prentice-Hall
   International, Inc., Englewood Cliffs, New Jersey, 1991.
2. Gerard J. Holzmann. Practical methods for the formal validation of SDL specifications. *Computer Communications*, 15(2):129–134, March 1992.
3. Gerard J. Holzmann. The model checker SPIN. *IEEE Transactions on Software
   Engineering*, 23(5):279–295, May 1997.
4. Gerard J. Holzmann and Joanna Patti. Validating SDL specifications: an experiment. In Ed Brinksma, Giuseppe Scollo, and Chris A. Vissers, editors, *Protocol Specification, Testing and Verification, IX, Proceddings of the IFIP WG 6.1 Ninth International Symposium on Protocol Specification, Testing, and Verification, Enchede,
   The Netherlands, 6–9 June, 1989*, pages 317–326, Amsterdam, 1990. North-Holland.
5. Markus Malmqvist. Methodology of dynamical analysis of SDL programs using
   predicate/transition nets. Technical Report B16, Helsinki University of Technology,
   Digital Systems Laboratory, April 1997.
6. Roberto Saracco, J.R.W. Smith, and Rick Reed. *Telecommunications Systems Engineering using SDL*. North-Holland, Amsterdam, 1989.

dSPIN: A Dynamic Extension of SPIN

Claudio Demartini[1], Radu Iosif[1], and Riccardo Sisto[1]

Dipartimento di Automatica e Informatica, Politecnico di Torino
corso Duca degli Abruzzi 24, 10129 Torino, Italy
demartini@polito.it, iosif@athena.polito.it, sisto@polito.it

Abstract. The SPIN extension presented in this article is meant as a way to facilitate the modeling and verification of object-oriented programs. It provides means for the formal representation of some run-time mechanisms intensively used in OO software, such as dynamic object creation and deletion, virtual function calls, etc. This article presents a number of language extensions along with their implementation in SPIN. We carried out a number of experiments and found out that an important expressibility gain can be achieved with at most a small loss of performance.

1 Introduction

It is nowadays a common approach to use concurrent programming along with object-oriented techniques in order to increase robustness and re-usability of concurrent software. A number of new problems in software design and verification arise due to the increase in program complexity, namely run-time complexity. As an obvious consequence, formal verification of this kind of software requires special features. A previous attempt to elaborate formal models of OO programs is presented in [3]. It regards the possibility of automatically generating PROMELA models of programs written in sC++, a concurrent extension of C++. However, the modeling approach used has an important number of limitations, in particular the lack of models for: object creation and deletion, pointer and reference variables, polymorphic function calls.

Our previous experience regarding the translation of Java programs into PROMELA is presented in [4]. One of the critical aspects in our model regards object creation. We discovered that dynamic object creation can be represented in PROMELA in several ways but always in exchange of an important increase in memory requirements for verification. The approach used for Java multithreading applications regarded both passive and active objects (i.e., *thread* objects) and used predefined vectors of a maximal size in order to keep the object data. An index into the vector was used as a pointer (reference) to the object. In addition to the fact that the number of created objects is strongly bound by the maximal vector size, the model does not cover type casting operations and polymorphism, because of the lack of underlying support for representing this kind of information within SPIN.

An analysis of the Java run-time system led us to the conclusion that implementing the following features in PROMELA would suffice in order to efficiently model any kind of Java construct[1]:

- object references.
- dynamic object creation.
- function definition and call.
- function code reference.

In the following we refer to the above presented mechanisms as *dynamic features*, intended as representations of dynamic information regarding the program. Here we distinguish between static and dynamic information, the former referring to the program information that can be known at compile-time using static analysis techniques (e.g., data flow analysis) while the later referring to information that occurs while the program is running.

The SPIN extension presented in this article is called dSPIN, which stands for *dynamic* SPIN. Its intention is to provide SPIN with a number of dynamic features which allow for object-oriented programs to be modeled in a natural manner and efficiently verified. The new features introduced by dSPIN can be divided into:

- **memory management** features concerning dynamic memory allocation and reference mechanisms.
- **functional management** features concerning function declaration, call and reference but also local scoping.

Even if the above mentioned mechanisms are currently implemented in both the SPIN simulator and model checker our attention focuses on the implementation of the model checker and, specifically on the changes made to the representation of the program state and transition system. We tried to exploit the standard philosophy as much as possible in order to achieve a high degree of compatibility with the SPIN distribution. Nevertheless, new aspects had to be introduced in order to ensure the correctness of dSPIN verifications and their compliance with the complexity reduction mechanisms used by SPIN.

The paper is organized as follows: Sect. 2 presents the language features, while Sect. 3 is concerned with their implementation in dSPIN. Sect. 4 discusses the backwards compatibility with the original software and finally Sect. 5 presents some experimental results.

2 The Language Features

In order to make this paper self-contained, the present section discusses the syntax and semantics of the main extensions added to PROMELA in dSPIN. A full description of the dSPIN language extension can be found in [5]. As already mentioned, we classify dynamic features into memory management and functional

---

[1] We did not mentioned exception handling because SPIN 3.2.4 already provides support for it by means of a different interpretation of the **unless** construct.

management features. Memory management regards the possibility of referring memory objects, namely statically declared and dynamically allocated variables, as well as memory allocation and release mechanisms. Functional management is concerned with function declaration and call, function code reference mechanism and local scoping (visibility) issues. The following covers the main issues of both classes of extensions.

2.1 Memory Management

The main extension concerning dynamic memory management is the memory reference mechanism, called briefly *pointer*. A pointer may hold at run-time a reference to a previously defined or dynamically generated object. By object we mean a variable of any type, including basic types, array types and user defined types. In order to make use of pointers one should be able to assign and read reference values, called *left values*, to and respectively, from them. Left values are produced by the left-value operator and the new object creation statement, presented later in this section.

Pointer Syntax and Semantics. A pointer variable is declared by prefixing its name with the & (ampersand) symbol in the declaration. Unless it is initialized in declaration, a pointer variable contains the null value, where null represents a dSPIN literal that can be used in programs in order to denote the value of an undefined pointer.

The use of pointers is quite simple because they do not need to be dereferenced. It is done automatically, according to the context. Let us consider first the case when a pointer variable occurs on the left-hand side of an assignment statement. In this case the assignment changes the pointer's left value only if the right-hand side of the assignment is a pointer variable, a left-value expression or a new object creation expression. Otherwise, an assignment to a pointer changes its *right value* that is, the value of the object to which it points. Any attempt to change the right value of an undefined (null) pointer generates a run-time error.

The second case to be considered is when a pointer occurs on the right-hand side of an assignment. If the left-hand side variable is a pointer then the pointer will evaluate to its left value, otherwise the pointer will evaluate to its right value, namely the value of the object to which it actually points. In the last case the pointer needs not be null, otherwise a run-time error will be raised.

Pointers can also be used along with comparison operators == and !=. An equality comparison between two pointers evaluates to true if and only if their left values are equal that is, if they point to the same object or they are both null. In all other types of expressions and statements, a pointer will evaluate to its right value.

The Left-Value Operator. The left-value operator is an unary operator (&) which takes as argument any kind of variable of a basic, array or structured type. It cannot be applied to a pointer variable. The left-value operator returns a reference to its argument. This reference can then be assigned to a pointer variable.

The New and Delete Statements. The new object creation statement, called briefly the *new* statement, allocates an amount of memory in order to hold a number of objects of any basic or structured type. The reference to the newly allocated area is assigned to a pointer variable. The formal syntax for the new statement is presented below:

```
<pointer> '=' new <type> [ '[' <bound> ']' ]
```

Here **pointer** stands for a pointer variable, **type** stands for any type name and **bound** is an integer specifying the size in number of objects to be allocated. The bound specifier is optional, the default size being of one object of the specified type.

The object deletion statement, briefly called the *delete* statement performs the reverse action i.e., it deallocates the memory space previously allocated by a new statement. The formal syntax of a delete statement is presented below:

```
delete '(' <pointer> ')'
```

where **pointer** stands for a pointer variable. Only heap variables can be used along with delete statements. Any attempt to delete a static variable raises a run-time error.

Another point to be stressed here concerns the executability of the new and delete statements. Both are always executable. The order in which objects can be deleted does not depend on the order they were created that is, a process will never block attempting to delete an object.

2.2 Functional Management

The main concept regarding functional management features is the *function*, defined in dSPIN as it is in most programming languages: a function is a parameterized sequence of code whose execution may be invoked at a certain point in the program and which, upon termination, makes control return immediately after the invocation point. dSPIN functions are executed synchronously that is, the caller process execution thread does not span, rather it is continued by the function call. The statements contained within the function are executed with interleaving along with other processes. The way functions are defined in dSPIN allows for recursiveness in a natural manner.

Functions represent also "objects" supporting a reference mechanism. Indeed, a function can be referred by a special kind of pointer, which provides a mean to model polymorphic function calls used in most object-oriented languages.

Function Definition and Call. The syntax of function definition is similar to the standard PROMELA **proctype** definition. Formally it looks like:

```
function <name> '(' <list> ')' [ ':' <type> ]
'{' ( <declaration> | <statement> )* <statement>+ '}'
```

where **name** stands for the function name, **list** stands for the formal parameter list and **type** is any type name (including pointer types), specifying the function return type. The return type is optional, which means that a function is not required to return a value i.e., it can be a procedure. A function definition also specifies the function body which consists of a number of declarations and statements. It is required for a function to contain at least one statement.

Upon declaration the name of a function can occur within a function call statement. In dSPIN statements of a function are executed with interleaving, reflecting the behavior of real concurrent programs.

There are three types of function invocation statement. The first one concerns only non-void functions i.e., functions for which the return type is specified in definition. Its formal syntax is shown below:

```
<variable> '=' <name> '(' <list> ')'
```

Here **variable** stands for a declared variable identifier, **name** stands for a declared function name, and **list** for the function actual parameter list. This statement causes function **name** to be called, its return value being assigned to **variable**.

A function may return a value by means of the dSPIN **return** statement, formally specified as:

```
return [ <expression> ]
```

where **expression** stands for any expression that can be atomically evaluated. The **return** statement causes control to leave the function body and return to the statement immediately below the invocation point. The return expression is only required when the **return** statement occurs within a non-void function definition.

For procedures i.e., functions for which the return type is not specified or the return value is not of interest at the invocation point, there is a more simple type of invocation:

```
<name> '(' <list> ')'
```

Here **name** stands for a procedure name and **list** for the actual parameter list. The above statement causes function **name** to be called with actual parameters from **list**, any possible return value being discarded.

The third and last type of function invocation statement was introduced in order to facilitate the writing of tail-recursive functions. It has the following formal syntax:

```
return <name> '(' <list> ')'
```

where **name** stands for a non-void function name and **list** specifies the actual parameter list for the function invocation. This statement causes the function **name** to be called, its return value being passed back as the return value of the caller function.

A process attempting to execute a function call statement will always pass to the first statement of the function without blocking. Analogously, a return statement is always executable. However, the executability of a function call statement depends on the executability of the statements residing inside the function body, therefore it cannot be evaluated a priori. For this reason, function call statements cannot be used within deterministic regions of code (i.e., **d_step** sequences).

Function Pointers. As previously mentioned, functions represent objects which can be referred using a special kind of variables called *function pointers*. A pointer to a function actually holds a reference to the beginning of the function code.

A function pointer is declared as a variable of a predefined type named **ftype**. Unless initialized in declaration, a function pointer is undefined i.e., its value is **null**. A function pointer can be assigned a reference to any declared function. Upon assignment, the function pointer can be used in any form of function invocation statement, instead of the function name.

Local Scopes. The notion of function introduces also the concept of *local scope* for variables. Variables can be declared inside a function, being visible only within the function scope. Moreover, a local scope can be declared inside a process, function or local scope by enclosing the program region into curly braces. Local scopes can be nested and the same variable name can be used in different scopes without conflicts. Variables defined within a local scope are automatically initialized when the control enters the scope.

3   Implementation Issues

This section presents some issues regarding the implementation of the dynamic features discussed in Sect. 2 in dSPIN. As a first remark, let us note that almost all language extensions previously mentioned require dynamic memory space that is, the ability to dynamically increase or decrease the amount of memory used by the current program state. This appears obvious in the case of **new** and **delete** statements and moreover, function calls require the caller process to expand in order to hold the function actual parameters and local variables. A linear representation of the current state (i.e., state-vector representation) would not be convenient for our purposes, because every dynamic increase or decrease of the memory space could require the relocation of many components of the state (e.g., processes, queues, variables), affecting the overall performance of the model checker. Our solution was to adopt a different representation for the current

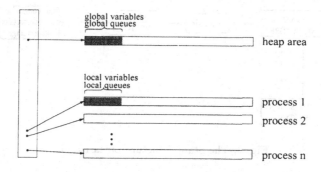

Fig. 1. The State Structure

state. This representation is non-linear, rather composed of a number of different vectors. In the following we will refer to the current state representation as the *state structure*. Fig. 1 depicts the general organization of the state structure.

All memory areas that may shrink or expand are organized into separate vectors of variable sizes. There is one vector for each currently active process, which we refer to as *process vector* and another global one called *heap area* used to hold global data and dynamically created objects. Global variables and queues reside at the beginning of the heap area, while local variables and queues are kept at the beginning of the process vector.

Static variables (i.e., variables explicitly declared in the program) are assigned an offset into the containing vector, global variables being represented by heap offsets, while local variables being defined by offsets into the process vector that contains them. This representation of variables somehow contrasts with the standard SPIN representation because SPIN directly converts PROMELA variables into C variables of the corresponding type. In dSPIN we use type information to compute the storage size of a variable and determine its offset.

An important point which needs to be stressed here regards the way in which the state structure representation affects state comparisons and storage performed by the model checker during verification runs. The standard version of SPIN takes great advantage from the linear state representation (i.e., state-vector) in order to optimize the run-time performance of the model checker. Indeed, the comparisons between states are implemented as byte-vector comparisons. Moreover, state-space storing procedures (e.g., hash indexing store, minimized automaton store[2]) are byte-vector operations. For example, the computation of a hash index takes only one pass through the vector in order to accomplish its task. As previously discussed, the state structure representation keeps the state information organized into several vectors of various sizes. Making the state comparison and store routines iterate through all vectors that make up the state structure greatly decreases the run-time performance of the model

---

[2] dSPIN considers only the storing techniques used up to and including SPIN version 3.2.0

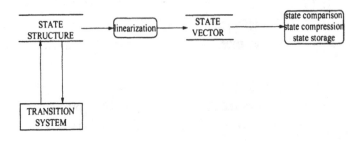

Fig. 2. The State Structure Linearization

checker. Also state compression can be difficult to implement when using a non-linear structure.

The implementation solution used in dSPIN interfaces the state structure representation with linear comparison, compression and storing techniques by first performing a linearization of the state. The linear representation of the state is subsequently referred to as the *state vector*. It is obtained from the state structure by copying the relevant state information from the heap area and process vectors into the state vector. The state vector uniquely identifies the state that is, every state change into the state structure is reflected into the corresponding state vector. This is then used along with state comparison and storing routines instead of the original state structure representation. Fig. 2 shows the use of the state structure along with standard SPIN comparison, compression and storage routines.

3.1 Implementation of New and Delete Operations

As already mentioned, dynamically allocated objects are modeled into the heap area. A dynamic object is represented by an integer index into two tables that keep the information needed in order to locate the object. The first table holds the offset of the object into the heap area, while the second one holds the object size. In the following, we will refer to the first table as the *offset table* and to the second one as the *size table*. The representation of dynamic objects somehow resembles the representation of message channels within standard SPIN.

A new operation takes as parameters a type specifier and a number of elements of the specified type in order to compute the storage size of the object. The heap area is then increased by the size increment in order to contain the newly created object, the first free slot into the offset and size tables is found and the retrieval information is written into the tables. In order to avoid false partial matches of the state structure the type of a newly created object is encoded at the end of the object area. Finally, the new operator returns the table index of the object that is subsequently used to compute the actual reference to the object data.

A delete operation receives as parameter a reference to the object that is intended to be deleted. Such a reference specifies the index number of the object

that is, its index into the offset and size tables. The heap area is decreased by a decrement equal to the size of the object. Unless the deleted object was placed at the end of the heap area, a compaction of the heap area is needed in order to avoid memory losses caused by fragmentation. In practice, the compaction is a simple operation which involves only the relocation of the objects and message channels situated after the deleted object into the heap area by decreasing their offset values by the size of the deleted object. The run-time overhead of heap compaction is therefore limited.

3.2 Implementation of Object References

The object reference mechanism called pointer was presented in Sect. 2. Let us recall that a pointer can hold a reference to a statically declared local or global variable or to a heap variable. We distinguish among three kinds of object reference: the *local variable reference*, the *global variable reference* and the *heap variable reference*. The implementation of object references follows a symbolic approach that is, rather than storing the physical memory address into the pointer variable we have chosen to encode the information needed to locate the object into the pointer by using a symbolic format. This approach allows for an easy run-time check of dangling references. In the following, we model pointers as unsigned 32-bit integers[3]. The first two bits of the integer are used to encode the reference type, which may be one of the above mentioned.

A reference to a local variable uses the next 6 bits in order to encode the declaring process identifier. This allows for local variables from at most 2^6 processes to be referred. The last 24 bits will hold the local variable offset into the process vector, allowing for a maximum of 2^{22} different 32-bit integer objects to be referred inside a process vector.

The global variable reference uses all remaining 30 bits for the representation of the variable offset within the heap area. This allows for a maximum of 2^{28} different 32-bit integer objects to be referred inside the heap area.

The heap variable reference uses the remaining 30 bits in order to keep the object index number that uniquely identifies the heap object. This allows for a maximum of 2^{30} different heap objects to be referred.

3.3 Implementation of Functional Management Mechanisms

It was mentioned in the presentation of the state structure that every active process in the system is represented by a separate vector of a variable size. This implementation choice was inspired by the real world run-time systems that use a separate stack for every process in order to hold the actual values of function parameters and local variables during a function call. Fig. 3 shows in more detail the organization of the process vector as implemented in dSPIN.

The process vector is composed of a static area situated at the beginning, which we will refer to as the *prefix*. It contains information regarding control

---

[3] The implementation of pointers on different architectures requires minimal changes.

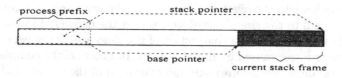

Fig. 3. The Process Vector

flow, such as process type and current state number. As in the standard version of SPIN, this information is needed in order to identify the current process transition from the transition table. Stack management is performed by means of two variables, called *stack pointer* and *base pointer*, residing also in the prefix area. The remainder of the process vector is referred to as the *process stack*. The top offset of the process stack is pointed to by the stack pointer. The area between the offset pointed to by the base pointer and the top offset is called the *current stack frame*. It contains information regarding the currently executing function, namely local variables and actual parameters, as well as function return information.

Sect. 2 briefly mentioned a couple of aspects regarding the semantics of function calls. The first one we recall here states that the instructions contained in a function are executed with interleaving along with other processes. As a consequence of this, a function is represented by means of a separate finite state machine having its own entry into the global transition table. A process that makes a function call temporarily suspends the execution of its finite state machine and starts executing the function FSM. After a return from the function, the execution of the caller process FSM is resumed. The second aspect regarding the execution of function calls is that the caller process execution thread is actually continued by the call. In order to give a more detailed explanation of this, let us consider the linear sequence of states explored by the depth-first search during verification. Let us consider also that the system is in state S_a just before performing a function call. After firing the function call transition a new state S_{a1} is generated. This state reflects only the changes committed on the caller process stack by the function call transition but it has no relevance from the verification point of view that is, it does not carry information that may be useful in order to check system properties. Therefore it makes no sense to store this state in the state space. The first relevant state after the function call is generated by firing the first transition from the function body. Let us call this state S_b. Fig. 4 shows the behavior of the model checker during a function call.

The transitions depicted using dotted lines represent the function call and return from function transitions. In the following, we denote this kind of transition a *virtual transition*. Even if it does not create a new state into the state space, a virtual transition must be recorded on the trail stack in order to allow the model checker to unwind it by performing a backward move.

A function call transition increases the process stack size by first pushing the return information onto the stack that is, the current process type identifier and

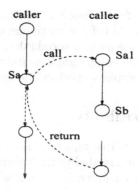

Fig. 4. The Function Call

state number. Following, the left value of the return variable is pushed onto the stack. This is a reference to the object meant to keep the function return value, if there is one. Finally, the current value of the base pointer is saved on the stack, the base pointer is set to the current value of the stack pointer, and the process prefix is actualized in order to reflect the control state change. This is done by storing into it the function type identifier and the identifier of the function FSM initial state in the process prefix area. At this point, the actual parameters are evaluated and their values pushed onto the stack. It is to be mentioned that each process local variable is uniquely identified by its offset relative to the beginning of the stack frame. When the base pointer is set to the stack pointer value a new stack frame is actually created, in order to hold the function parameters and local variables that are not visible from the caller process scope[4].

A return from function transition performs the reverse actions. First the current stack frame is popped from the stack by simply setting the stack pointer to the current value of the base pointer. Then the control flow information is retrieved from the stack in order to resume the caller process type identifier and state number. Finally the original stack frame is restored by assigning the base pointer with the previously saved value. If the function returns a value this is assigned to the object referred by the left value that was also saved on the stack. Subsequently, the model checker attempts to fire the transition immediately following the function call, resuming in this way the execution of the caller process FSM.

The implementation of local scopes also makes use of the process stack mechanism. A local scope can be seen as a parameterless function call for which no return information is needed because the transitions residing inside the scope are part of the same finite state machine as the ones situated outside it.

Sect. 2 presents the function reference mechanism, called function pointer. The implementation of function pointers uses a 32-bit integer value in order to represent the information needed to uniquely identify a function object. The

---

[4] The dSPIN language extension does not provide support for the dynamic binding of variables.

first 16 bits are used to encode the function identifier that is, its entry into the global transition table. This allow for a maximum of 2^{16} different functions to be referred. The last 16 bits are used to encode the state number of the function FSM initial state. The function pointer implementation uses a symbolic approach that allows for run-time consistency checks to be easily performed.

4 Backwards Compatibility

The previous section presented the implementation of the dSPIN language features and discussed some issues related to the correctness of formal verifications taking into account these new aspects. In the following, we will discuss the way in which our implementation choices affect the standard SPIN complexity reduction techniques, considering state compressions and partial order reductions. Some explanations regarding the run-time overhead introduced by dSPIN are also given.

4.1 Compliance with State Compressions

Sect. 3 presented the state representation used in dSPIN and its use along with the standard SPIN state comparison, compression and storage techniques. Let us recall that all these techniques are based on a linear representation of states in order to optimize the run-time performance of the model checker. In dSPIN a non-linear state representation is used along with the standard approach, which is made possible by linearization of the state structure. In the following, we consider the two main state compression techniques used in SPIN, namely byte-mask compression and recursive indexing compression (i.e., COLLAPSE mode) [6]. These compression modes are the main ones in the sense that all other compression routines (e.g., minimized automaton) take as input the state vector already compressed by one of byte-masking or recursive indexing routines. An important optimization of dSPIN was obtained by combining linearization with one of the two above mentioned techniques. In this way, the state vector obtained by applying linearization to the state structure representation is already in the compressed form and can be used for further compressions, comparisons and hash storing. The time taken up by linearization in this case is almost equal to the time needed by the standard SPIN byte-mask or recursive indexing, yielding a very small overhead in comparison with the original version. It is to be noted that linearization combined with byte-mask compression can be implemented using block copy operations yielding a further speed increase. In exchange, some redundant information is copied into the state vector as it is the case of rendezvous queues which, unlike in the original byte-mask compression are copied along with their containing vectors.

4.2 Compliance with Partial Order Reductions

The current version of SPIN uses a static partial order reduction of the interleavings between processes known as a *persistent set* technique [10]. The implementation of partial order reduction in SPIN is based on a static analysis of the processes in order to identify transitions that are *safe*. One case in which a transition is considered to be unconditionally safe regards any access to exclusively local variables, as discussed in [7]. While in the standard PROMELA language it is quite straightforward to find out if some identifier represents a local variable, in dSPIN this is not so. Indeed, an access to a local variable referred by a global pointer variable cannot be considered an unconditionally safe transition. Moreover, by-reference parameter passing in function calls introduces similar problems. As previously mentioned, a static analysis of the source code cannot determine exactly the dynamic information, still a conservative approximation of it can be obtained using data flow analysis techniques. Our solution, implemented in dSPIN uses an iterative algorithm in order to solve what is known as an *aliasing problem* [1]. The algorithm computes, for every non-pointer variable accessed at a certain point in the program, an *alias list* that is the list of all pointers that may refer it. The alias relation is symmetric, therefore every pointer variable at a certain point in the program also has an associated list of objects that it may point to. The safety condition is restricted. We consider a transition to be unconditionally safe if none of the accessed variables is global or has a global alias. More precisely, an access to a local variable that is aliased by a global pointer, as well as an access to a pointer that refers a global object are considered unsafe. By making this assumption we can only err on the conservative side, choosing not to apply partial order reduction in some cases where it still can be safely applied, but never applying it for unsafe transitions.

A concurrent program represented in dSPIN consists of a set of processes and functions. Every such entity is described by a reduced flow graph that is, a graph whose nodes represent sequences of statements and whose edges represent possible control flow paths. A node of such a flow graph is also known as a *basic block*. It is a sequence of consecutive statements in which flow of control enters at the beginning and leaves at the end without possibility of branching except at the end. Every basic block has an associated equation relating the alias relationships among all variables at the beginning of the basic block with the alias relationship at its end. The set of all such equations is known as the *data-flow equation system*. Solving the data flow equation system means finding the smallest conservative estimation of every basic block input and output relations. It is done by an iterative algorithm that is a slightly modified version of the ones described in [1]. The iteration is repeated for every process and function flow graph, one at the time, until a stable solution is found that is, no more changes occur to any input or output relation. In order to estimate the overall complexity of the algorithm let us consider for every process an extended flow graph obtained by adding to the original process flow graph the flow graphs of all functions that may be called during its execution. As pointed out in [1], the number of iterations through a depth-first ordered flow graph is bounded by the depth of the flow graph which is at most $logN$, where N represents the number of basic blocks in the extended flow graph. As a consequence, the complexity of the entire data flow computation is $O(NlogN)$ where N represents here the maximum number of basic blocks over all process extended flow graphs.

5 Experimental Work

We have applied dSPIN to perform verification of a number of standard SPIN specifications in order to make a performance comparison between the tools. The experience we had analyzing standard examples is reported in the first part of this section. The remainder reports a number of tests carried out with a dSPIN specification of a concurrent B-tree structure in order to give a glimpse of the tool's capability of verifying programs that make use of dynamic information. [5]

Table 1 shows a comparison of the results obtained by verifying a number of specifications with dSPIN and standard SPIN. All examples are taken from the standard SPIN distribution and are denoted by the corresponding file name.

Table 1. Standard Examples

File	States	Transitions	Memory (Mb)	Time (sec)
i. Using dSPIN				
leader	108	108	1.373	0.1
leader2	28898	42274	7.065	1.1
sort	6965	6965	10.193	0.8
pftp	678785	917632	187.184	35.9
erathostenes	444602	628697	180.121	24.3
ii. Using standard SPIN				
leader	108	108	1.493	0.1
leader2	28898	42274	6.613	1.9
sort	6965	6965	9.276	1.9
pftp	678785	917632	191.957	59.3
erathostenes	444602	628697	109.628	38.8

While the number of states and transitions are exactly the same in both cases, we notice that dSPIN sometimes tends to use a slightly larger amount of memory in exchange of a small verification speedup. The cause of this overhead resides in our current implementation of byte-masking compression that uses block copy operations in order to increase speed but at the same time copies from the state structure some redundant information, as discussed in Sect. 4. However, the memory overhead is limited and in most cases it does not increase with the global number of states.

[5] All analysis time reports are obtained from the Unix **time** command on a 256 Mb RAM UltraSparc 30 at 300MHz workstation. Small times (under 0.5 seconds) tend to be inaccurate because of the system overhead.

The experiments regarding the modeling of dynamic aspects have been carried out using a B-tree structure [8] accessed concurrently by updater processes that insert values into it. The system model was specified using pointer variables as well as dynamic object creation and deletion operations. The mutual exclusion protocol follows the approach described in [2]. Each node has an associated lock channel used to ensure exclusive access to its data. When performing insertion into a node, an updater process holds only the locks to its ancestors considered to be *unsafe* (i.e., the safety property is verified for all nodes that do not split due to an insertion). When a certain depth of the tree is reached, the updater processes stop their execution, in order to avoid an unbounded growth of the data structure. The B-tree example considered here is highly scalable, the scaling parameters being the B-tree order, referred to as K, the B-tree maximum depth, referred to as D and the number of updater processes, referred to as P.

Table 2 shows the results obtained by performing analysis of the model for some different configurations of the scaling parameters. The last column of the table specifies the compression modes activated by the corresponding compilation options. Complexity increases exponentially with the maximum depth of

Table 2. The B-Tree Example

K, D, N	States	Transitions	Memory (Mb)	Time (min:sec)	Options
2, 2, 2	9215	18354	3.022	0:02.0	COLLAPSE
2, 2, 3	300577	895141	9.886	1:44.2	COLLAPSE
2, 2, 4	2.87937e+06	1.12389e+07	66.417	23:27.6	COLLAPSE
2, 3, 2	719925	1.50269e+06	40.330	3:03.5	COLLAPSE
2, 3, 3	1.152e+06	3.40875e+06	3.150	5:54.9	BITSTATE
4, 2, 2	13019	25490	3.283	0:2.8	COLLAPSE
4, 2, 3	691256	2.0539e+06	19.060	4:03.2	COLLAPSE
4, 2, 4	1.54303e+06	5.50518e+06	2.824	8:31.9	BITSTATE
4, 3, 2	651896	1.30644e+06	4.009	2:27.3	BITSTATE
4, 3, 3	1.26746e+06	3.72083e+06	4.018	6:45.1	BITSTATE

the B-tree and the number of processes too. The most trivial cases were verified using the recursive indexing (i.e., COLLAPSE) compression mode, while the others were analyzed approximatively using the supertrace technique (i.e., BITSTATE).

6 Conclusions

An extension of the model checker SPIN, providing support for modeling and verification of programs that use dynamic mechanisms was presented. Here the term "dynamic" has roughly the same meaning it has in the context of compiler development, identifying the information that occurs exclusively at run-time. In order to support the representation of dynamic information, some new concepts were introduced at the front-end level, among them: pointer variables, new object creation and deletion statements, function declarations and calls, function pointers and local scopes. The implementation of these language extensions uses an alternative representation for states that is interfaced with the existing state compression and storage techniques of the standard SPIN version. Nevertheless, new approaches had to be used for the representation of variable references and function calls. The correctness of verifications performed in the presence of the new language features has also been discussed. As pointed out, systems that make use of the dynamic extensions can be verified at the expense of a limited memory overhead by taking advantage of all standard state compression techniques. The number of cases where partial order reductions can be applied is smaller with dSPIN than with SPIN, due to the use of pointers and function calls. The applicability of partial order reductions is driven by a conservative approximation of the variable alias relationship, which is computed by a polynomial complexity data-flow analysis algorithm.

Experiments carried out in order to make a comparison between dSPIN and the standard version of SPIN showed that the overhead in memory space and execution speed can be neglected. Moreover, experience with a non-trivial dynamic data structure used in a concurrent environment gives a glimpse of the tool's capability of modeling and verifying programs that use dynamic mechanisms.

References

1. Alfred V. Aho, Ravi Sethi, Jeffrey D. Ullman: Compilers, Principles, Techniques and Tools. Addison-Wesley (1986)
2. R. Bayer and M. Schkolnick: Concurrency of Operations on B-Trees. Acta Informatica, Vol. 9. Springer-Verlag (1977) 1–21
3. Thierry Cattel: Modeling and Verification of sC++ Applications. Proceedings of the Tools and Algorithms for the Construction and Analysis of Systems, Lisbon, Portugal, LNCS 1384. Springer-Verlag (April 1998) 232–248
4. C. Demartini, R. Iosif, and R. Sisto: Modeling and Validation of Java Multithreading Applications using SPIN, Proceedings of the 4th workshop on automata theoretic verification with the SPIN model checker, Paris, France (November 1998) 5–19
5. R. Iosif: The dSPIN User Manual.
   http://www.dai-arc.polito.it/dai-arc/auto/tools/tool7.shtml
6. Gerard J. Holzmann: State Compression in SPIN: Recursive Indexing and Compression Training Runs. Proceedings of the 3rd workshop on automata theoretic verification with the SPIN model checker, Twente, Holland (April 1997)
7. Gerard J. Holzmann: An Improvement in Formal Verification. Proceedings FORTE 1994 Conference, Bern, Switzerland (October 1994)
8. Knuth, D.E.: The Art of Computer Programming. Vol. 3. Sorting and Searching. Addison-Wesley (1972)
9. Bjarne Stroustrup: The C++ Programming Language. Addison-Wesley (1991)
10. Pierre Wolper and Patrice Godefroid: Partial-Order Methods for Temporal Verification. CONCUR '93 Proceedings, Lecture Notes in Computer Science, Vol. 715. Springer-Verlag (August 1993) 233–246

Author Index

Lecture Notes in Computer Science

For information about Vols. 1–1610
please contact your bookseller or Springer-Verlag

Vol. 1650: K.-D. Althoff, R. Bergmann, L.K. Branting (Eds.), Case-Based Reasoning Research and Development. Proceedings, 1999. XII, 598 pages. 1999. (Subseries LNAI).

Vol. 1651: R.H. Güting, D. Papadias, F. Lochovsky (Eds.), Advances in Spatial Databases. Proceedings, 1999. XI, 371 pages. 1999.

Vol. 1652: M. Klusch, O.M. Shehory, G. Weiss (Eds.), Cooperative Information Agents III. Proceedings, 1999. XI, 404 pages. 1999. (Subseries LNAI).

Vol. 1653: S. Covaci (Ed.), Active Networks. Proceedings, 1999. XIII, 346 pages. 1999.

Vol. 1654: E.R. Hancock, M. Pelillo (Eds.), Energy Minimization Methods in Computer Vision and Pattern Recognition. Proceedings, 1999. IX, 331 pages. 1999.

Vol. 1655: S.-W. Lee, Y. Nakano (Eds.), Document Analysis Systems: Theory and Practice. Proceedings, 1998. XI, 377 pages. 1999.

Vol. 1656: S. Chatterjee, J.F. Prins, L. Carter, J. Ferrante, Z. Li, D. Sehr, P.-C. Yew (Eds.), Languages and Compilers for Parallel Computing. Proceedings, 1998. XI, 384 pages. 1999.

Vol. 1661: C. Freksa, D.M. Mark (Eds.), Spatial Information Theory. Proceedings, 1999. XIII, 477 pages. 1999.

Vol. 1662: V. Malyshkin (Ed.), Parallel Computing Technologies. Proceedings, 1999. XIX, 510 pages. 1999.

Vol. 1663: F. Dehne, A. Gupta. J.-R. Sack, R. Tamassia (Eds.), Algorithms and Data Structures. Proceedings, 1999. IX, 366 pages. 1999.

Vol. 1664: J.C.M. Baeten, S. Mauw (Eds.), CONCUR'99. Concurrency Theory. Proceedings, 1999. XI, 573 pages. 1999.

Vol. 1666: M. Wiener (Ed.), Advances in Cryptology – CRYPTO '99. Proceedings, 1999. XII, 639 pages. 1999.

Vol. 1667: J. Hlavička, E. Maehle, A. Pataricza (Eds.), Dependable Computing – EDCC-3. Proceedings, 1999. XVIII, 455 pages. 1999.

Vol. 1668: J.S. Vitter, C.D. Zaroliagis (Eds.), Algorithm Engineering. Proceedings, 1999. VIII, 361 pages. 1999.

Vol. 1671: D. Hochbaum, K. Jansen, J.D.P. Rolim, A. Sinclair (Eds.), Randomization, Approximation, and Combinatorial Optimization. Proceedings, 1999. IX, 289 pages. 1999.

Vol. 1672: M. Kutylowski, L. Pacholski, T. Wierzbicki (Eds.), Mathematical Foundations of Computer Science 1999. Proceedings, 1999. XII, 455 pages. 1999.

Vol. 1673: P. Lysaght, J. Irvine, R. Hartenstein (Eds.), Field Programmable Logic and Applications. Proceedings, 1999. XI, 541 pages. 1999.

Vol. 1674: D. Floreano, J.-D. Nicoud, F. Mondada (Eds.), Advances in Artificial Life. Proceedings, 1999. XVI, 737 pages. 1999. (Subseries LNAI).

Vol. 1675: J. Estublier (Ed.), System Configuration Management. Proceedings, 1999. VIII, 255 pages. 1999.

Vol. 1976: M. Mohania, A M. Tjoa (Eds.), Data Warehousing and Knowledge Discovery. Proceedings, 1999. XII, 400 pages. 1999.

Vol. 1677: T. Bench-Capon, G. Soda, A M. Tjoa (Eds.), Database and Expert Systems Applications. Proceedings, 1999. XVIII, 1105 pages. 1999.

Vol. 1678: M.H. Böhlen, C.S. Jensen, M.O. Scholl (Eds.), Spatio-Temporal Database Management. Proceedings, 1999. X, 243 pages. 1999.

Vol. 1679: C. Taylor, A. Colchester (Eds.), Medical Image Computing and Computer-Assisted Intervention – MICCAI'99. Proceedings, 1999. XXI, 1240 pages. 1999.

Vol. 1680: D. Dams, R. Gerth, S. Leue, M. Massink (Eds.), Theoretical and Practical Aspects of SPIN Model Checking. Proceedings, 1999. X, 277 pages. 1999.

Vol. 1682: M. Nielsen, P. Johansen, O.F. Olsen, J. Weickert (Eds.), Scale-Space Theories in Computer Vision. Proceedings, 1999. XII, 532 pages. 1999.

Vol. 1684: G. Ciobanu, G. Păun (Eds.), Fundamentals of Computation Theory. Proceedings, 1999. XI, 570 pages. 1999.

Vol. 1685: P. Amestoy, P. Berger, M. Daydé, I. Duff, V. Frayssé, L. Giraud, D. Ruiz (Eds.), Euro-Par'99. Parallel Processing. Proceedings, 1999. XXXII, 1503 pages. 1999.

Vol. 1687: O. Nierstrasz, M. Lemoine (Eds.), Software Engineering – ESEC/FSE '99. Proceedings, 1999. XII, 529 pages. 1999.

Vol. 1688: P. Bouquet, L. Serafini, P. Brézillon, M. Benerecetti, F. Castellani (Eds.), Modeling and Using Context. Proceedings, 1999. XII, 528 pages. 1999. (Subseries LNAI).

Vol. 1689: F. Solina, A. Leonardis (Eds.), Computer Analysis of Images and Patterns. Proceedings, 1999. XIV, 650 pages. 1999.

Vol. 1690: Y. Bertot, G. Dowek, A. Hirschowitz, C. Paulin, L. Théry (Eds.), Theorem Proving in Higher Order Logics. Proceedings, 1999. VIII, 359 pages. 1999.

Vol. 1691: J. Eder, I. Rozman, T. Welzer (Eds.), Advances in Databases and Information Systems. Proceedings, 1999. XIII, 383 pages. 1999.

Vol. 1692: V. Matoušek, P. Mautner, J. Ocelíková, P. Sojka (Eds.), Text, Speech and Dialogue. Proceedings, 1999. XI, 396 pages. 1999. (Subseries LNAI).

Vol. 1693: P. Jayanti (Ed.), Distributed Computing. Proceedings, 1999. X, 357 pages. 1999.

Vol. 1694: A. Cortesi, G. Filé (Eds.), Static Analysis. Proceedings, 1999. VIII, 357 pages. 1999.

Vol. 1698: M. Felici, K. Kanoun, A. Pasquini (Eds.), Computer Safety, Reliability and Security. Proceedings, 1999. XVIII, 482 pages. 1999.

Vol. 1699: S. Albayrak (Ed.), Intelligent Agents for Telecommunication Applications. Proceedings, 1999. IX, 191 pages. 1999. (Subseries LNAI).

Vol. 1701: W. Burgard, T. Christaller, A.B. Cremers (Eds.), KI-99: Advances in Artificial Intelligence. Proceedings, 1999. XI, 311 pages. 1999. (Subseries LNAI).

Vol. 1702: G. Nadathur (Ed.), Principles and Practice of Declarative Programming. Proceedings, 1999. X, 434 pages. 1999.

Vol. 1704: Jan M. Żytkow, J. Rauch (Eds.), Principles of Data Mining and Knowledge Discovery. Proceedings, 1999. XIV, 593 pages. 1999. (Subseries LNAI).

Vol. 1705: H. Ganzinger, D. McAllester, A. Voronkov (Eds.), Logic for Programming and Automated Reasoning. Proceedings, 1999. XII, 397 pages. 1999. (Subseries LNAI).